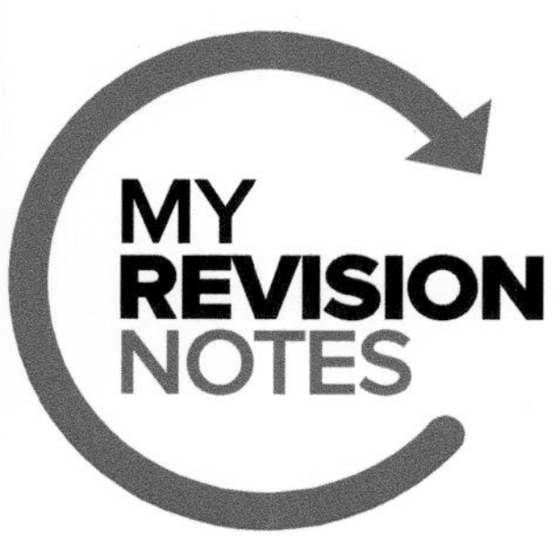

A-level

LAW

2ND EDITION

Clare Wilson
Craig Beauman

HODDER
EDUCATION
AN HACHETTE UK COMPANY

Orders: please contact Hachette UK Distribution, Hely Hutchinson Centre, Milton Road, Didcot, Oxfordshire, OX11 7HH. Telephone: +44 (0)1235 827827. Email education@hachette.co.uk Lines are open from 9 a.m. to 5 p.m., Monday to Friday. You can also order through our website: www.hoddereducation.co.uk

ISBN: 978 1 3983 5204 9

First published in 2017

This edition published in 2022 by

Hodder Education,

An Hachette UK Company

Carmelite House

50 Victoria Embankment

London EC4Y 0DZ

www.hoddereducation.co.uk

Impression number 10 9 8 7 6 5 4 3 2

Year 2026 2025 2024 2023 2022

Cover photo © graham oakes/Shutterstock.com

Illustrations by Aptara Inc

Typeset in Bembo Std 11/13 pt by Aptara Inc

Printed and bound by CPI Group (UK) Ltd, Croydon, CR0 4YY

A catalogue record for this title is available from the British Library.

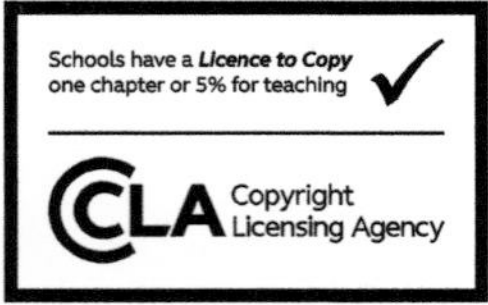

Get the most from this book

Everyone has to decide their own revision strategy, but it is essential to review your work, learn it and test your understanding. Revision doesn't begin seven or eight weeks before the exam, it begins on the first day and every day of class. These Revision Notes will help you to do that in a planned way, topic by topic. Use this book as the cornerstone of your revision and don't hesitate to write in it – personalise your notes and check your progress by ticking off each section as you revise.

A key strategy is to write your own questions, look at previous question papers and get a 'flavour' of how AQA examiners write the questions. Try writing your own scenario/problem questions based on those available on the AQA website.

Tick to track your progress

Use the revision planner on pages iv–v to plan your revision, topic by topic. Tick each box when you have:

- revised and understood a topic
- tested yourself
- practised the exam questions and checked your answers online.

You can also keep track of your revision by ticking off each topic heading in the book. You may find it helpful to add your own notes as you work through each topic.

Features to help you succeed

Exam tips

Expert tips are given throughout the book to help you polish your exam technique in order to maximise your chances in the exam.

Typical mistakes

The author identifies the typical mistakes candidates make and explains how you can avoid them.

Now test yourself

These short, knowledge-based questions provide the first step in testing your learning. Answers are available online.

Definitions and key words

Clear, concise definitions of essential key terms are provided where they first appear.

Key words from the specification are highlighted in blue throughout the book.

Revision activities

These activities will help you to understand each topic in an interactive way.

Exam practice

Practice exam questions are provided for each topic. Use them to consolidate your revision and practise your exam skills.

Exam summaries

Descriptions of the types of questions you can expect in the examination.

This second edition contains three new features:

Stretch and challenge

A series of activities and questions to challenge your thinking and help you to aim for the higher grades.

Evaluation points

Boost your evaluative skills with these activities and discussion points.

End-of-unit summaries

These bring together the whole content of the unit, containing a bulleted list for you to review quickly before the exam. This 'retrieval practice' allows you to practise recall of learnt information and skills.

Online

Go online to check your answers to the now test yourself and exam practice questions at www.hoddereducation.co.uk/myrevisionnotes

My revision planner

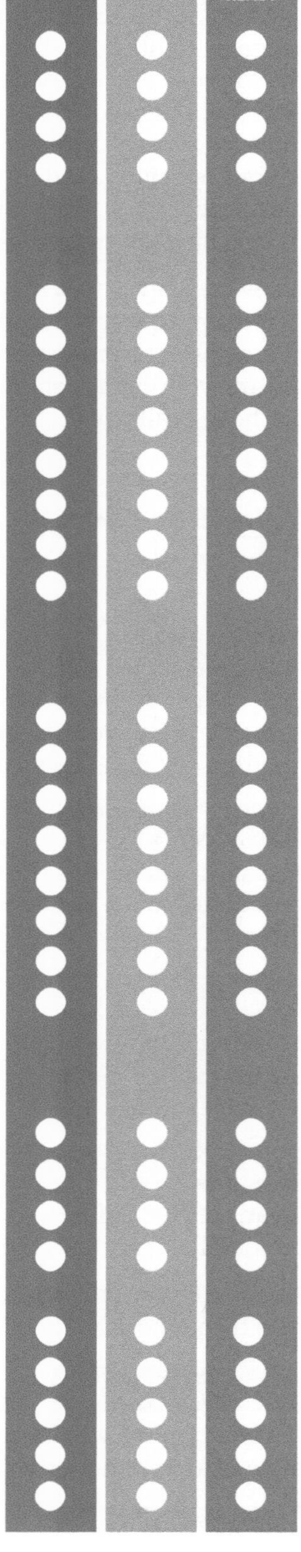

1 The nature of law and the English legal system

1 1.1 The nature of law
15 1.2 The rule of law
18 1.3 Law making
41 1.4 The legal system

2 Criminal law

61 2.1 Rules of criminal law
63 2.2 Theory in criminal law
65 2.3 General elements of liability
69 2.4 Fatal offences against the person
77 2.5 Non-fatal offences against the person
82 2.6 Property offences
88 2.7 Preliminary offence: attempt
91 2.8 Defences

3 Tort

105 3.1 Rules of tort law
107 3.2 Theory of tort law
110 3.3 Liability in negligence
117 3.4 Occupiers' liability
121 3.5 Nuisance and the escape of dangerous things
127 3.6 Vicarious liability
130 3.7 Defences
135 3.8 Remedies

4 Law of contract

141 4.1 Rules of contract law
143 4.2 Theory of contract law
146 4.3 Essential requirements of a contract
157 4.4 Contract terms (1): General
161 4.5 Contract terms (2): Specific terms implied by statute in relation to consumer contracts
164 4.6 Contract terms (3): Exclusion clauses
168 4.7 Vitiating factors
172 4.8 Discharge of a contract
176 4.9 Remedies

5 Human rights

183 5.1 Rules in human rights law

185 5.2 Theory of human rights

187 5.3 Human rights in international law

189 5.4 Human rights in the UK prior to and after the Human Rights Act 1998

193 5.5 European Convention on Human Rights 1953

203 5.6 Restrictions

206 5.7 Enforcement

209 5.8 Human rights and English law

213 5.9 Reform of the protection of human rights in the UK

218 Glossary

221 Index

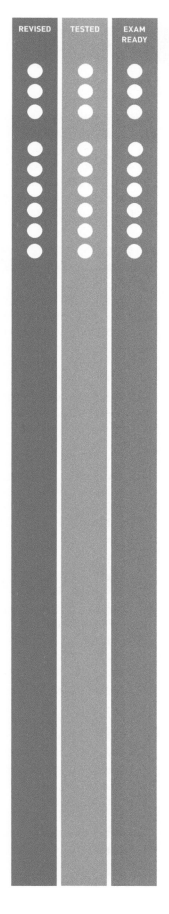

Countdown to my exams

From September

Attend class in person or via the internet if necessary; listen and enjoy the subject; make notes. Make friends in class and discuss the topics with them. Watch the news. Also refer to the *A-level Law Review* for further clarification of topics, exercises and case law updates.

6–8 weeks to go

- Start by looking at the specification – make sure you know exactly what material you need to revise and the style of the examination. Use the revision planner on pages iv–v to familiarise yourself with the topics.
- Organise your notes, making sure you have covered everything on the specification. The revision planner will help you to group your notes into topics.
- Work out a realistic revision plan that will allow you time for relaxation. Set aside days and times for all the subjects that you need to study and stick to your timetable.
- Set yourself sensible targets. Break your revision down into focused sessions of around 40 minutes, divided by breaks. These Revision Notes organise the basic facts into short, memorable sections to make revising easier.

REVISED

2–6 weeks to go

- Read through the relevant sections of this book and refer to the exam tips, exam summaries, typical mistakes and key terms. Tick off the topics as you feel confident about them. Highlight those topics you find difficult and look at them again in detail.
- Test your understanding of each topic by working through the 'Now test yourself' questions in the book. Look up the answers online.
- Make a note of any problem areas as you revise and ask your teacher to go over these in class.
- Look at past papers. They are one of the best ways to revise and practise your exam skills. Write or prepare planned answers to the exam practice questions provided in this book. Check your answers online at **www.hoddereducation.co.uk/myrevisionnotes**.
- Use the revision activities to try out different revision methods. For example, you can make notes using mind maps, spider diagrams or flash cards.
- Track your progress using the revision planner and give yourself a reward when you have achieved your target.

REVISED

One week to go

- Try to fit in at least one more timed practice of an entire past paper and seek feedback from your teacher, comparing your work closely with the mark scheme.
- Check the revision planner to make sure you haven't missed out any topics. Brush up on any areas of difficulty by talking them over with a friend or getting help from your teacher.
- Attend any revision classes put on by your teacher. Remember, he or she is an expert at preparing people for examinations.

REVISED 

The day before the examination

- Scan through these Revision Notes for useful reminders, for example, the exam tips, exam summaries, typical mistakes and key terms.
- IMPORTANT: Check the time (is it morning or afternoon?) and place of your examination. Keep in touch with other students in your class.
- Make sure you have everything you need for the exam – pens, highlighters and water.
- Allow some time to relax and have an early night to ensure you are fresh and alert.

REVISED 

My exams

A-level Law Paper 1

Date: ....

Time: ....

Location: ....

A-level Law Paper 2

Date: ....

Time: ....

Location: ....

A-level Law Paper 3

Date: ....

Time: ....

Location: ....

Assessing AQA A-level Law

As a student of A-level law, it is important to understand HOW you are to be examined at the end of two years of study. In consequence, there are three key measures that you need to understand:

- the 'assessment objectives' used to mark an exam
- the command words used in exam papers
- the format of the exam papers themselves.

AQA Assessment objectives

REVISED

Assessment objectives (AOs) are set by OFQUAL and measure how students meet certain criteria in their exam responses:

- **AO1**: *Demonstrate knowledge and understanding of the English legal system and legal rules and principles.*

  This AO is used to examine your understanding of how well you can discuss or explain the law – the rules, the statutes, the common law decision of judges, and so on, in an extended piece of writing.
- **AO2**: *Apply legal rules and principles to given scenarios in order to present a legal argument using appropriate legal terminology.*

  This AO is used to examine your understanding of how well you can apply legal rules, statutes and the common law to a fictitious problem/scenario situation.
- **AO3**: *Analyse and evaluate legal rules, principles, concepts and issues.*

  This AO is used to examine your own assessment, and that of well-established assessment of the rules, the statutes, the common law and decision of judges in an extended piece of writing.

AQA Command words

REVISED

A command word is used at the beginning of an exam question. It 'frames' or specifies exactly what you are to do and how to answer a question. An understanding of the question's command word will avoid wasting time in an exam.

The most frequently used command words used for AQA A-level law papers, along with the number of marks for associated questions, are:

1. **Select**
   - Used in multiple-choice questions, worth 1 mark.
   - AO1
   - Questions 1–5 on all papers.
   - Meaning: Display knowledge and understanding of a specific aspect of the nature of law, the ELS or substantive law.
2. **Explain**
   - Used in extended questions, worth 5 marks.
   - AO1
   - Question 6 on all papers.
   - Meaning: Display knowledge and understanding of a specific aspect of the nature of law, the ELS or substantive law.
3. **Suggest**
   - Used in scenario/problem questions, worth 5 marks.
   - AO1 (2 marks) + AO2 (3 marks)
   - Question 7 on all papers.
   - Meaning: Display and apply knowledge and understanding of rules and principles of substantive law to support or deny a conclusion given in the instructions.

4 **Advise**
  - Used in scenario/problem questions, worth 10 marks.
  - AO1 (3 marks) + AO2 (4 marks) + AO3 (3 marks)
  - Question 8 on all papers.
  - Meaning: Display knowledge and understanding, supported by analysis and evaluation, and application of relevant rules and principles of substantive law to construct a legal argument on which advice as to criminal or legal liability is given.

5 **Examine**
  - Used in extended questions, worth 15 marks.
  - AO1 (5 marks) + AO3 (10 marks)
  - Question 9 on all papers.
  - Meaning: Analyse some aspect of non-substantive law to provide a detailed basis for a required evaluation of substantive law.

6 **Consider**
  - Used in scenario/problem questions, worth 30 marks.
  - AO1 (10 marks) + AO2 (10 marks) + AO3 (10 marks)
  - Question 10 on all papers.
  - Meaning: Display knowledge and understanding, supported by detailed analysis evaluation and application of relevant rules and principles, to construct a legal argument allowing a well-reasoned conclusion.

AQA Exam papers

REVISED

The AQA A-level law specification is examined in three equally weighted (100 marks) papers of two hours, duration, each sat at the end of the course. Each paper is therefore worth 33.3 per cent of the overall assessment.

Paper 1 The nature of law, the English legal system and criminal law

100 marks split into two parts:
- the nature of law, the English legal system (25 marks)
- criminal law (75 marks).

Paper 2 The nature of law, the English legal system and tort law

100 marks split into two parts:
- the nature of law, the English legal system (25 marks)
- tort law (75 marks).

Paper 3A The nature of law, the English legal system and contract law

100 marks split into two parts:
- the nature of law, the English legal system (25 marks)
- contract law (75 marks).

Paper 3B The nature of law, the English legal system and human rights law

100 marks split into two parts:
- the nature of law, the English legal system (25 marks)
- human rights law (75 marks).

1 The nature of law and the English legal system

1.1 The nature of law

This chapter explores the differences between rules that are enforceable by law and rules that are followed as part of normal human behaviour.

It contrasts civil and criminal law, as well as identifying the main sources of law. Law and society are examined together with law and morality, and the extent to which the law achieves justice.

The nature of law is assessed in all three exam papers.

The nature of law

REVISED 

The distinction between enforceable legal rules and principles and other rules and norms of behaviour

Law is made up of rules and regulations that are enforceable by the state. This means they are:

+ made by the state, and
+ administered by state organisations, for example, Her Majesty's Court Service.

We obey laws because we have to.

Other rules, such as the rules of football or of social etiquette, are not laws because they are not enforceable by the state. We obey these rules because we choose to in certain situations.

There are four categories of legal rules and regulations, as outlined in the table below.

Revision activity

In the context of the UK, to what does the word 'state' refer?

Exam tip

These are key issues which you will need to compare and contrast throughout this chapter.

Table 1.1.1 Categories of legal rules and regulations

Category	Purpose	Example
Procedural laws	Prescribe the framework in which other laws are made and enforced.	The Police and Criminal Evidence Act 1984 provides a procedure to be followed by the police in order to make a lawful arrest; other procedural laws dictate how a trial is to be run, who can access financial assistance when going to court etc.
Substantive laws	Create and define legal rights and obligations.	Criminal offences are substantive laws, but so are other laws such as employment rights or the law relating to divorce.
Public laws	Govern the relationship between the state and its citizens.	Public laws include criminal laws and most procedural laws as they define the powers of Parliament, government and other key institutions of the state, such as the police and courts.
Private laws	Create rights enforceable between individuals; they are mainly substantive in nature.	The law of trespass allows you to restrict access to your property.

Differences between criminal and civil law

Criminal law

Criminal laws create criminal offences and punish those who commit them. These laws attract the attention of the Criminal Justice Service (CJS), which includes:

- the police
- the Crown Prosecution Service (CPS)
- the criminal courts
- Her Majesty's Prison Service
- Her Majesty's Probation Service
- the National Offender Management Service.

The Crown prosecutes the defendant. The defendant may be found guilty, provided the jury/magistrates have no reasonable doubt.

Criminal law fits into both the substantive and public categories outlined above. There are courts that specialise in criminal law (see Chapter 1.4).

Civil law

Civil laws create rights that are enforceable between private individuals. This means that enforcement agencies such as the police do not get involved in these laws. Civil laws therefore do not aim to punish but to compensate those whose rights have been violated.

The claimant can sue the defendant. The defendant may be found liable on the balance of probabilities.

Civil laws fit into the substantive category above. There are courts that specialise in civil law (see Chapter 1.4).

Now test yourself

TESTED 

1 Decide which type and category the following laws fit into:
- theft
- rules of evidence
- conventions that dictate how an Act of Parliament should be made
- wills
- health and safety law.

2 In which type of law are the police likely to be involved?

3 What is the aim of criminal law?

4 Is the criminal or civil law standard of proof higher?

5 Select the true statement about civil and criminal law:

A The same unlawful conduct may sometimes be both a crime and a breach of the civil law.

B Civil law is based on common law rules, whereas criminal law is based on statutory rules.

C Issues of law are always decided by juries, in both civil and criminal law cases.

D Judges of the Supreme Court do not hear appeals in civil law cases.

Exam summary

You are most likely to be asked specific multiple-choice questions in this area, such as Q5 above.

However, there is an expectation that this is underpinning knowledge for all other questions, and you must ensure you refer to the correct criminal or civil terminology when answering longer questions on the substantive law areas.

Revision activity

Name as many different law-making bodies as you can.

Prosecutes: legal term for bringing a criminal charge against a defendant.

Guilty: legally responsible for a specified wrongdoing.

Reasonable doubt: the criminal standard of proof which means the prosecution must provide sufficient evidence for the jury or magistrates to be certain of the defendant's guilt – if they are not, then they have reasonable doubt.

Claimant: legal term for a person or organisation starting a civil claim in the courts.

Sue: take civil legal proceedings against a defendant.

Defendant: legal term for a person defending or responding to a legal claim (called a respondent in some aspects of civil law).

Liable: held to be legally responsible for a breach of the civil law.

Balance of probabilities: the civil standard of proof which means the claimant must satisfy the court that their version of events is more likely than not.

Revision activities

1 Name two of the criminal law courts.

2 Name two of the civil courts.

Exam tip

Make sure you do not mix up the terminology used in criminal and civil law.

Different sources of law

You will find much more detail on this topic in Chapter 1.3.

Custom

Rules that come about through custom or practice involve the disapproval of the community rather than formal punishment if they are broken. The individual may also become conditioned to accept the rules, so they are enforced by a feeling of self-guilt.

Some such rules may 'harden into rights' and be so widely accepted that they become the law.

The early common law developed out of customs that were commonly accepted.

Statute

The UK Parliament is based in the Palace of Westminster and made up of the monarch, the House of Commons and the House of Lords. Laws passed here are known as Acts of Parliament or statutes.

Most new law – and all law that could attract controversy, for example, increased police powers in relation to terror suspects – is made by Parliament.

Statute laws are easy to identify as the clues are in the names, for example the Human Rights Act 1988 (see Chapter 5).

Devolved bodies

The UK Parliament has delegated some of its law-making power to other organisations in specific matters, such as:

- the European Union (see Chapter 1.3)
- the Scottish Parliament
- the Welsh Government
- the Northern Ireland Assembly
- local councils, such as local borough or county councils.

Laws passed by local councils often only apply in a small geographical area, for example, a by-law banning ball games on an area of parkland (see Chapter 1.3).

Common law

'Common law' refers to laws that have been developed by judicial decisions.

An example of a common law crime is murder. This means it has never been defined in an Act of Parliament, but instead developed froms ancient custom and is still developing through the decisions of judges in the highest courts. These decisions are known as 'precedents' (see Chapter 1.3).

Lord Reid said famously: 'There was a time when it was thought almost indecent to suggest that judges make law – they only declare it ... But we do not believe in fairy tales anymore.'

Stretch and challenge

Consider how the decision in *R (AR) v Chief Constable of Greater Manchester* (2018) illustrates the importance of maintaining the balance between conflicting interests.

Exam summary

You are unlikely to be asked a specific question on this area, but more detailed information on parliamentary law making, delegated legislation and judicial precedent will be asked about (see Chapter 1.3). In addition, there is an expectation that you will know the sources of each substantive law you refer to.

Now test yourself

6 What are statutes?
7 Who is needed to make statutes?
8 Who makes the common law, and how?

TESTED

Law and society

REVISED

The role law plays in society

Law can be described as a mechanism of social control. It comprises rules for keeping order in all societies. These rules develop from the behaviour that society has, over time, accepted as 'appropriate' or 'normal'.

A rule is something that determines the way in which we behave. We either:

- submit ourselves to the rule voluntarily, as is the case with moral rules (see pages 8–9), or
- have to follow the rule as it is enforceable in some way, as is the case with the law.

The aim of criminal law is to maintain law and order. Therefore, when a person is found guilty of an offence, that offender will be punished. There is also the aim of trying to protect society, and this is the justification for sending offenders to prison.

Civil law upholds the rights of individuals and organisations. The courts can order compensation to put the parties back to the position they would have been in if their rights had not been violated.

The effect of law on enforceable rights and the balance required between competing interests

This topic is assessed in Paper 3.

What are rights/interests?

In this context, rights and interests are defined by Rudolf von Jhering and Roscoe Pound as 'principles identified by individuals and/or states as being of fundamental importance'.

Individuals' interests (private interests) might include:

- survival
- safety
- freedom
- justice
- privacy
- healthcare
- education.

We now associate many of these areas with human rights law.

The state's interests (public interests) are less complex – generally just:

- physical security
- financial security.

When do interests conflict?

Individuals can conflict with:

- other individuals, for example, a starving man's method of survival may be to steal another person's bread
- the state, for example, a suspected terrorist's interest in freedom will conflict with the state's interest in security.

How does the law balance conflicting interests?

Conflict between individuals' interests is generally dealt with by substantive laws, such as theft in our example above.

Conflict between an individual's interests and the state's interests is generally dealt with by procedural laws, such as the rule in the Terrorism Act 2006 that allows the police to hold a suspected terrorist for up to 14 days without charge, as in our example above.

Exam tip

Your exam responses should show that you know about the key theorists in this area and the differences between them, and that you understand the important areas of substantive and procedural law. Always use key cases to illustrate your points.

Table 1.1.2 Key theorists on enforceable rights and balancing conflicting interests

Jeremy Bentham (1748–1832)	+ Bentham devised the concept of utilitarianism, also known as the 'greatest happiness principle'. + He was a leading theorist in the philosophy of law and a political radical whose ideas included freedom of expression, equal rights for women, the right to divorce and the decriminalising of homosexual acts. He called for the abolition of slavery, the death penalty and physical punishment, and was an early advocate of animal rights. + He was strongly in favour of the extension of individual legal rights and opposed the idea of natural law ('God-given' in origin), calling it 'nonsense upon stilts'.
Rudolf von Jhering (1818–92)	+ Von Jhering explored the 'struggle for law'. He conceived of jurisprudence as a science to be utilised for the further advancement of the moral and social interests of mankind.
Roscoe Pound (1870–1964)	+ Pound is associated with social engineering, emphasising the importance of social relationships in the development of law. + He stated that a lawmaker acts as a social engineer by attempting to solve problems in society using law as a tool.

Table 1.1.3 Key cases for balancing competing interests

Case	Use as an example of:
Miller v Jackson (1977)	Conflict of individual rights: the cricket club wanted to play cricket; its neighbours wanted to stop balls flying into their gardens.
Kennaway v Thompson (1981)	The use of partial injunctions and damages in order to strike a balance between the rights of the neighbours and the social interest of sport.
Evans v UK (2006)	Individuals' conflicting rights over the destruction or otherwise of embryos created from them both.
R v T (1990)	Substantive law, for example, a defence attempting to balance the conflicting interests of the defendant and the victim.
DPP v Majewski (1976)	Restriction of the use of a 'defence' for policy reasons.

Key areas of substantive and procedural law

- Nuisance (see Chapter 3.5)
- Bail (see page 44)
- Treatment of suspects by the police (see page 44)
- Criminal trial process (see page 44–5)
- Automatic disclosure of criminal convictions
- Cautions
- Consent (see Chapter 3.7)
- Intoxication (see Chapter 2.8)

Revision activity

Identify whether areas of law are procedural or substantive.

Link them to the cases in the table – does the law successfully engineer a balance of the interests?

The meaning and importance of fault in civil and/or criminal law

Fault is an integral part of English civil and criminal law. Indeed, it has often been said that fault is the common thread that runs through all English law.

This topic will be assessed in Paper 1 and/or Paper 2.

Fault in civil law

Negligence – one of the largest areas of civil law – relies on the defendant breaching a duty of care owed to the victim (see Chapters 3.1–3.3). This breach is where the fault lies.

To be found to have breached the duty of care, the defendant must be seen to have fallen below the standards of the 'reasonable person', making this a kind of objective fault.

The defendant can have different levels of fault, depending on a multitude of factors. Key cases here include *Paris v Stepney Borough Council* (1951) and *Latimer v AEC* (1953).

Reasonable person: sometimes known as the 'man on the Clapham omnibus', the reasonable person is a hypothetical ordinary person, used by the courts to decide whether a party has acted as a reasonable person would do. The reasonable person is a reasonably educated, intelligent but nondescript person, against whom the defendant's conduct can be measured.

Fault may be transferred from one person to another – known as vicarious liability (see Chapter 3.6). It can also be shared between the two parties – known as contributory negligence (see Chapter 3.7).

Just as there are some crimes with no fault requirement (strict liability offences), there are also some civil torts with no fault requirement – see *Rylands v Fletcher* (1868) in Chapter 3.5.

Other key cases here include *Froom v Butcher* (1976) and *Mohamud v WM Morrison Supermarkets plc* (2016).

Fault in criminal law

An act must be accompanied by fault to equal a crime. An act without fault is an accident and so, in the majority of cases, nobody can be found guilty of a crime.

However, there are two types of offence that do not require fault:

- strict liability offences
- absolute liability offences.

These offences are there to regulate society and protect the vulnerable, for example, parking offences or sexual intercourse with a child under the age of 13.

The laws governing these offences are strictly monitored, so as to ensure that people are not unjustly found guilty of an offence over which they had no control (see page 46). A key case here is *Sweet v Parsley* (1970).

In crime, there are different levels of fault (see Chapters 2.1–2.6). These levels tend to reflect how seriously the crime is viewed, as opposed to the outcome.

For instance:

- someone who intends to kill their victim will be charged with murder – see *R v Janjua and Choudhury* (1998)
- if the defendant was negligent, they would be charged with gross negligence manslaughter – see *R v Adomako* (1995).

As murder carries a mandatory life sentence and gross negligence manslaughter only carries a maximum life sentence, this demonstrates that sentencing reflects the fault of the defendant and not what happened to the victim.

Fault can be reduced or removed completely if the defendant can successfully plead a defence (see Chapter 2.8).

Revision activity

Research the facts of *R v Hart* (2000) and *R v Huntley* (2004).

How many victims did each defendant kill? Which was given the most severe sentence? Do you agree with this outcome?

Importance of fault

Fault was first introduced into negligence law in *Cambridge Water v Eastern Counties Leather* (1994). Before that, fault was not always necessary for damages to be paid.

Some civil legal systems operate a non-fault-based system. For instance, in New Zealand all taxpayers contribute to a fund that pays the victims of accidents and other incidents resulting in injuries to the victim. However, to apply an entirely no-fault system would require higher taxes for everyone.

Fault has always been a part of criminal law. It is necessary to justify sentencing, as it would be unjust to penalise someone for an act when the outcome was not their fault. It simply would not be possible to have a criminal legal system without fault.

Equally, a criminal system that did not have some regulatory offences without fault would grind to a halt – the courts would be full of motorists being prosecuted for speeding or parking on double yellow lines, whereas in the UK's system of strict liability for these offences, they can be dealt with by post (see Chapter 2.3).

Revision activity

Use the headings and subheadings from this section to make up questions of your own that have two or more requirements. Test yourself or your study buddy on how to respond to them.

Typical mistakes

Often, questions on fault will ask you to do at least two things, for example, 'Explain what is meant by fault and its importance'. If you ignore the word 'and', your answer will not gain the higher marks.

Table 1.1.4 Key cases on fault

Case	Use as an example of:
Sweet v Parsley (1970)	Strict liability being avoided. Judges inserted the word 'knowingly' to prevent the offence being one of strict liability.
R v Janjua and Choudhury (1998)	The different levels of fault acceptable to establish the *mens rea* of murder, from direct intent to kill to oblique intent GBH.
R v Adomako (1995)	The lowest type of fault possible in criminal law – negligence. This was a gross negligence manslaughter case involving an anaesthetist who failed to take adequate care of a patient.
Paris v Stepney Borough Council (1951)	Fault in civil law. The employer knew of the employee's condition (one eye) and failed to provide safety equipment.
Latimer v AEC (1953)	Fault in civil law. The employer took sufficient steps to keep his staff safe – he was not required to take unreasonable steps.
Froom v Butcher (1976)	Fault can be shared in negligence using the principle of contributory negligence. Here, the claimant was injured in an accident caused by the defendant, but the claimant was not wearing a seatbelt and so contributed to his own injuries.
Mohamud v WM Morrison Supermarkets plc (2016)	Fault can be transferred to the employer, who can be legally responsible for the actions of an employee. Morrisons supermarkets was liable when its employee attacked the claimant.
Cambridge Water Co. Ltd v Eastern Counties Leather plc (1994)	Establishing the requirement of fault in negligence and stating that damage must be reasonably foreseeable

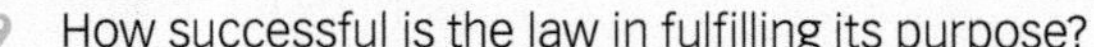

Now test yourself TESTED

9 How successful is the law in fulfilling its purpose?
10 Why is it important that the balancing of competing interests is seen to be done?
11 Why is having a number of offences without fault important for efficiency purposes? Why are these offences regarded as a problem?
12 What effect does a defence have on the fault element of a crime?

Exam summary

In the exam, you MAY be asked:

- a short question (5 marks) about one of the areas that has been addressed by this topic
- a maximum-length question (30 marks), part of which requires the application of substantive law, but part of which goes on to question how effective this area of law is at balancing conflicting interests, for example.

Law and morality

REVISED

This will be assessed in Paper 2 and/or Paper 3.

The distinction between law and morality

Laws are rules and regulations that are objective and not necessarily fault-based, for example, speeding.

Morals are subjective personal codes of values or beliefs that are based on levels of fault and determine what is right or wrong, for example, lying.

In some situations, it is possible for there to be an overlap of the two, such as murder which is both against the law and morally wrong.

However, there are other situations that cause tension between legal and moral rules, for example, abortion and euthanasia.

The diversity of moral views in a pluralist society

The UK is a pluralist society, where there is more than one:

- culture
- race
- religion
- political party
- language
- ethnic origin
- set of customs and traditions
- social class.

Stretch and challenge

Read this case to develop your understanding of law and morality: *R (on the application of Conway) v Secretary of State for Justice* (2018). You can find good analysis at **https://ukhumanrightsblog.com/2018/07/09/the-right-to-die-who-decides/**.

In an effective, progressive pluralist society, diversity should be celebrated, not simply tolerated. However, this can lead to tensions: should the law involve itself in matters of moral importance to some groups?

Relationship between law and morality

Table 1.1.5 Relationship between law and morality

Laws	Morals
+ Made by formal institutions, e.g. Parliament and the courts. + (But think of common law: does this have its basis in morality?)	+ Evolve as society evolves, no formal creation. + (Were the Ten Commandments in the Bible or the Koran an attempt to create a formal moral code?)
+ Can be instantly made or repealed. + (However, this often takes time and public pressure: the Human Rights Act was passed in 1998, years after the United Nations Declaration of Human Rights in 1948.)	+ Change with society's attitudes; slow transitional period. + (Sometimes change is rapid, such as during the 1960s. Within a decade, contraception, sex outside marriage and the use of recreational drugs became widely acceptable.)
+ Existence can be established. + (But does this make them right? The defence to many war crimes was that the defendants were merely obeying the law.)	+ Only vaguely defined. + (There may be general agreement on some issues such as murder, but not on others such as abortion.)
+ Breaking them attracts some form of sanction/ punishment/remedy enforced by the state.	+ Breaching moral standards merely results in social condemnation, as opposed to an organised system of enforcement.
+ Society's attitude to the law is irrelevant. + (See recent disputes over the 'tampon tax'. However, in a democracy this can only be a short-term position.)	+ Morals reflect society's values and beliefs.
+ Obligatory	+ Subjective
+ Not necessarily fault-based (i.e. strict liability)	+ Fault-based

The legal enforcement of moral values

Lord Devlin devised four key principles for Parliament to bear in mind when deciding which moral 'offences' ought to be prohibited by law and which ought not:

1. The individual freedom to be allowed must be consistent with the integrity of society.
2. The limits of such tolerance are not static, but lawmakers should be slow to change laws which protect morality.
3. Privacy must be respected as far as possible.
4. The law is concerned with minimum rather than maximum standards of behaviour: i.e. the law sets down a minimum standard of behaviour; society's standards should be higher.

There has been much academic and legal debate about whether the law should be used to enforce moral values. Broadly, there are two differing philosophies:

- positivism
- natural law theory.

Positivism

Positivism maintains that laws and morals should be kept separate.

Table 1.1.6 Key theorists for positivism

Aristotle	The law should be 'reason, free from passion'.
Jeremy Bentham	Natural law theory is 'nonsense upon stilts'.
John Stuart Mill	'The only purpose for which power can be rightfully exercised over any member of a civilised society against his will is to prevent harm to others. His own good, either physical or moral, is not a sufficient warrant.'
H.L.A. Hart	'Is it morally permissible to enforce morality? Deprivation of freedom causes pain to the individual. Individuals should not be so deprived, unless it is justifiable in the interests of society.' 'Laws that merely enforce morals should cease. Laws should only intervene where immorality causes harm to the society or harm to the individual concerned.'
Wolfenden Report 1978	'Unless a deliberate attempt is made by society, acting through the agency of law, to equate the sphere of crime with that of sin, there must be a realm of private morality and immorality which is, in brief and crude terms, not the law's business.'

Natural law theory

Natural law theory maintains that the law should be used to enforce moral values.

Table 1.1.7 Key theorists for natural law theory

St Thomas Aquinas	Natural law theory is a 'dictate of right reason'.
James Fitzjames-Stephens	'The immorality of an action is good reason for it to be a crime and the law should be a persecution of the grosser forms of vice.'
Lord Devlin	'The suppression of vice is as much the law's business as the suppression of subversive activities.' 'It is an error of jurisprudence to separate crime from sin.'
Lon Fuller	Referring to laws made by Germany under the Nazi regime, 'some laws are so immoral that they must be invalid'.
Viscount Simonds	'There remains in the courts of law a residual power to enforce the supreme and fundamental purpose of the law, to conserve not only the safety and order but also the moral welfare of the state.'

It is difficult in practice to take a theoretical position on this argument, particularly because we live in a pluralist society. Judges are often faced with tough decisions which are matters of life and death – the arguments then become much more difficult to polarise.

In 2000, the case of conjoined twins Jodie and Mary came before the court. The only way to save Jodie's life was for doctors to perform surgery which would kill Mary. Lord Justice Ward said: 'This is a court of law, not a court of morals.'

Because these matters can be very divisive, political parties and politicians often prefer not to publicly state their positions for fear of alienating voters.

Evaluation point

Research these theorists, adding dates to create a timeline. How does the period of time add context to their arguments?

Revision activity

Consider the recent cases regarding baby Charlie Gard and Tony Nicklinson on the rights to receive treatment or to die. Create a timeline of the attempts to pass the Assisted Dying Bill and try to fit the successes and failures around the theories.

Revision activity

Why do you think living in a pluralist society can make these sorts of decisions more difficult?

Stretch and challenge

What mechanism is used in Parliament to pass controversial law without political parties having to state an option?

Table 1.1.8 Key cases for positivism and natural law

Case	Facts	Useful quotes or points	Decision based on positivism or natural law?
R v Wilson (1996)	D branded his initials on his wife's buttocks with a hot knife, at her request. Her skin became infected and she sought treatment from a doctor, who reported the matter to the police. The husband was charged with ABH.	Russell LJ: 'Consensual activity between husband and wife, in the privacy of the matrimonial home, is not, in our judgment, a proper matter for criminal investigation, let alone criminal prosecution.'	Positivism
R v Brown (1993)	Ds engaged in sadomasochism, including physical torture.	Lord Templeman: 'Pleasure derived from the infliction of pain is an evil thing.'	Natural law
R v Human Fertilisation and Embryology Authority ex parte Blood (1997)	Blood's husband contracted meningitis and lapsed into a coma. Samples of his sperm were taken for later artificial insemination. Her husband died shortly after the samples were obtained.	As the husband's consent was not given, Blood was not permitted to use the sperm. However, she later used an EU rule and was permitted to use it abroad.	Positivism
Gillick v West Norfolk and Wisbech Health Authority (1986)	G sought a declaration that it would be unlawful for a doctor to prescribe contraceptives to girls under the age of 16 without the knowledge or consent of the parent.	The court refused to grant it, setting out guidelines for when children can give consent to medical procedures. This is now known as 'Gillick competency'.	Positivism
Shaw v DPP (1961)	D published a ladies' directory of the services offered by prostitutes.	The supreme and fundamental purpose of the law is to conserve not only the safety and order but also the moral welfare of the state.	Natural law
Knuller v DPP (1973)	D published a magazine in which advertisements were placed by homosexuals seeking to meet other like-minded individuals to engage in sexual practices.	The House of Lords doubted the correctness of the decision in *Shaw* but declined to depart from it.	Natural law
R v Gibson and Sylveire (1990)	Ds exhibited a pair of earrings made with freeze-dried human foetuses at the Young Unknowns Gallery in London.	This was the first occasion on which the charge of outraging public decency had been preferred in more than 80 years.	Natural law
Pretty v DPP (2001)	Pretty attempted to change the law so she could end her own life because of the pain and problems caused by her terminal illness, motor neurone disease.	Lord Bingham: 'The task of the committee in this appeal is not to weigh or evaluate or reflect those beliefs and views or give effect to its own but to ascertain and apply the law of the land as it is now understood to be.'	Natural law
R v Cox (1992)	Cox was a consultant and had been treating V for years. As her rheumatoid arthritis became worse, she pleaded with him to end her life. He administered a fatal injection to stop her heart.	D was found guilty but given a suspended sentence.	Natural law
Evans v UK (2007)	Evans wanted to use embryos fertilised by her ex-partner; he refused.	Despite the emotional issues at stake, consent must be applied.	Positivism
R v Dudley and Stephens (1884)	Ds were shipwrecked and stranded in a small boat with a young cabin boy. When food ran out, they drew straws to see which one of them would be killed so that the others could eat him. Ds ate the cabin boy and were convicted of murder.	Law and morality are not the same, and many things may be immoral which are not necessarily illegal, yet the absolute divorce of law from morality would be of fatal consequence.	Natural law

Exam tip

If an exam question contains the words 'should' or 'ought', you need to weigh up the arguments – both the theoretical ones and those presented by the reality of hearing such sensitive matters in court – and write a conclusion.

As long as your conclusion is supported by a balanced analysis of the arguments, it should not matter whether you agree or disagree.

Typical mistake

In a question such as 'Explain the relationship between law and morality and whether the law should enforce moral values', candidates sometimes fail to answer both parts.

Now test yourself

TESTED 

13 What is meant by pluralism?
14 What are the earliest examples of law you can think of? Do they still exist in some form today?
15 Who are the key positivists?
16 Who are the key opponents of positivism? What are their arguments known as?

Exam summary

In the exam, you MAY be asked:

+ a short question (5 marks) about one of the areas that have been addressed by this topic
+ a maximum-length question (30 marks), part of which requires the application of substantive law, but part of which goes on to question whether this area of law has its basis in morality, for example.

Stretch and challenge

Read '*Where law and morality meet*' by Matthew H Kramer (2004) at **philpapers.org**.

Law and justice

REVISED

This will be assessed in Paper 1 and/or Paper 3.

The meaning of justice

Justice is the idea that the law is 'fair' in how it seeks to punish wrongs and protect rights. The idea comes from John Rawls' book, *A Theory of Justice* (1971), who put this rather metaphysical concept into words:

1 The social contract: social cooperation relies on a contract which people have made among themselves. The principles of justice are to be viewed as the result of a binding contract among the members of society.
2 Greatest equal liberty: this includes basic freedoms such as speech.
3 Difference principle: social and economic inequalities are fair and just, but only if they work for the benefit of the least advantaged in society. People have different interests and demands but will have some individual conception of 'good'. However, the specific content of 'good' may not be developed.

Typical mistake

It is really important to link theory to practical application. Often candidates only reference the theorists and not cases. Ensure you include both.

Revision activity

Copy and complete this table.

Type of justice	Explanation	Examples from across your study
Formal justice	The existence of independent institutions and processes.	
Substantive justice		Requirement for MR in crime and the application of defences.
	Fair allocation of resources.	Equality laws, welfare stare.
Corrective justice		Remedies in tort, putting claimant in back in the position as if the tort had not occurred.

Theories of justice

Philosophers from as early as Aristotle's time have attempted to pin down the meaning of justice, with some similarity between them.

> **Evaluation point**
>
> Research these types of justice and make notes on their advantages and disadvantages.

Table 1.1.9 Key theorists for law and justice

Aristotle	+ For Aristotle, justice was about distribution and proportionality. This is quite close to current ideas about social justice and can been seen in many human rights issues. + Key case: *Lindsay v Commissioners of Customs and Excise* (2002).
Aquinas	+ A natural law thinker, Aquinas was followed by Fuller and Rawls. He had ideas of 'justice as fairness'.
Jeremy Bentham	+ Bentham coined the idea of utilitarianism, a concept later developed by John Stuart Mill. This works on the principle that the purpose of law is to achieve the greatest happiness for the greatest number of people. + This clearly indicates the law's purpose is to create a balance, but that the individual's good may be sacrificed in favour of the good of the whole. + Examples of this are clear in policy decisions, such as *R v Brown* (1993) (see page 30), where the good of society (not to be corrupted) outweighed the concerns of the individuals involved (to consent to whatever activity they choose).
Karl Marx	+ Marx argued that in a capitalist society all laws are unjust. Justice can only be achieved by redistribution of wealth. + This perhaps led to Rawls' simple idea of a social contract.
Robert Nozick	+ Nozick's theory of 'entitlement' holds that society is just if everyone is entitled to the holdings they possess. Unfortunately, not everyone follows these rules: 'Some people steal from others, or defraud them, or enslave them, seizing their product and preventing them from living as they choose, or forcibly exclude others from competing in exchanges.' + This is in sharp contrast with Marx and Rawls.

> **Stretch and challenge**
>
> Read the six models of distributive justice put forward by Chaim Perelman. Link these to the types and theorists in Table 1.1.9.

> **Exam tip**
>
> You will be rewarded for any attempt to evaluate any particular idea of justice, for example, the utilitarian's concern for society rather than the individual.

The extent to which the law (civil and/or criminal) achieves justice

In most legal disputes, one party will usually see that justice has been done, while the other may wholeheartedly disagree. Whether or not the legal rules achieve justice is a subjective concept.

Even judges can disagree about the scope of their role in trying to achieve justice. In his autobiography, *The Family Story*, Lord Denning wrote that:

> 'My root belief is that the proper role of the judge is to do justice between the parties before him. If there is any rule of law which impairs the doing of justice, then it is the province of the judge to do all he legitimately can to avoid the rule, even to change it, so as to do justice in the instant case before him.'

In *Tito v Waddell* (No.2) (1977), Sir Robert Megarry VC took an opposing view:

> 'The question is not whether the plaintiffs ought to succeed as a matter of fairness or ethics or morality. I have no jurisdiction to make an award to the plaintiffs just because I reach the conclusion ... that they have had a raw deal. This is a Court of Law and Equity (using "equity" in its technical sense), administering justice according to law and equity, and my duty is to examine the plaintiffs' claim on that footing.'

> **Evaluation point**
>
> Research these theorists, adding dates to create a timeline. How does the period of time add context to their arguments?

How legal rules strive to achieve justice

Procedural justice

Procedural law puts systems in place in an attempt to ensure justice – it provides a framework in which all should be equal before the law.

Everyone is entitled to put their case in court.

- Financial assistance should exist for accessing lawyers and the courts.
- The rules of evidence ensure the material presented in court is reliable, for example, confession evidence of a defendant intimidated by police will not be admissible – see *R v Miller* (1992).
- The right to trial by jury can ensure justice being done in an individual case rather than a policy or 'floodgates' type verdict – *see R v Ponting* (1985).
- Judges, magistrates and juries must not be biased or appear to be biased – see *R v Bingham JJ ex parte Jowitt* (1974).
- Corrective justice, not the Aristotle theory but rather the notion that there is a right to a 'second opinion', provides a system of appeals, judicial review and the Criminal Cases Review Commission (CCRC) to ensure justice has been done.
- Within this framework, disputes are resolved by applying substantive laws to produce the most 'just' results.

Revision activity

Research the Criminal Cases Review Commission and briefly explain its role.

Stretch and challenge

Who said, 'the law, like a tavern, should be open to all' and what did they mean by this?

Evaluation point

Have a look at the consequences of the Legal Aid, Sentencing and Punishment of Offenders Act 2012 (LASPO): is the law still open to all?

Substantive justice

This kind of justice is achieved by the application of legal rules themselves. For example:

- In criminal law, there are defences to justify the actions of the defendant, and the partial defences to murder ensure the defendant still shoulders some responsibility but not all.
- When sentencing, the accused should be treated consistently with their level of fault (see Chapters 1.1 and 2.2).
- In civil law, concepts such as the standard of care owed by a professional above that of an ordinary person help to achieve justice.

Failures in achieving justice

Where rules have failed to achieve justice

- The mandatory life term for murders allows no judicial flexibility to recognise different levels of seriousness of offence. *In R v Canning* (2002), the trial judge described his sentence as 'a classic example of injustice'.
- The rules on joint enterprise: *R v Jogee* (2016) corrected a historic mistake which had exposed people to being found guilty of the most serious offences on the weakest legal basis.

Stretch and challenge

Read the facts and sentencing remarks in *R v Wallace* (2018).

Revision activity

Research these cases and create a grid 'attaching' them to an idea of justice, for example, by showing that there was a denial of natural justice.

Miscarriages of justice

The following cases are notorious instances of where justice was not achieved:

- Timothy Evans
- Alan Turing
- the Birmingham Six
- the Guildford Four
- Stephen Lawrence.

These cases stick in our memory because they are unusual. They are, after all, a tiny minority of the cases that pass through our criminal and civil justice systems. Perhaps it is fair to conclude that most of the system is just and achieves just results most of the time – this is a state of affairs to satisfy most utilitarians.

Stretch and challenge

Link these miscarriages of justices (and any other similar cases you may have learned about) to the types of justice. Can these cases be used to illustrate and evaluate these types?

Table 1.1.10 Key cases regarding the law and justice

Case	Facts	Principle of justice
Lindsay v Commissioners of Customs and Excise (2002)	The practice of customs officials to confiscate cars as well as the goods being smuggled in them was held to be disproportionate.	Aristotle
R v Miller (1992)	The police asked 300 questions of the suspect. The interview was held to be oppressive.	Procedural justice – police powers
R v Ponting (1985)	D, an MOD civil servant, passed documents showing the government had lied about the sinking of the ship *General Belgrano* during the Falklands War to an opposition MP to raise it in Parliament. D was charged under the Official Secrets Act. He was acquitted.	Procedural justice – trial by jury
R v Bingham JJ ex parte Jowitt (1974)	D was charged with speeding. His evidence contradicted evidence from a police officer. Finding D guilty, the chairman said: 'My principle in such cases has always been to believe the evidence of the police officer.' The Divisional Court quashed the conviction; this remark suggested bias and that D had not had a fair trial.	Procedural justice – the process must be free from bias.
Glynn v Keele University (1971)	A student was seen sunbathing nude, but he was not given a hearing at all; instead, he was sent a letter fining him £10 and he was suspended. Although the student had not suffered any injustice, he should have been given the opportunity to test the evidence.	Procedural justice – there must be reasonable opportunity to test the evidence.
R v Thames Magistrates' Court ex parte Polemis (1974)	A Greek sea captain was not given time to prepare his defence to an allegation of polluting docks with oil. He received his summons at 10.30 a.m. and the case was heard at 4 p.m.	Procedural justice – there must be reasonable opportunity to test the evidence.
Re Pinochet (1998)	Chilean dictator, Augusto Pinochet, tried to evade extradition to Spain. One of the House of Lords judges was associated with a charity that had campaigned to have Pinochet brought to justice.	Procedural justice; natural justice – there can be no suggestion of bias (in Latin, *nemo judex in res sua*)
R v B (A-G Ref. No. 3 of 1999) (2000)	This case looked at whether DNA profile evidence, which should have been destroyed under s 64(3B)(b) of the Police and Criminal Evidence Act 1984, could be admitted in evidence. The Court of Appeal ruled that it could not.	Procedural justice – evidence must be obtained fairly.
R v Mason (1987)	A confession obtained by deceit was wrongly admitted. An appeal was allowed; confession obtained by deceit should be rejected.	Procedural justice – evidence must be obtained fairly.
R v Wilson (1996)	See page 10.	Procedural justice; defences must be allowed and there must be an ability to distinguish precedents.
Miller v Jackson (1977)	See page 5.	Cumming-Bruce LJ: the court had to 'strike a fair balance'; damages were awarded instead of an injunction.
R v Dudley and Stephens (1884)	See page 10.	Utilitarianism not used here; individual justice is not sacrificed for the good of the majority – though the sentence was commuted and therefore reflective of Ds' ordeal.

Now test yourself TESTED

17 Define 'justice'.
18 How did Lord Denning and Sir Robert Megarry differ in their opinions about the role of the judge in achieving justice?
19 What is meant by 'substantive justice'?
20 Why are utilitarians happy about the law's efforts in achieving justice? What do you think?

Exam summary

In the exam, you MAY be asked:
+ a mid-length question (10–15 marks) about the meaning of a particular element of substantive law and then asked to consider whether that achieves justice
+ a maximum-length question (30 marks), part of which requires the application of substantive law, but part of which goes on to question whether this area of law achieves justice.

1.2 The rule of law

The rule of law is examined in outline as an introduction to human rights. It will be assessed in Paper 3.

The rule of law is a symbolic idea, with no single definition but much significance. Lord Bingham, one of the UK's most senior judges, wrote a book on the subject that explores the concept in great depth.

The Constitutional Reform Act 2005 makes reference to it in s 1, saying '[the] Act does not adversely affect the existing constitutional principle of the Rule of Law'.

Stretch and challenge

Read the introductory text for the Constitutional Reform Act 2005 to find out its purpose.

The constitutional doctrine of the rule of law

So, what is the rule of law? In broad terms, it means:
+ No person shall be sanctioned except in accordance with the law.
+ All shall be equal before the law.
+ There shall be fairness and clarity of the law.

The rule of law is therefore a safeguard against dictatorship:
+ The government and its officials are accountable under the law.
+ No single branch of government can exercise unlimited power.
+ There are checks and balances, including an independent judiciary, to maintain these principles.

Three academic views are summarised below.

A.V. Dicey

Broadly in line with the points above, Dicey felt there were three elements that created the rule of law:
1 An absence of arbitrary power on the part of the state: the state's power must be controlled by the law and can be challenged by judicial review. This includes preventing the state from having wide discretionary powers, because discretion can be exercised without proper checks and balances.
2 Equality before the law: no one is above the law regardless of how powerful they are; the law deals with them in the same way as it would anyone else. Those who carry out functions of state are accountable in the law for their actions. However, this does not take into account differences in wealth – real equality can only be achieved with some form of financial help from the state for those needing to access justice (see page 54).

3 Supremacy of ordinary law: this is different from the concept of parliamentary supremacy (see page 21), which may contradict the idea of arbitrary power above.

F.A. von Hayek

Von Hayek followed Dicey's principles but felt that the rule of law had become diluted because, provided actions of the state are permitted by an Act of Parliament, anything done in accordance with this Act is lawful. He also pointed out that regulating economic activity, as modern governments do, is in conflict with the rule of law.

Joseph Raz

Raz saw the rule of law as acting to minimise the danger of the use of discretionary power in an arbitrary way. He thought the rule of law was that law must be capable of guiding the individual's behaviour.

Some of his key principles are:

- There should be clear rules and procedures for making laws.
- The independence of the judiciary must be guaranteed.
- The principles of natural justice should be observed; these require an open and fair hearing with all parties being given the opportunity to put their case.
- The courts should have the power to review the way in which the other principles are implemented, to ensure that they are being operated as demanded by the rule of law.

> **Evaluation point**
>
> Research these theorists, adding dates to create a timeline. How does the period of time add context to their arguments?
>
> Whose position is closest to your own feelings?

Rule of law and law making

REVISED

Under the rule of law, the process by which laws are made must be open and fair.

Laws made by Parliament go through a process outlined on page 18–19. This process includes debates, votes and other checks and balances to ensure no element of the state is exercising arbitrary power.

Parliament can also delegate its powers, giving other bodies (known as secondary bodies) power to make regulations. In order to do this, Parliament must pass an Act granting power to make regulations. Then Parliament has powers to scrutinise and check those regulations. Finally, the regulations can be challenged in the courts through judicial review, to ensure the secondary body has not gone beyond the powers granted by Parliament (see page 23).

Independence of the judiciary ensures that judges can prevent/restrict arbitrary exercise of power (especially by government officials/agents) and resolve disputes strictly according to the law in a fair manner (see page 21).

Rule of law and the legal system (procedural law)

REVISED

In criminal procedure:

- every defendant has the right to a fair trial
- independence of the judiciary guarantees freedom of judges from improper influence/interference
- trial by peers (by magistrates or a jury) is important to maintaining fairness and protecting citizens' rights
- no person can be imprisoned without a trial: this is known as *habeas corpus* (in countries where the rule of law is disregarded, people are likely to be detained without a trial, particularly if they are opponents of the government).

In civil procedure:

- in theory, everyone can resolve their disputes effectively through the civil justice system

> **Exam tip**
>
> To prepare for questions on the rule of law, use the cross references given here.
>
> When revising, it might help to create spider diagrams showing the rule of law's relationship with other areas of law. Remember to include examples and make that link!

- the system should be free from discrimination and from corruption, for example, not improperly influenced by public officials
- the system should be accessible and affordable.

There are alternative ways of resolving civil disputes, which are much cheaper to use (see page 42–43).

Revision activity

Add the points you made on page 13 about LASPO (Legal Aid, Sentencing and Punishment of Offenders Act 2012) here too.

Rule of law and substantive law

REVISED

Human rights

Human rights, including the right to a fair trial, are central to the modern interpretation of the rule of law (see Chapters 5.1–5.7).

Criminal law

The aim of criminal law is to maintain law and order by creating criminal offences. For all of these offences, the law has to be clear and the prosecution has to prove that the defendant has committed an offence beyond reasonable doubt.

When a person is found guilty of an offence, that offender will be punished. There is also the aim of trying to protect society, which is the justification for sending offenders to prison.

All offences have a maximum penalty and the courts cannot impose a higher penalty than this.

Civil law

Through tort, the aim of civil law is aimed at protecting individuals' rights. It gives the right to claim compensation for damage caused by breaches of the law. Although everyone has the right to claim, so there appears to be equality before the law, the financial restrictions brought about by LASPO can make it difficult for many to bring a claim.

Through contract law, civil law recognises that people should be free to make what agreements they wish. However, it also recognises that consumers may have very little freedom or power when making contracts with big businesses, and therefore there is not really equality between the parties. This inequality has been balanced in the Consumer Protection Act 1987 and the Consumer Rights Act 2015.

Revision activity

Read the introductory text for the Consumer Protection Act 1987 and the Consumer Rights Act 2015 and make a note of their purpose in bringing equality.

Now test yourself

TESTED

1. What does the rule of law safeguard us against?
2. What impact can wealth have on 'equality before the law'?
3. Why is judicial independence important to the rule of law?
4. Show two ways in which criminal procedure complies with the rule of law.
5. Show two ways in which civil procedure complies with the rule of law.
6. What is the relationship between the rule of law and human rights?
7. How does the rule of law place limitations on how judges deal with defendants who have been found guilty?

Exam tip

In this section on the nature of law, while it is perfectly fine for different candidates to reach different conclusions, your conclusion should be balanced, reasoned and address the question. Use the words of the question to construct your conclusion.

Exam summary

There is an expectation that you understand the rule of law and its purpose throughout the specification and all the papers. You could be asked short- or mid-answer questions about the relationship between the rule of law and procedural matters, such as:

- 'Explain two elements that may be considered to be aspects of the rule of law.'
- 'Briefly explain why the independence of the judiciary is important in relation to the rule of law.'

Typical mistake

Do not work on the different areas of this topic in isolation. It is really important to view the rule of law holistically and to use examples from across the substantive chapters to show your understanding.

1.3 Law making

Law making covers an important set of topics, not only to gain an understanding of the legal system, but also to appreciate the impact of sources of law on substantive areas of law such as criminal law and tort law.

Law making is examined below by its various sources: Parliamentary law making, delegated legislation, statutory interpretation, judicial precedent, law reform and EU law.

Parliamentary law making

REVISED

This will be assessed in Paper 2.

The structure for parliamentary law making

The UK Parliament, based in the Palace of Westminster in London, is a tripartite body comprising the monarch, the House of Lords and the House of Commons.

It is also a bicameral legislature – the legislators are divided into two separate assemblies, chambers or houses.

Monarch

The UK is a constitutional monarchy. This means the queen (or king) is bound to exercise powers and authority only within the limits prescribed by the law.

Rules are not in a written constitution in the UK as they are in some other countries, but originate in the conventions, practices and precedents of Parliament, which form what is known as the Constitution of the United Kingdom.

The monarch is a ceremonial figurehead – a theoretical source of executive power who does not actually exercise executive powers. Executive powers may be exercised in the monarch's name by Parliament and the government.

No person may accept significant public office without swearing an oath of allegiance to the monarch. However, he or she is bound by constitutional convention to act on the advice of the government in making these appointments.

Political theorist Walter Bagehot identified three main political rights which a constitutional monarch may freely exercise, namely the right to be consulted, encourage and warn.

Revision activity

How many public organisations can you name that 'belong' to the monarch?

House of Commons

By convention the seat of government, the House of Commons is Parliament's only democratically elected element.

The UK is divided into 650 constituencies, each of which votes for a Member of Parliament (MP) to represent it. This vote is known as a general election and must be held at least every five years.

The government is formed by the political party with a majority of MPs in the House of Commons, and it is the leader of this political party who is invited by the monarch to be his/her Prime Minister. Because it has a majority, it is the government which has the main say in formulating new Acts of Parliament.

House of Lords

The House of Lords is a non-elected body made up of:

- 92 hereditary peers, who inherited their title and will pass it down through their family
- around 700 life peers, appointed on a non-partisan basis by the House of Lords Appointments Commission
- the 26 most senior bishops in the Church of England.

Prior to 1999 there were about 750 hereditary peers. After reforms of the House of Lords, the right of the remaining 92 to sit in the House of Lords will not pass down with their title.

Because the House of Lords is non-elected, the House of Commons can override it under powers contained in the Parliament Acts of 1911 and 1949. This is known as imperfect bicameralism, as the two houses are not equal in power.

Revision activity

Research the Parliament Acts of 1911 and 1949.

Why were they introduced and how do they limit the House of Lords' power?

Green and White Papers

Each government department (sometimes known as a 'ministry', such as the Ministry of Defence, or a 'department', such as the Department for Education) is responsible for an area of government.

If a change in the law is being considered, it will draft ideas for change. These draft documents are known as Green and White Papers:

- Green Paper – a consultative document issued by the government putting forward proposals for reform of the law and often inviting suggestions.
- White Paper – a document issued by the government stating its decisions as to how it is going to reform the law; this is for information, not consultation.

Formal legislative process

While a new law is making its way through the formal stages of becoming an Act of Parliament, it is known as a Bill. There are three types of Bill, outlined in the table below.

Table 1.3.1 Types of Bill

Public Bills	These involve matters of public policy affecting the whole country or a large section of it. Most government Bills are in this category, for example, the Legal Aid, Sentencing and Punishment of Offenders Act 2012.
Private Members' Bills	Individual (private) MPs introduce a Bill. They can be from any political party and are known as 'backbenchers' because they do not sit in the front row in the House of Commons with the government. There are two ways a private MP can introduce a Bill: + by ballot + through the 'ten-minute' rule.
Private Bills	These are designed to create a law which will affect only individual people or corporations. They do not affect the whole community.
Hybrid Bills	These are a cross between Public Bills and Private Bills. They are introduced by the government, but if they become law they will affect a particular person, organisation or place.

Stretch and challenge

Make a link with the section on 'Law and morals': when are Private Members' Bills used in this context?

Revision activity

Research how private MPs can introduce Bills. Find some Acts that started as Private Members' Bills.

Checks and balances

As discussed in Chapter 1.2, there have to be checks and balances built into the process of a Bill becoming an Act, to prevent any abuses of power.

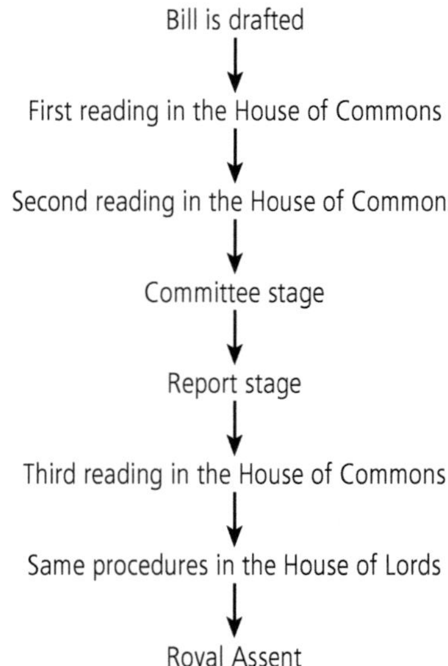

Figure 1 Flow chart of the passing of an Act of Parliament starting in the House of Commons

Revision activity

Write a sentence explaining each stage of the legislative process.

Influences on Parliament

So where do the ideas come from for new laws? As already mentioned, this is often government policy, but who influences this?

Table 1.3.2 Influences on Parliament

Type of influence	Example of its success	Advantages	Disadvantages
Political When a general election is called, the political parties publish a manifesto, which amounts to a promise of what new laws they will introduce.	The Hunting Act 2004 followed the promise by the Labour Party to outlaw fox hunting if elected (also a great example of using the Parliament Acts 1911 and 1949).	Each political party has its proposals ready. A government majority means that most of the Bills it introduces will be passed.	While it is easy to make a promise, it is much more difficult when in power to fulfil that promise, particularly without an overall majority (as the Conservative/Liberal Democrat coalition found in 2010–15).
Media When there is strong public opinion about an issue, the government may bow to it. Where an issue is given a high profile in the media, it may add to the weight of public opinion.	Following the Dunblane massacre in 1996, private ownership of handguns was banned.	The UK's free press is able to criticise government policy or bring any other issue to the attention of the government using public opinion.	Responding too quickly to high-profile incidents leads to poorly drafted law, e.g. the Dangerous Dogs Act 1991. Media companies can manipulate the news to create public opinion.
Pressure groups Sectional: represent the interests of a particular group of people Cause: promote a particular cause	In 2007, laws against smoking in public places were introduced because of public and medical opinion.	Pressure groups often bring important scientific discoveries to the government's attention, e.g. the damage being done by greenhouse gases and other pollutants.	There are occasions when two pressure groups have conflicting interests, e.g. the League Against Cruel Sports wanted to ban fox hunting but the Countryside Alliance wanted it to continue.

Type of influence	Example of its success	Advantages	Disadvantages
Public opinion These are the views of members of the general public in the UK. This is a strong influence upon Parliament, as those aged over 18 are entitled to vote in general elections.	Public opinion was mixed as to whether or not the UK should leave the EU. In a national referendum in 2016, the majority of those who voted chose to leave the EU. This allowed Parliament to legislate in 2017 to allow this to happen.	Where the majority of the public has certain beliefs or demands, then Parliament can safely pass legislation on that issue.	Gauging public opinion can be notoriously difficult. Realistically, no one can definitively say that the majority of the public believe one way or another in a specific issue.
Lobbyists/lobbying firms These are usually professionals or organisations who try to persuade or influence governments to enact, amend or repeal legislation that affects their or their representatives' interests.	Most multinational companies have or use lobbyists, e.g. Bell Pottinger Private.	Like any service industry, citizens or organisations can approach a lobbyist to represent and present their interests direct to government ministers or their departments, where lobbyists have political contacts.	Lobbyists are expensive and, in consequence, may only represent those citizens or groups who can afford to pay for their services. Accusations of dubious and corrupt methods, e.g. 'cash for questions', have been made against lobbyists.

The Law Commission is the UK's main law reform body, which recommends or researches law reform on behalf of the government (see page 35 for how it influences changes to the law).

Doctrine of parliamentary supremacy (sovereignty) and its limitations

A.V. Dicey said:

> 'The principle of Parliamentary sovereignty means ... that Parliament ... has the right to make or unmake any law whatever; and, further, that no person or body is recognised by the law of England as having a right to override or set aside the legislation of Parliament.'

This means that Parliament cannot control the actions of its future self and the courts have no power to question the legality of an Act of Parliament. A key case here is *British Railways Board v Pickin* (1974). However, there are a number of current Acts that do give the courts power to declare new parliamentary laws incompatible with them, thus contradicting the rule above. These are outlined in the table below.

Revision activity

Research the details of *British Railways Board v Pickin* (1974). Why is this case important?

Typical mistake

Do not forget that Parliament is ultimately supreme. It can repeal these Acts, thus regaining its original power, without an additional majority.

Table 1.3.3 Acts allowing a declaration of incompatibility

Act	Provision	Case example
Human Rights Act 1998	Section 4: the courts have the power to declare an Act incompatible with the European Convention on Human Rights.	*H v Mental Health Review Tribunal* (2001) declared that the Mental Health Act 1983 was incompatible.
European Communities Act 1972 (ECA)	Section 2: where EU law exists on a particular subject, it can override any inconsistent UK law, including Acts of Parliament.	*Factortame v Secretary of State for Transport* (1990) cases held the Merchant Shipping Act 1988 to be contrary to EU law.

In devolving some of its powers to the Scottish Parliament, Welsh Government and Northern Ireland Assembly (in the Scotland Act 1998, Wales Act 1998 and Northern Ireland Act 1998 respectively), the UK Parliament has handed over much self-governance to Scotland, Wales and Northern Ireland.

However, because Parliament can do anything and cannot be controlled by previous parliaments, in theory there is no reason why Parliament cannot simply repeal the Human Rights Act, the European Communities Act (ECA), the Scotland Act, the Welsh Act and the Northern Ireland Act, thus regaining its supremacy.

This happened to the ECA as part of Brexit, the UK's withdrawal from the European Union. Repealing the others would not be considered politically wise, even if technically possible.

Now test yourself TESTED

1 Which bodies make up Parliament?
2 What is a constitutional monarchy?
3 What is the difference between a Green Paper and a White Paper?
4 Which is the most effective influence on Parliament?
5 Is Parliament actually sovereign?

Exam summary

In the exam, you MAY be asked:

- multiple-choice questions about the parliamentary process and the difference between types of Bill and the stages through Parliament
- questions which require longer answers on the role of the House of Lords or the doctrine of parliamentary supremacy.

Delegated legislation

This will be assessed in Paper 3.

Parliament is incredibly busy and does not always have the time or expertise to deal with every new law that is required. Therefore, it delegates some of its law-making powers to secondary bodies, allowing them to make new laws on Parliament's behalf. These new laws are sometimes known as secondary legislation.

In order to delegate its power to a secondary body, an Act of Parliament is passed giving the secondary body the power to carry out tasks. These Acts are known as parent Acts or enabling Acts and are regarded as primary legislation.

People must obey these new laws: they have the same effect as if Parliament itself had written them.

Typical mistake

Do not forget to refer to the parent Act that gives the secondary body its power.

Delegated legislation: secondary legislation – laws passed in a specific area by a secondary body to which Parliament has passed its power.

Types of delegated legislation

The different types of delegated legislation are outlined in the table below.

Revision activity

What by-laws can you think of in your local community?

Table 1.3.4 Types of delegated legislation

Type	Secondary body	Reason	Example
Orders in Council	Privy Council (PC)	There can be a quick response in emergency situations.	+ The Constitutional Reform Act 2005 allows the PC to alter the number of judges in the Supreme Court. + The Civil Contingencies Act 2004 gives the PC power to make law in times of emergency when Parliament is not sitting.
Statutory instruments (SIs) also known as Ministerial Regulations	Government ministers	Over 3000 SIs are made each year. Parliament could not cope with this volume or complexity, which is best left to the departments with expertise and responsibility in specific areas.	+ The Building Regulations 2010 are incredibly complex, made by the Department for Communities and Local Government under the Building Act 1984. + Police powers are made by the Ministry for Justice under the Police and Criminal Evidence Act 1984.
By-laws	Local authorities and public corporations for matters within their jurisdiction, e.g. the British Airports Authority	Parliament has neither the time nor the local knowledge to deal with these types of matter.	+ The drinking ban zone is a Designated Public Place Order. It was put in place by local councils under the Criminal Justice and Police Act 2001. Within the designated area, alcohol consumption is restricted in any open space, other than licensed premises. + Other examples include 'no ball games', 'no parking' etc.

Parliamentary controls on delegated legislation

Parliament's first attempt to control delegated legislation made in its name comes with the drafting of the parent Act. This should be clear, unambiguous and give 'what' and 'how' instructions that are open to very little interpretation.

In controversial areas, such as human embryology, Parliament can also insist that the draft delegated legislation is subject to parliamentary scrutiny and vote before coming into force, by including a requirement for an Affirmative Resolution Order (ARO) in the parent Act.

Delegated legislation is designed to save parliamentary time, but AROs can defeat this object and could not possibly be used for all 3,000 SIs a year. In the absence of an ARO, Parliament has 40 days to pass a Negative Resolution Order to prevent an SI coming into force. If Parliament misses this deadline, only primary legislation or repealing the parent Act can remove the delegated legislation.

Evaluation point

Find out about the Legislative and Regulatory Reform Act 2006. How does this change the controls on delegated legislation?

There is also a Delegated Powers Scrutiny Committee in the House of Lords, which considers whether the provisions of any Bills going through Parliament delegate legislative power inappropriately. It reports its findings to the House of Lords before the committee stage of the Bill, but it has no power to amend Bills.

Finally, there is a Joint Scrutiny Committee, whose role is simply to scrutinise SIs. They are looking for SIs that are retrospective in effect, badly worded or attempting to impose taxation.

Judicial controls on delegated legislation

These controls require a party affected by the delegated legislation to apply to the Queen's Bench Division of the High Court for a judicial review. This review could find the delegated legislation to be *ultra vires* (UV) and therefore void (without legal effect). There are two types of UV, outlined in the table below.

Ultra vires: a Latin term meaning 'beyond the powers', i.e. the secondary body has exceeded the powers given to it by the parent Act.

Table 1.3.5 Types of *ultra vires* (UV)

Type of UV	Description	Key case
Procedural UV	The secondary body has exceeded its powers and failed to follow the procedural instructions in the parent Act.	*Agricultural Training Board v Aylesbury Mushrooms Ltd* (1972) (see Table 1.3.6)
Substantive UV	The secondary body has gone beyond the powers granted to it and made more regulations than permitted.	*R v Secretary of State for Health ex parte Pfizer Ltd* (1999) (see Table 1.3.6)

Furthermore, the judicial review can conclude that a piece of delegated legislation is without legal effect because it is 'outrageous in its defiance of logic' – see *Associated Provincial Picture Houses Ltd v Wednesbury Corporation* (1948).

Stretch and challenge

Look up the facts of *Associated Provincial Picture Houses Ltd v Wednesbury Corporation* (1948). Do you agree that the corporation's behaviour was unreasonable?

Table 1.3.6 Summary of parliamentary and judicial controls on delegated legislation

Type of control	Explanation	Example
Parent Act	This should give clear instructions: who can make the delegated legislation, how they should go about it and to what extent they can make the delegated legislation.	The Police and Criminal Evidence Act 1984 gives the Ministry of Justice powers to alter police powers.
Affirmative Resolution Order	Some SIs will not become law unless specifically approved by Parliament. The need for an affirmative resolution will be included in the parent Act.	An affirmative resolution is required before new or revised police Codes of Practice under the Police and Criminal Evidence Act 1984 can come into force.
Negative Resolution Order	Other SIs will be subject to a negative resolution, which means that the relevant statutory instrument will be law unless rejected by Parliament within 40 days.	Paraffin (Maximum Retail Prices) (Revocation) Order 1979.
Joint Scrutiny Committee	This examines SIs and reports back to Parliament if: + it imposes a tax or charge – this is because only an elected body has such a right + it appears to have retrospective effect which was not provided for by the parent Act + it appears to have gone beyond the powers given under the enabling legislation + it makes some unusual or unexpected use of those powers.	The Code of Practice (Picketing) Order 2017 reportedly failed to comply with proper legislative practice.
Procedural *ultra vires*	Judicial review states the delegated legislation has failed to follow the 'how' instructions in the parent Act.	*Agricultural Training Board v Aylesbury Mushrooms Ltd* (1972): the Horticultural Society was obliged to 'consult' all interested parties before bringing in new regulations but did not consult the mushroom growers.
Substantive *ultra vires*	Judicial review states the delegated legislation has failed to follow the 'to what extent' instructions in the parent Act and so the secondary body has gone beyond its powers.	*R v Secretary of State for Health ex parte Pfizer Ltd* (1999): the government lacked the power to ban the prescription of Viagra on the NHS for cost reasons – the ban was void.
Wednesbury unreasonableness	Judicial review states the delegated legislation is 'so outrageous in its defiance of logic'.	*Associated Provincial Picture Houses Ltd v Wednesbury Corporation* (1948).

Exam tip

An exam question may ask about the reasons for the use of delegated legislation – the introduction on page 22 and the advantages of delegated legislation in the next section will enable you to craft an answer to that question.

Advantages and disadvantages of delegated legislation

Table 1.3.7 Advantages and disadvantages of delegated legislation

Advantages	Disadvantages
Granting law-making powers to others saves much parliamentary time. Parliament could not possibly make all of these laws itself.	Delegated legislation lacks publicity. Over 3,000 SIs are made each year. It is impossible for the public to keep up with this, but ignorance of the law is no defence.
Laws can be made quickly to respond to emergency situations.	Parliamentary controls on delegated legislation are not always very effective. The Scrutiny Committee cannot possibly scrutinise all of them.
Parliament can concentrate on producing parent Acts, giving a broad outline and leaving the detail to others.	There is danger of the delegated bodies sub-delegating (passing the work onto someone else to do).
Local people are experts in local issues and so can produce detailed local laws given the framework.	The doctrine of parliamentary sovereignty is eroded, as judges are able to void delegated legislation by using *ultra vires*.

Advantages	Disadvantages
Delegated legislation is often used as a fast way of implementing directives from the EU.	Delegated legislation is not a democratic source of law, as it is often made by people who are not democratically elected.
Ministers making laws is considered a contradiction of the doctrine of the separation of powers, i.e. the executive doing the legislature's job.	Judges cannot exercise their control over delegated legislation without a member of the public taking legal action, which is time consuming and expensive.
	The House of Lords has recently stated that the Government's 'escalating' use of delegated powers instead of primary legislation is 'constitutionally objectionable'. The EU (Withdrawal) Act 2018 and the Childcare Bill were singled out as examples.

Stretch and challenge

Develop your knowledge and analysis of delegated legislation by reading the Select Committee on the Constitution, *'The Legislative Process: The Delegation of Powers 16th Report of Session 2017–19'* (20 November 2018, HL Paper 225). Available at: **https://publications.parliament.uk/pa/ld201719/ldselect/ldconst/225/225.pdf**

Evaluation point

While there are significant disadvantages, could Parliament possibly manage all of the legislative burden itself? Why not? Link back to the reasons for and advantages of delegated legislation.

Revision activity

Use the points in this table to write model answers on the advantages and disadvantages of delegated legislation, then try a combination essay – 'Write a critical evaluation of delegated legislation'. Remember to include examples that you have researched.

Now test yourself

TESTED

6 What is the difference between primary and secondary legislation?
7 Why does Parliament need to delegate some of its powers?
8 What type of delegated legislation is sometimes called ministerial regulations? Why?
9 What does *ultra vires* mean?
10 How does delegated legislation undermine parliamentary sovereignty?

Exam summary

In the exam, you MAY be asked:

- multiple-choice questions about the type or purpose of delegated legislation
- questions requiring short to mid-length answers about the controls or advantages and disadvantages of delegated legislation, such as why delegated legislation is necessary (an 'advantages' question in disguise!).

Statutory interpretation

REVISED

This topic will be assessed in Paper 1 and explores how judges interpret the language used in Acts of Parliament. This is necessary because sometimes:

- an act contains ambiguous words – see *Fisher v Bell* (1961)
- words used are too broad – see *R (Miranda) v Home Secretary* (2016)
- the progress of technology means the words may need to be considered in light of new advances – see *Royal College of Nursing v DHSS* (1981)
- there has been an error in drafting – see *R v Burstow* (1997).

Exam tip

You are unlikely to be asked specifically about these points, but they will aid your overall understanding and ability to evaluate this topic.

Rules of statutory interpretation

In order to interpret words, over time judges have come up with rules to guide them. No rule is obligatory and judges can use which they prefer. Often, bodies such as the Judicial Studies Board issue guidelines as to the preferred approach.

Table 1.3.8 explains the difference between the literal rule, golden rule, mischief rule and the purposive approach.

Literal rule: where judges use the exact meaning of words when interpreting statute, no matter how absurd the outcome.

Golden rule: where judges decide that the literal rule produces absurd results when interpreting statute.

Mischief rule: a rule of statutory interpretation used to prevent the mischief an Act is aimed at.

Purposive approach: where judges look to see what is the purpose of the law when interpreting statute.

Typical mistake

An evaluation without cases to boost your answer will not score highly. Make sure you illustrate each rule with relevant cases and explain why the word needed to be interpreted.

Table 1.3.8 Rules of statutory interpretation

Rule	Explanation	Cases
Literal rule	+ Popular in the late nineteenth and early twentieth centuries, this gives the literal and grammatically correct meaning to the section, regardless of how absurd the result. + Lord Reid: 'We are seeking not what Parliament meant, but the true meaning of the words they used.'	+ *Whiteley v Chappell* (1868) + *London and North Eastern Railway Co. v Berriman* (1946) + Also see *R v Judge of the City of London Court* (1892) for a quote from Lord Esher.
Golden rule	+ An extension of the literal rule, where words will be given their literal meaning unless the result would be absurd. + Lord Wensleydale in *Grey v Pearson* (1857): 'The ordinary sense of the words is to be adhered to, unless it would lead to absurdity, when the ordinary sense may be modified to avoid the absurdity but no further.' + Narrow approach: the court may only choose between the possible meanings of the word. If there is only one, then that must be taken. + Wide approach: where the words only have one clear meaning which would lead to an absurd result, the court will use the golden rule to modify the words in order to avoid the absurdity.	+ *Adler v George* (1964) + *Re Sigsworth* (1935)
Mischief rule	+ Originating from Heydon's Case (1584), this rule looks back to the gap in the previous law and interprets the Act so as to cover the gap. + Use the mischief rule if it 'is possible to determine from the Act the precise "mischief" the Act was to remedy [and it] is possible to say with certainty what additional words would have been inserted' – Lord Diplock in *Jones v Wrotham Park Settled Estates* (1980).	+ *Smith v Hughes* (1960) + *Royal College of Nursing v DHSS* (1981)
Purposive approach	+ This is currently popular and recommended by the Law Commission and the EU. The judges look to see what is the purpose of the law. + This is an extension of the mischief rule because the judges are not just looking to see what the gap was in the old law but deciding what they believe Parliament meant to achieve with the new law.	+ *R v Registrar-General, ex parte Smith* (1990) + *R v Coleman* (2013)

Aids to statutory interpretation

In addition to the rules above, there are also a number of 'aids' judges can use.

Internal/intrinsic aids

Internal/intrinsic aids are 'inside the Act' and include:

+ preamble/introductory text/long title, which may give some clues that will help with the mischief rule or purposive approach
+ explanatory notes included in the margin to show what a section is about
+ a glossary of key terms in some Acts.

Revision activity

Look up the case of *Lawton v Fleming-Brown* (2006). What rule and what type of aid was used? Do you agree with the outcome? Show how a different rule may have achieved the opposite result.

External/extrinsic aids

External/extrinsic aids are 'outside the Act' and include:

- the historical context of the Act, for example, the Offences. Against the Person Act 1861 uses the word 'grievous'; this word is no longer in common usage, but it was when the law was drafted
- dictionaries and textbooks; in *R v Jewell* (2014), Lady Justice Rafferty referred to Smith and Hogan's *Criminal Law* textbook
- previous commercial practice
- treaties with international law – in order to give continuity to the meaning of words
- Hansard, after Lord Denning's debate with Lord Diplock, culminating with the decision in *Pepper v Hart* (1993) regarding tax on perks; see also *Tuppen v Microsoft* (2000) for another example of the use of Hansard by the courts
- the Interpretation Act 1978, which gives some statutory guidance – 'he' will always include 'she' and singular will always include plural.

Stretch and challenge

Read para 58 in the judgment of *R v Taj* (2018). Which aid does this case provide an example of? Where else would this case be useful?

Table 1.3.9 Key cases for statutory interpretation

Case	Facts	Relevant rule
Fisher v Bell (1961)	Ambiguous words: statute made it a criminal offence to 'offer' flick knives for sale. It was held that goods on display in shops are not 'offers' in the technical sense but an invitation to treat.	Literal rule
R (Miranda) v Home Secretary (2016)	Words used are too broad: stop powers under Schedule 7 of the Terrorism Act 2000. The meaning of the word 'terrorism' was in question, as it could have a very broad or a very narrow meaning. When considering this, the judge said: 'It is unlikely that Parliament would have intended to make such a distinction.'	Purposive approach
Royal College of Nursing v DHSS (1981)	The progress of technology means the words may need to be considered in light of new advances. The Abortion Act 1967 provided that it would be an absolute defence for a medically registered practitioner (i.e. a doctor) to carry out abortions, provided certain conditions were satisfied. It was held this could include nurses.	Mischief rule
R v Burstow (1997)	There has been an error in drafting – 'inflict' in s 20 OAPA1861 simply means cause.	Golden rule
Whiteley v Chappell (1868)	A statute made it an offence 'to impersonate any person entitled to vote'. D used the vote of a dead man; he was not guilty as a dead person was not a person entitled to vote.	Literal rule – example of an absurd result
London and North Eastern Railway Co. v Berriman (1946)	A railway worker was killed while oiling the track. A statute provided compensation payable on death for those 'relaying or repairing' the track – oiling did not count.	Literal rule – example of an absurd result
Adler v George (1964)	Under the Official Secrets Act 1920, it was an offence to obstruct a member of the armed forces 'in the vicinity' of a prohibited palace. The defendant was actually in the prohibited place, rather than 'in the vicinity' of it, at the time of the obstruction.	Golden rule – narrow
Re Sigsworth (1935)	A son murdered his mother, who had not made a will. Under the statute setting the law on intestacy, as her only child he was entitled to inherit her entire estate. The literal rule would lead to a repugnant result; therefore, the golden rule was applied and he inherited nothing.	Golden rule – wide
Smith v Hughes (1960)	Ds were prostitutes charged under the Street Offences Act 1959, which made it an offence to solicit in a public place. The prostitutes were soliciting from private premises in windows or on balconies and so could be seen by the public.	Mischief rule

Case	Facts	Relevant rule
R v Registrar-General, ex parte Smith (1990)	The applicant had statutory right to a birth certificate at 18, but it was suspected that he wanted this in order to find and murder his mother. The court, despite the plain language of the Adoption Act 1976, applied the purposive approach saying: 'Parliament could not have intended to promote serious crime.'	Purposive approach
R v Coleman (2013)	D burgled a narrow boat. The purpose of the Power of Criminal Courts (Sentencing) Act 2000 was to punish burglars on their third offence and so the Act should be interpreted to mean the same as s 9(4) of the Theft Act 1968.	Purposive approach
Pepper v Hart (1993)	The court had to decide whether a teacher at a private school had to pay tax on the perk he received in the form of reduced school fees. A statement in Hansard made at the time the Finance Act was passed quoted his exact circumstance as an example of where tax would not be payable.	Use of Hansard

Impact of EU law on statutory interpretation

The purposive approach is preferred by most EU countries when interpreting their own legislation. It is also the approach adopted by the European Court of Justice in interpreting EU law.

Therefore, UK judges having to use the purposive approach for EU law for over 40 years has made them more likely to apply it to UK law.

Now the UK has left the EU, this will no longer apply. However, judges are likely to continue to use the purposive approach.

Stretch and challenge

1 Read and make notes on the case of *R v D* (2019).
2 To see the continued influence of EU law, consider the use of the General Data Protection Regulations (GDPR) to interpret the Data Protection Act 2018.

Impact of the Human Rights Act 1998 on statutory interpretation

Section 3 of the Human Rights Act 1998 states that, as far as it is possible to do so, legislation must be read and given effect in a way that is compatible with the rights in the European Convention on Human Rights. See *Mendoza v Ghaidan* (2002), which involved interpreting the Rent Act 1977 in terms that were compatible with Convention rights.

Advantages and disadvantages of the different approaches to statutory interpretation

These points are included in Table 1.3.10.

Table 1.3.10 Advantages and disadvantages of the different approaches to statutory interpretation

Rule	Advantages	Disadvantages
Literal rule	+ It respects parliamentary sovereignty. + It provides certainty, as the law will be interpreted exactly as it is written. This makes it easier to know what the law is and how judges will apply it. + Focuses the mind of Parliament, forcing them to be clear in their language. + Respects the Separation of Powers doctrine as the judges have minimal or no legislative function. + Takes advantage of the consistency provided by external aids such as the dictionary and other Acts, as well as reinforcing useful internal aids such as explanatory notes.	+ Where it leads to unjust results, such as in *London and North Eastern Railway Co. v Berriman* (1946), it can hardly be said to be enacting the will of Parliament. + It assumes every Act will be perfectly drafted. + Michael Zander calls it 'irresponsible'. + Can undermine Parliament's intentions rather than further them. + It is based on erroneous assumptions regarding meaning in language. + Not all Acts have the benefit of explanatory notes.

Rule	Advantages	Disadvantages
Golden rule	+ It provides a way of avoiding the worst problems created by the literal rule while attempting to respect parliamentary sovereignty.	+ Two approaches could lead to further inconsistency. + There is no definition of an absurd result. + Michael Zander calls it a 'feeble parachute'.
Mischief rule	+ It responds positively to loopholes in the law. + It is more likely to produce a 'just' result because judges try to interpret the law in the way that Parliament meant it to work. + Reinforces the importance of explanatory notes.	+ Judges are going beyond their authority by filling in gaps, i.e. contradicting parliamentary sovereignty. + It may lead to uncertainty, as it is impossible to know when judges will use the rule and what result it might lead to. This makes it difficult for lawyers to advise clients on the law. + Not all Acts have the benefit of explanatory notes.
Purposive approach	+ It is most likely to lead to justice in individual cases. + It allows judges to respond to new technology, as in *R (Quintavalle) v Human Fertilisation and Embryology Authority* (2003). + It gives judges discretion on when and how to avoid the absurdity of the literal rule.	+ How can judges know what Parliament's intentions were? + It allows unelected judges to 'make' law, as they are deciding what they think the law should be rather than using the words that Parliament enacted. + It leads to the same uncertainty as the mischief rule.

Stretch and challenge

Find out who Michael Zander is. Why is his opinion respected?

Revision activity

In recent years the UK Supreme Court published its judgment in the controversial case of *Isle of Wight Council v Platt* (2017).

Using all the information you have learned in this chapter, research this case. Consider the Act and the words that were interpreted, how the justices went about reaching their decision and the rules they used to do so.

Exam tip

Use the cases throughout this section to illustrate your discussion of the advantages and disadvantages of different methods of statutory interpretation.

Now test yourself

TESTED

11 Why do statutes need to be interpreted?

12 Why is the literal rule used?

13 Which rule evolved from the literal rule?

14 Which case allowed the use of Hansard?

15 Why does the purposive approach contradict the principle of parliamentary supremacy?

Exam summary

In the exam, you MAY be asked:

+ multiple-choice questions on the rules and aids for statutory interpretation
+ questions which require longer answers that analyse the impact of these rules and aids.

Judicial precedent

This will be assessed in Paper 1.

The doctrine of judicial precedent

English law has developed from custom and the decisions of judges in cases. This system of law is known as common law.

The decisions of judges in cases are known as precedents. Therefore, precedent is an important source of law where past decisions of judges create law for future judges to follow.

The doctrine of precedent means that courts must follow decisions of the courts above. This is known as *stare decisis* (see page 32).

So, where the point of law in a previous case and current case is the same, the court hearing the current case should follow the decision in the previous case. This concept of treating similar cases in the same way promotes the idea of fairness and provides certainty.

There are two types of precedent: binding and persuasive.

Binding precedent

For this system to work, there has to be a hierarchical court structure. This means our courts are tiered or ranked according to their seniority, and the higher ones bind the lower ones.

Therefore, a binding precedent is a decision in an earlier case and a higher court which must be followed in later cases.

Persuasive precedent

Persuasive precedent is a decision which does not have to be followed by later cases, but which the judge may decide to follow. Persuasive precedents may:

- come from courts that do not bind, such as the Judicial Committee of the Privy Council
- come from courts lower down the hierarchy
- be a part of the decision known as *obiter dicta* (see page 32).

Exam tip

All the cases you learn in this course are precedents. Use as many as you can to illustrate your points, but remember it is the point of law that is important, not necessarily the facts of the case.

Doctrine: for judicial precedent, doctrine means the 'principle, operation and rules' of precedent.

Binding precedent: a case from a senior court that must be followed in future cases.

Persuasive precedent: usually in the form of *obiter dicta*, persuasive precedent is part of the judgment that should be followed in similar cases but is not binding. However, a reason for deciding not to follow it must be given.

Hierarchy of the courts

Table 1.3.11 Hierarchy of the courts

Court	Bound by	Binding on	Cases	Comment
Judicial Committee of the Privy Council	No one, not even itself	All domestic courts of the Commonwealth, including England	*Grant v Australian Knitting Mills* (1936) *The Wagon Mound* (1961)	Regarded as persuasive precedent only in England (but very persuasive).
Supreme Court	European Court of Justice on EU issues Not itself	All other UK courts	*R v Brown* (1993) *Donoghue v Stevenson* (1932)	Supreme Court has not been bound by its own decisions since a Practice Statement in 1966. Also now has the power to reopen appeals, e.g. *Re Pinochet Ugarte* (1999).

Court	Bound by	Binding on	Cases	Comment
Court of Appeal (Civil Division)	Supreme Court (1) Itself with exceptions (2)	All lower courts and itself (2)	(1) *Broome v Cassell* (1971) and *Miliangos v George Frank (Textiles) Ltd* (1976) (2) *Young v Bristol Aeroplane Co. Ltd* (1944) gave the three rules on when it need not follow its own decisions.	1 Tried to challenge the rule that the Court of Appeal is bound by the House of Lords/Supreme Court – House of Lords rejected this. 2 Need not follow its own decisions where: + the previous decision was made *per incuriam* (in error) + there are two conflicting previous decisions (obviously cannot follow both) + there is a later conflicting Supreme Court decision.
Court of Appeal (Criminal Division)	Supreme Court Itself	All lower courts Itself		Prepared to be flexible in its approach to binding itself and will not follow its previous decisions where to do so would cause injustice.
Queen's Bench Division of the High Court	Supreme Court Court of Appeal Itself	High Court generally Lower courts Itself		Follows very similar rules to the Court of Appeal Criminal. Division in terms of binding itself.
Chancery and Family Divisions of the High Court	Supreme Court Court of Appeal Themselves	High Court generally Lower courts Themselves		
High Court	Supreme Court Court of Appeal Divisional courts Not itself	Lower courts Not itself		

The County Court, Crown Court and Magistrates' Courts do not create precedents as:

+ there are far too many cases going through them
+ they do not publish judgments that could be used.

Practice Statement 1966

When the Supreme Court replaced the House of Lords in 2009, the Constitutional Reform Act 2005 transferred the House of Lords' powers to the Supreme Court.

In *Austin v London Borough of Southwark* (2010), the Supreme Court confirmed that the power to use the Practice Statement had been transferred to it.

Practice Direction 3 and 4 of the Supreme Court state:

> 'The Practice Statement is "part of the established jurisprudence relating to the conduct of appeals" and "has as much effect in [the Supreme] Court as it did before the Appellate Committee in the House of Lords."'

Therefore, the Supreme Court does not have to follow its own previous decisions, but it must explain why if it chooses not to.

Stare decisis

Stare decisis is the fundamental principle of precedent and simply means that a decision in an early case will stand as guidance for all future cases.

The decision made by the court is known as the 'judgment'. This contains the decision and an explanation of how it was reached.

Ratio decidendi

This is the part of the judgment which forms the precedent for future cases.

All of the points of law you learn throughout the substantive sections that come from cases are the *ratio decidendi*. For example, that words can prevent an action from being an assault can be found in the *ratio decidendi* of *Tuberville v Savage* (1669).

Obiter dicta

Obiter dicta comprises the rest of the judgment apart from the *ratio decidendi*. Judges in future cases do not have to follow it, but it can give very useful guidance.

A key case is *Hill v Baxter* (1958), where the example of being attacked by a swarm of bees gives useful guidance for the need for a voluntary act and the defence of automatism.

Stare decisis: 'let the decision stand'.

Ratio decidendi: 'the reason for the decision'.

Assault: where the defendant intentionally or recklessly causes the victim to apprehend immediate unlawful personal violence.

Obiter dicta: 'other things said'.

Automatism: an act done by the muscles without any control by the mind, such as a spasm, a reflex action or a convulsion; or an act done by a person who is not conscious of what they are doing.

Law reporting

In order to follow past decisions, there must be an accurate record of what those decisions were. These records are called law reports and have existed since the thirteenth century. The judgment is noted down, word-for-word, and then published.

The accuracy is overseen by independent lawyers, as these reports effectively underpin the whole of the principle of precedent – without them, we would have no record to follow.

The codes you see at the end of case names are the references for locating the report for each case, for example, *Tuberville v Savage* [1669] EWHC KB J25. These codes are called citations and tell you which reports to access (EWHC is the High Court). These are published weekly in *The Times* newspaper and annually in leather-bound volumes.

All High Court, Court of Appeal, Supreme Court (and House of Lords for 1996–2009) cases are now reported on the internet.

Revision activity

Find as many other different codes as you can while researching cases throughout this book. How many can you find? Can you work out to which court they refer?

Operation of judicial precedent: following, overruling and distinguishing

When faced with a precedent set in an earlier case, judges have a number of options. The precedent can be:

- followed
- overruled or
- distinguished.

These options are explained in Table 1.3.12.

Table 1.3.12 Options for dealing with precedents

Option	Explanation	Example
Follow	+ The judge applies the same principle of law to the current case. + If the decision is by a court above or on the same level as the present court, then the judge must normally follow the previous precedent.	*Michael v Chief Constable of South Wales* (2015) followed *Hill v Chief Constable of West Yorkshire* (1988).
Overrule	+ The court in a later case states that the decision in an earlier case is wrong. + Overruling may occur when a higher court overrules a decision made in an earlier case by a lower court. + For example, when the Supreme Court overrules a decision of the Court of Appeal or when the Supreme Court uses the Practice Statement to overrule a past decision of its own.	*R v Jogee* (2016) overruled *R v Powell and R v English* (1999).
Distinguish	+ A judge avoids following a precedent. + If a judge finds that the material facts of the current case are sufficiently different from the case setting a precedent for a distinction to be drawn between the two, they are not bound by the previous case.	*Merritt v Merritt* (1971) distinguished *Balfour v Balfour* (1919). In *White Lion Hotel v James* (2021) the window sash was broken, in *Geary v JD Weatherspoon* (2011) the banister was not.

Advantages and disadvantages of judicial precedent and the operation of precedent

These are shown in Table 1.3.13.

Table 1.3.13 Advantages and disadvantages of judicial precedent and the operation of precedent

Advantages	Disadvantages
+ Certainty – it allows the law to be predictable, which in turn promotes alternative dispute resolution (**ADR**) in civil cases. + Consistency – like cases are decided alike, promoting a sense of justice. + Fairness – the certainty and consistency allow parties involved in cases to see how the decision was arrived at and that it is fair in the circumstances. + Precision – the exact details of the law are known by all parties. + Flexibility – bad precedents can be avoided using the Practice Statement, for example, *Young v Bristol Aeroplane Co. Ltd* (1944). + Time-saving – the predictability makes ADR more likely, thus saving parties (and the courts) time and money. + Details can be added to statutory provisions, such as *R v Clinton* (2012), clarifying the position on sexual infidelity. + The law can evolve to meet changing social attitudes, as it did by establishing an offence of rape within marriage in R v R (1991).	+ Rigidity – binding decisions can restrict decisions made in the interests of individual justice. + Complexity – judgments are very long and difficult to read, and it is not always easy to identify the *ratio decidendi* and *obiter dicta*. + Illogical distinctions – some cases are distinguished on very minor or controversial points. This could be argued in *R v Brown* (1993) and *R v Wilson* (1996); the defence of consent was allowed in *Wilson* but not in *Brown*, arguably on the basis of sexuality. + Slowness of growth – the development of precedent depends on accidents of litigation, i.e. waiting for a similar case to come along in order to develop the law further. + A bad precedent needs another case or an Act of Parliament to correct it, as in *Smith* (1961), and the Criminal Justice Act 1967 which reset intention as a subjective test. + Not a democratic source of law – unelected judges are making and developing key legal principles. Lord Mance in *Robinson v Chief Constable of West Yorkshi*re (2018) said, 'The courts are not a Law Commission but, in recognising the existence of any generalised duty in particular circumstances, they are making policy choices.'

Evaluation point

While there are significant disadvantages, could justice prevail without a system of precedent? Why not? Link back to the section on the doctrine of judicial precedent.

ADR: alternative dispute resolution, one of the key Woolf reform recommendations.

Table 1.3.14 Key cases for judicial precedent

Grant v Australian Knitting Mills (1936)	Persuasive nature of decisions of the Judicial Committee of the Privy Council.
The Wagon Mound cases (1961)	Persuasive nature of decisions of the Judicial Committee of the Privy Council.
R v Brown (1993)	House of Lords/Supreme Court precedent; also for distinguishing with *R v Wilson* (1996).
Donoghue v Stevenson (1932)	House of Lords/Supreme Court precedent creating the test for duty of care; it has never been overruled, but has been restricted.
Young v Bristol Aeroplane Co. Ltd (1944)	The judgment in this case gave the exceptions to the rule that the Court of Appeal must follow itself.
Conway v Rimmer (1968)	First use of Practice Statement 1966, avoided following *Duncan v Cammell Laird* (1942).
R v Shivpuri (1986)	First use of Practice Statement 1966 in a criminal case, avoided following *Anderton v Ryan* (1985).
Herrington v British Railways Board (1972)	Use of Practice Statement 1966 to overrule *Addie v Dumbreck* and establish a duty to trespassers.
Pepper v Hart (1993)	Use of Practice Statement 1966 to allow the use of Hansard in statutory interpretation.
Knuller v DPP (1973)	House of Lords deciding not to use the Practice Statement 1966.
R v G and R (2003)	House of Lords establishing the current definition of recklessness, overruling *MPC v Caldwell* (1982).
Michael v Chief Constable of South Wales (2015)	Followed *Hill v Chief Constable of West Yorkshire* (1988) in that it is not fair, just and reasonable to impose a duty on the police to protect future victims of crime.
R v Jogee (2016)	Overruled *R v Powell and R v English* (1999) on the use of the principle of joint enterprise in criminal law.
Merritt v Merritt (1971)	Distinguished *Balfour v Balfour* (1919) in relation to the binding nature of financial arrangements between spouses.

Now test yourself

TESTED

16 What is a binding precedent?

17 If a judge is not following a persuasive precedent, what should they do?

18 What does the Practice Statement 1966 do?

19 What does *stare decisis* mean?

20 Which of the following kinds of statement made in a judgment in a case would best be described as *obiter dicta*?

- A Statements about the application of the law.
- B Statements about the important facts in the case.
- C Statements about the result of the case.
- D Statements about the application of the law to facts which are a little different from those in the case.

21 Where is a judgment published?

Exam summary

In the exam, you MAY be asked:

- multiple-choice questions such as Q20 above
- questions requiring short or mid-length answers on why the *ratio decidendi* of a case may sometimes be difficult to establish, using examples.

You will always be required to make reference to the important precedents in every area of substantive law you have studied.

Law reform

REVISED

This will be assessed in Paper 2.

The work of the Law Commission

The Law Commission was set up in 1965 by the Law Commissions Act 1965. It is a full-time body, consisting of a Chair (who is a High Court Judge), four other Law Commissioners and support and research staff.

Its stated aim is to ensure that the law is:

- fair
- modern
- simple
- cost-effective.

Revision activity

Section 3 of the Law Commissions Act 1965 sets out the role of the Law Commission. Find this section and make some notes on it.

Reform

To 'reform' the law means to update the law. The Law Commission can choose areas that it considers need updating or areas can be referred to it by the government via the Lord Chancellor.

Its first step is to open a consultation, which sets out the current law and why it needs to be reformed. For example, a consultation was launched in July 2017 regarding wills, which states: 'The law of wills needs to be modernised to take account of the changes in society, technology and medical understanding that have taken place since the Victorian era.'

This consultation will invite responses from interested parties and will include the problems with current law, suggestions for reform and questions for interested parties to consider, as well as examples of how the area of law operates in other countries.

After a suitable time for responses to the consultation, the Law Commission will then issue a report. This will often contain a draft Bill that Parliament could begin to put through the formal process of creating an Act, if it so chooses.

Codification

Codification means reviewing all the law on one topic, creating a complete code of law then integrating all relevant laws into a new Act of Parliament.

When the Law Commission was first set up, its aim was to codify – rewrite – all of family law, contract law, landlord and tenant laws and the law of evidence. However, the enormity of this task meant the idea was shelved.

That said, in 1985 the Law Commission published a draft criminal code following many years of research and writing. It included all of the main general principles of criminal law. However, the government has never implemented it and the Law Commission stated in 2008 that in future it would concentrate on smaller areas, as there is more chance the government will then adopt these.

Consolidation

Consolidation means drawing all the existing provisions in an area of law together into one Act. It is different to codification, as the law is not reviewed or changed; it is simply brought together.

On 27 July 2017, a new consultation was launched by the Law Commission to tidy up sentencing law – to 'modernise the law, bring greater transparency and improve efficiency'. This has led to the Sentencing Code enacted by the Sentencing Act 2020.

Repeal

The repeal of an Act of Parliament means that the Act ceases to be law. Only Parliament can repeal an Act of Parliament, but the Law Commission can advise Parliament about which Acts should be repealed. Its job is to identify which Acts are no longer needed – such as the Statute of Marlborough 1267 passed during the reign of Henry III!

> **Exam tip**
>
> Have a look at the Law Commission's website: **www.lawcom.gov.uk**.
>
> Make a note of the topics the Law Commission is currently working on. Can you make connections with the other areas of law you are studying? Your exam response will be boosted if you can demonstrate up-to-date knowledge and connections between topics.

This is the area of the Law Commission's work where it has seen most success: 19 Bills have been enacted since 1965, which repeal more than 3000 Acts.

Advantages and disadvantages of reform through the Law Commission

Table 1.3.15 Advantages of reform through the Law Commission

Advantage	This means:	Evidence
It saves Parliament's time.	Parliament has time to deal with political matters, leaving this relatively uncontroversial, but time-consuming and vital work, to a separate body.	Over 3000 Acts have been examined, found to be redundant and repealed.
Law is researched by legal experts.	Practical recommendations are made.	The Chair is a High Court or an Appeal Court Judge, appointed to the Commission by the Lord Chancellor and Secretary of State for Justice for up to three years. The other four Commissioners are experienced judges, barristers, solicitors or teachers of law.
There is consultation before drawing up proposals.	All interested parties have a chance to have their say.	Publication: *The Sentencing Code* Publication date: 27 July 2017; response date: 26 January 2018. On 1 December 2020 the Sentencing Code came into effect in England and Wales, consolidating existing sentencing procedure law into a single Sentencing Act.
Whole areas of law are considered.	The impact of any new law on related areas is fully explored.	In 2012, the Law Commission published a paper on Contempt of Court, which covered: + contempt in the face of the court + court reporting + juror misconduct and internet publications + scandalising the court.
It can bring the law on one topic together in one Act.	The law is easier to find and therefore more accessible to all.	Powers of the Criminal Courts (Sentencing) Bill
It simplifies and modernises the law.	The law is easier to understand and therefore more accessible to all.	Simplification of Criminal Law: Public Nuisance and Outraging Public Decency (Law Com No. 358)

Table 1.3.16 Disadvantages of reform through the Law Commission

Disadvantage	This means:	Evidence
The government is slow to implement the reforms.	Large areas of work can be wasted as they are not politically important.	Offences Against the Person (Law Com No. 218)
Some reforms may never be implemented.	A great amount of time, and therefore public money, have been wasted on research and preparation which is not put into place to benefit the public, despite experts identifying a need.	Liability for Psychiatric Illness (Law Com No. 249)
There is a lack of parliamentary time to discuss the proposed reforms.	Suggestions for reform may not be thoroughly debated and discussed before being enacted.	The Coroners and Justice Act 2009 cherrypicked elements of Law Com No. 290, and Parliament did not properly scrutinise what the implications of this would be.
Parliament may make changes to the proposed reforms without the benefit of legal expertise.	The legal expertise that went into the suggestions for reform is ignored.	Link to the evaluation of the homicide reforms contained in the Coroners and Justice Act 2009.

Typical mistake

Do not confuse a 'statement' with an actual advantage/disadvantage. You need to explain why your statement is positive or negative and support it with evidence – a case, an example or a statistic, where possible.

Revision activity

The Criminal Justice and Courts Act 2015 is a good example of an Act coming about as a result of Law Commission proposals.

Look up this Act and make a note of its provisions – link these to the material in Chapter 1.4. Then answer the following:

- Do you agree with the provisions?
- Why do you think the Law Commission suggested them?
- Why do you think Parliament enacted them?
- Can you find any prosecutions under these provisions?

Now test yourself

TESTED 

22 What is the Law Commission and what is its remit?

23 When and how was the Law Commission established?

24 Give an example of a Law Commission success.

25 Give an example of where the Law Commission's work has not been implemented.

Exam summary

In the exam, you MAY be asked:

- multiple-choice questions on the role of the Law Commission and the codification of specific areas of law
- about which areas of substantive law have come about as a consequence of Law Commission proposals
- essay questions on the link between those substantive topic areas and the Law Commission

The European Union

REVISED

This will be assessed in Paper 3.

The EU was formed in 1957. The UK joined the EU in 1973 by signing the Treaty of Rome.

Permission for the UK government to adopt the principles of this treaty was given by Parliament passing the European Communities Act 1972, which followed a referendum.

Typical mistake

It is a mistake to think EU law was imposed upon the UK. The UK was a senior member of the EU and had at least as much say in new EU law as other Member States.

Stretch and challenge

How is a referendum different from other national elections? Can you think of any other significant referendums in recent UK history?

In 2016, the UK voted by referendum to leave the EU. Known as Brexit, the UK left on 31 January 2020.

The institutions of the EU and their functions

Table 1.3.17 EU institutions

Institution	Function	Make-up

Council	+ Principal law-making body of the EU.
	+ Voting in the Council is by qualified (or double) majority, which is reached if:
	  + 55 per cent of Member States vote in favour, and
	  + the proposal is supported by Member States representing at least 65 per cent of the total EU population.
		+ The government of each nation sends a representative to the Council, usually the Foreign Minister.
		+ A minister responsible for the topic under consideration often attends, so the precise membership will vary with the subject being discussed, e.g. the Minister for Agriculture will attend if the issue involves agriculture.

Commission	+ Proposes new laws to be adopted by the Parliament and the Council. + Responsible for the administration of the EU. + Ensures that treaty provisions etc. are properly implemented by Member States. + Can refer the matter to the Court of Justice of the EU where there is a failure to do so. + Responsible for the EU's budget and supervises how the money is spent.	+ Each Member State has one Commissioner, who must act independently of their national origin. + They are appointed for a five-year term and can only be removed during their term of office by a vote of censure by the EU Parliament. + Each Commissioner heads a department with responsibility for an area of EU policy, e.g. agriculture.
European Parliament	+ MEPs form political groups with those of the same political allegiance. + Meets once a month. + Has standing committees which discuss proposals made by the Commission and then report to the full Parliament for debate. + Can now co-legislate on an equal footing with the Council and can approve or reject proposals made by the Commission. + Decides on international agreements. + Decides on whether to admit new Member States. + Reviews the Commission's work programme and asks it to propose legislation.	+ There are 751 members of the European Parliament (MEPs). + It is directly elected by the electorate of the Member States in elections which take place every five years. + The number of MEPs from each country is determined by the size of the population of the country.

Institution	Function	Make-up
Court of Justice of the European Union	+ Decides whether a Member State has failed in its obligations, e.g. *Re Tachographs: The Commission v United Kingdom* (1979). + Hears references from national courts for preliminary rulings on points of EU law; this is very important, as rulings made by the Court of Justice of the European Union are binding on courts in Member States; this ensures that the law is uniform throughout the EU – see *Factortame v Secretary of State for Transport* (1990).	+ The Court sits in Luxembourg, with one judge from each Member State. + For a full court, 11 judges will sit. + For other cases, the Court sits in chambers of five judges or three judges. They are assisted by 11 Advocates General, who take a case, research it and impartially present the issues that arise to the Court.

Sources of EU law

There are three sources of EU law:

- treaties
- regulations
- directives.

These are outlined in the Table 1.3.18.

Table 1.3.18 Sources of EU law

Source	Effect	Cases to research
Treaties	+ Primary legislation + Automatically part of a Member State's law. + Before it was repealed as part of Brexit, see s 2(1) of the European Communities Act 1972, which allows individuals to directly rely on treaty provisions.	+ *Van Duyn v Home Office* (1974) + *Macarthys Ltd v Smith* (1980) + *Diocese of Hallam Trustee v Connaughton* (1996)
Regulations	+ Binding on Member States. + Automatically apply in each Member State.	+ *Re Tachographs: The Commission v United Kingdom* (1979)
Directives	+ Member States have to pass their own laws to implement directives, within a time limit set by the European Commission. + Delegated legislation usually used in the UK.	+ **Vertical direct effect**: *Marshall v Southampton and South West Hampshire Area Health Authority* (1986). + **Horizontal direct effect**: *Francovich v Italian Republic* (1991).

The impact of EU law on the law of England and Wales

EU law applied to the court structure in England and Wales. While the UK was a member of the EU, the Supreme Court had to refer questions of EU law to the Court of Justice of the European Union.

The Court of Justice of the European Union was also important because its attitude to interpretation was followed by English courts. In *Von Colson v Land Nordrhein-Westfalen* (1984), it was said that 'national courts are required to interpret their national law in the light of the wording and the purpose of the directive'.

Section 2 of the European Communities Act 1972 provided that where EU law exists on a particular subject, it could override any inconsistent UK law, including Acts of Parliament. The *Factortame v Secretary of State for Transport* (1990) cases held the Merchant Shipping Act 1988 to be contrary to EU law.

Vertical direct effect: an individual can claim against the state even if the directive is not yet implemented.

Horizontal direct effect: directives give an individual rights against other people, provided they have been implemented.

On the face of it, this was a major limitation on the doctrine of parliamentary supremacy. However, as we have seen through the process of Brexit, Parliament preserved its supremacy by retaining its ability to repeal the European Communities Act, in what became known as the Great Repeal Bill.

Table 1.3.19 Key cases on EU law

Case	Facts	Relevant area	*Ratio decidendi*
Re Tachographs: The Commission v United Kingdom (1979)	Regulations to fit tachographs to certain vehicles were not being enforced.	Role of the ECJ	The regulations were enforced by the EU.
Factortame v Secretary of State for Transport (1990)	Multiple cases related to fishing rights and the restrictions of free movement of trade.	Supremacy of EU law	The Merchant Shipping Act had to be repealed, as it conflicted with EU law.
Van Duyn v Home Office (1974)	A Dutch national wished to enter the UK to take up work with the Church of Scientology.	Effect of treaties	A state is precluded from refusing its own nationals the right of entry or residence.
Macarthys Ltd v Smith (1980)	A woman claimed equal pay with a male counterpart who was not currently employed but had been previously.	Effect of treaties	The principle that men and women should receive equal pay for equal work, enshrined in Article 119 of the Treaty of Rome, is not confined to situations in which men and women are contemporaneously doing equal work for the same employer.
Diocese of Hallam Trustee v Connaughton (1996)	Very similar facts to *Macarthys Ltd v Smith* (1980).	As above	As above
Marshall v Southampton and South West Hampshire Area Health Authority (1986)	This involved a challenge to the different retirement ages of men and women.	Conflict of law between a national legal system and EU law.	There is no horizontal effect of treaties.
Francovich v Italian Republic (1991)	Italy had not implemented directives to protect workers in insolvency cases.	Effect of directives	The state must impose directives to avoid being liable for the consequences.
Von Colson v Land Nordrhein-Westfalen (1984)	A female German national was refused employment at a prison on the basis of her gender, contrary to the Equal Treatment Directive.	Effect of directives	A national court's duty to interpret national law in accordance with EU law means directives become almost horizontally effective.

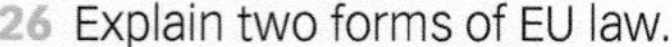

Now test yourself TESTED

26 Explain two forms of EU law.
27 Which institution is made up of members elected directly by the people of the Member States?
28 Which institution's membership varies depending on the topic under discussion?
29 Explain the impact of membership of the EU on UK law.

Exam summary

In the exam, you MAY be asked multiple-choice questions about the differences between the institutions of the EU and the types of EU law.

1.4 The legal system

The nature of law and the legal system are key topic areas assessed across all three AQA exam papers.

For the legal system, you will need to identify and explain:

- civil courts and other forms of dispute resolution
- criminal courts and lay persons
- legal personnel and the judiciary
- access to justice and funding.

Civil courts and other forms of dispute resolution

REVISED 

Civil courts

The civil courts deal with non-criminal matters, such as contract, tort and human rights issues. They are designed to deal with disputes between individual citizens and/or organisations.

Examples of disputes include disagreements arising under contract, family or employment law.

The civil justice system was largely reformed in the 1990s. There are two key civil courts of first instance:

- the County Court
- the High Court, for more complex and substantial cases.

The civil courts deal with a wide variety of small or simple claims, for example, faulty goods, up to multi-million-pound claims between corporations. Most criminal cases do not end up in court, as many are dealt with through alternative dispute resolution (ADR).

Civil courts: courts that deal with non-criminal matters.

First instance courts: courts where trials are initiated, rather than held on appeal.

Reform of the civil justice system

Following historic public criticisms of the civil justice system, Lord Woolf's report, *Access to Justice* (1996), suggested major reforms to the civil justice system. These reforms had an overriding objective to enable the civil courts to deal with cases in a more 'just' way than they had been historically. The reforms included:

- allowing individual judges greater autonomy in the handing of case management
- introducing a 'track' system in the County Court, to put claims in a hierarchical order depending upon the value of the claim
- encouraging other forms of dispute resolution, including alternative dispute resolution (ADR).

Exam tip

You need a clear understanding of the civil courts' structures, procedures and appeal systems. It might help you to visit as many types of civil court as you can, to observe their workings in practice.

Revision activity

Identify which courts have both civil and criminal jurisdiction.

Stretch and challenge

Using the following webpage, consider whether Lord Woolf's 1996 report into civil justice reform was justifiable: **www.judiciary.uk/wp-content/uploads/2013/03/lj-jackson-cjreform-adr.pdf**

The three-track system

When a claimant applies to go to court to make a civil litigation claim and after a defence is received from the other side, the county court will allocate the claim to the most appropriate track (depending on the value of the claim):

- small claims track for straightforward claims of not more than £10,000 excluding personal injury
- fast track for claims between £10,000 and £25,000
- multi-track for claims over £25,000 and not more than £50,000
- High Court for more complex claims over £50,000.

Typical mistake

Do not muddle the three tracks when it comes to the financial limits and the key types of cases they hear. Exam questions might ask about which court(s) an appeal will go to after it is heard in one of the tracks – be clear on the differences.

However, recent digitalisation of the civil claims procedure means that many civil cases involving the recovery of money owed can be done via the GOV.UK website. This is known as 'making a court claim'. Again, the amount claimed is crucial here and dictates how a claim is to be made. While a claimant can still use the paper N1 form to make a claim, it is simpler and quicker to use the online system:

- For claims of £10,000 or less, claimants can use the GOV.UK online system or the traditional N1 claim form.
- For claims between £10,001 and £100,000, claimants can use the Money Claim Online (MCOL) online system or use the traditional N1 form.

Revision activity

Print out and complete an N1 form. This will help you appreciate the idea of simplicity and understand its requirements.

Alternatively, have a look at the online system at **www.gov.uk**.

Civil courts appeal system

If either party in a case is dissatisfied with the decision made by the judge at first instance, then it is possible to appeal.

- A first appeal from a decision of the small claims court or the fast track is heard by a next-level judge. If the case was first heard by a District Judge, the appeal will be to a Circuit Judge. If first heard by a Circuit Judge, then the appeal is to a High Court Judge.
- It is possible for a second appeal from the decision of a Circuit Judge or High Court Judge to the Court of Appeal (Civil Division), but this would be in exceptional circumstances and only with the Court of Appeal's permission.
- An appeal from a decision of the multi-track, whether heard by a District or Circuit Judge, is to the Court of Appeal (Civil Division).
- An appeal from the High Court is to the Court of Appeal (Civil Division) or on rare occasion to the Supreme Court (called a 'leapfrog' appeal) where a point of general public importance is present.
- It is possible for a further appeal from the Court of Appeal (Civil Division) to the Supreme Court, but only if either court gives permission.
- A final appeal is possible for a case to be referred to the European Court of Justice, under Article 234 of the Treaty of Rome, if a point of EU law is involved.

Revision activity

Draw a chart showing the civil courts' appeal routes from:

- the County Court
- the High Court.

Other forms of dispute resolution

There are two main alternatives to the civil courts:

- tribunals
- ADR – negotiation and mediation.

Exam tip

Make sure you understand the outline of the tribunal structure, the role of tribunals and the roles of negotiation and mediation.

Tribunals

Structure

Tribunals are separated at first instance into seven divisions dealing with specific areas of law and four divisions for appeals.

First-tier tribunals hear cases at first instance and upper tribunals hear appeals from the first tier.

There is a possible appeal route to the Court of Appeal and from here an appeal route to the Supreme Court.

A separate first-tier tribunal and upper tribunal exist for disputes involving employment law.

Revision activity

Using the internet, draw a flowchart to reflect the tribunals' structure in England and Wales.

Role

The system of administrative tribunals runs alongside the civil courts system.

Tribunals were established to deal with a wide variety of specific areas of social and welfare legislation which impact everyday life, for example, school exclusions, immigration issues or employment rights.

Stretch and challenge

Role play the following situation in a fictional tribunal: You are a year 12 student who has been permanently excluded from college. You were permanently excluded for organising a protest on the college site over the lack of adequate hygiene stations at the college during the COVID-19 pandemic.

Negotiation

Table 1.4.1 Role of negotiation

Description	The most basic form of ADR, where an individual attempts to resolve the issue directly, privately and possibly face to face with the other party.
Advantage over litigation	Potentially the quickest, cheapest, most informal way of settling a dispute between parties, as no court or lawyers are involved.
Disadvantages compared to litigation	+ Requires confrontation with the other party. + If the dispute is not settled, the case may go to court, which will involve costs and the court may insist the parties go back to negotiation before trial.
Examples	+ Noise caused by neighbours. + Returning faulty goods to a shop. + Receiving poor service from a tradesperson.

ADR: Mediation

Table 1.4.2 Role of mediation

Description	+ Slightly more formal than negotiation, but still a relatively informal method of dispute resolution. + A neutral third-party mediator attempts to resolve the issue (possibly face to face) with both parties, without giving their opinion.
Advantages over litigation	+ The parties are, in effect, in control of proceedings and decisions. + Based on common sense rather than decisive legal rules.
Disadvantages compared to litigation	+ Will only work if both parties agree and cooperate. + Many decisions may not ultimately be binding on both parties.
Examples	+ Businesses negotiating or renegotiating contracts. + Marriage guidance to avoid separation or divorce.

Now test yourself

TESTED

1. List three areas of law that would be dealt with in the civil courts.
2. List two key reforms that were introduced after Lord Woolf's report, *Access to Justice* (1996)
3. Look at the chart below and complete the missing court or value of claim.

Court	Claim value
Small claims	
	Between £10,000 and £25,000
Multi-track	
	Over £50,000

4. Explain the role of tribunals in the civil justice system.
5. Explain the role of the tribunal system.
6. Give three ways that alternative dispute resolution (ADR) is different from using the civil courts.
7. Explain what is meant by negotiation and mediation.

Exam summary

In the exam, you MAY be asked:

+ multiple-choice questions about the civil courts and other forms of dispute resolution
+ to explain the purpose of the civil courts, the types and practices of the civil courts or tribunals and negotiation and/or mediation
+ to write an analysis of the civil courts, tribunals, negotiation or mediation as a standalone, short or mid-range question.

Criminal courts and lay people

REVISED

The criminal courts system is designed to uphold laws which forbid certain types of behaviour. Carrying out those behaviours risks punishment, which creates a civilised society.

There are two key criminal courts of first instance: the Magistrates' Court and the Crown Court.

Criminal process

There are three key criminal processes in the criminal courts' system:

- being charged with a crime: bail and remand
- trial in the Magistrates' Courts and/or Crown Court
- the Crown Prosecution Service.

Being charged with a crime

If a person is charged with a crime, they are given a 'charge sheet' which outlines the offence(s) they are charged with. The police then decide whether the person can go home until the trial, known as bail, or are kept in custody until taken to court for their first hearing.

Bail

There is a rebuttable presumption that bail should be granted under s 4 of the Bail Act 1976.

After being arrested, a suspect can be released on bail at the police station after being charged with an offence.

Bail can be issued by the police or any court before which the defendant appears, usually either the Magistrates' Court or Crown Court.

It will remain in place until their court hearing.

It can also be refused if there are sufficient grounds.

It can be refused upon arrest and granted later in court and vice versa.

Conditions can be applied to the bail, for example:

- live at a particular address
- do not contact certain people
- give your passport to the police so you cannot leave the UK
- report to a police station at specific, agreed times each week.

Failure to comply with these conditions means the suspect can be arrested again and remanded in prison until their court hearing.

Remand

If bail is refused, for example, the person is charged with a serious crime, then the accused person will go to prison until their first hearing at a Magistrates' court.

Trial in the Magistrates' Court

Around 97 per cent of all criminal cases are dealt with in a Magistrates' Court, with more than 90 per cent being concluded here. The court's key functions include:

- trying summary offences and most either-way offences
- sentencing defendants if found guilty – powers are limited but reflect the seriousness of the crimes under its jurisdiction
- dealing with the first hearing of indictable offences such as the granting of bail or making reporting restrictions before being sent to the Crown Court
- granting or refusing bail in summary or either-way trials
- trying cases in the Youth Court for defendants aged 10–17.

Criminal courts: there are two levels – the Magistrates' Court, which deals mainly with 'summary offences', and the Crown Court, which deals mainly with indictable offences.

Bail: a form of security, either a sum of money or a promise in exchange for the freedom of an arrested person as a guarantee that they will appear in a criminal court when required.

Custody: where a person is under arrest or on remand in prison awaiting trial or while serving a custodial sentence in prison.

Rebuttable presumption: a conclusion that a judge will take in court unless the opposite point is raised and proven.

Exam tip

Here you must have a basic understanding of the criminal processes, including the classification of offences and the criminal appeal system.

Revision activities

1. Read s 4 of the Bail Act 1976 and summarise the section's main constituent parts.
2. Identify the Magistrates' Courts in your local area and the geographical area each one serves.

Revision activity

Identify the Magistrates' Courts in your local area and the geographical area each one serves.

Trial in the Crown Court

In 1971, a system of Crown Courts was established to deal with those criminal cases not tried fully in the Magistrates' Courts.

The Crown Courts deal with the most serious, indictable offences, and some triable-either-way offences. It also deals with appeals against a Magistrates' Court conviction or sentence and cases passed from a Magistrates' Court for trial or sentencing.

The Crown Court normally has:

- a jury that decides guilt
- a single judge who decides the sentence if a person is found guilty.

Stretch and challenge

As a class, nominate a student to contact your local magistrates' association and arrange a Zoom or Teams meeting with a senior magistrate to discuss an evaluation of their role in the criminal justice system.

Crown Prosecution Service

The Crown Prosecution Service (CPS) is responsible for prosecuting most criminal cases in England and Wales. It:

- decides which cases are to be prosecuted
- determines the most appropriate offences with which to charge the defendant
- prepares cases and presents them in court.

Under the Code for Crown Prosecutors, a decision to prosecute is made if the merits of the case pass a two-fold test:

1. The evidential burden test: there must be sufficient evidence to prosecute.
2. The public interest stage test: the prosecution must be in the public interest.

Factors influencing the CPS to prosecute would include:

- a premeditated decision to commit a crime
- use of a weapon
- the defendant was in a position of authority or trust
- vulnerability of the victim
- the defendant has previous convictions.

Revision activity

Browse the CPS website (www.cps.gov.uk) and see if you can find out further information about the Code for Crown Prosecutors.

Exam tip

You might be asked to explain three factors influencing the CPS to prosecute a suspect or assess the likelihood of a suspect being prosecuted in an example scenario. You will need to remember these factors and be able to spot them in a scenario.

Classification of criminal offences

Table 1.4.3 Classification of criminal offences

Classification of offence	Trial court	Examples of offences	Sentencing powers of court
Indictable	Initial hearing in Magistrates' Court, then transferred to Crown Court for trial.	+ Murder + Manslaughter + Robbery + Section 18 wounding/GBH	Up to the maximum set by specific offence by common law or statute.
Triable-either-way	Plea before Magistrates' Court or Crown Court.	+ Theft and burglary + Section 20 & ABH + Drugs offences	Up to maximum set by specific offence (but see below for magistrates' maximum sentencing powers).
Summary	Magistrates' Court	+ Common assault + Most motoring offences + Minor criminal damage	Up to six months' imprisonment for a single offence or up to 12 months in total for two or more offences; and/or a fine, generally of up to £5000.

Stretch and challenge

Using your local newspaper's website, research an example of a person convicted with a summary, triable-either-way and an indictable offence.

Revision activity

Create and illustrate a diagram on A3 paper identifying the three classifications of offence.

Criminal appeal system

The criminal courts system provides potential appeal routes for defendants in all cases and to the prosecution in certain situations. It does not matter if you initially pleaded guilty or not guilty. A judge will look at an appeal application and decide whether to grant or refuse an appeal.

In any case, an appeal must be made within 28 days of either the conviction if appealing against conviction or the sentence if appealing against sentence. Again, a form can be downloaded from the GOV.UK website.

Revision activity

Create a flowchart poster showing the different appeal routes from the Crown Court.

Table 1.4.4 Appeals from the Magistrates' Court to the Crown Court

Available to	Only the defence.
Reason for appeal	Against sentence and/or conviction.
Appeal heard by	Panel of a single Circuit Judge and two magistrates.
Further appeal possible?	Generally no, but possible to appeal to the Queen's Bench Divisional Court purely on a point of law. Possible further appeal to the Supreme Court (see below).
Result of appeal	Appeal quashed, confirm appeal or remit case back to the Magistrates' Court.

Table 1.4.5 Appeals from the Magistrates' Court to the Queen's Bench Divisional Court (QBD)

Available to	The prosecution and the defence.
Reason for appeal	On a point of law by way of case stated.
Appeal heard by	Panel of two or three High Court Judges, which might include a Court of Appeal Judge.
Further appeal possible?	Possible appeal by the prosecution or the defence to the Supreme Court on a point of law of general public importance. Must have leave to appeal by either the Supreme Court or QBD.
Result of appeal	Appeal quashed, confirm appeal or remit case back to the Magistrates' Court.

Table 1.4.6 Appeals from the Crown Court (1)

By whom?	Defendant
Reason for appeal	Rare, but possible – against sentence and/or (unsafe) conviction.
Where heard?	Court of Appeal (Criminal Division) within six weeks of conviction and must be granted permission. Fresh evidence can be heard at this appeal.
Further appeal possible?	Again, rare but possible, to the Supreme Court on a point of law of general public importance. Must have leave to appeal.
Result of appeal	Appeal quashed or confirm appeal.

Table 1.4.7 Appeals from the Crown Court (2)

By whom?	Prosecution
Reason for appeal	Against the acquittal of the defendant if the prosecution is unhappy with the decision or by the Attorney-General to clarify a point of law relevant to the acquittal. Against sentence if the Attorney-General considers the sentence to be unduly lenient.
Where heard?	Court of Appeal (Criminal Division)
Further appeal possible?	Rare, but possible. To the Supreme Court on a point of law of general public importance. Must have leave to appeal.
Result of appeal	Appeal quashed or confirm appeal.

Criminal court powers and sentencing of adult offenders

The term 'sentencing' means any punishment given to an offender who has been convicted. An adult offender is anyone aged 21 years or older who has been convicted of an offence.

There are four main types of adult sentences:

+ Imprisonment: the offender's behaviour is so serious that none of the other sentences will suffice. Offenders serve half of their sentence in prison and the other half on licence in the community.
+ Community sentences: offenders are made to carry out between 40 and 300 hours of demanding work in the community or undergo treatment for issues like drug addiction.
+ Fines: these are for less serious offences and, by far, the most common type of sentence. The amount depends on the severity of the crime.
+ Discharges: this is where the court feels that simply being brought in front of a judge or magistrate is enough punishment. Conditions can be set with a discharge, for example, to stay out of trouble, and if the offender commits another crime, the first crime will be taken into consideration if sentenced.

Typical mistake

Do not use incorrect or out-of-date information. As part of your self-study or homework, make sure you research relevant websites, for example, GOV.UK.

Exam tip

You might be asked to explain one or more of the four main types of sentence available to adult offenders or assess which sentences would be available to a judge in sentencing an adult defendant in a scenario.

Stretch and challenge

Consider which of the four types of adult sentencing would be the most appropriate in each case:

+ Adam is caught speeding at 80 mph on a motorway.
+ Belinda stabs her partner in a fit of rage.
+ Sajira is caught spray painting her name on the wall of an underpass.
+ David, who is homeless, steals a sandwich from a supermarket.

Revision activity

Look at Table 1.4.3 Classification of criminal offences on p 45.

Identify the sentences available to judges in each of the offences listed under the 'examples of offences' column. For example, for an adult convicted of murder there are four 'starting points': 15, 25 or 30 years or a whole life order.

Identify whether a magistrate or judge has the authority to pass the sentence in each example.

Revision activity

Where possible, visit your local Magistrates' Court and Crown Court and observe a morning's worth of cases.

The role of lay people in the criminal courts

Lay people are 'legally unqualified' persons in the criminal justice system who play an important role in the decision-making process.

There are two main types:

+ magistrates – part-time, unsalaried 'judges' who decide guilt and sentence offenders
+ juries – drawn from the electorate, they decide the guilt of offenders in the Crown Court.

Lay people: in the criminal justice system, lay people are either magistrates or juries. 'Lay' in this circumstance means legally 'unqualified'.

Magistrates: ordinary people who work unpaid (except for expenses), hearing cases in their community. They deal with the vast majority of criminal cases.

Magistrates

Role and powers

The role of magistrates is to:

+ sit, usually, in benches of three, including two 'wingers' and a Presiding Justice who acts as Chair
+ listen to evidence given in court and follow structured guidelines in their decision-making process
+ try summary and relevant either-way offences, sentence guilty defendants or send the case to the Crown Court for sentencing if they think their sentencing powers are insufficient
+ carry out preliminary hearings, such as early administrative hearings for indictable offences, remand hearings and applications for bail.

Exam tip

You might be asked to discuss the role of a lay magistrate in the criminal justice system, so knowing four or five key roles is crucial to success.

See page 44 for more information on the powers of magistrates in criminal courts.

Magistrates have powers to decide the guilt or innocence of an accused person and to impose these sentences:

- an absolute or conditional discharge
- a custodial sentence of between five days and six months
- a suspended sentence
- a community order
- a fine
- an order for compensation
- a disqualification or banning order, for example, a driving ban.

Typical mistake

Do not confuse the role of magistrates with that of juries or vice versa.

Revision activity

Research the facts, decision and impact of *Bushell's* Case (1670).

Juries

Role in criminal courts

Only around two per cent of criminal trials use juries. Juries:

- sit in the Crown Court as a panel of 12 persons
- decide the verdict only of the defendant – guilty or not guilty
- decide the facts of the case
- listen to the judge who will direct a jury on points of law
- are independent and act without fear of pressure from the judge to either convict or decide a verdict quickly – see *Bushell's* Case (1670).

Advantages and disadvantages of using juries in criminal courts

Table 1.4.8 Advantages and disadvantages of using juries in criminal courts

Advantages	Disadvantages
Public confidence is instilled due to the traditional idea of being judged by ordinary members of society rather than professional judges.	Slow and expensive – having to explain points of law increases the time taken and the cost of the judges and legal personnel.
Jury equity upholds democracy and freedom of will – see *R v Ponting* (1985) and *R v Grobbelaar* (1997).	Unpopular – the compulsory nature of jury service means many jurors would rather not serve due to its impact on their working or family life.
Open system of justice – the process is public and assumes no legal knowledge of jurors as points are explained.	Outside influences – arguably media and social media coverage can influence jurors, or jurors can be 'nobbled' – see *R v Twomey* (2010).
Privacy of decision-making process – juries decide the verdict in private without outside pressures.	No explanation of verdict – the decision is made in secret and no reason is given for the decision, or bizarre methods are used to reach the decision – see *R v Young* (1995).
The random selection process allows a cross-section of community to be picked from.	Failure to understand the case – due to the complex nature of the law, it is possible juries do not follow the issues clearly.
Neutrality – a jury should be impartial and, as a panel of 12, any individual prejudices should be cancelled out.	Lack of neutrality – a complete cancelling of bias, especially racism, is speculative at best and highly unlikely – see *Sander v UK* (2000).

Now test yourself TESTED

8 Give a simple definition of bail.
9 Identify two conditions that could be applied to bail.
10 List the key functions of a Magistrates' Court as a criminal court.
11 Identify and explain one of the types of punishment for adult offenders.
12 Explain the term 'lay people' with regard to criminal cases.
13 Name the different sentencing powers of a magistrate.
14 List three advantages of using a jury.

Evaluation point

Consider the following statement: 'The jury system is unfair on defendants. They are simply made up of people who are forced to serve, retired people killing time and pro-police conservatives.' Do you agree or disagree?

Exam summary

In the exam, you MAY be asked:

- multiple-choice questions about the criminal processes, the classification of offences and lay people
- to explain the purpose of the criminal courts and the role of magistrates and/or the value of juries in criminal trials
- to write an analysis of the criminal courts, role of magistrates or value of juries, as standalone, short or mid-range questions or as part of a criminal law extended scenario question.

Legal personnel

REVISED

Role of legal personnel

Role of barristers

Barristers at the Bar are self-employed legal advocates who generally practise out of chambers in court. Their role includes:

- when required, being briefed by a solicitor on behalf of a client or approached directly in certain civil matters
- rights of audience in all courts to represent clients, particularly the Crown Court or higher courts
- acting as a specialist legal advisor, giving clients independent and objective advice and opinion on the merits of a case, called 'counsel's opinion'
- if appointed as Queen's Counsel (QC), handling very serious or complex cases
- drafting legal documents for court
- working for the CPS or large businesses who have legal departments.

Typical mistake

Remember that while many of the roles of barristers and solicitors overlap, they are very different in many cases. Questions may ask for the differences between the role of a solicitor and a barrister.

Role of solicitors

Solicitors' roles largely depend on what type of firm (small or large) that they are employed in. The work can include:

- acting as a 'first contact' with clients needing legal advice on a range of specialist areas, for example, conveyancing or family matters
- acting as advocates for clients, generally in the lower courts such as the Magistrates' Court or County Court
- organising a barrister for their client if the case goes to Crown Court or higher court (some solicitors have rights of audience in all the courts)
- writing letters on their client's behalf on legal matters
- drafting contracts or other legal documents such as wills
- generally, working in private practice, but can work for large businesses that have a legal department or local authorities.

Role of legal executives

Legal executives are qualified lawyers and usually specialise in one particular area of law. They generally work alongside solicitors and provide a similar role.

The work can include:

- acting as a first contact with clients needing legal advice in straightforward cases
- limited rights of audience acting as advocates for clients, generally in lower courts such as the County Court
- giving legal advice to clients on a range of specialist areas, for example, personal injury and debt recovery
- handling legal aspects of a property transfer
- drafting contracts or other legal documents such as wills.

Revision activity

Draw a Venn diagram or chart for the similarities and differences between the three types of **legal personnel**.

Legal personnel: a collective term which includes solicitors, barristers and legal executives. Traditionally, barristers had 'rights of audience' (the right to exclusively practice) in certain courts such as the Crown Court where solicitors did not. This is now no longer the case.

Regulation of legal personnel

Regulation of the legal profession is vital in order to ensure a safe, secure and responsible environment for lawyers and their clients.

If there were no specific regulation, lawyers could potentially act unprofessionally or negligently without recourse and their clients would have little or no redress against them.

The regulation is governed mainly by the Legal Services Act 2007.

Regulation: a process whereby the actions of individuals or a collective are overseen and governed by an authorised organisation.

Regulation of barristers

Barristers are regulated by the Bar Standards Board, whose duties include:

- setting the education and training requirements of barristers and continuing training requirements throughout their career
- setting the standards of conduct for barristers
- monitoring the service provided by barristers
- handling complaints against barristers, taking disciplinary action where required.

Regulation of solicitors

Solicitors are regulated by the Solicitors' Regulatory Authority which protects and helps the public by:

- setting the standards for qualifying as a solicitor
- monitoring performance of solicitors
- setting the rules for professional conduct
- handling complaints against solicitors who do not follow the Authority's rules
- operating a compensation fund for clients who have lost money as a result of a solicitor's dishonesty.

Regulation of legal executives

Legal executives are regulated by the Chartered Institute of Legal Executives (CILEX) which:

- oversees the education, qualification and practice standards of legal executives
- takes action against legal executives who do not meet those standards.

Stretch and challenge

Imagine you are a careers adviser. Abdul, Bob and Chantelle all want to enter the legal profession, but for different reasons. Abdul doesn't want to go to university and wants to start a job straight after leaving college. Bob and Chantelle are happy to go to university, but Bob wants to work in an office for a charity, whereas Chantelle wants to argue cases in court. Advise which of the three legal professions would suit each student.

Revision activity

Using the internet, research the governing body websites for each type of legal personnel.

Table 1.4.9 Summary of the regulation of legal personnel

	Barristers	Solicitors	Legal executives
Governing body	Bar Council	Law Society	Chartered Institute of Legal Executives (CILEx)
Regulatory body	Bar Standards Board	Solicitors' Regulatory Authority	CILEx Regulation
Powers of regulatory body	+ Fined + Individual sanctions + Suspension + Disbarment from working	+ Fined + Written rebuke + Reprimand + Severe reprimand	+ Reject a complaint + Impose conditions on future work + Exclude from membership + Fined + Ordered to pay costs of the case
Client liability	No contractual liability but can be sued for negligence – see *Hall v Simons* (2000).	Contractual liability and can be sued for negligence – see *White v Jones* (1995).	Contractual liability and can be sued for negligence.

Legal Services Board

The Legal Services Board was created under the Legal Services Act 2007 and oversees the regulation of lawyers in England and Wales. It operates as a second check to the regulatory bodies of the three types of legal personnel.

It suggests reform and recommendations to modernise the legal services market.

Legal Ombudsman

If the dispute between client and lawyer cannot be resolved between themselves or the relevant regulatory body, then the case could be referred to the Legal Ombudsman. This is an independent scheme that resolves complaints about lawyers from clients in a fair and effective way. It helps to drive improvements to legal services.

Now test yourself TESTED

15 Explain three roles undertaken by a barrister.
16 Explain three roles undertaken by a solicitor.
17 Explain three roles undertaken by a legal executive.
18 Explain how the work of a barrister is regulated.
19 Explain three key differences between a barrister and a solicitor.
20 Look at the following chart in relation to legal personnel and decide whether the statement is true or false by placing a tick in the correct column.

	True	False
Barristers, and not solicitors, generally have rights of audience in the Crown Courts or higher.		
Barristers cannot be approached directly by clients. Only a solicitor can speak directly to a barrister.		
Solicitors can work for small high-street firms, larger city firms and for large multi-national businesses.		
Legal executives have the same rights of audience as barristers.		
Legal executives are not allowed to draft legal documents such as wills; only solicitors are allowed to carry out this task.		

Exam summary

In the exam, you MAY be asked:

- multiple-choice questions about legal personnel
- to explain the roles and regulation of the legal profession
- to write an analysis of the roles and regulation of the legal profession as standalone, short or mid-range questions, or as part of a criminal law extended scenario question.

The judiciary

REVISED

The judiciary is split between the civil courts and the criminal courts. However, the higher up the hierarchy, the more likely judges can sit in either civil or criminal cases, depending upon where they are needed. Their main role is to adjudicate either over transgressions of the law in criminal trials or in disputes in civil cases.

Judiciary: collective term for all the different types of judge in the English legal system.

Types of judge and their roles

There are different types of judge. They can be divided into:

- inferior (Crown Court and below)
- superior (High Court and above).

The differences relate to their role, their appointment and how they are dismissed.

Table 1.4.10 Type and role of judges

Court	Type of judge	Role of judge in civil and criminal courts
Supreme Court	✚ Justices of the Supreme Court ✚ Head of the Supreme Court: President of the Supreme Court	Hear appeals on points of law in both civil and criminal cases.
Court of Appeal	✚ Lord Justices of Appeal ✚ Criminal Division Head: Lord Chief Justice ✚ Civil Division Head: Master of the Rolls	✚ Hear appeals in criminal cases against conviction and/or sentence. ✚ Hear appeals in civil cases on finding of liability and/or amount awarded.
High Court	✚ High Court Judges (Puisne Judges) ✚ Head of Chancery Division: Chancellor of the High Court ✚ Head of Family Division: President of the Family Division ✚ Head of the Queen's Bench Division: President of the Queen's Bench Division	✚ Judges sit in one of three High Court Divisions. ✚ Hear large-value, first-instance civil cases to decide liability and remedy. ✚ Hear appeals from lower courts in both civil and criminal cases.
Crown Court	✚ High Court Judges (for serious cases) ✚ Circuit Judges ✚ Recorders (part time)	✚ Hear complex and serious criminal cases. ✚ Hear appeals from Magistrates' Courts. ✚ Try criminal cases with a jury. ✚ Decide the law. ✚ Assist the jury on points of law. ✚ Pass sentences.
County Court	✚ Circuit Judges ✚ Recorders (part time) ✚ District Judges (small claims court)	✚ Hear civil cases. ✚ Decide liability and remedies.
Magistrates' Court	✚ District Judges (Magistrates' Court)	✚ Hear low- to medium-level criminal cases. ✚ Decide verdict. ✚ Pass sentences. ✚ Hear civil cases: some family work, licensing appeals.
Tribunals	✚ Tribunal Judges ✚ Head: Senior President of Tribunals	✚ Hear cases on specific civil issues, such as employment disputes.

Stretch and challenge

Using the Supreme Court's official website (**www.supremecourt.uk/index.html**), research the educational background of the Justices. Consider the similarities of their educational backgrounds.

Independence of the judiciary

Security of tenure

It is a long-established principle in the English legal system that:

- ✚ judges should not be under the control of the government (the executive)
- ✚ judges should not be removed as a government changes, in order to serve a new government's purpose or desire
- ✚ individual judges are not criticised in parliamentary debates
- ✚ any judicial removal mechanisms and the length of tenure should be firmly established in law.

There is no minimum age to be appointed as a judge, but:

- ✚ in most cases, they must be able to serve for a 'reasonable length of service', which in practice is for a minimum of five years
- ✚ judges must retire by the time they are 70 years old (some judges can work longer, but no judge is allowed to serve after they reach 75 years of age).

Judges hold office 'during good behaviour' and can be removed if there is an allegation of misconduct:

- For High Court Judges and Court of Appeal Judges, removal is by petition to the Crown following an address presented to both Houses of Parliament by virtue of the Act of Settlement 1701.
- There is a similar process to remove Supreme Court Judges, but this kind of judge can appear before a tribunal before any parliamentary motion is tabled (Constitutional Reform Act 2005).
- Circuit and District Judges can be removed by the Lord Chancellor on the grounds of misconduct or incapacity, but he/she can only do so if the Lord Chief Justice agrees.

Revision activity

Using the internet, research any instances where judges have been dismissed and for what reasons.

Immunity from suit

On the grounds of public policy, judges are given immunity from suit – see *Sirros v Moore* (1975). This means that they are free from any legal action while serving correctly in their capacity as a judge.

However, this does not prevent a complaint being raised against a judge because of their behaviour, language or conduct. It is therefore possible for a judge to be removed from office in certain circumstances.

Independence from the Executive

In court, judges have to be independent from any external pressures, so that the defendant is seen to have a fair trial. The doctrine of separation of powers states that the judiciary must remain separate from the government and Parliament.

It is important that the public see that judges are independent. Judges must be impartial and free from any political bias or influence.

The Executive: the UK's democratically elected government.

The judiciary should ignore pressure from **the Executive** to:

- manoeuvre or coerce a judge into making certain pro-Executive (government) decisions
- force a judge to rule against those who oppose the Executive's policies or plans.

Other influences judges must ignore are:

- Parliament (the legislature)
- other judges, particular senior judges, unless bound by law such as precedent
- pressure groups
- their own self-interest, opinions and beliefs – see *Re Pinochet* (1998)
- the media.

Stretch and challenge

The concept of the independence of the judiciary was famously supported by Baron de Montesquieu. Carry out a basic background search of this famous 18th century French judge and his beliefs in this area.

Reasons for and advantages of judicial independence

Judicial independence is important to:

- ensure that the verdict, or decision in the case, is only decided upon by evidence of the facts and the law as it stands
- ensure that in jury trials, juries decide the verdict based on facts and not on any other influence
- deliver fair and impartial justice
- protect citizens and their rights against unlawful actions of government, state-run agencies or any person or organisation that tries to infringe or remove their rights.

Methods for achieving judicial independence

Some argue that judges are above the law. Nevertheless, judicial independence is protected in several ways:

- Judges have immunity from being prosecuted for any acts they perform while carrying out their judicial function.
- Judges have immunity from being sued for defamation from anything they say about anyone involved in the court case, for example, comments they may make about the defendant or witnesses.
- As a precaution, any errors made by a judge can be appealed against rather than being a rigid, permanent decision.
- Judges' salaries and pension rights are not set by the Executive but by independent bodies.

Evaluation point

Consider the following statement: 'The belief in an independent judiciary is ridiculous. Inferior judges are not independent to the decisions of superior judges who are not independent to the decisions of the Lord Chancellor and the Executive.' Do you agree or disagree?

Now test yourself

TESTED 

21 Explain the role of a judge in the Supreme Court.
22 Explain the role of a judge in the Court of Appeal Civil Division.
23 Discuss what is meant by the term 'security of tenure' in relation to the judiciary.
24 Discuss what is meant by the term 'immunity from suit' in relation to the judiciary.
25 Look at the following chart in relation to the judiciary and decide whether the statement is true or false by placing a tick in the correct column.

	True	False
District Judges sit in both the Crown Court and the High Court.		
Inferior judges include those of the Supreme Court.		
Superior judges can be removed by the Lord Chancellor, provided the Lord Chief Justice consents to the dismissal.		
It is important that the Executive has control over the judiciary or else judges might make decisions which go against government policy.		

Evaluation point

Consider the following statement: 'The methods of achieving judicial independence are simply to avoid judges being accountable for their decisions.'

Exam summary

In the exam, you MAY be asked:

- multiple-choice questions about the judiciary
- to explain the types, role and independence issues of the judiciary
- to write an analysis of the types, role and independence issues of the judiciary as standalone, short or mid-range questions, or as part of a criminal law extended scenario question.

Access to justice and funding of legal services

REVISED

This topic refers to

- how a litigation is paid for
- who pays for the litigation
- whether there are any alternative methods of 'funding' advice.

Litigation: the process of taking action, normally in a civil dispute.

One of the central beliefs of the English legal system is the idea that there must be equality before the law. This means that guilt or liability in a court is proved or disproved on the basis of the facts and the relevant law. This must be irrespective of a person's status or wealth, and therefore an inability to pay for legal services must never bar citizens from bringing an action or defending themselves in court.

However, going to court is an expensive matter and many people cannot afford the high costs of lawyers. On many occasions, even if citizens can afford to go to court, they cannot afford the best lawyers, such as Queen's Counsel, because of their expense.

Typical mistake

Do not confuse access to justice with alternative dispute resolution (ADR). Access to justice is about financial access to the courts and not looking for alternative ways to settle disputes.

Alternative sources of legal advice

REVISED

Sometimes free legal advice is available to members of organisations via a subscription to a general service, as outlined in the table below.

Exam tip

You might be asked to explain alternative sources of legal advice.

Table 1.4.11 Alternative sources of legal advice

Alternative source of legal advice	Method of assistance	Examples of alternative sources of legal advice
Helplines	Via telephone or online access direct to an operator qualified to provide advice.	RAC/AA (motoring organisations); Disability Law Service (advice for many organisations and people with disabilities).
Citizens Advice	Town-centre-based legal advice agency providing general legal advice face to face, via telephone or online.	Over 3500 locations throughout the country and at **www.citizensadvice.org.uk**.
Law centres	Free access to legal advice from solicitors.	45 locations in England and at **www.lawcentres.org.uk**.
Trade unions	Specific, targeted advice on issues relevant to the trade union – generally on employment issues.	National Union of Teachers; British Medical Council (doctors); National Union of Journalists.

Stretch and challenge

Find out where your nearest Citizens Advice office is situated. Using the website **www.citizensadvice.org.uk**, identify the current most common areas of Bureau advice.

Private funding

This is where an individual pays for their own litigation in some form or another.

Exam tip

You might be asked to explain one of the methods of private funding of legal services.

Own resources

Private funding requires citizens to pay for legal services themselves. Using their own resources to pay legal fees or raising the funds via a loan or remortgaging a home can put people into financial difficulties or prevent many people from pursuing a case.

Insurance

It is not uncommon for people to take out insurance to pay for court costs in civil cases and, in some situations, in anticipation of criminal cases.

There are two types of insurance for advice and representation:

- 'before the event' – in anticipation of fighting or defending a legal case
- 'after the event' – to insure against losing a case and having to pay the other side's costs as well as damages.

Examples can be found under household insurance and motor insurance policies as optional extras.

Some conditional fee agreements insist on insurance being taken out.

Conditional fee agreements (CFAs): 'no win, no fee' arrangements.

Conditional fee agreements (CFAs)

Table 1.4.12 Outline of conditional fee agreements

Purpose	+ CFAs were introduced as an alternative way to privately fund a civil case. + The client only pays the solicitor's fees if they win, and pays nothing if they lose.
Method	+ An agreement is struck between the client and their solicitor that any costs are paid from the compensation received if they win the case, along with a 'success fee'. + Until 2013, the 'success fee' could be recovered from the losing party, but this was stopped and instead will be taken from their client's compensation.
Advantages	+ They offer a further alternative to private funding of a case. + They remove the anxiety of having to pay huge costs. + Any deductions for costs are set at 25 per cent. + Insurance can be taken out to compensate for any losses. + They are widely available. + There is no payment up front or in advance to begin a case.
Disadvantages	+ Solicitors generally charge a higher fee to cover the risk of losing the case. + Court costs may still need to be paid that are not covered in the arrangement. + Certain firms are contracted to take on certain publicly funded cases such as clinical negligence, restricting the pool of potential firms available. + They encourage the 'cherry-picking' by solicitors of those cases that stand a greater chance of winning. + Arguably lawyers might use tactics to win at all costs, including tactics of a dubious nature. + Lawyers will generally insist on insurance being taken out, precluding many poorer clients from accessing CFAs.

Stretch and challenge

Complete the table below on conditional fee arrangements. In this situation, there is a success fee of £2000 if the case is won, or a 25 per cent cap on success fee:

Result of case	Client pays	Explanation
Case is lost.	£?	no win, no fee
Case won. Client gets £40,000 in damages.	£?	25% cap
Case is won. Client gets £4000 in damages.	£?	25% cap

Exam tip

You might be asked to explain or compare three advantages (or disadvantages) of a conditional fee agreement, or you might be asked to assess the merits of using a conditional fee agreement to fund a civil case in a scenario question.

Public funding – criminal and civil state funding

The Legal Aid Agency provides civil and criminal legal aid and advice in England and Wales to help people deal with their legal problems. Their role is to:

+ ensure that legal aid services from solicitors, barristers and the not-for-profit sector are available to the general public
+ fund the Civil Legal Advice Service
+ publish statistical evidence about the decisions made on whether or not to fund a case
+ run the Public Defender Service for criminal cases.

Table 1.4.13 The Civil Legal Advice Service and Public Defender Service

	Civil Legal Advice Service	Public Defender Service
Role	Provides free and confidential advice in civil law matters such as debt, housing and domestic abuse.	Provides: + a range of services within the criminal defence market + free, full representation of defendants from the police station through to the courts, even on appeal + free advice and assistance when a person is under arrest at any time + an advocacy service with access to 25 advocates, including seven QCs.
Merit tested?	Yes, via the **www.gov.uk** website.	Yes, via a 'means test' which looks at a person's household income, capital and outgoings.
Advantages	+ Funding of cases for those on no income or low income. + Fundamental right to the agency's services as part of the welfare state in England and Wales. + A stepped contribution process, allowing fairer access to justice for those unable to pay or those on low to mid-range salaries.	
Disadvantages	+ Penalises those in employment who have to contribute or are refused legal aid because of moderate to high wages. + Very strict means test. + Funding capped by government, which traditionally results in criminal funding taking priority over civil funding due to potential loss of liberty in criminal cases. + Less attractive to qualified solicitors as fee rates are lower than private clients. + Arguably seen as a quick entry into the profession by new, inexperienced solicitors. + Civil legal aid unavailable for employment tribunal cases.	

Now test yourself

TESTED

26 Explain how Citizens Advice can be considered an alternative source of legal advice.

27 Explain two advantages of using a conditional fee agreement.

28 Explain one disadvantage of using a conditional fee agreement.

29 Read each statement below carefully and decide which type of private funding of legal services it refers to, then complete the table.

Statement	Type of private funding
Client re-mortgages home to pay for legal services.	
No win, no fee.	
Offered by companies, e.g. motoring companies.	

Exam tip

You might be asked to explain the Civil Legal Advice Service or the Public Defender Service.

Exam summary

In the exam, you MAY be asked:

+ multiple-choice questions about access to justice and funding
+ to explain the alternative sources of legal advice available and public or private funding of cases
+ to write an analysis of alternative sources of legal advice available and public or private funding of cases as standalone, short or mid-range questions, or as part of a criminal law extended scenario question.

Revision activities

Make sure that you have worked through all previous MCQs and short answer questions on the legal system from the AQA website.

Also, look at back-copies of the *A Level Law Review* which contains examples of AQA-style MCQs.

Write your own MCQs and short answer questions on the legal system using the style set by AQA. Don't make the answers too simple or too obscure. Follow the specification and pick out key areas that a question-setter might use to set an exam question.

Exam practice

The content of this chapter will be distributed across all three papers as shown in the table below.

Paper 1 – Crime	Paper 2 – Tort	Paper 3 – Contract/HR
Nature of law – legal and other rules; civil/criminal distinction and sources	Nature of law – legal and other rules; civil/criminal distinction and sources	Nature of law – legal and other rules; civil/criminal distinction and sources
		The rule of law
Statutory interpretation	Parliamentary law making	Delegated legislation
Judicial precedent	Law reform	European Union
The criminal courts and lay people	The civil courts and other forms of dispute resolution	
Legal personnel – roles of barristers, solicitors and legal executives; regulation		
The judiciary: types of judge. Role of judges in criminal courts	The judiciary: types of judge. Role of judges in civil courts	The judiciary: types of judge. Role of judges in civil courts (contract) and in criminal courts (human rights)
		Independence of the judiciary
Access to justice and funding in criminal system	Access to justice and funding in civil system	Access to justice and funding in civil system (contract) and in criminal system (human rights)
Law and society – fault Law and justice	Law and society – fault Law and morality	Law and society – balancing conflicting interests Law and justice Law and morality

Nature of law

In Paper 3, for Nature of Law you will be asked:

- one of the two short 5-mark scenario questions
- two 10- or 15-mark questions: one of these will be a Nature of Law essay requiring an extended answer which shows a clear, logical and sustained line of reasoning, leading to a valid conclusion.
- an extended scenario, worth 30 marks: you will need to apply criminal law, analyse a related Nature of Law topic and create a valid conclusion.

Law making and legal systems

Questions on these topics will be spread across the papers as indicated above. You will answer:

- five multiple-choice questions
- short answer questions worth 5 marks
- 10- and 15-mark questions, usually combining the substantive element with the content of this chapter.

Multiple-choice questions (1 mark each)

1 Proposed new legislation affecting the whole of the country, but which is promoted by a minority interest group, is most likely to be brought to Parliament as a:

- A Government Bill
- B Private Bill
- C Private Members' Bill
- D White Paper

2 A local council intends to introduce a law banning dogs from walking on beaches in its area in the summer months. From the following list, choose the best form of legislation for the council to use:

- A Statutory instrument
- B Order in Council
- C By-law
- D Act of Parliament

3 Which statement most accurately describes the effect of an EU treaty on UK law?

- A It has horizontal direct effect.
- B It automatically becomes part of UK law.
- C It only gives the state rights.
- D It does not become law until the UK Parliament approves the treaty.

4 Which of the following statements about magistrates in criminal trials is correct?

- A Magistrates are paid a salary for their work in court.
- B Magistrates are legally qualified professionals.
- C Magistrates can send convicted citizens to prison.
- D Magistrates try indictable cases, such as murder or robbery.

5 In the criminal courts, which one of the following judges will not sit in the Crown Court to hear indictable cases?

- A District Judge
- B Circuit Judge
- C Recorder
- D High Court Judge

'Short answer' 5-mark questions

6 Explain what is meant by a Private Members' bill and how they are introduced to Parliament.

7 Explain two differences between the civil and criminal law.

8 Explain two advantages and one disadvantage of using juries in criminal courts.

9 Explain two of the key roles of a barrister as a member of the legal profession.

10-mark questions

10 Explain how a barrister's work is regulated.

11 Explain the process of passing an Act of Parliament starting in the House of Commons.

15-mark questions

These are likely to be Nature of Law questions linked to the substantive element. The substantive element is in brackets, and you could practise answering this question with a variety of different substantive elements.

12 Examine the meaning of 'justice' and discuss the extent to which (application of the rules on sexual infidelity in the loss of control defence) may achieve justice.

13 Examine the meaning and significance of 'fault' within criminal law and discuss the extent to which offences of strict liability criminalise those who are not at 'fault'.

End-of-unit summary

Nature and role of law

- The difference between enforceable legal rules and principles and other rules and norms of behaviour.
- The links between law, morality and justice.
- The differences between civil and criminal law.
- An overview of the development of English Law: custom, common law, statute law.
- The definition and importance of the rule of law.
- The definitions of morals and law, where they overlap and differ.
- The function of morals and law, where they overlap and differ.
- The main legal theories underpinning the law, such as legal positivism and natural law.
- Pluralism as a key factor in shaping the approach to morality in our society.
- Cases and issues where morality and law have clashed in the courts.
- The main arguments and issues in the Devlin-Hart debate and the application of the main arguments to specific issues and cases.
- Evaluation of law and morality.
- The meaning of justice.
- Theories of justice.
- The extent to which the law achieves justice.
- Evaluation of law and justice.
- The elements that make up the rule of law.
- The role of the rule of law in law making.
- The role of the rule of law in substantive areas, with examples and evaluation.

Law making

- How Bills come into being – Green and White papers.
- Different types of Bill and when and why they are used.
- Stages of the legislative process, in both Houses.
- An evaluation of the process.
- What delegated legislation is and why it is important (this is also an evaluation point).
- The three types of delegated legislation, including the relevant secondary body, with a reason and example for each.
- How Parliament places controls on delegated legislation – with types of control and examples.
- How effective these are (this is also an evaluation point).
- How the courts control delegated legislation – with types including *ultra vires*, and examples.
- An evaluation of delegated legislation – drawing a conclusion that it is flawed but necessary.
- What statutory interpretation is and why it is necessary (this is also an evaluation point).
- The rules of statutory interpretation explained and illustrated with examples.
- The intrinsic and extrinsic aids – what they mean, where they can be found and examples of their use.
- The continued impact of EU membership on statutory interpretation.
- The impact of the Human Rights Act 1998 on statutory interpretation.
- An evaluation of the rules and approaches to statutory interpretation – drawing a conclusion that they are flawed but necessary.
- An understanding of the basic purpose and doctrine of judicial precedent.
- The meaning of *stare decisis*; the importance of judgment and law reporting in this context.
- The meaning of *ratio decidendi*, illustrated by a case example.
- The meaning of *obiter dicta*, illustrated by a case example.
- An understanding of the hierarchical structure of the courts, including their 'binding' relationships.
- The impact and use of the Practice Statement 1966.
- Types of precedent with explanations and examples.
- An evaluation of judicial precedent – drawing a conclusion that it is flawed but an essential element to the perception of justice.
- The specific influences on Parliament, explained and illustrated with real examples.
- The role and make up of the Law Commission.
- The impact of the work of the Law Commission, illustrated with real examples.

- An evaluation of all different influences on Parliament.
- Very brief understanding of the timeline of the EU.
- The membership, role and functions of each of the institutions of the EU.
- The sources and types of EU law, illustrated with examples.
- The role of the EUCJ on citizens' rights, supported by examples.
- The impact of membership of the EU on parliamentary sovereignty, illustrated by examples – particularly *Factortame*.

The legal system

- The track system.
- The civil courts' appeals process.
- Tribunals' structure and the role of tribunals.
- The classification of offences.
- The criminal appeal system.
- The criminal courts' powers and sentencing of adult offenders.
- The role and power of magistrates.
- The role of juries.
- The strengths and weaknesses of using juries.
- The differences in the roles of legal personnel.
- A basic understanding of the regulation of the legal profession.
- The types of judges.
- The role of judges in the civil and criminal courts.
- The independence of the judiciary.
- The reasons for an independent judiciary.
- How the independence of the judiciary is maintained.
- Basic understanding of alternative sources of legal advice.
- Private funding of legal cases.
- Public funding of legal cases

2 Criminal law

2.1 Rules of criminal law

Criminal law is a substantive area of law and is assessed in Paper 1. It comprises a series of common law rules and statutes which define conduct that is prohibited in our society because it threatens or causes harm to public safety.

Rules and principles

It is important that you are able to define and explain the principles of criminal law and are competent in applying these principles. The course requires you to understand the rules and theory in criminal law before carrying out an examination of the key principles of *actus reus* and *mens rea*.

This chapter gives background material for what will be assessed in this paper. It revises the rules and principles concerning general elements of criminal liability. Specific elements and crimes are dealt with in greater detail in Chapters 2.2–2.8.

Defining crime

Lord Atkin defined crime in *Proprietary Articles Trade Association v Attorney-General for Canada* (1931) as 'the act prohibited with penal consequences'. Therefore, there are two elements:

- The act must be prohibited (forbidden by the state).
- The act must attract penal consequences (it must be punished by the state).

Usually, the state will create a crime by passing an Act of Parliament in the manner shown on page 20, for example, the Fraud Act 2006. However, some crimes are created by the common law using the doctrine of precedent as shown on page 30. For example, the law of murder has never been set down by Parliament but has been developed over time by judges.

This is quite rare nowadays; most new crimes are set down by Parliament to respond to new circumstances, such as the outlawing of 'revenge porn' by the Criminal Justice and Courts Act 2015. However, the case of *R v R* (1991) created a 'new' crime of marital rape.

'Punished' means that the state must have provided a maximum or mandatory sentence to be imposed if a person is convicted of a criminal offence.

There are many different types of crime, but all will have these two points in common.

Stretch and challenge

See what new offences you can find – have they been made by Parliament or the courts? Identify either the Act of Parliament or name of the case that established them.

Revision activity

Find an example of an offence against the person, a property offence and a regulatory offence. For each, find both the source (Act or case) and the sentence.

General elements of criminal liability

The fundamental principle of English criminal law was stated by Edward Coke in the seventeenth century as '*actus non facit reum nisi mens sit rea*'. This means 'an act is not guilty unless the mind is also guilty'.

As a consequence, most crimes will have both:

- an *actus reus* (AR) – a guilty act, and
- a *mens rea* (MR) – a guilty mind.

These two elements must occur at the same time in order for a crime to have been committed.

Actus reus: a guilty act.

Mens rea: a guilty mind.

Revision activity

Create a table for every offence you have studied in this course, showing the source, the *actus reus*, the *mens rea* and the sentence (see the example below).

Offence	Source	*Actus reus*	*Mens rea*	Sentence
Criminal damage	Section 1 of the Criminal Damage Act 1971	Destroys or damages any property belonging to another	Intention or recklessness	Maximum ten years' imprisonment

A person is guilty of attempting to commit an offence under s 1(1) of the Criminal Attempts Act 1981 if they perform an act which is more than merely preparatory to the commission of the offence, with the intention of committing an offence. The offence consists of both *actus reus* (an act more than merely preparatory) and a *mens rea* (intention to commit an offence – recklessness is not sufficient). For further detail on attempt, see page 88.

Liability for offences against the person, property offences and attempt

REVISED

Defending crime – removing liability

Although the defendant may have committed the *actus reus*, without the appropriate *mens rea* they cannot be guilty. So, if someone kills another person but does not, or cannot, intend to kill them, they cannot be guilty of murder (they might be guilty of a different offence though).

In addition, there are a number of general defences that may be available even if the defendant has both the *actus reus* and *mens rea*. These will lead to a 'not guilty' verdict.

For A-level, you have to study general defences of self-defence/prevention of crime, duress by threats, duress of circumstance, insanity, automatism and intoxication. This list of defences can be split into two categories known as:

- 'capacity defences' – the defendant could not form the *mens rea*
- 'necessity defences' – the defendant did form the *mens rea* but has an 'excuse' for doing so.

These are discussed in greater detail in Chapter 2.8.

Revision activity

Put each defence listed here into the relevant category – capacity defence or necessity defence.

Exam tip

Familiarise yourself with these technical terms and use them throughout your answers.

Proving criminal liability

Burden of proof

A defendant is innocent until proven guilty. This means it is the prosecution's responsibility to provide evidence in court that the defendant had both the *actus reus* and *mens rea* of the offence with which they have been charged.

Standard of proof

The prosecution must provide evidence of the defendant's guilt 'beyond all reasonable doubt'. This means that the jury or magistrates (depending on how serious the offence is and the type of court dealing with it) should only convict if they are satisfied on the evidence, so that they are sure of the defendant's guilt.

This is a higher standard than in civil law, as here a person's liberty is at stake.

Burden of proof: a defendant is innocent until proven guilty.

Standard of proof: the defendant's guilt must be proved 'beyond all reasonable doubt'.

Evaluation point

Consider how general and partial defences impact on the burden and standard of proof. Do you think this is fair?

Typical mistake

Make sure that you use technical language and don't confuse it with the language of civil law.

Now test yourself TESTED

1 What are the two ways in which new crimes can be created?
2 Which two elements are common to all crimes?
3 Why are there two elements to most crimes?
4 What is the impact of a successful defence?
5 What is the difference between a capacity defence and a necessity defence?
6 Is the burden in criminal law higher or lower than in civil law? Why is this?

Exam summary

In the exam, you MAY be asked:

+ multiple-choice questions about the elements of an offence, the types of defence or the burden of proof
+ mid-length questions that require you to decide whether the elements of an offence are present
+ full-length questions requiring you to advise a client on the *actus reus, mens rea* and any appropriate defences relating to an offence they have been charged with – for these you will need the information here and in the relevant substantive law section.

2.2 Theory in criminal law

This chapter gives background material for what will be assessed in Paper 1. It revises the theory of criminal liability. Specific elements and crimes are dealt with in detail in Chapters 2.3–2.8, but also link closely to Chapters 1.1 and 1.2.

Harm as the basis for criminalising conduct

REVISED

This concept is explored more thoroughly on pages 7–11, where law and morality are discussed.

The idea that harm to others is the only justifiable basis for imposing criminal liability is associated with the work of John Stuart Mill's, *On Liberty* (originally published in 1859).

Other theorists, including H.L.A. Hart in his book, *Law, Liberty and Morality* (1968), have suggested that stopping somebody from harming themselves can also be a justification for criminalising conduct. This approach is referred to as paternalism.

Paternalism: the state is justified in protecting individuals from harm.

Legal moralism: immoral conduct is criminalised for better social cohesion.

Evaluation point

Consider whether social cohesion is actually being achieved. What does the Black Lives Matter movement show us about how effective the law is at ensuring social cohesion?

Revision activity

Read this in conjunction with fault and law and morality. Make sure you can identify where each offence deals with fault and if is it is based on paternalism or legal moralism.

The view that behaviour which is offensive but not harmful could be criminalised was developed and explored by Joel Feinberg in *The Moral Limits of the Criminal Law* (1984–88).

Criminalising conduct on the basis of its lack of morality – without the need to establish harm or offensiveness – is known as legal moralism. In his book, *The Enforcement of Morals* (1965), Patrick Devlin argues that a society's shared morality holds it together and so it is proper to criminalise immoral conduct for the sake of social preservation.

Stretch and challenge

Consider these two contrasting theories. Which one are you most comfortable with and why?

Typical mistake

Do not forget to mention these key terms and theorists throughout. It will show a deeper understanding of the underlying principles.

Autonomy, fault and individual responsibility

REVISED

This concept is closely linked to the information in Chapter 1.1 on fault.

In a legal context, autonomy means being responsible, independent and able to speak for oneself free of influences. This means most adults who are not suffering from debilitating illness or under oppressive and constricting conditions (see the defences in Chapter 2.8) are considered to be autonomous – and therefore responsible for their own actions and their consequences.

Autonomous: legally capable of making one's own decisions and therefore legally responsible for their consequences.

Principles in formulating rules of criminal law

REVISED

This concept is closely linked to Chapter 1.2 on the rule of law.

There are a number of ideals that should be adhered to when new criminal laws are introduced.

Fair labelling

This means that crimes should be defined to reflect their wrongfulness and severity.

Fair labelling is important in two ways:

+ Description – the crime must be properly described, include all the necessary elements, be clear and be communicated.
+ Differentiation – the crime must be clearly distinguished from other crimes, particularly in relation to fault and social condemnation (for example, the difference between murder and manslaughter).

Fair labelling is essential in securing public confidence in the law and a sense of justice.

Correspondence

The correspondence principle means that the result which the defendant intends or foresees should match the result which actually occurs. A defendant should not be held liable for an act unless they meant to do it, or at least knowingly ran the risk of it (see Chapters 2.1 and 2.3).

The Law Commission has criticised the current laws of actual bodily harm (ABH) (s 47 of the Offences Against the Person Act 1861) and grievous bodily harm (GBH) (under s 20) in that they do not conform to the 'correspondence principle'.

Maximum certainty

This is key to the rule of law (see Chapter 1.2). Legal certainty means that decisions are made according to legal rules (they are lawful). This means providing citizens with the ability to organise their behaviour in such a way that does not break the law, as well as protecting them from arbitrary use of state power.

No retrospective liability

The means that the law does not apply back in time. Precedent does of course apply in the individual case it concerns (see page 21), but not in general terms.

Parliamentary laws should not apply retrospectively, but it is possible by virtue of the doctrine of parliamentary sovereignty (see page 21).

An example of a retrospective criminal law is the Criminal Justice Act 2003. This Act allows the retrial of people acquitted of murder if there is 'new, compelling, reliable and substantial evidence' that the acquitted person really was guilty. This applies retroactively and can be used to re-prosecute people who were acquitted before the Act came into effect in 2005 or even before it was passed in 2003. As a result, the defendants who were acquitted in the murder of Stephen Lawrence were allowed to be retried, even though this murder occurred in 1993 and the defendants had been acquitted in 1996 – see *R v Dobson and Norris* (2012).

Revision activity

Create a spider diagram or mind map showing the links between this and other chapters and challenge yourself to use these phrases in every piece of written work you do in the related sections.

Now test yourself

1. In the context of criminalising conduct, what is meant by 'paternalism'?
2. What is legal moralism?
3. What did Devlin mean by 'social preservation'?
4. When might a defendant not be considered autonomous?
5. Why is fair labelling essential?
6. Why do s 47 and s 20 of the OAPA 1861 fail to conform to the correspondence principle?
7. Why is it important for law makers to adhere to the rules of law making?

TESTED

Exam summary

You are unlikely to be asked direct questions about any of these issues, but they are all underlying principles across the course.

Once you have read this chapter, refer to the others it makes reference to and ensure you are confident in using these words, concepts or issues when writing about those areas.

2.3 General elements of liability

Most crimes require *actus reus* and *mens rea* occurring contemporaneously (at the same time). This chapter will identify the key elements, definitions and cases required.

Actus reus

REVISED 

Conduct

Acts and omissions

Usually, the *actus reus* relates to what the defendant is 'doing', and that conduct must cause a consequence. However, sometimes it can also relate to what the defendant omits doing or that they are simply 'being', rather than actually 'doing' anything.

Omission means failure to act. There is a general rule in English law that a 'failure to act' does not amount to an *actus reus*. This is often referred to as the lack of a 'Good Samaritan' law – the law does not place an obligation on you to act.

However, in order to achieve justice, there are a number of exceptions to this rule where there is a duty to act:

- Statutory duty to act, for example, s 1 of the Children and Young Persons Act 1933 (as amended) or s 170 of the Road Traffic Act 1988.
- Duty arising from special relationship – *R v Gibbons and Proctor* (1918).
- Duty arising from the assumption of care for another – *R v Stone and Dobinson* (1977).
- Duty arising from contract of employment – *R v Pittwood* (1902).
- Duty arising from official position – *R v Dytham* (1979).
- Duty to avert a danger of one's own making – *R v Miller* (1983).

State of affairs

In some circumstances, a defendant can commit an offence by simply 'being' rather than 'doing' – these are known as 'state of affairs' offences.

Having an offensive weapon in a public place is an example (s 1 of the Prevention of Crime Act 1953). The defendant does not have to do anything with the weapon, nor does it have to be visible. It is enough just to have it in one's possession in a public place.

Revision activity

In which other section will you find the case of *Hill v Baxter*? Make the link.

Voluntariness and involuntariness

In carrying out the *actus reus*, the defendant must be acting voluntarily. Consider the cases of *R v Mitchell* (1983) and *R v Larsonneur* (1933). It cannot be as a consequence of a fit or reflex action.

In *Hill v Baxter* (1958), Devlin J in *obiter dicta* gave an example of a driver driving dangerously who is being attacked by a swarm of bees not being liable for the subsequent accident as his actions were not voluntary.

There is a requirement that in order for a defendant to be criminally liable, their actions must be voluntary. Where voluntary conduct is lacking, there can be no link between the defendant and any subsequent harm.

Exam tip

It is essential to make the link between the facts of the case and the point it is making.

Typical mistake

Do not write too much about the facts of the cases – practise summarising the key points in seven words or fewer.

Causation

Where a consequence must be proved, the prosecution has to show that the defendant's conduct was:

- the factual causation of that consequence, and
- the legal cause of that consequence.

However, on its own this rule is not enough. There has to be legal causation too – see the Supreme Court ruling in *R v Hughes* (2013).

Factual causation: but for the defendant's action, the victim would not have suffered that consequence.

Stretch and challenge

Watch this YouTube clip *about R v Broughton* (2020) and add this case into the appropriate rule of causation: **www.youtube.com/watch?app=desktop&v=6utQz8a7ZBo**.

Revision activity

Compare the cases of *R v White* (1910) and *R v Pagett* (1983) to show how the rule on causation works.

Even where the rules on causation are established, the defendant may be excused criminal liability if there is a subsequent intervening act, known as a *novus actus interveniens*, which breaks the chain of causation.

Novus actus interveniens: where a subsequent intervening act breaks the chain of causation.

Consequences

A crime can be an 'action', such as speeding, or it can be a 'consequence', such as murder where the consequence is a 'dead human being'.

Most offences against the person – crimes where someone is injured/killed – are 'consequence' crimes.

Where the consequence is not directly caused by the defendant's action (there is another factor involved) the rules of causation apply.

Exam tip

Look out for scenarios in the exam that are very similar to the facts of the cases in the revision activity. You will be expected to use these as precedents and follow them.

Revision activity

Copy and complete the table.

Rule	Explanation	Case	Facts
'*De minimis*' conduct was more than a 'minimal' cause	'More than a slight or trifling link' between conduct and consequence.	*R v Kimsey* (1993)	
Thin skull			V refused a blood transfusion on religious grounds; D was responsible for her subsequent death.
Intervening acts	Act of a third party, or V's own act or A natural but unpredictable event.	*R v Roberts* (1972) *R v Williams* (1992) *R v Marjoram* (2000)	
Medical intervention	Does not break the chain unless 'extraordinary and unusual' or 'palpably wrong'.	*R v Cheshire* (1991) *R v Jordan* (1956)	
'Operating' and 'substantial' cause	D's acts need not be the sole cause or even the main cause of death, provided that their acts contributed significantly to the death.	*R v Smith* (1959) *R v Jordan* (1956)	

Additional fault elements

REVISED

Mens rea: intention and subjective recklessness

Most crimes require the defendant to have a degree of fault. Different levels of *mens rea* are attached to crimes to indicate the level of fault required for a defendant to be guilty of that offence.

The highest level of fault is intention and this can be further split into direct intent, oblique intent or subjective recklessness.

Intention: a decision to bring about the criminalised act.

Subjective recklessness: the defendant commits an act knowing there is a risk of the consequence happening.

Table 2.3.1 Types of intention

	Description	Key case
Direct intent	It was the defendant's decision to bring about the prohibited consequence (the AR). It was their aim and purpose.	*R v Mohan* (1976)
Oblique intent	There are two elements to this type of intent: + the prohibited consequence (the AR) is virtually certain, and + the defendant realises this.	*R v Woollin* (1998) *R v Matthews and Alleyne* (2003) said the court has the option to find intention if these tests are satisfied, but is not obliged to do so.
Subjective recklessness	The defendant appreciates the risk of the prohibited consequence (the AR) and continues anyway. This is sometimes known as 'basic intent', which can be a little confusing – so if you come across a referral to 'crimes of basic intent', it means crimes where recklessness is a sufficiently high MR.	*R v Cunningham* (1957)

Evaluation point

Consider how MR reflects blameworthiness and why this is important.

Negligence

Negligence is a failure to meet the standards of the reasonable person. It is rarely sufficient for a *mens rea* in criminal law, but there are exceptions such as gross negligence manslaughter. A key case in this area is *R v Adomako* (1994).

Transferred malice

Mens rea can be transferred from the intended victim to the actual victim where the defendant misses their intended target or the domino rally effect occurs. Key cases here are *R v Latimer* (1886), *R v Mitchell* (1983) and *R v Gnango* (2011). However, *mens rea* can only be transferred where the *actus reus* remains the same – see *R v Pembliton* (1874).

Revision activities

1 Create a bar chart, with degrees of fault on the y axis and types of *mens rea* on the x axis. Create bars for the types of *mens rea* and include their definitions and cases.

2 Find the key facts in the cases mentioned under 'Transferred malice' and summarise in 10 words or fewer.

No fault: strict liability

REVISED 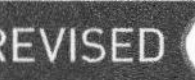

Offences requiring no fault are called strict liability offences (SLOs) and exist to regulate society and protect the vulnerable. Examples of SLOs are given in Table 2.3.2 below.

Table 2.3.2 Examples of strict liability offences

Case	Facts	How the SLO protects society
PSGB v Storkwain Ltd (1986)	The appellant had allowed prescription drugs to be supplied on production of fraudulent prescriptions.	Supply of medicines must be carefully regulated.
Winzar v Chief Constable of Kent (1983)	D was 'found drunk on a highway', having been removed from a hospital by the police officers who then arrested him in their police car.	Drunken and anti-social behaviour must be deterred, especially as MR might not be able to be formed if drunk.
Callow v Tillstone (1900)	A butcher was convicted of selling unfit meat, despite the fact that he had had the meat certified as safe by a vet before the sale.	Food safety is paramount.
Harrow LBC v Shah (1999)	National Lottery tickets were sold to a person under the age of 16.	Gambling is a matter of social concern.
R v Prince (1875)	The appellant was charged with taking an unmarried girl under the age of 16 out of the possession of her father. He believed on reasonable grounds that the girl was aged 18.	Protection of children is a matter of social concern.
Alphacell Ltd v Woodward (1972)	A factory owner was convicted of causing polluted matter to enter a river. He was unaware of the pollution.	Safety and pollution are matters of social concern.
R v Blake (1997)	D operated a pirate radio station without a licence.	Radio bands are used by emergency services and so any unauthorised use must be prevented.

As these offences are contrary to the normal rules of criminal law, judges treat them with caution. See the following key cases and note how they limit the application of SLOs: *Sweet v Parsley* (1969) and *Gammon Ltd v A-G of Hong Kong* (1984).

Evaluation point

Ensure you are able to evaluate these offences in the context of fault – consider the positives and negatives of their existence and purpose.

Stretch and challenge

Consider the facts of *London Borough of Hounslow v Aslim* (2018) in light of the protection of society principles above.

Coincidence of *actus reus* and *mens rea*

REVISED

This is the contemporaneity rule, meaning 'at the same time'. Therefore, there is a general rule in English law that the *actus reus* and the *mens rea* must occur at the same time.

However, judges have shown themselves to be flexible with this rule in the interests of justice.

Table 2.3.3 Avoiding the need for contemporaneity

Case	Facts	How the rule was avoided
Fagan v MPC (1969)	D accidentally drove onto a police officer's foot. The officer shouted at him to get off. D refused to move.	Driving onto the foot and remaining there was part of a continuing act.
Thabo-Meli v R (1954)	When defendants formed the intention to kill, there was no AR as the man was still alive. When they threw him off the cliff, there was no MR as they cannot intend to kill someone they believed was already dead.	The act of beating him and throwing him off the cliff was one continuing act/single transaction.
R v Church (1965)	During a fight, the appellant knocked the victim unconscious. He tried to wake her for 30 minutes to no avail. He believed she was dead and threw her body into a river. Medical evidence revealed that the cause of death was drowning.	The act of beating her and throwing her in the river was one continuing act/single transaction.

Now test yourself

TESTED

1 Why is there generally no liability for a failure to act?
2 Why should a defendant be liable for the death of a victim who refuses life-saving medical treatment?
3 Identify both the objective and subjective elements of the definition of oblique intent.
4 What is meant by 'basic intent'?
5 When can *mens rea* not be transferred?
6 Why do *actus reus* and *mens rea* have to occur at the same time?

Exam tip

To score highly, you will need to make links with the other topics, so ensure you have a mind map showing these links to revise from.

Exam summary

In the exam, you MAY be asked:

- multiple-choice questions about different types of *mens rea* or the lack of it, specific elements of *actus reus* and the meaning of contemporaneously occurring *actus reus* and *mens rea*
- questions requiring short to mid-length answers explaining the differences in types of *mens rea* or the fact that it can be transferred, rules of *actus reus* (perhaps omissions or causation), and the meaning and exceptions to the contemporaneity rule
- full-length questions that require you to apply the types of *mens rea*, rules of *actus reus* or principles of contemporaneity to a scenario and come to a conclusion about the likely outcome.

2.4 Fatal offences against the person

This topic deals with specific offences and will refer to the theoretical concepts and general elements throughout, so you will need a sound understanding of Chapters 2.1–2.3 in preparation for this.

Exam tip

When using cases in scenario/application questions, remember IDEA:

- **I**dentify the point of law.
- **D**escribe the point of law.
- **G**ive a case example.
- **A**pply the point/case to the facts of the scenario.

Murder

REVISED

Murder is a common law offence.

It is an indictable offence, therefore triable only by jury in the Crown Court, and carries a mandatory life sentence (this does not necessarily mean life imprisonment).

It requires *actus reus* and *mens rea*.

Murder: the unlawful killing of a human being with malice aforethought (Edward Coke's definition in the sixteenth/seventeenth century).

Actus reus of murder

The *actus reus* of murder is 'the unlawful killing of a human being'.

Table 2.4.1 Components of the *actus reus* for murder

Component of the *actus reus*	Explanation
Unlawful	This relates to the presence of a defence (see Chapter 2.8, as it is possible for a killing to be lawful if it is legally justified, such as in self-defence). Key case: *R v Clegg* (1995)
Killing	This means 'causing death'. It is irrelevant how D has caused V's death; it could be an act or an omission.
Causing	The usual rules and cases of causation apply. See Chapter 2.3: be prepared to use any or all of the rules in this chapter for an answer about murder. For example, the act or omission must be a substantial cause of death, but it need not be the sole or main cause of death. It must have 'more than minimally, negligibly or trivially contributed to the death' – Lord Woolf MR in *R v HM Coroner for Inner London ex parte Douglas-Williams* (1999).
Death	This is a medical test and not a legal one. It currently means 'brain stem death'. Illness or disability, no matter how extreme, does not prevent a person being a human being, and therefore euthanasia is still murder. Key cases: *R v Malcherek and Steel* (1981) and *R v Inglis* (2011)
Human being	The test is 'when' is a human being, not 'what' is a human being: when is a human being capable of existence independent of the mother? This means being born alive and breathing through its own lungs. Key cases: *Rance v Mid-Downs Health Authority* (1991) and *A-G Ref. No. 3 of 1994* (1997)

Stretch and challenge

Consider the impact of suicide on causation here – see *R v BW* (2018).

Revision activity

Can you think of any reasons why the test for defining a human being may be controversial?

Typical mistake

In a scenario question, the victim will always be both human and dead, so do not waste too much time discussing these points. Concentrate on the causation/omission element to score a higher mark.

Revision activity

See http://www.lawlaughs.com/trials/washedead.html for a light-hearted moment on the proof of death.

Mens rea of murder

The *mens rea* of murder is 'malice aforethought'.

Lord Mustill said in 1998: 'The law of homicide is permeated by anomaly, fiction, misnomer and obsolete reasoning.' He was partly referring to the phrase 'malice aforethought'. What this actually means is 'intent to kill or cause grievous bodily harm'. This can be:

- direct intent to kill
- oblique intent to kill
- direct intent to cause really serious harm
- oblique intent to cause really serious harm.

Key cases here include *DPP v Smith* (1961), *R v Saunders* (1985) and *R v Janjua and Choudhury* (1998).

Revision activity

As you work through this topic, make notes and explore any issues of the law which you think may be open to criticism. You might be required to write about them.

Table 2.4.2 Key cases for *actus reus* and *mens rea*

Case	Facts	Relevant area of murder	*Ratio decidendi*
R v Clegg (1995)	A soldier used excessive force, killing a joyrider who failed to stop at a checkpoint.	AR – 'unlawful'	D's lack of 'wicked or evil' motive did not preclude his actions from being unlawful.
R v Malcherek and Steel (1981)	Doctors switched off life-support machines as neither victims were showing any activity in their brain stem.	AR – 'death'	Confirms 'brain stem' as the current medical test for death.
R v Inglis (2011)	D killed her son who was in a persistent vegetative state following an accident.	AR – 'death' and 'human being'	'A disabled life, even a life lived at the extremes of disability, is not one jot less precious than the life of an able-bodied person.'
A-G Ref No. 3 of 1994 (1997)	A pregnant woman was stabbed in the abdomen. The baby was born alive but died 112 days later due to its premature and traumatic birth.	AR – 'human being'	'Murder or manslaughter can be committed where ... the child is subsequently born alive, enjoys an existence independent of the mother, thereafter dies.'
DPP v Smith (1961) *R v Saunders* (1985) *R v Janjua and Choudhury* (1998)	The wording is more relevant than the facts, but Janjua and Choudhury stabbed their V several times with a five-inch blade.	MR – 'intent to cause really serious harm'	*DPP v Smith* (1961): 'grievous means no more and no less than 'really serious'. *R v Saunders* (1985): the word 'serious' could safely be omitted. *R v Janjua and Choudhury* (1998): the trial judge should decide whether or not to include 'really'.

Voluntary manslaughter

REVISED

Loss of control and **diminished responsibility** are defences, not offences, so there is no *actus reus* and *mens rea* required. They are partial defences to murder only – they cannot be used for any other crime and they reduce a murder conviction to one of manslaughter.

Very often a jury will be given a choice to convict of murder rather than manslaughter.

Loss of control: a partial defence, reducing a murder conviction to one of manslaughter.

Diminished responsibility: a partial defence, reducing a murder conviction to one of manslaughter.

Loss of control

Loss of control is described in s 54 of the Coroners and Justice Act 2009. There is a three-stage test:

- the defendant must lose control
- because of a qualifying trigger, and
- a person of their sex and age, with a normal degree of tolerance, might have reacted in the same way in the same circumstances.

A key case here is *R v Clinton* (2012).

Unlike diminished responsibility, which simply amended existing law (see below), this is a totally new defence. Be aware of Lord Thomas CJ in *R v Gurpinar and Kojo-Smith* (2015) who stated, 'it should rarely be necessary to look at cases decided under the old law of provocation'.

Section 54(1)(b)

It does not matter whether or not the loss of control was sudden, but control must have been lost. It can still be put before a jury even where there has been delay between the trigger incident and the murder.

In *R v Jewell* (2014), Lady Justice Rafferty held: 'Loss of control is considered by the authors of *Smith and Hogan* 13th edition to mean the loss of an ability to act in accordance with considered judgment or a loss of normal powers of reasoning.'

Revision activity

Make the link with statutory interpretation and use this as an example.

Section 55

This section defines what is meant by qualifying trigger:

It can be the defendant's fear of serious violence from the victim, though this violence cannot be incited by the defendant – see s 55(6)(a). The defendant will have to show that they genuinely feared that the victim would use serious violence, whether or not that fear was reasonable. This is known as the 'fear trigger'.

Alternatively, it can be something done and/or said by the victim that constituted circumstances of an extremely grave character (the breakdown of a relationship is not, by itself, sufficient – *R v Hatter* (2013)) and caused the defendant to have a justified sense of being wronged (in *R v Bowyer* (2013), D had no justifiable sense of being wronged, given that he was committing a burglary at the time of the offence). This is for the jury to determine, having applied an objective test. This is known as the 'anger trigger'.

The defence is not available to those who act in a considered desire for revenge (s 54(4)), even if the defendant loses self-control as a result of one of the qualifying triggers – see *R v Dawes* (2013).

Sexual infidelity cannot by itself qualify as a trigger, but it can be taken into account as part of a bigger picture– see *R v Clinton* (2012).

Also 'things said' can include admissions of sexual infidelity (even if untrue), as well as reports of it by others.

Section 54(1)(c)

This section requires that a person of the defendant's sex and age, with a normal degree of tolerance and self-restraint and in the circumstances of the defendant, might have reacted in the same or similar way. This is a question for the jury to decide.

Additional characteristics may be relevant when assessing the circumstances of the defendant and the impact on the defendant of sexual infidelity is not excluded, although under s 54(3) circumstances which relate to the defendant's general capacity to exercise tolerance and self-restraint are to be disregarded.

Burden of proof

If the defendant raises the issue of loss of control and the judge believes that a jury, properly directed, could reasonably conclude that the defence might apply, then the burden is on the prosecution to prove beyond reasonable doubt that there was no loss of control.

Table 2.4.3 Key cases for loss of control

Case	Facts	Relevant area of loss of control	*Ratio decidendi*
R v Clinton (2012)	D killed his ex-wife following taunts, revelations about affairs and mental illness.	All elements	Sexual infidelity can add to a defence where there exist other qualifying triggers. Aspects: + whether things done or said amounted to extremely grave circumstance + a justifiable sense of being wronged under s 55(4) + examining the defendant's circumstances under s 54(1)(c).
R v Dawes (2013)	D attacked V with a bottle after finding him asleep with his estranged wife. V took the bottle and attacked D, who grabbed a kitchen knife and fatally stabbed V.	Qualifying triggers	Qualifying triggers based on s 55(3)(4) and (5) still apply despite D's bad behaviour, unless his actions were intended to provide him with the excuse or opportunity to use violence.
R v Asmelash (2013)	D was intoxicated when he murdered the victim.	Alcohol and drugs	D cannot rely on loss of control when self-administered drugs or alcohol impaired his normal judgement.
R v Rejmanski (2017)	D had been a soldier and was taunted about his service in Afghanistan.	Qualifying triggers	In principle, post-traumatic stress disorder (PTSD) could justify loss of control.

Diminished responsibility

Section 52 of the Coroners and Justice Act 2009 amends s 2 of the Homicide Act 1957 and is a four-stage test:

+ Was the defendant suffering from an abnormality of mental functioning?
+ If so, had this arisen from a recognised medical condition?
+ If so, had it substantially impaired their ability either to understand the nature of their conduct or to form a rational judgement or to exercise self-control (or any combination)?
+ Does it thus explain their behaviour?

Where there is unchallenged medical evidence, the judge should withdraw the charge of murder from the jury – see *R v Brennan* (2014).

Abnormality of mental functioning

This means a state of mind so different from that of ordinary human beings that the 'reasonable person' would term it abnormal. It covers the ability to exercise willpower or to control physical acts in accordance with rational judgement. It is a question for a jury.

Recognised medical conditions

These can be found in the World Health Organization's *International Classification of Diseases*. However, *R v Dowds* (2012) states that just because a recognised medical condition appears in the lists does not necessarily mean that it is capable of being relied upon to show an abnormality of mental functioning.

Impairment must be substantial

There must be evidence of this and it must be raised by defence. The abnormality of mental functioning must have substantially impaired the defendant's ability to:

+ understand the nature of the defendant's conduct, or
+ form a rational judgement, or
+ exercise self-control.

Key cases include *R v Golds* (2014), *R v Simcox* (1964) and *R v Lloyd* (1967). See the quote below (originally from *Simcox*, reiterated in *Golds*):

> 'Do we think, looking at it broadly as common-sense people, there was a substantial impairment of his mental responsibility in what he did? If the answer is "no", there may be some impairment, but we do not think it was substantial.'

Explanation

Abnormality of mental functioning provides an explanation for the defendant's behaviour, if it was at least a significant contributory factor in causing the defendant to act as they did. It does not need to be the only cause or even the most important factor in causing the behaviour, but it must be more than a merely trivial factor.

The defence should not be able to succeed where the defendant's mental condition made no difference to their behaviour – when they would have killed regardless of their medical condition.

The effects of alcohol do not amount to an abnormality of mental functioning. However, the defendant may be able to show diminished responsibility from brain damage caused by alcohol.

Key cases here include *R v Atkinson* (1985), *R v Tandy* (1989) and *R v Dietschmann* (2003).

Evaluation point

Consider how far the relatively new law on voluntary manslaughter from the Coroners and Justice Act addresses the problems it set out to solve.

Burden of proof

The defendant has to prove diminished responsibility on the balance of probabilities – the civil standard (in contrast to loss of control, see above).

Table 2.4.4 Key cases on diminished responsibility

Case	Facts	Relevant area of diminished responsibility	*Ratio decidendi*
R v Golds (2014)	D, who had a history of mental disorder, killed his partner by inflicting 22 stabs wounds on her following an argument.	Substantial impairment	The court should leave interpretation of the word 'substantial' to the jury, but can advise that substantial means big or large.
R v Dietschmann (2003)	D killed a friend who had broken his watch, which was a gift from a dead relative. D was medicated for suicidal thoughts relating to the relative's death.	Abnormality and alcohol	If D's mental abnormality substantially impaired his mental responsibility despite drinking alcohol, he is not guilty of murder but can be guilty of manslaughter.

Involuntary manslaughter

REVISED

Involuntary manslaughter is a common law offence and so has an *actus reus* and *mens rea*:

- The *actus reus* elements of murder of causing the death of a human being are the same and so not repeated here.
- These offences are charged when the *mens rea* of murder cannot be satisfied, but a lower level of *mens rea* does exist.

Unlawful act manslaughter: an offence requiring the death to have been caused by the defendant's unlawful conduct, rather than deliberately.

Unlawful act manslaughter

This is an unlawful and dangerous act that causes the death of a human being.

Actus reus of unlawful and dangerous act manslaughter

The killing must be the result of the defendant's act not omission – see *R v Lowe* (1973).

The act must be unlawful (criminal), for example, arson, robbery or assault – see *R v Franklin* (1883). However, the act need not be directed against the victim or any person. It can include assisting in the administration of a drug – see *R v Rodgers* (2003).

The unlawful act must be dangerous, which means all sober and reasonable people would realise it would subject the victim to the risk of physical harm, though not necessarily serious harm, whether or not the defendant realised this. It is irrelevant if the defendant had a mistaken belief that what they were doing was not dangerous. Key cases here include *R v Church* (1965) and *R v Ball* (1989).

The unlawful and dangerous act must cause the death, so the normal rules of criminal causation apply. Key cases here include *R v Williams* (1992) and *R v Carey* (2006).

Mens rea of unlawful and dangerous act manslaughter

It is only necessary to establish the *mens rea* of the unlawful act. No additional *mens rea* is required for the subsequent death – see *R v Lamb* (1967).

Table 2.4.5 Key cases for unlawful and dangerous act manslaughter

Case	Facts	Relevant area of unlawful and dangerous act manslaughter	*Ratio decidendi*
R v Lowe (1973)	The appellant's child died from neglect.	AR – 'act'	There must be an unlawful 'act'. It cannot be committed by an omission.
R v Church (1965)	D knocked the victim unconscious and thought she was dead. He threw her body into a river. The cause of death was drowning.	AR – 'dangerous'	The unlawful act must be such as all sober and reasonable people would inevitably recognise must subject the other person to the risk of some harm resulting therefrom, albeit not serious harm.
R v Ball (1989)	D grabbed his gun and shot what he thought were blank cartridges at V. The cartridge was live and she died from her injury.	AR – 'dangerous'	The appellant's intention, foresight or knowledge is irrelevant.
R v Carey (2006)	V ran just over 100 metres away from B after a bullying incident but then collapsed and died of ventricular fibrillation, caused by the run. V had heart disease.	AR – 'causation'	X commits an unlawful act which is dangerous – it is recognised by reasonable persons as subjecting Y to the risk of some physical harm which in turn causes the death.
R v Lamb (1967)	One boy shot and killed another while playing with a gun, mistakenly thinking that the gun would not go off.	MR of the unlawful act	As there was no assault, there was no unlawful and dangerous act manslaughter.

Gross negligence manslaughter

Gross negligence manslaughter is where the death is a result of a grossly negligent act or omission on the part of the defendant. Although it is a serious crime, it includes some civil law tests.

The key case for this offence is *R v Adomako* (1994) which gave a four-stage test, known as the Adomako test. However, in recent times this has been further developed in the following cases: *R v Rudling* (2016), *R v Sellu* (2016), *R v Bawa-Garba* (2016), *R v Rose* (2017), *R v Zaman* (2017), *R v Winterton* (2018), *R v Pearson* (2019), *R v Kuddus* (2019), *R v Broadhurst* (2019).

This development culminated in *R v Broughton* (2020).

Revision activity

For a summary of the facts in *Broughton*, see www.youtube.com/watch?app=desktop&v=6utQz8a7ZBo.

Gross negligence manslaughter: an offence requiring the death to have been caused by the defendant's gross negligence, rather than deliberately.

Exam tip

You do not need to know the names of all the cases in between *Adomako* and *Broughton*, but it is good to know that there has been a lot of recent development.

The result of this development is that six elements have been identified that the prosecution must prove before a defendant can be convicted of gross negligence manslaughter, shown in Table 2.4.6.

Table 2.4.6 Elements to be proven for gross negligence manslaughter

Element	Explanation
1	+ The defendant owed an existing duty of care to the victim. + This requires foreseeability, proximity, fairness, justice and reasonableness – see *Donohue v Stevenson* (1932). + The duty can arise from a contract of employment – see *R v Pittwood* (1902). + The duty can exist if the deceased and the defendant were engaged in an unlawful activity together – see *R v Wacker* (2003) and *R v Willoughby* (2004). + The risk must be a serious and obvious risk of death, not merely serious injury – see *R v Misra and Srivastava* (2005).
2	+ The defendant negligently breached that duty of care. + This is an objective test and so is based upon what a reasonable person would do in the defendant's position at the time of the breach. + An unqualified person is not to be judged at a lower standard than a qualified person. Therefore, the lack of skill will not be a defence if the conduct is deemed negligent. + If, however, the defendant has particular skills and knowledge of a danger that the reasonable person would not have, their actions should be judged in the light of those skills or knowledge.
3	+ At the time of the breach there was a serious and obvious risk of death – see *R v Singh* 1999. + Serious, in this context, qualifies the nature of the risk of death as something much more than minimal or remote. Risk of injury or illness, even serious injury or illness, is not enough. + An obvious risk is one that is present, clear and unambiguous. It is immediately apparent, striking and glaring, rather than something that might become apparent on further investigation.
4	+ It was reasonably foreseeable at the time of the breach of the duty that the breach gave rise to a serious and obvious risk of death. + As it is an objective test, it does not matter that the defendant did not appreciate the risk (the foreseeable risk of death). + The risk would have been obvious to a reasonable person in the defendant's position – see *R v DPP ex parte Jones* (2000), *A-G Ref. No. 2 of 1999* (2000).
5	+ The breach of the duty caused or made a significant (more than minimal) contribution to the death of the victim.
6	+ In the view of the jury, the circumstances of the breach were truly exceptionally bad and so reprehensible as to justify the conclusion that it amounted to gross negligence and required criminal sanction – see *R v Misra & Srivastava* (2005).

Table 2.4.7 Key cases for gross negligence manslaughter

Case	Facts	Relevant area of gross negligence manslaughter	*Ratio decidendi*
R v Adomako (1994)	During an operation, an oxygen pipe became disconnected and the patient died. The anaesthetist appellant failed to notice or respond to obvious signs of disconnection.	The basis of the offence	The law of negligence applies to ascertain whether D has been in breach of a duty of care towards V. If breach is established, did it cause the death of V? If so, was it gross negligence and therefore a crime?
R v Misra and Srivastava (2005)	V was D's patient. V developed an undiagnosed and untreated infection in a wound, despite obvious symptoms.	Breach must be gross	Jury to decide whether D's behaviour was grossly negligent and consequently criminal.
R v Broughton (2020)	D failed to summon help after supplying his girlfriend with drugs that eventually caused her death.	Six rules above were stated (para 5)	There was insufficient evidence to be sure that D's failure to obtain medical help caused V to die.

Revision activity

Practise applying the law relating to these offences/defences to a given scenario. For example: 'Consider the criminal liability of Oliver for the manslaughter of Marcus and for the murder of Noah.'

- Oliver will be charged with ... (identify the offences)
- This comes from ... (identify the sources)
- The *actus reus* of this offence is ... (state the *actus reus*, then use the IDEA method to work through each element of it – do not forget causation)
- The *mens rea* of this offence is ... (state the *mens rea*, then use the IDEA method to work through each element of it – do not forget to look out for transferred malice here)
- The defences Oliver may seek to rely on are ... (use the IDEA method to work through appropriate defences; these may be the partial defences examined in this topic or general defences dealt with in Chapter 2.8)
- Conclusion (your own)

Revision activity

Create a spider diagram showing the links between this chapter and Chapters 1.1–1.3.

Stretch and challenge

To prepare for the exam, read these Law Commission reports:

- Legislating the Criminal Code: Involuntary Manslaughter (Law Com No. 237)
- Murder, Manslaughter and Infanticide (Law Com No. 304).

Note the problems identified by the Law Commission, the extent to which they have since been addressed by Parliament and with what degree of success.

Now test yourself

TESTED 

1 What is the lowest *mens rea* possible for a murder conviction?
2 What does 'malice aforethought' actually mean?
3 For the purpose of the offence of murder, how is 'human being' defined?
4 What things will prevent a 'trigger' from qualifying?
5 What is the difference in the way that ss 52 and 54 of the Coroners and Justice Act treat the previous law?
6 How is abnormality of mental functioning determined?
7 What is the test for 'dangerous' in unlawful and dangerous act manslaughter?
8 Why is the *mens rea* only for the unlawful act, not for the death?
9 Which tests are used to determine duty in gross negligence manslaughter?

Exam summary

In the exam, you MAY be asked:

- multiple-choice questions on the elements of murder, loss of control or diminished responsibility, and either unlawful act manslaughter or gross negligence manslaughter
- questions requiring short to mid-length answers explaining the meaning of elements of the offence, or the importance of general criminal theory rules to it (such as the rules of causation), the meaning of the elements of loss of control or diminished responsibility in relation to one of the concepts, the elements of unlawful act manslaughter or gross negligence manslaughter, and causation and omissions.
- long-answer questions that require you to apply these principles to a criminal scenario.

2.5 Non-fatal offences against the person

This chapter deals with specific offences and will refer to theoretical concepts and general elements throughout, so you will need a sound understanding of Chapters 2.1–2.3 in preparation for this.

Typical mistake

The police use the word 'assault' to mean many things. Ignore these; we are interested in the theory of the law, not how it is used by the police.

Assault

REVISED 

Assault is a common law offence.

It is a summary offence, therefore triable only in the Magistrates' Court.

It carries a maximum sentence of six months' imprisonment according to s 39 of the Criminal Justice Act 1988.

Revision activity

Look back at gross negligence manslaughter on page 74 and make the link.

Actus reus of assault

The victim must apprehend immediate unlawful personal violence. These elements are broken down in Table 2.5.1.

Table 2.5.1 Components of the *actus reus* for assault

Component of *actus reus*	Explanation	Key cases
Apprehend	'Apprehend' means the victim need not be put in fear but must be aware that they are about to be subjected to violence. If the victim does not anticipate unlawful personal violence, there is no assault.	*R v Lamb* (1967)
	There does not need to be an actual threat.	*Logdon v DPP* (1976)
	The conduct that causes the victim to apprehend can be actions, words or even silence.	*R v Constanza* (1997) and *R v Ireland* (1997)
	Words can also negate an assault.	*Tuberville v Savage* (1669)
Immediate	'Immediate' is satisfied if the victim did not know what the defendant was going to do next.	*Smith v Chief Constable of Woking* (1983)
Unlawful	'Unlawful' relates to the presence of a defence. See Chapter 2.8, as it is possible for an assault to be lawful if it is legally justified, e.g. in self-defence.	
Personal violence	'Personal violence' means the victim needs to apprehend the level of force that amounts to a technical battery, i.e. touching is sufficient.	

Mens rea of assault

The *Mens rea* of assault is

- the intention to cause the victim to apprehend immediate unlawful personal violence, or
- being reckless as to whether such apprehension is caused – see *R v Parmenter* (1991).

Exam tip

Remember to use the definitions set out in Chapter 2.3 when discussing the *mens rea* of all offences.

Evaluation point

Make notes and explore any issues of the law which you think may be open to criticism – you may be required to write about them

Battery

REVISED

Battery is a common law offence.

It is a summary offence and therefore triable only in the Magistrates' Court.

It carries a maximum sentence of six months' imprisonment according to s 39 of the Criminal Justice Act 1988.

Battery: the intentional or reckless application of unlawful force upon a victim (definition from *R v Ireland* (1997)).

Actus reus of battery

This requires the application of unlawful physical force.

Table 2.5.2 Components of the *actus reus* for battery

Component of *actus reus*	Explanation	Key cases
Application	'Application' need not be direct.	*DPP v K* (1990)
Unlawful	'Unlawful' relates to the presence of a defence – see Chapter 2.8, as it is possible for an assault to be lawful if it is legally justified (such as in self-defence).	*Collins v Wilcock* (1984) stated there could be implied consent where there was jostling in crowded places, handshakes, back slapping, and tapping to gain attention, provided no more force was used than reasonably necessary in the circumstances.
Physical force	Any touching will suffice; it need not necessarily be hostile, rude or aggressive.	*Faulkner v Talbot* (1981)

Mens rea of battery

This is intention to apply unlawful physical force or being reckless as to whether such force is applied – see *R v Parmenter* (1991).

Stretch and challenge

In the summer of 2021, Professor Chris Whitty, at the time the Government's Chief Medical Officer and face of daily news briefings, was subject to some unwanted attention whilst walking in London. Research this incident, the nature of the offences and charges.

Table 2.5.3 Key cases for assault and battery

Case	Facts	Assault or battery?	*Ratio decidendi* (where not given above)
R v Lamb (1967)	V did not believe the gun would go off, therefore he did not apprehend immediate unlawful personal violence.	AR assault – 'apprehend'	No assault had been committed.
Logdon v DPP (1976)	D pointed an imitation gun at V in jest. V was terrified. D then told her it was not real.	AR assault – 'apprehend'	There does not need to be an actual threat for an assault to be committed.
Tuberville v Savage (1669)	D put his hand on his sword and stated, 'if it were not assize-time, I would not take such language from you'.	AR assault – 'apprehend'	Words can prevent an apprehension.

Case	Facts	Assault or battery?	*Ratio decidendi* (where not given above)
Smith v Chief Constable of Woking (1983)	A peeping tom claimed V could not have been frightened of personal violence as he was outside the house and she was inside.	AR assault – 'apprehend'	The basis of her fear was that she did not know what the defendant was going to do next.
R v Parmenter (1991)	D assaulted his baby son.	MR 'recklessness'	It is necessary to establish that D appreciated the risk. It is not sufficient that he should have foreseen a risk of injury.
DPP v K (1990)	A boy put acid in a hand dryer that caused injury to the next user of the dryer.	AR battery – 'application'	Battery need not be direct.

Exam tip

In a scenario answer, identify:

- the offence
- its source
- the elements of the AR and MR (with case examples).

Then apply the elements to the question.

Offences Against the Person Act 1861

REVISED 

Section 47: Assault/battery occasioning ABH

Although this offence is set out in s 47 of the Offences Against the Person Act 1861, the common law has had to develop rules around this to give more detail. It is a triable-either-way offence and carries a maximum sentence of five years' imprisonment.

Actus reus of s 47 assault/battery occasioning ABH

This requires an assault or battery which causes actual bodily harm.

Table 2.5.4 Components of the *actus reus* for ABH

Component of *actus reus*	Explanation	Key cases
Assault or battery	Either will suffice, but all of the elements of assault or battery must be present.	*R v Chan-Fook* (1994)
Causes	The assault or battery must cause actual bodily harm. The usual rules and cases of causation apply – see Chapter 2.3.	*R v Roberts* (1971)
Actual bodily harm (ABH)	This means hurt or injury calculated to interfere with the health or comfort of the victim. It need not be permanent but should not be so trivial as to be wholly insignificant. ABH can include psychiatric injury and the cutting of hair.	*R v Miller* (1954) *R v Chan-Fook* (1994)

Typical mistake

The *actus reus* of ABH is in three parts: the assault or battery, the causation link and the resulting harm. Candidates often forget the first two of these and just concentrate on the resulting harm.

Stretch and challenge

Research *R v Chan-Fook* (1994) and find out why Chan-Fook was found not guilty.

Mens rea of s 47 assault/battery occasioning ABH

This is intention or reckless as to the assault or battery. There is no additional *mens rea* for the harm caused – see *R v Roberts* (1971).

Typical mistake

Do not forget to focus on all three parts of the *actus reus* of ABH: the assault or battery, the causation link and the resulting harm.

Wounding and GBH

Wounding and GBH are found under two separate sections of the Offences Against the Person Act 1861 (OAPA): ss 20 and 18.

Section 20 wounding and GBH

> 'Whosoever shall unlawfully and maliciously wound or inflict any grievous bodily harm on any other person, either with or without a weapon or instrument, shall be guilty of a misdemeanour.'

A conviction under s 20 represents the lesser offence which is triable either way and carries a maximum penalty of five years' imprisonment. The main differences between the offences relate to the *mens rea*.

Actus reus of s 20 *wounding and GBH*

This requires the defendant to unlawfully wound or inflict GBH on another person.

Table 2.5.5 Components of the *actus reus* for s 20 wounding and GBH

Component of *actus reus*	Explanation	Key cases
Unlawfully	Some wounding or GBH may be classed as lawful. This covers those who are acting in self-defence or prevention of crime, and in limited circumstances where the victim has consented (such as medical procedures and where the injury results from properly conducted games and sports).	
Wound	A wound exists where there is a break in the continuity of the skin causing external bleeding.	*Moriarty v Brookes* (1834) *C v Eisenhower* (1984)
Inflict	'Inflict' simply means 'cause'.	*R v Burstow* (1997)
GBH	'Grievous bodily harm' means really serious harm, such as long-term/permanent injury or injury requiring extensive treatment. It can also include: + less serious injuries if the victim is vulnerable, e.g. particularly old or young + multiple ABHs + psychiatric injury, but it must be a recognisable illness.	*DPP v Smith* (1961) *R v Bollom* (2004) *R v Brown and Stratton* (1997) *R v Burstow* (1997) *R v Dhaliwal* (2006)

Mens rea of s 20 *wounding and GBH*

This requires the defendant to have the intention to cause or be reckless as to the causing of some harm. There is no need to establish that they intended or were reckless as to causing serious harm – see *R v Savage* (1991) and *R v Parmenter* (1991).

Section 18 wounding and GBH

> 'Whosoever shall unlawfully and maliciously by any means whatsoever wound or cause any grievous bodily harm to any person, with intent to do some grievous bodily harm to any person, or with intent to resist or prevent the lawful apprehension or detainer of any person, shall be guilty of felony.'

Section 18 is a more serious offence than s 20, is indictable and carries a maximum sentence of life imprisonment.

Actus reus of s 18 *wounding and GBH*

Despite the use of the different verbs – 'inflict' in s 20 and 'cause' in s 18 – there is very little difference between the *actus reus* of s 20 and that of s 18. For the purposes of your course, it is safe to assume they mean the same thing.

Mens rea of s 18 wounding and GBH

This requires either intent to cause GBH or intent to resist or prevent the lawful detainer (arrest) of any person.

Table 2.5.6 Key cases for OAPA

Case	Facts	Relevant area OAPA	*Ratio decidendi* (where not given above)
R v Roberts (1971)	V jumped out of a moving car to escape D's unwanted sexual advances.	Section 47 ABH – 'causation' and MR	Escape from physical danger is not 'daft' and does not break the chain. The MR for the assault or battery is sufficient; no additional MR is required for the harm caused.
Moriarty v Brookes (1834)	V suffered a cut to the skin under his eye in a dispute in a pub.	AR – 'wounding'	If the skin is broken and there was bleeding, that is a wound.
C v Eisenhower (1984)	Pellets from D's air gun caused bruising and rupturing of internal blood vessels of V's eye, but there was no breaking of the skin.	AR – 'wounding'	There needs to be a break in the continuity of the whole skin.
R v Bollom (2004)	The injuries to a 17-month-old baby consisted of various bruises and abrasions.	AR – 'GBH'	Vulnerable victim of GBH
R v Brown and Stratton (1997)	V sustained a broken nose, lost three teeth and suffered swelling to her face, lacerations to her eye and concussion.	AR – 'GBH'	Multiple ABHs
R v Burstow (1997)	D engaged in harassment against V. As a result, she suffered a severe depressive illness.	AR – 'GBH'	Psychiatric injury
R v Savage (1991)	D threw a pint of beer over V in a pub. The glass slipped out of D's hand and cut V's wrist.	MR s 20	It is sufficient that D intended or could foresee that some harm will result.

Evaluation point

To prepare for the exam, read the Law Commission report, *Reform of Offences Against the Person* (Law Com No. 361). Note:

- the problems identified by the Law Commission
- the extent to which they have since been addressed by Parliament
- how successfully they have been addressed.

Stretch and challenge

Look up *R v Golding* (2014). Why was this relatively minor illness classed as GBH?

Now test yourself TESTED

1 What does apprehend mean?
2 Why was the defendant not guilty in *R v Lamb* (1967)?
3 What is the lowest form of *mens rea* possible for assault?
4 Why is tapping someone on the shoulder generally not an offence?
5 How much harm must the force used cause for battery?
6 What case would you use as precedent for throwing a piece of chalk at someone amounting to a battery?
7 What is the highest form of *mens rea* required for battery?
8 Give two reasons why the defendant *in R v Roberts* (1971) was responsible for the victim's injuries.
9 A ruptured spleen causing internal bleeding could amount to which offence/s?
10 Can bodily harm be caused by infection? What problems can you foresee with this?
11 What is the difference between s 20 and s 18 wounding and GBH? Why is this so?

Exam summary

In the exam, you MAY be asked:

- multiple-choice questions about individual elements of assault, battery or individual elements of non-fatal OAPA
- to apply the law relating to assault, battery or OAPA to a given scenario
- to write an analysis of assault, battery or OAPA, possibly linking to a topic in Chapter 1.1.

2.6 Property offences

This chapter relates to two key areas under property offences:
- theft under s 1 of the Theft Act 1968
- robbery under s 8 of the Theft Act 1968.

Exam tip

Make sure you have accurate knowledge of sections 1–6 and 8 of the Theft Act 1968. You need to be able to support any interpretation of these sections with relevant and, where possible, recent case law.

Typical mistake

Be selective in discussing the sections of the Theft Act. It is not necessary to recite every part of each section if irrelevant. For example, do not state every defence under s 2, or discuss wildflowers or untamed wild creatures under s 4, if they are irrelevant to the specific exam question.

Theft

REVISED

Theft is defined under s 1(1) of the Theft Act 1968:

> 'A person is guilty of theft if he dishonestly appropriates property belonging to another with the intention of permanently depriving the other of it; and "thief" and "steal" shall be construed accordingly.'

Section 1(1) is the specific charge for theft. Sections 2–6 provide further interpretation of these elements.

Evaluation point

The Theft Act 1968 was a consolidating Act in that it brought together scores of individual theft type offences relating to different ways and different types of property that could be stolen. Section 1(1) of the Act introduced a single 'catch-all' offence of theft.

Actus reus of theft

The *actus reus* of theft is established by proving:
- the appropriation
- of property
- belonging to another.

Stretch and challenge

Using the internet, research the cases of *Lawrence v MPC* (1972) and *R v Gomez* (1993) and explain the decisions.

Appropriation (s 3)

Appropriation is defined under s 3(1) as: 'Any assumption by a person of the rights of an owner [which] includes, where he has come by the property (innocently or not) without stealing it, any later assumption of a right to it by keeping or dealing with it as owner.'

The definition of appropriation is very wide. It does not mean 'misappropriates', and so includes situations even where the owner has consented to the appropriation – see *Lawrence v MPC* (1972) and *DPP v Gomez* (1993) where an 'adverse interference or usurpation' of the rights of the owner are not required.

Property (s 4)

Property is defined under s 4(1): 'Property includes money and all other property, real or personal, including things in action and other intangible property.'

The definition under s 4(1) is very wide and includes money and personal property. It also includes property that is illegally held such as Class A drugs – *R v Smith* (2011).

The rest of s 4 defines, *inter alia*, 'property' which cannot be stolen:
- land
- mushrooms, flowers, fruit or foliage growing wild unless picked for financial gain
- wild creatures, unless tamed, in captivity or in the possession of another
- confidential information (held on paper) – see *Oxford v Moss* (1979), but note the decision in *Akbar* (2002).

Stretch and challenge

Using the internet, research the cases of *Oxford v Moss* (1979) and *Akbar* (2002) and explain the decisions and rationale behind the sentencing in *Akbar*.

Belonging to another (s 5)

Belonging to another is defined under s 5(1): 'Property shall be regarded as belonging to any person having possession or control of it, or having in it any proprietary right or interest'.

The wide definition under s 5 includes anyone:
- with possession or control. This covers the situation where the appropriation is not from the owner, but from someone who has the owner's permission to have the property in their possession
- who has given the property to the defendant subject to an obligation it is to be dealt with in a certain way: *Davidge v Bunnett* (1984)
- who has given it to the defendant by mistake and the defendant is under an obligation to restore it to them: *A-G Ref. (No.1 of 1983)*(1985).

The definition does not require property to be lawfully held, so a charge of theft would be made out where a person appropriates illegal drugs from another. Even where the property is appropriated by the true owner or person who has the right of ownership, they may still be guilty of theft – see *R v Turner* (1971).

Revision activity

1 Make a list of items that you think would be defined as personal property under s 4(1).
2 Using the internet, research and compare the cases of *Davidge v Bunnett* (1984) and *A-G Ref. (No. 1 of 1983)* (1985).

Table 2.6.1 Key cases on the *actus reus* of theft

Case	Facts	Section of the Theft Act 1968	*Ratio decidendi*
R v Pitham and Hehl (1977)	D sold furniture belonging to another person but did not come into actual possession of the property.	'Appropriation' – s 3	Appropriation – selling was a right of the owner which D interfered with. Not all rights have to be interfered with.
R v Morris (1983)	D swapped price labels on two items in a supermarket.	'Appropriation' – s 3	Switching price labels and trying to pay the lower price was an appropriation, an interference of the owner's rights.
R v Smith and others (2011)	S and two friends robbed V of some heroin V was trying to sell to S. S argued illegal drugs were not 'property' since the possession was illegal.	'Property' – s 4	Property is defined under s 4 as including all tangible property which does not preclude illegally held property.
R v Turner (1971)	D took his car without paying from a garage after repairs had been carried out.	'Belonging to another' – s 5	The question as to who has the 'better right' to the car was irrelevant, and D was convicted of theft. The garage was still 'in possession or control'.
R (on the application of Ricketts) v Basildon Magistrates' Court (2010)	D took bags containing donated items left outside a charity shop intended for sale in the shop and bags from behind the shop. D claimed they were abandoned.	'Belonging to another' – s 5	The bags, and their contents, outside the shop remained the property of the donor, while those behind the shop were the property of the charity.

Mens rea of theft

The *mens rea* of theft is established by proving:

- dishonesty, and
- the intention to permanently deprive.

Dishonesty (s 2)

The Theft Act does not define 'dishonestly', but specifies that an appropriation is not dishonest, providing three 'defences' if the person doing it believes:

- they have a legal right in law to deprive the other of it, or
- the owner would agree to the taking of it if they knew about it, or
- if the person to whom the property belongs cannot be discovered by taking reasonable steps.

When Parliament passed the 1968 Act, it felt that the definition of dishonesty should be left to the common sense of magistrates or a jury and be decided on a case-by-case basis. Parliament felt that the changing nature of the public's opinion as to what is meant by 'dishonestly' precluded a specific definition in the Act.

In *Ivey v Genting Casinos* (2017), a civil case, the Supreme Court established a preferred definition for 'dishonestly', that of the civil law. In summary:

1. Decide what the individual knew about what they were doing and what the surrounding circumstances were.
2. Then, assuming that state of knowledge, decide whether the ordinary decent member of society would say what was done was dishonest, and if so, the behaviour does not become honest simply because the defendant has different or lower standards.

Although *Ivey* was a Supreme Court civil case and its decision remained purely *obiter* on the criminal courts, in *DPP v Patterson* (2017), a Divisional Court decision, the court uncharacteristically adopted the *Ivey* definition of dishonesty as the true definition, over that of the previous Court of Appeal decision in *Ghosh* (1982).

The matter was finally resolved by the Court of Appeal as to the true test of criminal dishonesty in *Barton and Booth* (2020) where the Lord Chief Justice stated:

> 'We wish to endorse the respondent's submission that the test of dishonesty formulated in Ivey remains a test of the defendant's state of mind – his or her knowledge or belief – to which the standards of ordinary decent people are applied. This results in dishonesty being assessed by reference to society's standards rather than the defendant's understanding of those standards.'

Revision activity

In your own words, what do you think the word 'dishonest' means?

Stretch and challenge

Do you agree with the Lord Chief Justice's definition as quoted here? Research the case of *R v Barton and Booth* (2020).

Intention of permanently depriving (s 6)

The section gives guidance as to what may fall within an intent to permanently deprive. It does not provide any exhaustive definition, which is purely a question of fact for the jury or magistrate.

Examples given under s 6(1) include where:

- the person treats the thing as their own to dispose of regardless of the other's rights
- a borrowing or lending of the thing may amount to an intention to permanently deprive if it is for a period and in circumstances equivalent to an outright taking or disposal.

Under s 6(2), there is intention to permanently deprive the owner of the thing even if it is returned but some of its value has diminished, for example:

- selling a person's property back to them, pretending to be the true owner
- using some of the charge out of a person's batteries or eating part of someone's chocolate bar and giving the rest back
- returning a concert, gig or raffle ticket after it has been used.

In *Vinall* (2012), the Court of Appeal stated:

> 'What section 6(1) requires is a state of mind in the defendant which Parliament regards as the equivalent of an intention permanently to deprive, namely "his intention to treat the thing as his own to dispose of regardless of the other's rights".'

Where property is taken without an intent to permanently deprive, such as joyriding a motor-vehicle and the vehicle is destroyed, for example, by crashing it or by fire, it may still be an intent to permanently deprive even where the property is no longer in a form that can be used – *Mitchell* (2008).

Table 2.6.2 Key cases on the *mens rea* of theft

Case	Facts	Section of Theft Act	*Ratio decidendi*
R v Lawrence (1972)	D, a taxi driver, took £7 for a £1 fare from an Italian tourist who spoke little English and was unfamiliar with the currency. V had held his wallet open and D took the £7.	'Dishonestly' under s 2(1)(b)	Belief or absence of belief that the owner consented to the appropriation is relevant to the issue of dishonesty.
R v Small (1988)	D took a car which had been left for two weeks with the windows open, keys left in the ignition, a flat battery and no petrol.	'Dishonestly' under s 2(1)(c)	A belief unreasonably held can be an honest belief.
R v Velumyl (1989)	D borrowed over £1050 from the safe at work, with the intention to pay it back the following Monday. This was against company rules.	'Intention to permanently deprive' – s 6	Held as an intention to permanently deprive as the exact money could not be replaced.
Lavender v DPP (1994)	D removed two doors from a council house to replace two broken doors at his girlfriend's council house.	'Intention to permanently deprive' – s 6	D intended to treat the doors as his own, regardless of the council's rights.
Ivey v Genting Casinos (UK) Ltd (2017)	D, a professional gambler, had 'won' £7.7m at a casino. The casino owners refused to pay, saying he had cheated.	'Dishonestly' under s 2	The Supreme Court installed the civil test for dishonesty as the preferred test under the criminal law. This test was adopted by the CA (Criminal Division) in *Barton and Booth* (2020).

Now test yourself

TESTED

1. What are the key elements of the *actus reus* of theft?
2. What are the key elements of the *mens rea* of theft?
3. Explain two reasons why the definition of 'dishonestly' may sometimes be difficult to establish.
4. Explain the differences between s 5(3) and s 5(4) of the Theft Act 1968.
5. List five ways that a textbook can be appropriated to satisfy s 3 of the Theft Act 1968.
6. Sections 1–7 of the Theft Act provide a complicated definition for what is in practice a fairly straightforward crime. Discuss.

Exam summary

In the exam, you MAY be asked:

- multiple-choice questions about theft
- to explain and analyse the definitions of theft, in part or in whole, in short- or long-answer questions, for example, why s 2 of the Theft Act has had to be assisted by judicial precedent
- to apply the law on theft to a scenario situation and be able to consider the criminal liability of a defendant or defendants.

Robbery

REVISED

Robbery is defined under s 8 of the Theft Act 1968:

> 'A person is guilty of robbery if he steals, and immediately before or at the time of doing so, and in order to do so, he uses force on any person or puts or seeks to put any person in fear of being then and there subjected to force.'

Typical mistake

As s 8 is so long, it is easy to omit parts of the definition or incorrectly apply them. For a scenario question, remember the mnemonic ILAC:

- **I**ssues (spot what is going on in the scenario)
- **L**aw (define the relevant law for the issues)
- **A**pply (apply the law to the issues)
- **C**onclude (has the defendant committed the crime?)

Exam tip

Learn the definition under s 8 exactly as it is defined. Then learn how the *actus reus* can be broken down into its constituent parts, for example, (1) steals, (2) and immediately before or at the time of doing so etc.

Actus reus of robbery

Table 2.6.3 Components of the *actus reus* of robbery

Component of *actus reus*	Explanation
Steals	A theft under sections 1–6 Theft Act 1968 must be committed. No theft means there is no robbery.
immediately before or at the time of doing so	The timing of the force or threat of force must be before or at the time of the theft. Once the theft is complete, any force used subsequently cannot amount to a robbery, as later force misses the definition. However, this can be a continuing act – *Hale* (1978).
and in order to do so (steal)	The use or threat of force must be in order to steal.
uses force on any person or puts or seeks to put any person in fear of being then and there subjected to force.	D must apply force to V or threaten to apply force to V in order to steal.

Revision activity

Research the case of *Hale* (1978).

How does this case assist in establishing that:

- an appropriation is not a precise moment and is, in fact, a continuing act, and
- as a continuing act, it would be artificial to establish exactly when the precise moment ends?

Mens rea of robbery

The defendant must have the *mens rea* of theft – dishonesty (see *Barton and Booth* (2020)) and an intention to permanently deprive. There must be the intention to use force to steal.

Table 2.6.4 Key cases on robbery

Case	Facts	Element of robbery	*Ratio decidendi*
R v Robinson (1977)	D was owed £7 by V's wife. D approached V with a knife. D argued with V who dropped a £5 note which D picked up and kept.	'Steals'	As D had a genuine belief he had a right in law to the £5, and to deprive the owner of the money, he would not be dishonest under s 2(1)(a), even though he was not entitled to use a knife to recover the debt.

Case	Facts	Element of robbery	*Ratio decidendi*
R v Dawson and James (1976)	D pushed V so that V lost balance, so that D2 could take his wallet.	'Force' or threat of 'force'	CA upheld conviction: force is an ordinary word decided by the jury.
R v Clouden (1987)	D snatched a handbag out of V's hands. It was argued force was not on a person.	'Force' or threat of 'force'	Even though force was only slight, the judge was right to allow the jury to decide.
RP v DPP (2012)	D snatched a cigarette from V's hand.	'Force or the threat of 'force'	The QBD stated that there was, like a pickpocket, no direct physical contact between the D and the V.
R v Hale (1979)	D1 and D2 forced their way into a house. D1 tied up V while D2 took items from upstairs.	'immediately before or at the time of'	Theft was seen as a continuing act even though the force to tie up V was separate to the stealing.
R v Lockley (1995)	D was challenged leaving a shop after he took cans of beer. D pushed the shopkeeper and ran off.	'immediately before or at the time of'	Theft was seen as a continuing act even though the force to tie up V was separate to the stealing.

Evaluation point

Like the definition of theft under s1(1), the definition of robbery is a 'catch-all' definition. However, in doing so, the definition becomes long-winded, complicated and difficult to apply and establish in the ordinary world.

Stretch and challenge

Imagine you were a government agency in 1965 tasked with defining 'theft' and 'robbery'. What would be your own definitions of the two offences?

Now test yourself

TESTED 

7. List the essential elements of robbery.
8. Give three examples of how robbery can be committed.
9. Discuss what is meant by 'force' used in robbery.
10. Why was the defendant's appeal in *R v Robinson* (1977) successful, following his conviction for robbery?
11. Discuss the main similarity between *R v Hale* (1979) and *R v Lockley* (1995).
12. 'Section 8 of the Theft Act 1968 provides a complicated definition for what is in practice the fairly straightforward crime of robbery.' Examine the truth behind this statement.

Exam summary

In the exam, you MAY be asked:

- multiple-choice questions about robbery
- to explain and analyse the definitions of robbery, in part or in whole, in short- or long-answer questions
- to apply the law on robbery to a scenario situation and be able to consider the criminal liability of a defendant or defendants.

2.7 Preliminary offence: attempt

This chapter outlines three key areas of attempted crimes:

- *actus reus* of attempt
- *mens rea* of attempt
- attempting the 'impossible'.

Criminal law can punish a person who tries but fails to commit the full crime. The problem that has faced the courts is: at what point does an attempted crime start and at what point does an attempt become the full offence?

A person is guilty of attempting to commit an offence under s 1(1) of the Criminal Attempts Act 1981 if they commit an act which is more than merely preparatory to the commission of the offence, with the intent to commit the offence.

In each case, it is a question of fact as to whether the defendant has moved from the merely preparatory stage and gone sufficiently far enough towards committing the full offence, for the act to be considered an attempt. Specifically:

- Had the defendant actually tried to commit the offence?
- Or, had they simply got ready, got into position or equipped themselves to commit the offence?

Typical mistake

While pre-1981 Act common law cases provide some guidance, cases after 1981 give a more accurate interpretation of what is, or is not, an attempted crime. Do not unnecessarily discuss the pre-1981 common law tests.

Actus reus of attempt

REVISED

An attempt must be:

- a positive act, not an omission
- an act that is 'more than merely preparatory to the commission of the offence' (MTMP).

Therefore, an act which is 'merely preparatory' (MP) is not an attempt.

Exam tip

Learn the statutory definitions and the relevant MP and MTMP cases to support your answer. Use cases confidently and accurately. Many scenario questions will have their basis in an actual case, for example, *R v Campbell* (1990), which should give you a clear, if meandering, steer to the answer.

Revision activity

What is meant by an omission in criminal law? Refer back to page 65 to check your answer.

Table 2.7.1 Cases of merely preparatory (MP): getting into position or equipping themselves?

Case	Facts	Offence attempted	*Ratio decidendi*
R v Gullefer (1987)	D tried to stop a greyhound race to recover his stake, as his dog was losing.	Theft	CA: MP – D had to go and ask for his money back first.
R v Campbell (1990)	D approached a post office wearing a crash helmet with a knife and threatening note. He was arrested outside by police.	Robbery	CA: MP – D did not enter post office and threaten staff.
R v Geddes (1996)	D was seen in the boys' toilets and ran off when challenged. Later, his rucksack was found nearby containing rope, a large knife and masking tape.	False imprisonment	CA: MP – D had not tried to commit the crime itself.
R v Nash (1999)	Two letters in the street were addressed to 'Paper Boy', inviting V to engage in acts of gross indecency. A third letter offered employment. Police set up a 'sting' in the local park using a volunteer to meet D as per letter 3.	Procure an act of gross indecency	CA: letter 3 was MP; as it did not involve a request for an act of gross indecency, it could not be an attempt of such.

Case	Facts	Offence attempted	*Ratio decidendi*
MS, Application by the Prosecution for Leave of Appeal (2021)	D was stopped 85 miles from Dover while heading to board a ferry to France. She had been denied from taking her child out of the country.	Child abduction	The CA stated that 'geographical proximity' was not a sole deciding factor and that each case MUST be looked at on its own facts. The case was sent back to Crown Court in 2021.

Table 2.7.2 Cases of more than merely preparatory (MTMP): actually trying to commit the offence?

Case	Facts	Offence attempted	*Ratio decidendi*
R v Boyle and Boyle (1987)	D1 and D2 were found standing next to a door with a broken lock and hinge.	Burglary	MTMP – all they had to do was enter the building to commit the full crime.
R v Jones (1990)	D got into V's car and pointed a shotgun at him.	Murder	MTMP – all he had to do was pull the trigger to commit the full crime.
A-G Ref. (No. 1 of 1992) (1993)	D dragged V into a shed to have sex with her but could not maintain an erection.	Rape	MTMP – all he had to do was penetrate V to commit the full crime.

Revision activity

Using the internet, research the case of *R v Khan* (1990). How did this case extend the law on attempts?

Stretch and challenge

Select three fully established criminal cases that you are familiar with, for example, *Fagan* (1969), *Pagett* (1983) and *Latimer* (1886). Theoretically, establish the point of 'mere preparation' and where they were 'more than merely preparatory'.

Mens rea of attempt

REVISED

For an attempted crime, the prosecution must prove an intent to commit the full offence. However, in certain crimes, an intent may suffice for the full crime, and it may also suffice for an attempt. See *A-G Ref. (No. 3 of 1992)* (1994) and *R v Khan* (1990) below.

Table 2.7.3 Key cases on the *mens rea* of attempt

Case	Facts	Offence attempted	*Ratio decidendi*
R v Whybrow (1951)	D wired a soap dish next to the bath to electrocute V.	Murder	CA: *mens rea* is an intent to kill for attempted murder.
R v Millard (1987)	D was arrested after pushing against a wooden fence at a football match.	Criminal damage	No attempt, no intent and recklessness will not suffice.
A-G Ref. (No. 3 of 1992) (1994)	D threw a petrol bomb at a car containing four men.	Arson with intent to endanger life	Need intent to damage property but could be reckless as to endanger life.
R v Khan (1990)	D was convicted of attempted rape, being unsuccessful in trying to have sex with the victim.	Rape	Conviction upheld, despite trial judge's direction that the Crown only had to prove an intent to have sex knowing V was not consenting or not caring.

Case	Facts	Offence attempted	*Ratio decidendi*
R v Pace and Rogers (2014)	D1 and D2 bought what they suspected as being stolen scrap metal. The metal was not stolen but sold to them by the police as test purchases (*R v Khan distinguished*).	Conversion of criminal property	CA stated D must have an intent to commit all the elements of the offence, not just some of them. A suspicion was insufficient.
MS, Application by the Prosecution for Leave of Appeal (2021)	D was stopped by police 85 miles from Dover intending to board a ferry with her child. D had been refused permission to take her child out of the country.	Child abduction	The original judge had rejected the attempted crime, saying 85 miles was too far away. This was rejected by the Court of Appeal, stating that D could have 'embarked upon' the crime some considerable distance from Dover and indeed when she had left her home in Stoke.

Attempting an 'impossible' crime

REVISED

The Criminal Attempts Act 1981 introduced a new offence of attempting the impossible but drew a distinction between an offence which is factually impossible, which became an offence, and an offence which is legally impossible, which is not an offence.

- Factually impossible: if on the facts, the commission of the crime was impossible, although the defendant believed it to be possible, then they can still be convicted of an attempted crime. See *Shivpuri* (1986) below.
- Legally impossible: if the defendant believes they are committing an offence, but they are in fact not committing an offence, then they cannot be convicted of the offence they think they are committing.

Evaluation point

Exam scenario questions on attempts can include an attempting the impossible situation. Candidates should appreciate the difference between factually impossible (a crime) and legally impossible (not a crime). Factually impossible crimes are quite commonly set as part of a larger scenario situation.

Table 2.7.4 Cases of attempting the 'impossible'

Case	Facts	Offence attempted	*Ratio decidendi*
Anderton v Ryan (1985)	D admitted to police that she bought a video recorder which she thought was stolen.	Handling stolen goods	HL (House of Lords): quashed conviction, ignoring the 1981 Act. D could not be convicted for something she believed but turned out to be wrong.
R v Shivpuri (1986)	D, a drugs courier, was arrested with what he thought was heroin but was actually a harmless vegetable-type substance.	Knowingly concerned in dealing with a controlled drug	Overruling *Anderton* above, D was convicted of attempting the impossible.
R v Jones (2007)	D tried to solicit young girls for sex, including 'Amy' who he thought was 12, but was, in fact, an undercover female police officer.	Inciting a child under 13 to engage in sexual activity	Even though 'Amy' was not a real 12-year-old girl, D was still convicted for attempting the impossible.

Revision activity

Would the defendant in *R v Jones* (2007) have been convicted of such an offence before the passing of the 1981 Act?

Stretch and challenge

Research the case of *R Shivpuri* (1986). Do you agree or disagree with Lord Bridge's judgment?

Now test yourself TESTED

1 Explain why there is a law on attempted crimes.
2 Discuss why the decisions *in R v Geddes* (1996) and *R v Campbell* (1990) are controversial.
3 Discuss why the decisions in *R v Millard* (1987) are controversial.
4 Explain the purpose behind the law on attempting the impossible.
5 'The Criminal Attempts Act 1981 has provided clarity to the law on attempted crimes.' Examine the truth behind this statement.

Exam tip

To answer a scenario/problem-type question, learn the statutory definition of an attempted crime and the relevant MP and MTMP cases to support your answer.

Many AQA scenario questions will have their basis in an actual case, for example, *R v Campbell* (1990), which should give you a clear steer to the answer.

Exam summary

In the exam, you MAY be asked:

+ multiple-choice questions about the law on attempted crimes
+ to explain and analyse the definition of attempted crimes, in part or in whole, in short- or long-answer questions, for example, the difference between MP and MTMP acts
+ to apply the law on attempted crimes to a scenario situation and be able to consider the criminal liability of a defendant or defendants, even where impossibility may have occurred.

2.8 Defences

Defences 1: Capacity defences

REVISED 

The AQA specification examines three key common law mental capacity defences:

+ insanity (insane automatism)
+ automatism (non-insane automatism)
+ intoxication.

Insanity (insane automatism)

Section 2 of the Trial of Lunatics Acts 1883 states that if at the time of committing an offence the defendant was insane, then the jury shall return a special verdict of not guilty by reason of insanity.

The common law definition of insanity

The definition of insanity is contained in the M'Naghten rules of 1843:

> 'The defendant must prove that at the time of the offence he was labouring under such a defect of reason, arising from a disease of the mind, that he did not know the nature and quality of the act he was doing, or, if he did know it, that he did not know that what he was doing was wrong.'

Starting point for the defence

The law here has developed mainly through the common law but also by statute. There are a number of procedural rules:

+ The defendant is presumed sane.
+ The prosecution, defence or judge can raise the issue of insanity.

Typical mistake

Do not muddle which case supports which capacity defence or which exact element of the definition it supports. Also, make sure you match case names accurately to the facts.

Exam tip

Make sure you accurately memorise the definitions for each of the three defences and are able to support each constituent part with a case or cases.

Evaluation point

Evaluation is important here: make sure you can evaluate and comment upon the advantages and disadvantages of each defence.

- The burden of proof is on the defendant to prove on a balance of probabilities.
- The judge decides whether the defendant is fit to plead.

Due to the social stigma, antiquated definition, huge advances in mental health care and the introduction of the diminished responsibility defence, insanity is rarely raised as a defence to crimes.

Revision activity

Why do you think being labelled 'insane' carries a social stigma?

The M'Naghten rules

The defendant must satisfy each part of the rules. See Table 2.8.1.

Table 2.8.1 The M'Naghten rules

Part of the rules	Explanation
'Labouring under a defect of reason' (*mens rea*)	+ Being deprived of the power to reason, not just failing to use it. + This does not include absentmindedness or being confused – *R v Clarke* (1972).
'Arising from a disease of the mind' (*actus reus*)	+ A legal term and not a medical term. + Must be supported by medical evidence. + Broad definition covering organic or functional, permanent or transient and intermittent issues. + Must be caused by an internal factor existing at the time of the act – *R v Kemp* (1957).
'Did not know the nature and quality of the act' (*actus reus*)	+ Means the physical nature and consequences, not the moral quality of the act – defendant is delusional. + May be due to a state of unconsciousness or impaired unconsciousness, or lack of understanding or awareness due to a mental condition while conscious.
'Or, if he did know it, that he did not know that what he was doing was wrong' (*mens rea*)	+ Defence will fail if the defendant understood their actions were legally wrong, even if they had a mental illness at the time of the act. + Does not mean morally wrong – *R v Windle* (1952) and *R v Johnson* (2007).

Consequences of an insanity verdict

While a common law defence, the consequences of a successful defence are statutory. If a defendant is found to have been insane, the jury should return the special verdict 'not guilty by reason of insanity', which amounts to an acquittal.

For murder, the sentence is indefinite hospitalisation under s 24(1)(3) of the Domestic Violence, Crime and Victims Act 2004.

For all other offences, s 5 of the Criminal Procedure (Insanity) Act 1964 (as amended by the 2004 Act) sets out three disposal options:

- hospital order
- supervision order
- absolute discharge.

Exam tip

Unless the question asks for the cases to be explained chronologically, it is not so important to remember the case dates. Detailed facts are not needed, but an accurate explanation of the case's legal point is vital.

Table 2.8.2 Key cases on insanity

Case	Facts	Element of insanity	Legal point
R v M'Naghten (1843)	M killed a government official while suffering from extreme paranoia.	Whole definition	The law was criticised; after the case, judges formulated the test for insanity.
R v Clarke (1972)	C took items from a shop and forgot to pay for them. She argued this was due to her diabetes.	'Defect of reason'	D is required to be deprived of the powers of reasoning and not simply be confused or absentminded.
R v Kemp (1957)	K had hardening of the arteries and attacked his wife with a hammer.	'Disease of the mind'	The defence is concerned with the mind and not the brain.
R v Quick (1973)	Q, a diabetic, attacked a patient after taking his insulin but not eating sufficient food.	'Disease of the mind'	The disease of the mind must originate from an internal source. This was external: the insulin.

Case	Facts	Element of insanity	Legal point
R v Hennessy (1989)	H was a diabetic and failed to take insulin for three days, during which he took a car without consent.	'Disease of the mind'	The disease of the mind must originate from an internal source. This was internal: the diabetes.
R v Burgess (1991)	B attacked his girlfriend after falling asleep.	'Disease of the mind'	Sleepwalking is an internal factor and therefore insanity.
R v Coley (2013)	D, a heavy cannabis user and 'gamer', stabbed a neighbour to death while having 'a brief psychotic episode'.	Whole definition	CA: due to the external factor (the cannabis) it was not insanity and, as such, a case of voluntary intoxication.
Loake v DPP (2017)	L had sent a large number of texts to her ex-husband.	Availability of defence	Insanity is available as a defence for anyone who possesses the *mens rea* for an offence and satisfies the M'Naghten rules.

Reform proposals for the insanity defence

The Law Commission published a discussion paper, *Criminal Liability: Insanity and Automatism* in 2013, outlining their reform proposals:

- To term a person with a disability such as diabetes or epilepsy 'insane' seems arbitrary and outdated. The very name is 'off-putting or even offensive'.
- There is a mismatch between modern psychiatry and the legal definition.
- The decisions in *R v Quick* (1973) and *R v Hennessy* (1989) were described as 'odd'.
- The internal/external requirement made the potential 'scope of the defence . . . surprisingly wide'.
- Sleepwalking cases led to inconsistency, with some defendants given the 'special verdict' while others were acquitted.

Stretch and challenge

Using the internet, compare the cases of *R v Windle* (1952) and *R v Johnson* (2007).

Automatism (non-insane automatism)

Automatism is where a person's consciousness is so impaired that they are acting in a state of physical involuntariness. Therefore, they cannot be held responsible for their involuntary actions, however unfortunate the result, as there is no *mens rea*.

Automatism was defined by Lord Denning in *Bratty v A-G for Northern Ireland* (1963) as:

> 'an act which is done by the muscles without any control by the mind such as a spasm, a reflex action or a convulsion; or an act done by a person who is not conscious of what he is doing such as an act done whilst suffering from concussion or whilst sleepwalking.'

The evidential burden of proof is on the defence to prove automatism. If successful, it results in a complete acquittal – see *Hill v Baxter* (1958) and *R v C* (2007).

The legal burden of proof is on the prosecution.

There must be an external factor – this is essential in proving automatism. Examples include being struck on the head by an object, slipping on ice, being overcome by a sudden illness, hiccups, a coughing fit, or a temporary loss of control due to a radical event such as being attacked by a swarm of bees (see *Kay v Butterworth* (1945)).

There must be a total loss of control – any impaired, reduced or partial control will invalidate the defence.

Typical mistake

Do not confuse the internal/external factor theory and, in particular, the cases that support the theory. Also, do not muddle the specific conditions that give rise to the defences. See the facts of *R v Quick* (1973) and *R v Hennessy* (1989), for example.

Stretch and challenge

Using the internet:

- Compare the cases of *R v Bailey* (1983) and *R v Hardy* (1984).
- Research the three rules of self-induced automatism that were decided in *R v Bailey* (1983).

Self-induced automatism

Automatism will not be successful as a defence if a defendant knows their conduct will bring about an automatic state, for example, through intoxication. In such situations, the defendant will usually have a defence to specific intent crimes. However, the defendant will not have a defence to basic intent crimes if it is their fault that they voluntarily placed themselves in such a situation.

There is an exception, where the defendant does not realise that their self-induced (voluntary) actions would cause automatism and they were not reckless – see R *v* *Hardy* (1984).

Revision activity

Using decided cases, make a list of external factors that can satisfy the defence of automatism.

Table 2.8.3 Key cases on automatism

Case	Facts	Element of automatism	Legal point
Bratty v A-G for Northern Ireland (1963)	D strangled and killed his girlfriend during a 'blackout'.	Definition	Legal test of automatism created by Lord Denning.
Hill v Baxter (1958)	D hit a car at a junction and said he remembered nothing.	Must be an external factor	The burden of proof for automatism is on the defence.
R v Quick (1973)	See page 92.		
R v Hennessy (1989)	See page 93.		
R v T (1990)	D took part in a robbery three days after being raped. She argued she was in a dream-like state and suffered PTSD.	Must be an external factor	External stress can give rise to automatism if severe enough.
A-G Reference No. 2 1992 (1993)	A truck driver drove in a trance-like state along the motorway's hard shoulder and hit and killed two people.	Must be a loss of total control	As there was some control, the CA dismissed automatism.
McGhee (2013)	M pleaded automatism against a charge of ABH and s 18, having drunk himself into an involuntary state.	Self-induced automatism	Defence rejected. Even if he was in an involuntary state, this was because of his voluntary fault.

Reform proposals for automatism defence

The Law Commission published a Discussion Paper, *Criminal Liability: Insanity and Automatism* in 2013, which proposed:

- abolishing the existing common law defence of automatism and replacing it with a new defence of automatism triggered 'only where there is a total loss of capacity to control one's actions which is not caused by a recognised medical condition and for which the accused was not culpably responsible'
- defendants who raised the defence due to a recognised medical condition which caused a lack of capacity (such as diabetes or epilepsy) would be required to plead the new 'recognised medical condition defence'
- a successful outcome in raising the new defence would lead to a complete acquittal
- the defence would continue to have the evidential burden, while the legal burden would remain with the prosecution.

Intoxication

Intoxication, whether voluntary or involuntary, is not necessarily a defence!

The issue arises when a person is so intoxicated, in either case, that they cannot form the *mens rea*. Allowing a defence for a person intoxicated with drugs or alcohol has to be balanced against public policy.

Why is intoxication a defence?

'Intoxication' covers the effects of alcohol, drugs and other substances such as solvents. It is not a defence *per se*, but it can throw doubt on the defendant's ability to form the required *mens rea* for an offence.

The 'defence' is based strongly on public policy. On the one hand, we cannot usually punish someone who cannot form the *mens rea*, but this must be balanced with punishing people who commit crimes after having become intoxicated.

There are two main ways of identifying intoxication in law:
- voluntary, or
- involuntary.

Voluntary intoxication

This is where the defendant chooses to take a substance, generally alcohol and/or drugs that they know can cause intoxication. In the case of drugs, the drug must be well known to cause unpredictability or aggressiveness.

In both *Bailey* (1983) and *Hardie* (1985), the Court of Appeal distinguished between 'dangerous' drugs and 'non-dangerous' drugs:
- Knowingly taking 'dangerous' drugs would equate to voluntary intoxication.
- Taking 'non-dangerous' drugs may count as voluntary intoxication, but this depends on whether the defendant understands the impact of the drug upon them.
- Voluntary intoxication can be a complete defence to specific intent crimes but will usually not be a defence to crimes of basic intent.

Involuntary intoxication

This is when the defendant was unaware they were taking an intoxicating substance and claims they had been 'spiked'. Also, substances such as prescription drugs may have unexpected or unforeseen effects on the defendant. Therefore:
- If the defendant while involuntarily intoxicated did not form the *mens rea*, then they are not guilty of the crime.
- If the defendant while involuntarily intoxicated did form the *mens rea*, then they can be guilty of the crime.

Intoxication – specific and basic intent crimes

Voluntary intoxication is never a defence to a crime of basic intent. If the defendant is so intoxicated so as to be incapable of forming the *mens rea*, they have a complete defence to specific intent crimes.

If the defendant is intoxicated but still has the intent to form the *mens rea*, they can be guilty of the offence. A drunken intent is still an intent (*R v Sheehan and Moore* (1975)).

Similarly, a person who drinks to give themselves 'courage' to commit an offence will still be guilty of any offence they commit.

The rationale behind basic intent crimes and disallowing intoxication as a defence is based on:
- the notion that becoming intoxicated is a reckless course of action
- sufficient evidence of *mens rea* for basic intent (recklessly committed) crimes such as ABH or common assault.

However, in *R v Harris* (2013), the Court of Appeal made an unusual *obiter* comment on subjective recklessness and voluntary intoxication:

> 'We see some force in the argument that voluntary intoxication ought not to be a defence to an offence involving recklessness, even subjective recklessness; it may fall for decision in a later case whether Lord Lane's view in Stephenson (1979) correctly represents the law now that Caldwell recklessness has passed away'.

Evaluation point

In essay questions, always use the best cases to illustrate the points being made. For your evaluation, do not ignore the basic evaluative points, such as why intoxication is a defence.

Exam tip

Learn the common law definitions of intoxication clearly and make sure you have the correct category of intoxication along with accurate and stimulating evaluation of the defence.

Stretch and challenge

Research the case of *R v Lipman* (1970) and explain the difference between specific and basic intent crimes.

Table 2.8.4 Specific intent and basic intent crimes

Specific intent crimes	Basic intent crimes
+ Murder + Wounding/GBH with intent, s 18 + Theft and robbery	+ Common assault, s 47 + Manslaughter + Wounding/GBH, s 20

Reform proposals for intoxication

The Law Commission published the report *Intoxication and Criminal Liability* in 2009. The report made a number of recommendations, including the following:

- References to basic and specific intent should be abolished.
- The distinction between voluntary and involuntary intoxication should be retained.
- There should be a primary presumption that the defendant was not intoxicated and it should be up to the defendant to prove that they were.
- A secondary presumption would be that the defendant was voluntarily intoxicated.
- If the defendant states that they were involuntarily intoxicated, then they would have to prove that they were.

Table 2.8.5 Key cases on intoxication

Case	Facts	Element of intoxication	Legal point
DPP v Beard (1920)	B argued intoxication as a defence to murder.	Definition	D must be completely incapable of forming the *mens rea* for the defence to apply.
Attorney General for NI v Gallagher (1963)	D decided to kill his wife and bought some whisky and a knife. He drank some of the whisky before he killed her.	Definition	*Mens rea* was formed to kill his wife before the intoxication. 'Dutch courage' is no defence – a drunken intent is still an intent.
DPP v Majewski (1977)	D drank excessive amounts of alcohol and took drugs. He got into a fight.	Voluntary intoxication and basic intent crimes	His conviction for ABH was upheld due to his recklessness in getting intoxicated.
R v Kingston (1994)	K, a known paedophile, drank a drugged coffee and went on to abuse a young boy as part of an attempt by others to blackmail K.	Involuntary intoxication	Despite the involuntary intoxication, K still knew what he was doing, he just could not stop himself.
R v Coley (2013)	D, a heavy cannabis user and 'gamer', stabbed a neighbour to death while having 'a brief psychotic episode'.	Voluntary intoxication	CA: due to the external factor, the cannabis, it was a case of voluntary intoxication and no complete loss of control for automatism.

Now test yourself

TESTED 

1. Explain the M'Naghten rules and why they have proved to be controversial.
2. Explain the difference between the decisions in *R v Quick* (1973) and *R v Hennessy* (1989).
3. Explain the importance of the following cases:
   - *Hill v Baxter* (1958)
   - *R v T* (1990)
   - *A-G Ref. No. 2 1992* (1993).
4. Explain what is meant by self-induced automatism.
5. Why do the courts not see intoxication as a 'true' defence, but are forced to accept its operation due to the spilt between specific and basic intent crimes?
6. 'The 'defence' of intoxication is a balance between a defect in the defendant's *mens rea* and the need to protect the public.' Examine the truth behind this statement.

Evaluation point

Students should not be frightened or nervous about identifying their own concerns or support for the capacity defences. While examiners are looking for the established criticisms, a candidate's own legitimate criticisms are generally well received.

Exam summary

In the exam, you MAY be asked:
- multiple-choice questions about the law on capacity defences (insanity, automatism and intoxication)
- to explain and analyse the definitions of insanity, automatism and intoxication, in part or in whole, in short- or long-answer questions, for example, the differences and justifications behind insanity and automatism
- to apply the law on insanity, automatism and/or intoxication to a scenario situation and be able to consider the criminal liability of a defendant or defendants, for example, where the source of the defendant's actions is internally or externally caused.

Defences 2: Necessity defences

REVISED

The AQA specification examines three key common law necessity defences:
- self-defence and the prevention of crime
- duress by threats
- duress of circumstances (commonly linked to the necessity defence).

Prevention of crime: this is governed by ss 2 and 3 Criminal Law Act 1967.

Self-defence: using reasonable force in order to defend oneself.

Self-defence and the prevention of crime

The most basic form of self-defence, defending yourself, comes under the common law. It must be necessary to use force and reasonable to do so.

Those who are acting reasonably and in good faith will be entitled to a defence in order to defend themselves, their family or to prevent the commission of a crime.

Exam tip

Learn the definitions of each necessity defence. Some are more complicated than others and can appear confusing. In order to understand each case, apply the facts to its definition and see if you agree with the court's decision.

Coverage of the defence of self-defence

Self-defence is a defence available to crimes committed by force.

The basic principle was clarified in *Palmer* (1971):

> 'It is both good law and good sense that a man who is attacked may defend himself. It is good law and good sense that he may do, but only do, what is reasonably necessary.'

The operation of the defence was clarified in s 76 Criminal Justice and Immigration Act 2008 as to the test of reasonableness. It is a complete defence, including to murder, as the defendant's use of force is justified in the circumstances.

The defence is mainly common law and covers:
- actions needed to defend oneself from attack
- actions taken to defend another person.

Main rules or elements of the defence

There are two key elements to the defence:
- Was the use of force necessary in the circumstances – was force needed at all?
- Was the force used reasonable in the circumstance?

Typical mistake

It is easy to get confused with the elements of self-defence, especially as they can overlap with other defences, so make sure you have a clear and accurate definition.

1 Must be necessary to use some force

This is a subjective test, based on the defendant's genuine belief in those precise circumstances. The defendant can be mistaken but can still plead the defence.

Pre-emptive strike is possible and allowable. The defendant can prepare for an attack and there is no duty to retreat.

2 The degree of force must be reasonable

This is an objective test. A jury must ask themselves, based on the facts the defendant believed them to be: would a reasonable person regard the force as reasonable or excessive?

Lord Morris provided further clarification in *Palmer* (1971) as to what was reasonable force: that a defendant 'in a moment of unexpected anguish' may not have been able to 'weigh to a nicety the exact measure of his defensive action'.

However, even if an act was deemed necessary, the resulting action may not be seen as reasonable. The reaction to the threat is always integral to the reasonableness of the force used – *Clegg* (1995).

A mistake of fact while intoxicated will prevent the defence's application to an act – *O'Grady* (1987).

Revision activity

1. Explain why 'householders' are given special consideration in self-defence cases.
2. Research the case of *R v Bird* (1985). Explain whether you think it was necessary to use self-defence.

Householders and use of self-defence

In 2018, the Crown Prosecution Service and the National Police Chiefs' Council issued a joint public statement, 'Householders and the use of force against intruders', on the use of force in such circumstances. The statement is unequivocal: a householder must have acted honestly and instinctively and thought it necessary in the 'heat of the moment'. This is the strongest evidence for them having acted lawfully and in self-defence, in reaction to an intruder or 'home-invasion'.

Section 76 Criminal Justice and Immigration Act 2008 allows a householder to use 'disproportionate force' in self-defence. This is judged on a case-by-case basis, but the degree of force will not be seen as reasonable in each circumstance if the householder's actions were seen as grossly disproportionate.

Pre-emptive strikes, the duty to retreat and revenge

There is no law to say that a person cannot, in the right circumstances, hit another person first in an act of self-defence rather than wait to be attacked – *Deana* (1909).

Failure to retreat and avoid conflict does not preclude the application of the defence and provide evidence the defendant was not acting in self-defence. Such evidence is relevant to the test of reasonableness, but it is not necessary for the defendant to walk away – *Bird* (1985).

The act of revenge does not rule out the possibility of the defence of self-defence – *Rashford* (2005). However, if a person starts the violence, they cannot rely upon the defence to render their actions lawful.

Evaluation point

Self-defence is a complicated and controversial topic. With its roots and development largely in the common law, any use of self-defence will always remain controversial.

Coverage of the defence of prevention of crime

The common law approach to self-defence is relevant to the defence of prevention of crime, which is statutorily defined under section 3 Criminal Law Act 1967:

> 'A person may use such force as is reasonable in the circumstances in the prevention of crime . . .'

Therefore, the amount of force used in order to stop or prevent a crime, and whether or not a defendant can use force in doing so, mirrors the test in self-defence.

Stretch and challenge

Research the case of Norfolk farmer Tony Martin: *R v Martin (Anthony)* (2002). Consider the jury's decision to reject his defence of self-defence. Do you agree or disagree with their decision and why?

Table 2.8.6 Key cases for self-defence

Case	Facts	Element of self-defence	Legal point
R v Bird (1985)	B gouged out V's eye during a major row after V hit B.	Duty to retreat	B's conviction was quashed. Evidence of a retreat is helpful but not essential.
R v Williams (1987)	W grabbed V, an off-duty police officer, whom he mistakenly thought was attacking a youth.	Mistaken use of self-defence/prevention of crime	An honest but mistaken belief will allow the defence to operate. The conviction was quashed.

Case	Facts	Element of self-defence	Legal point
A-G Ref. (No. 2 of 1983) (1984)	D kept petrol bombs for protection after his shop had been attacked several times during riots.	Pre-emptive strike	A person is entitled to make preparations in self-defence for a future attack against them.
R v Clegg (1995)	C, a soldier, shot and killed a joyrider whom he thought was a terrorist.	Excessive force	C was not acting in self-defence, as the last shot was excessive force as the 'threat' had passed.
R v Martin (Anthony) (2002)	M shot and killed a burglar.	Excessive force	It was not self-defence, as M shot when V was making his escape.
R v Hussain (2010)	H chased and caught a burglar that he found in his house. H beat the burglar with a cricket bat.	Excessive force	It was not self-defence; violence was just used as retribution. The burglary was over and no one was in danger.
R v Oye (2013)	H was arrested after behaving oddly in a café. He threw plates at police officers and fought with them when arrested.	Psychological characteristics are not relevant	Self-defence was rejected, but an insanity plea was allowed.
R v Taj (2018)	D fatally wounded V who he believed, wrongly, was a terrorist about to plant a bomb. D had a history of drug abuse, mental illness and was 'under the influence' at the time.	Mistaken use of self-defence	The trial judge withdrew the defence from the jury and the CA upheld his conviction for murder, rejecting mistaken self-defence while intoxicated.

Duress

Duress by threats is a common law defence and therefore its entire definition is based on various decisions of judges rather than statute.

Purpose of the defence

The defence operates where the defendant argues that they were forced to commit a crime due to a direct threat aimed, usually, at themselves. It is deemed a credible defence, due to being 'founded on a concession to human frailty' where a person's will is overcome by threats.

So, if the defendant had not been threatened, they would not have committed the offence. The defendant does not deny committing the crime but was forced into doing it.

This defence is available to all crimes committed by a defendant under duress, other than murder, attempted murder and probably treason. It is rarely successful – courts are reluctant to believe that the defendant had to commit a crime and could not have walked away or sought help.

Definition and rules

The definition has evolved over time.

1. The starting point is the two-part *Graham* (1982) test which must be satisfied:
   - Was the defendant compelled to act because they reasonably believed they had a good reason to fear death or serious injury?
   - Would a sober person of reasonable firmness, sharing the same characteristics as the defendant, have acted in the same way?
2. There must be either a threat of death or serious injury (GBH).
   - A threat of serious psychological injury will not suffice – *Baker* (1997).
   - The threat must be convincing, so a person of reasonable firmness with the defendant's characteristics would have given in – *Howe* (1987).
   - The threat must be objectively reasonable and subjectively genuine – *Hasan* (2005).

Exam tip

Ensure you learn each of the elements of this defence and can discuss the need for each. Being able to justify or criticise each element will create a more accurate response in an essay.

Duress by threats: a common law defence whereby someone commits a crime because they were subject to a threat of death or serious injury.

Revision activity

Is there ever really any justification to committing a crime if someone threatens you unless you carry it out? Examine the truth behind this statement.

- In considering the defendant's characteristics, pregnancy, serious physical disability or a recognised mental illness may be relevant. Age and gender will be taken into account, but a low IQ will not be – *Bowen* (1996).

3 There can be a combination of threats, but a threat of death or serious injury must be present and play a major part in the defendant's rationale for committing the crime.
4 The threat can include the defendant, a close family member of their immediate family or people the defendant is responsible for – *Wright* (2000).
5 If there is a safe avenue of escape, then this must be pursued, although there may be exceptions to this rule – see *R v Gill* (1963) and *R v Hudson and Taylor* (1971).
6 The threat must be effective and be operational when the defendant carries out the crime. The threat of death or serious harm must be 'an imminent danger of physical injury' – *Quayle* (2005).
7 There must be a nexus between the crime nominated and the crime committed – *Cole* (1994).
8 The defence will usually fail if the defendant associates with people who are known to make threats, for example, criminal gangs or terrorists – see *R v Sharp* (1987) and *R v Shepherd* (1987).

Typical mistake

Do not forget to mention certain key elements of this defence, such as the requirement of a nexus between the crime and the threat.

Reform of duress

The Law Commission's Consultation Paper, *A New Homicide Act*, in 2005 suggested that this should be a partial defence to murder, but when the Law Commission reported in 2006, they stated it should be a full defence to murder and attempted murder.

A Ministry of Justice Report in 2008, *Murder, Manslaughter and Infanticide: Proposals for Reform of the Law*, made no specific reference to duress by threats in relation to murder, ignoring the earlier recommendations.

Revision activity

Using the internet, compare the cases of:

- *R v Sharp* (1987) *and R v Shepherd* (1987)
- *R v Gill* (1963) and *R v Hudson* and Taylor (1971).

Table 2.8.7 Key cases on duress by threat

Case	Facts	Element of duress by threats	Legal point
R v Howe (1987)	H was party to the torture and killing of a man. He later did the same while on his own. H said he had been threatened to do so.	Availability	The defence was refused for murder, as one person's life is not worth more than another's.
R v Gotts (1992)	G, 16, was threatened by his father into stabbing his mother to death.	Availability	There was no defence to attempted murder.
R v Valderrama-Vega (1985)	V imported cocaine, threatened with the exposure of his homosexuality, death and financial ruin.	Type of threat	All threats can be considered but must contain a threat of death. Other kinds of threat are insufficient.
R v Wright (2000)	W was arrested with cocaine but said she had it because her boyfriend had been threatened.	Personal responsibility for another	Persons to whom the threat is made include those outside the immediate family.
R v Graham (1982)	G lived with his wife and his homosexual lover, K. G helped K kill his wife. G said he was frightened of K.	'Graham' suitability of defence test	A test of general suitability was created.
R v Hasan (2005)	H associated with a violent drug dealer and was threatened into carrying out a burglary/robbery.	Imminence	The threat must be, or be believed to be, immediate or almost immediate.
R v Cole (1994)	C robbed a building society to repay a debt after he and his family were threatened.	Nexus	C chose this course of action to repay debt; there was no threat or duress.
R v Batchelor (2013)	B claimed he had been threatened by armed men over a period of time to repay money they said was owed.	Failure to seek police protection	Defendant could have sought police protection over a period of two and a half years, so the treat was not imminent or immediate.

Case	Facts	Element of duress by threats	Legal point
R v Brandford (2016)	B was charged with conspiracy to sell class A drugs. She argued that her boyfriend had been threatened by a third party that 'something bad would happen to him' unless he transported the drugs and she was simply avoiding him being injured or killed by doing this instead.	Indirect threats of violence or death	The CA stated that such threats could be valid but agreed with the trial judge who had rejected the defence at trial, saying that the words were vague, they lacked immediacy and she had ample time to go to the police.

Duress of circumstances (necessity)

Duress of circumstances is a common law defence. Most of its definition is based on the decisions of judges rather than statute.

This is sometimes referred to as the defence of 'necessity'. Lord Woolf CJ in *Shayler* (2001) stated that the distinction between necessity and duress of circumstance had largely been 'ignored and blurred by the courts' and were essentially the same defence.

Duress of circumstances: a common law defence whereby someone commits a crime because of the circumstances in which they found themselves.

Scope of the defence

For this defence, the defendant was forced to react due to the circumstances they found themselves in, rather than from a direct threat of death or serious injury. This defence has evolved to compensate for the restrictive nature of duress by threats.

In *Re A (Children) (Conjoined Twins: Surgical Separation)* (2001), the Court of Appeal approved the following definition:

'An act, which would ordinarily be considered a crime, but may excuse the defendant if they can show that:

- it was done to avoid consequences which could not otherwise be avoided, and if they had been followed would have inflicted inevitable and irreparable evil upon themselves or others
- no more was done than was reasonably necessary
- the evil inflicted was not disproportionate to the evil avoided.'

Typical mistake

The reason behind the defence of duress of circumstances can be difficult to understand. It is not a direct threat of death or violence, but a perceived danger of death or serious injury in the circumstances.

In addition, the two-part *Martin* test must be satisfied:

1. From an objective point of view, the accused acted reasonably and proportionately to avoid a threat of death or serious harm, and
2. The same two-part *Graham* test applies.

Originally, the defence was raised against driving offences, but this has been extended on a case-by-case basis.

Exam tip

Learn the cases for the two duress defences to see the differences between them. The *Graham* test applies to threats and the *Martin* test applies to circumstances.

Table 2.8.8 Key cases on duress of circumstances

Case	Facts	Element of duress of circumstances	Legal point
R v Willer (1986)	W drove on a pavement to avoid being attacked by youths. There was no threat to carry out a crime.	Origins	The jury should be allowed to consider some type of duress in such circumstances.
R v Conway (1988)	C drove fast after he thought he had been shot at.	Origins	Duress was available if, from an objective point of view. D was acting to avoid a threat.
R v Martin (1989)	M drove while disqualified because his wife threatened suicide if he did not take their son to work.	Test	CA adapted the two-part *Graham* test.

Case	Facts	Element of duress of circumstances	Legal point
R v Pommell (1995)	P was found with a gun at his house, saying he had taken it from a man and intended to hand it in.	Extent and availability	CA said whether duress of circumstance applied was a matter for the jury.
DPP v Davis (1994)	D drove while intoxicated to avoid being attacked.	Extent and availability	Convictions were quashed. Duress of circumstances was available.
R v Cairns (1999)	V threw himself on the bonnet of C's car. C warned V to get off. C drove and braked. V fell off and was seriously injured.	Extent and availability	There was a reasonable perceived threat of death or serious injury and the defence was allowed.

Stretch and challenge

Using the internet, explain the decision *in R v Pommell* (1995).

Evaluation point

The difference between duress of circumstance and the defence of necessity can seem confusing. The two defences have simply evolved as defence counsels have sought to manipulate shortcomings in the common law not addressed by statute law.

Now test yourself

TESTED 

7 What are the two situations, relevant to the AQA specification, in which self-defence can be used?

8 Explain how the courts decide whether it was necessary to use force in self-defence and whether it was reasonable to do so.

9 Explain why there is a defence of duress by threats.

10 What is the *Graham* test and why was it introduced?

11 Explain the differences between the defences of duress by threats and duress of circumstances.

12 Explain how the defence of duress of circumstances was extended in *R v Martin* (1989).

Exam summary

In the exam, you MAY be asked:

- multiple-choice questions about the law on necessity defences (self-defence, duress by threats and duress of circumstances)
- to explain and analyse the definitions of self-defence, duress by threats and duress of circumstances, in part or in whole, in short- or long-answer questions, for example, the justifications and restrictions placed on duress by threats and duress of circumstances.

Revision activity

Make sure that you have worked through all previous MCQs and short-answer questions on the legal system from the AQA website.

Also, look at back-copies of the *A Level Law Review* which contain examples of AQA-style MCQ.

Write your own MCQs and short-answer questions on the legal system using the style set by AQA. Don't make the answers too simple or too obscure. Follow the specification and pick out key areas that a question-setter might use to set an exam question.

Exam practice

In Paper 1 you need to answer:

- five multiple-choice questions – at least two of these will be criminal law questions
- two short five-mark scenario questions will follow – one of these will be a criminal law question
- two 10- or 15-mark questions: a scenario and an essay. You will need to provide an extended answer which shows a clear, logical and sustained line of reasoning, leading to a valid conclusion.
- an extended scenario, worth 30 marks, that will require comprehensive application of the law to facts leading to a valid conclusion.

Multiple-choice questions (1 mark each)

1 Which of the following statements about strict liability offences is false?

A D cannot be guilty of a strict liability offences if she was not negligent.

B D will not usually be guilty of a strict liability offence if his conduct was involuntary.

C Some offences impose strict liability as to one *actus reus* element but require *mens rea* as to another.

D Strict liability is often imposed in 'regulatory' offences.

2 Which one of the following statements about the defence of insanity is true?

A The 'defect of reason' must be caused by an external factor.

B The defences cannot succeed if D understood the nature and quality of his act.

C The 'disease of the mind' can result from physical disease.

D The burden of proof is on the prosecution.

3 Which of the following statements about theft is true?

A The Act provides a clear definition of dishonesty.

B An appropriation is defined as 'assuming all of the rights of the owner'.

V Property does not include tangible items such as money or illegal drugs.

D Belonging to another can include a person who has temporary control of the property such as a garage or cloakroom attendant.

4 Which of the following statements about robbery is false?

A D cannot be guilty of robbery if they have not committed theft.

B D will not be guilty of robbery unless the use or threat of force is used in order to steal.

C D must apply force, or threaten force, in order to steal to be guilty of robbery.

D Robbery is a basic intent crime.

5 Which of the following statements about self-defence are false?

A During an act of violence against a person, there is an absolute duty to retreat.

B The defence will not operate where a person 'throws the first punch' to avoid conflict.

C Any use of force must be reasonable in the circumstances.

D Householders are given more protection than the person 'on the street' who uses force to protect themselves.

Short answer 5-mark questions

6 Explain the doctrine of transferred malice. Illustrate your answer with cases.

7 Alan borrowed a book from his friend Balsem a week ago. Balsem asks for the book back, but Alan says he has given it to her mother 'yesterday'. In fact, Alan still has the book. An hour later, feeling guilty, he gives the book to Balsem's mother.

Suggest why, in law, Alan probably did not commit the *mens rea* of theft when he returned the book.

8 Kaira intended to throw acid at Laboni's face. She hid in a shop doorway and as Laboni approached, Kaira threw the acid at her. Laboni suffered serious burns as a result.

Identify and explain the *actus reus* of the offence Kaira is likely to be charged with.

9 'The defence of the prevention of crime under s 3 Criminal Law Act 1967 is clear and unambiguous.' Examine the truth behind this statement.

10-mark questions

10 William has been threatened by his girlfriend, Delia, that unless he steals a very expensive painting from an art gallery, she will pour paint over his neighbour's car. She says that she will tell the neighbour it was William who did it. The last time Delia threatened William, she persuaded her brother, who has a series of convictions for violence, to punch William in the face. William reluctantly steals the painting but is arrested by the police while he tries to escape.

Advise William on whether he could avoid criminal liability for the theft/burglary by pleading duress by threats.

11 Ranya has fallen out with Saachi and decides to teach her a lesson. Ranya hides behind a wall and as Saachi passes, Ranya sticks her foot out to trip Saachi. Saachi's leg makes contact with Ranya's foot and she does trip. The trip causes Saachi to fall and she bangs her head, resulting in mild concussion.

Identify and apply the elements of the offence Ranya is likely to be charged with.

15-mark questions

12 Examine the meaning of 'fault' and discuss its impact on the application of the rules of self-defence.

13 Hope is at a party when she sees her ex-boyfriend. He pins her against the wall and says: 'Get out of this house or I'll do you in!' Hope, who is holding a bottle of beer, smashes it against his face, causing a deep cut to his cheek.

Suggest why, in law, Hope will be able to successfully raise the defence of self-defence against a charge of wounding under the Offences Against the Person Act 1861.

30-mark questions

14 Denzel was furious as his neighbour, Victor, had blocked his drive. He banged on Victor's door. Victor began to open the door but when he saw who was there, he tried to close it again. Denzel pushed the door hard, Victor fell back and hit his head on a coat peg in the hallway. When the ambulance arrived, the crew dropped Victor on the way to the vehicle. On arrival at hospital, Victor was misdiagnosed with mild concussion. The following day, he died from brain damage. The effects of the concussion were more serious for him because he suffered from brittle bone disease, which meant that his skull did not adequately protect his brain.

Consider the criminal liability of Denzel for the involuntary manslaughter of Victor (including whether there was a break in the chain of causation).

15 Shauna and her partner Luca live in a block of flats. One morning on his way to work, Luca is walking through the main entrance when Grace, a neighbour, stands in his way and says: 'Where are you off to, gorgeous?' Luca is nervous as he knows Grace can be violent and shoves her so hard that she falls, banging her head against the floor. Luca runs off to work.

Later that day, when Luca returns home from work, he tells Shauna what had happened earlier with Grace. Angry and upset, Shauna goes to Grace's flat and kicks in her front door, shouting, 'Where are you? I'm going to kill you!' Grace gets a knife from the kitchen and holds it up as Shauna approaches. Shauna picks up a plant pot and throws it at Grace. The plant pot hits Grace in the chest. Grace runs at Shauna and stabs her, killing her instantly.

Luca, who has followed Shauna, grabs Grace and restrains her until the police arrive.

Consider whether the defences of self-defence and the prevention of crime will assist Luca or Grace if they were to be charged with any crimes.

End-of-unit summary

- Explain the burden of proof in criminal law.
- Explain the standard of proof in criminal law.
- Identify AR.
- Recognise the difference between conduct and consequence crimes.
- Explain when an omission can amount to an AR.
- Recognise when causation is relevant.
- Explain and apply the rules of causation.
- Identify MR.
- Recognise the importance of fault and its relationship with voluntary acts and state of affairs.
- Explain direct intent and oblique intent.
- Understand subjective recklessness and how it differs from intent.
- Explain when negligence in an appropriate MR.
- Explain and evaluate strict liability offences.
- Apply the principle of transferred malice.
- Apply the contemporaneity rule.
- Explain and apply the elements of AR common to all fatal offences.
- Explain and identify MR of murder.
- Understand the impact of the Coroners and Justice Act 2009 on the Homicide Act 1957.
- Explain and apply the elements of loss of control. Illustrate this with cases.
- Explain and apply the elements of diminished responsibility. Illustrate this with cases.
- Differentiate and evaluate the burden of proof in the two partial defences.
- Explain and apply the elements of AR of unlawful act manslaughter.
- Explain and apply the elements of MR of unlawful act manslaughter.
- Explain and apply elements of gross negligence manslaughter.
- Explain and apply elements of the AR of assault.
- Explain and apply elements of the MR of assault.
- Explain and apply elements of the AR of battery.
- Explain and apply elements of the MR of battery.
- Explain and apply elements of the AR of ABH.
- Explain and apply elements of the MR of ABH.
- Explain and apply elements of the AR of GBH.
- Explain and apply elements of the AR of malicious wounding.
- Explain and apply elements of the MR of s 20.
- Explain and apply elements of the MR of s 18.
- Explain and apply the elements of the AR and MR of theft.
- Explain and apply the elements of the AR and MR of robbery.
- Explain and apply the elements of the AR and MR of attempted crimes.
- Explain and apply attempting the impossible.
- Explain and apply the defence of insanity.
- Explain and apply the defence of automatism.
- Explain and apply the defence of intoxication.
- Explain and apply the defence of self-defence/ prevention of crime.
- Explain and apply the defence of duress.
- Explain and apply the defence of duress of circumstance.
- An evaluation of the non-fatal offences and their sentencing, including the history of reform and its impact (or lack thereof).
- An evaluation of the defence of intoxication, including suggestions for reform.
- An evaluation of self-defence, including suggestions for reform.
- An evaluation of the defence of consent, including suggestions for reform.

3 Tort

3.1 Rules of tort law

Tort is a substantive area of law and is assessed in Paper 2.

It makes up 75 of the 100 marks available in this paper.

Torts are established by both common law rules and Acts of Parliament. They form part of what is known as private law, because the state does not get involved in them. They are not crimes that are investigated and prosecuted by public bodies to protect us all – instead, they provide redress and compensation when we suffer damage to our person, property or enjoyment of our land through the non-criminal actions of others.

You will need to:

- be able to define and explain the principles, defences and remedies in tort law, and to be competent in applying these
- understand the rules and theory in tort before examining the key principle of negligence, including where the damage created is purely economic or psychiatric in nature
- examine the statutory impact where the damage is suffered by a visitor or trespasser to an occupier's land, and the land-based torts of nuisance and *Rylands v Fletcher*
- apply the defences of consent or contributory negligence while considering whether the tortfeasor was employed and acting in the course of employment (which would warrant a claim in vicarious liability)
- advise how damages are calculated in a given scenario and make links to support the theoretical sections in the English legal system and law-making chapters.

This chapter is background material for what will be assessed in Paper 2. Chapters 3.3–3.8 give the substantive detail on tort law.

General principles

Civil law is concerned with settling disputes between parties. It is not to punish wrongdoing.

There are many different areas of civil law including:

- tort law
- contract law, which deals with the sale of goods and services
- family law
- employment law.

Tort law allows a person to claim compensation when they have been injured or their property has been damaged. The individual parties involved in a civil claim are the 'claimant' and the 'defendant'.

The state is not usually concerned with tort law, as the action is between the persons involved in the incident. If the claimant is successful in proving their case, they will ask the court to award a remedy.

Typical mistake

Do not mix up the terminology used in criminal and civil law!

Tort law: an area of the law that allows a person to claim compensation when they have been injured or their property has been damaged.

Revision activity

The defendant is not called 'guilty' in civil law. What word do we use instead?

Rules and principles concerning liability and fault

REVISED

Burden and standard of proof

In civil law, the burden of proving that the defendant is liable is on the claimant. The standard of proof in civil cases is 'the balance of probabilities'. This means that it is more likely than not that the claimant is telling the truth.

The claimant merely has to establish that the defendant was at fault for the incident and responsible for the damage.

The civil courts of first instance are different from those that deal with criminal law.

Stretch and challenge

Identify the civil courts and determine how the appropriate court is selected.

Fault or no fault

Fault was first introduced into negligence law in *Cambridge Water v Eastern Counties Leather* (1994). Before that, fault was not always necessary for damages to be paid.

Fault means that there is some wrongdoing by the defendant, and is a requirement in torts such as:

- negligence
- occupiers' liability
- psychiatric damage
- pure economic loss caused by negligent misstatement.

However, it is not needed in torts such as:

- nuisance
- *Rylands v Fletcher*
- vicarious liability.

For these torts, the claimant does not need to show how and why the incident happened – simply that it did, and then establish a causal link to the damage suffered.

Defences and remedies

REVISED

Defences

As in criminal law, there are ways for a defendant to refute a claim. However, there are far fewer in civil law than in criminal law.

Defences generally divert blameworthiness away from the defendant back to the claimant, suggesting they were, to some degree, responsible for their own damage.

Exam tip

While you are unlikely to be asked a whole question in this area, it is underpinning knowledge that supports the whole topic and there is an expectation that you will be familiar with and competent in accurately using this terminology.

Remedies

Remedies for successful action can be:

- damages – money calculated to return the claimant to their original position before the tort had taken place (in so far as it is possible to do so with money), or
- injunctions – a court order to stop; this is most common in torts such as trespass and nuisance.

In civil cases, the general rule is that the loser pays the winner's legal costs in addition to their own costs, so it is a risky business. See Chapter 1.4 and make the link.

Evaluation point

As you work through this chapter, continually ask yourself, how successful is this area of law in balancing the conflicting interests of the parties?

Now test yourself TESTED 

1. Why is the burden in civil law lower than in criminal law?
2. Where is fault not always necessary in tort?
3. Where is fault required in civil law? Which case brought about this change?
4. What is the aim of damages?

Exam summary

While this material is underpinning knowledge for the substantive law of tort, you should be aware that you may be asked multiple-choice questions or short-answer questions on the key points, such as the burden of proof or the purpose of damages.

You will be expected to apply these principles alongside the substantive law in long-answer questions.

3.2 Theory of tort law

This is background material for what will be assessed in Paper 2. Chapters 3.3–3.8 give the substantive detail, including case information.

Typical mistake

Do not view this section in isolation – read about tort law alongside the relevant substantive chapters and also the English legal system chapters.

Exam tip

This chapter requires a basic understanding of the areas, but with a view to conducting analysis and evaluation. This suggests essay writing and making links with the relevant sections in Section 1 (The nature of law and the English legal system) that are assessed in Paper 2.

Policy decisions

REVISED 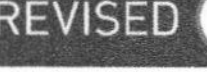

Factors governing duty of care

Most of the law relating to negligence is common law, which means it is developed by judges when deciding cases. When deciding whether to impose liability in an area not previously dealt with, judges exercise caution so as not to create an avalanche of new claims.

These types of decisions are known as 'policy decisions' – they are not made simply to achieve individual justice, but to create a precedent that is fair, just and reasonable.

The factors judges take into consideration are:

- loss allocation – who can afford to bear the loss? Is there any insurance? Is either body funded by the tax payer?
- floodgates – will imposing liability lead to a high volume of new claims? What would the impact of this be on insurance, the courts, public-funded bodies?
- the practical impact of imposing liability – will standards be raised as a consequence of this deterrent or will essential funds be diverted away from front-line activities to defend legal claims?

These issues often arise in the context of public-funded bodies and in particular in relation to the police, the CPS, local authorities and the emergency services.

Key cases in this area include *Caparo v Dickman* (1990), Hill *v Chief Constable of West Yorkshire* (1988) and *Michael v Chief Constable of South Wales* (2015).

However, in the recent Supreme Court judgment in Robinson *v Chief Constable of West Yorkshire* (2018), Lord Reed (para 55) reiterated that *Hill* is NOT:

> 'authority for the proposition that the police enjoy a general immunity from suit in respect of anything done by them in the course of investigating or preventing crime [and in fact] the liability of the police for negligence or other tortious conduct resulting in personal injury, where liability would arise under ordinary principles of the law of tort, was expressly confirmed'.

Also in *Robinson* (2018), Lord Mance stated (para 84):

> 'It would be unrealistic to suggest that, when recognising and developing an established category, the courts are not influenced by policy considerations ... Landmark examples are *Donoghue v Stevenson* ... in relation to physical injury, and *Hedley Byrne & Co Ltd v Heller & Partners Ltd* [in relation to economic loss].'

Stretch and challenge

Find out what Lord Reid said about fairy tales in *in Journal of the Society of Public Teachers of Law* (New Series), vol. 12, issue 1 (January 1972), pp. 22–29.

Evaluation point

Throughout this section, make links with and refer to judicial precedent.

Policy decisions and liability for pure economic loss and psychiatric injury

There are sound policy reasons for limiting claims made on the basis of pure economic loss and psychiatric injury.

The substantive law on both of these will be dealt with in Chapter 3.3.

Pure economic loss

If this were actionable, there would be no reasonable limit to a defendant's liability and the courts would become overwhelmed with claims.

The courts often quote US judge Benjamin N. Cardozo, who famously described it in *Ultramares v Touche* (1931) as 'a fear of an indeterminate number of claims by an indeterminate number of parties in indeterminate amounts of money for an indeterminate amount of time'.

A key case in this area is *Hedley Byrne and Co. Ltd v Heller and Partners Ltd* (1963).

Psychiatric injury

Psychiatric injury has been historically considered less serious than physical harm (this is now not the case), because of the fear of:

- opening the floodgates
- the potential for fraudulent claims being brought by people exaggerating their claims
- problems of proof and diagnosis, including the costs of expert opinion.

The claimant is often a secondary victim.

Finally, the courts argued that Parliament is better suited to dealing with this area.

Key cases in this area include *McLoughlin v O'Brian* (1983) and *Alcock v Chief Constable of South Yorkshire* (1992).

Factors governing the objective standard of care in an action for negligence

In *Vaughan v Menlove* (1837), the defendant built a haystack near his property line, adjacent to the claimant's property. The haystack caught fire and spread to the claimant's barns, stables and cottages. The court said:

> 'If the standard was that the defendant only needed to act "bona fide to the best of his own judgement", that would leave so vague a line as to afford no rule at all, the degree of judgement belonging to each individual being infinitely various. We ought to adhere to a standard which requires in all cases a regard to caution such as a man of ordinary prudence would observe.'

The test that compares the defendant to the reasonable person was born.

Factors governing the granting of an injunction as a remedy and the way in which conflicting interests are balanced

An injunction is a court order prohibiting a person from doing something or requiring a person to do something. It is used most commonly in nuisance and trespass.

The Supreme Court of Judicature Act 1925 (now repealed) stated in s 45 that 'an injunction may be granted ... in all cases in which it shall appear to the Court to be just or convenient'.

The court will weigh up the social usefulness of the activity against the 'harm' it is causing to the claimant.

Key cases in this area include *Miller v Jackson* (1977) and *Kennaway v Thompson* (1981).

Nature and purpose of vicarious liability

The most common vicarious liability is the liability of an employer for the torts of employees committed in the course of employment. This requires a connection between the employment duties and the employee's acts complained of.

In addition, in order to establish vicarious liability, it is necessary to show that an employee was employed.

This exists principally because the employer has the 'deepest pockets' and, as such, most employers will be insured against such liability.

Key cases in this area include *Ready Mixed Concrete Ltd v Minister of Pensions* (1968) and *Mohamud v WM Morrison Supermarkets plc* (2016).

Now test yourself

TESTED

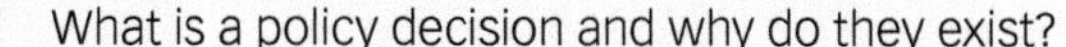

1. What is a policy decision and why do they exist?
2. Why has psychiatric damage been problematic in negligence in the past?
3. Why would a subjective test for negligence be inappropriate?
4. When might damages be paid in lieu of an injunction?
5. Why is it preferable to sue the employer rather than the employee?

Exam summary

While this material is underpinning knowledge for the substantive law of tort, be aware that you may be asked multiple-choice questions or short-answer questions on the key points such as the meaning of the 'reasonable person' or the purpose of policy decisions.

You will be expected to apply these principles alongside the substantive law in long-answer questions.

3.3 Liability in negligence

Liability for physical injury to people and damage to property

REVISED

Duty of care: the 'neighbour' principle and the Caparo test

If a duty does not already exist in law, such as that between road users, between teachers and students and between doctors and patients, then the tests shown in Table 3.3.1 are used to decide whether a new duty should be created.

Exam tip

For this part of the course you need to apply the law to given scenarios.

Table 3.3.1 Tests to decide whether a duty of care should be created

Original test (known as the neighbour principle)	New test
Donoghue v Stevenson (1932)	*Caparo v Dickman* (1990)
+ You must take reasonable care to avoid acts or omissions you can reasonably foresee are likely to injure your neighbour. + Your neighbour is anyone so closely and directly affected by your actions that you ought reasonably to have them in your contemplation.	+ The damage must be reasonably foreseeable. + There must be a relationship of proximity between the parties. + It must be fair, just and reasonable to impose a duty of care.

You can see that the new test updates the language from *Donoghue* and adds a new element.

Table 3.3.2 explains the new elements of the Caparo test that the new Supreme Court case of *Robinson v Chief Constable of West Yorkshire* (2018) tells us should be used 'only in a novel type of case, where established principles do not provide an answer'.

Established principles means 'the courts will consider the closest analogies in the existing law, with a view to maintaining the coherence of the law and the avoidance of inappropriate distinctions'.

Therefore, the Caparo test will be used only if there are no previous cases that are sufficiently similar.

Revision activity

For a light-hearted moment on this area of law, see **https://youtu.be/zWia3G-CzyLQ**.

Stretch and challenge

For an example of this, read or watch the Supreme Court video on *Darnley v Croydon NHS Trust* (2018).

Table 3.3.2 The Caparo test

Caparo test	Explanation
1 The damage must be reasonably foreseeable.	An objective test.
2 There must be a relationship of proximity between the parties.	Close in terms of time, space and relationship.
3 It must be fair, just and reasonable to impose a duty of care.	A policy test restricting the imposition of a duty, particularly where imposing a duty might place an unreasonable burden on the operations or budgets of the public services or might open the floodgates to an avalanche of claims.

Exam tip

It is vital to use the facts of the case to illustrate the point of law for all areas of negligence, for example, in relation to *Jolley v Sutton* (2002), 'it is reasonably foreseeable that a child will be injured by a boat left abandoned in a park'.

Table 3.3.3 Key cases for duty of care

Case	Facts	Point of law
Donoghue v Stevenson (1932)	A snail was found in ginger beer.	Neighbour principle.
Caparo v Dickman (1990)	Shares were misvalued.	Updated neighbour principle with three-part test, which includes a narrowing of the test.
Kent v Griffiths (2000)	An ambulance was late in attending a patient.	Damage was reasonably foreseeable.
Jolley v Sutton LBC (2000)	C, a child, was injured by a boat left abandoned in a park.	'It is reasonably foreseeable that a child will be injured by a boat left abandoned in a park.'
Bourhill v Young (1943)	The 'nosy fishwife' case: she chose to view the scene of an accident.	No proximity.
McLoughlin v O'Brian (1983)	C saw the aftermath of a serious accident involving her family and suffered psychiatric loss as a consequence.	There was proximity in this case, as C had no choice.
Hill v Chief Constable of West Yorkshire (1988)	C sued the police for failing to catch the serial killer who murdered her daughter.	It was not fair, just and reasonable for the police to owe a duty in the detection of crime. This was followed in *Michael v Chief Constable of South Wales* (2015).

Breach of the duty of care

An objective test comes from *Blyth v Birmingham Water Works* (1856): 'omitting to do something a reasonable man would do, or doing something a reasonable man would not do'.

Stretch and challenge

For an interesting read on the origin of the 'reasonable man' test, look up *Vaughan v Menlove* (1837).

Although this is an objective test, an appropriate degree of knowledge may be added to the reasonable person. So, a professional will be judged not by the standard of a reasonable person, but by the standard of a reasonable person of that profession. Key cases in this area include *Bolam v Frien Hospital Management Committee* (1957) (although this has now changed for advice given by healthcare professionals) and *Montgomery v Lanarkshire* (2015).

However, this does not apply to trainees in any skill, therefore the learner driver will be judged by the standard of a reasonable driver – see *Nettleship v Weston* (1971).

A child will be judged by the standard of a reasonable child – see *Mullin v Richards* (1998).

Stretch and challenge

For an interesting case about omissions in negligence see *Chief Constable of Essex v Transport Arendonk* (2020).

In determining whether the defendant acted reasonably, the court will consider four further factors, outlined in Table 3.3.4.

Table 3.3.4 Factors to ascertain whether the defendant acted reasonably

Factor	Explanation	Key case
Degree of risk involved	The greater the risk, the more precautions a defendant will have to take in order for their conduct to be judged as acting at the standard of a reasonable person.	*Bolton v Stone* (1951)
Cost of precautions	The court will not expect the cost of precautions to outweigh the risk involved. Therefore, a defendant does not have to take excessive measures to guard against minor risk. A reasonable person would take reasonable precautions given the circumstances.	*Latimer v AEC* (1952)
Potential seriousness of injury	The more serious the potential injury, the greater the level of care required in order to be judged as acting at the standard of a reasonable person.	*Paris v Stepney Borough Council* (1951)
Importance of the activity	Some risk may be acceptable if the risk undertaken is socially important.	*Watt v Hertfordshire County Council* (1954)

Typical mistake

Your exam answer will not score highly if you fail to make the link between the factors and the impact they have on the standard of the reasonable person.

Stretch and challenge

What risk is reasonably foreseeable, even obvious, of children being given metal golf putters? Read *Bosworth Water Trust v SRR & AB & JBW* (2018).

Table 3.3.5 Key cases for breach of the duty of care

Case	Facts	Point of law
Bolam v Frien Hospital Management Committee (1957)	C was undergoing ECT as treatment for his mental illness. The doctor did not give any relaxant drugs and C suffered a serious fracture.	A professional will be judged not by the standard of a reasonable person, but by the standard of a reasonable person of that profession.
Mullin v Richards (1998)	Two 15-year-old schoolgirls were fighting with plastic rulers. A ruler snapped and a splinter went into one girl's eye, causing blindness.	A child will be judged by the standard of a reasonable child.
Nettleship v Weston (1971)	D was a learner driver who injured C, her instructor.	Trainees will be judged by the standard of the competent professional.
Bolton v Stone (1951)	Should a cricket club have taken precautions to prevent the injury of a person outside the cricket ground from being hit by a cricket ball?	The greater the risk, the more precautions a defendant will have to take in order for their conduct to be judged as acting at the standard of a reasonable person.
Latimer v AEC (1952)	C worked at D's factory and slipped on the factory floor. The factory had become flooded. D had put up warning signs, mopped up and placed sawdust in the most used places to make it as safe as possible.	The court will not expect the cost of precautions to outweigh the risk involved.
Paris v Stepney Borough Council (1951)	C only had one eye. At work, a splinter of metal went into his sighted eye, causing him to become completely blind. The employer did not provide safety goggles.	The more serious the potential injury, the greater the level of care required in order to be judged as acting at the standard of a reasonable person.
Watt v Hertfordshire County Council (1954)	C was injured by equipment not secured due to the rush to save a life.	Some risk may be acceptable if the risk undertaken is socially important.

Damage

The resulting damage must be:

- caused by the breach – would not have happened 'but for' the breach – see *Barnett v Chelsea Hospital* (1969)
- not too remote from the breach – of a foreseeable type – see *The Wagon Mound* (1961).

However, the precise chain of events need not be foreseeable (see *Hughes v Lord Advocate* (1962)), nor is it necessary for the extent of the damage to be foreseeable; this is the thin skull test being used in negligence (see *Smith v Leech Brain* (1962)).

Evaluation point

Make the link with judicial precedent in Chapter 3.4 and policy development in Chapter 4.8.

Stretch and challenge

What is the impact of *novus actus interveniens* in *Clay v TUI* (2018)?

Read and makes notes on the causation issue in *Darnley v Croydon Health Services* (2018).

Add these to the key cases table.

Table 3.3.6 Key cases on damage

Case	Facts	Point of law
Barnett v Chelsea Hospital (1969)	A doctor failed to examine a man who had been poisoned. If he had done so, he still could not have saved his life.	Damage must have been caused by the breach.
The Wagon Mound (1961)	A ship leaked oil into Sydney Harbour which led to a fire, destroying a wharf and boats.	Damage must be of a foreseeable type.
Hughes v Lord Advocate (1962)	Two boys went to explore a manhole. An unforeseeable explosion occurred, causing them serious injury.	The precise chain of events leading to the damage need not be foreseeable.
Smith v Leech Brain (1962)	As a result of D's negligence, C incurred a burn to his lip. The lip contained pre-cancerous cells which were triggered by the injury sustained. He died three years later from cancer.	It is not necessary for the extent of the damage to be foreseeable.

Now test yourself TESTED

1. How and why did *Caparo v Dickman* (1990) change the neighbour principle?
2. What is the difference between *Bourhill v Young* (1943) and *McLoughlin v O'Brian* (1983)?
3. What impact would a highly dangerous situation have on the standard of a reasonable person?
4. How is factual causation tested?
5. What does 'remoteness of damage' mean?

Exam tip

Consider using the IDEA method:

- **I**dentify the point of law.
- **D**escribe the point of law.
- Give a case **e**xample.
- **A**pply the point/case to the facts of the scenario.

Exam summary

In the exam, you MAY be asked:

- multiple-choice questions about individual elements of negligence
- to apply the law relating to negligence to a given scenario, for example, 'If it could be proved that Jeffry owed a duty of care to George, and that Jeffry had breached that duty, discuss whether the damage to George's vintage motorcycle was too remote.'
- to write an analysis of negligence, possibly linking to a topic in Chapter 1.1, such as the relationship between justice and policy decisions.

Liability for economic loss and psychiatric injury

REVISED

Pure economic loss caused by negligent acts and negligent misstatements

Generally, no duty of care is owed to avoid causing another to suffer a loss which is purely economic, where the financial loss is not related to a personal injury or damage to property – see *Spartan Steel and Alloys Ltd v Martin* (1972).

However, where the economic loss is caused by a negligent misstatement (which includes advice) rather than a negligent act, liability may be imposed – see *Hedley Byrne and Co. Ltd v Heller and Partners Ltd* (1963).

According to *Hedley Byrne*, a defendant owes a duty of care to a claimant in the making of a statement (usually in the giving of advice), only if there is a 'special relationship' between them. This means:

- the defendant who made the statement possesses some special skill relating to the statement, and
- knows that it is highly likely that the claimant will rely on the statement, and
- the claimant does rely on it, thereby incurring financial loss, and
- it was reasonable for the claimant to so rely upon it.

Exam tip

You need to apply the law to given scenarios for this part of the course. See Chapter 3.2 for some background information about these two situations.

Stretch and challenge

Would it be reasonable to rely on advice given by a friend at a party?

Typical mistake

Do not forget to deal with the other two elements of negligence in pure economic loss and psychiatric injury, such as breach and damage.

Key cases here include *Chaudhry v Prabhakar* (1989), *Caparo v Dickman* (1990) and *JEB Fasteners v Bloom* (1983).

Table 3.3.7 Key cases on pure economic loss

Case	Facts	Point of law
Spartan Steel and Alloys Ltd v Martin (1972)	While digging a trench, D negligently cut off the electricity supply to C's steelworks. The value and profits of the 'melt' ruined by the power cut was allowed, but not on four further melts.	Recovery of damages for pure economic loss was not permitted as a 'matter of policy so as to limit the liability of the defendant' – Lord Denning.
Hedley Byrne and Co. Ltd v Heller and Partners Ltd (1963)	Hedley Byrne relied on a credit reference from Heller about a client and suffered financial loss when the client went into liquidation.	A negligent misstatement may give rise to an action for damages for economic loss.
Chaudhry v Prabhakar (1989)	D helped C purchase a car, not realising it was unroadworthy. C relied on his advice and therefore suffered economic loss.	As C believed D was knowledgeable about cars, there was reliance.
Caparo v Dickman (1990)	Shares were mis-valued.	D had no knowledge of C's existence, let alone reliance.
JEB Fasteners v Bloom (1983)	C acquired a company to make use of the directors.	C knew the financial state of the company and so could not claim reliance.

Psychiatric injury sustained by primary and secondary victims

Psychiatric injury is a long-term, diagnosed mental injury which is greater than shock or grief. The claimant must be suffering from a diagnosed psychiatric injury – see *Behrens and Ors v Bertram Mills Circus Ltd* (1957).

Grief, sorrow, fear, panic and terror do not amount to psychiatric injury – see *Hinz v Berry* (1970) and *Hicks v Chief Constable of South Yorkshire* (1992).

The court will adopt differing approaches to whether a duty is owed, depending on whether the claimant is a:

- primary victim – someone in the zone of physical danger, or
- secondary victim – someone not within the physical zone of danger but a witness of horrific events.

Whether the claimant is in the zone of physical danger and therefore a primary victim, is an objective test.

The claimant need only establish that physical harm was foreseeable. There is no requirement that psychiatric injury was foreseeable, provided personal injury was foreseeable – see *Page v Smith* (1996) and *McFarlane v E. E. Caledonia* (1994).

In order to establish a duty, secondary victims must fulfil the four Alcock tests. The victim must:

- have a close tie of love and affection with a primary victim – this will be presumed between parent and child and between spouses, but must be proved in other relationships
- witness the event with their own unaided senses – therefore television and radio broadcasts are not sufficient
- be proximate to the event itself or its immediate aftermath – from Lord Wilberforce in *McLoughlin v O'Brian* (1983) (see page 111): 'sight or hearing of the event or of its immediate aftermath'
- receive the psychiatric injury as the result of a shocking event – Lord Ackner in *Alcock v Chief Constable of South Yorkshire* (1992) called this 'the sudden appreciation by sight or sound of a horrifying event, which violently agitates the mind'; this therefore excludes psychiatric injury developed over time due to providing care for a primary victim.

In addition, following *Young v Downey* (2020), it is necessary for the secondary victim to appreciate that their loved one has, or might have been, injured in the incident witnessed.

Other than *Alcock v Chief Constable of South Yorkshire* (1992), another key case in this area is *Sion v Hampstead Health Authority* (1994).

Stretch and challenge

Brian Harrison, Robert Alcock, Mr and Mrs Copoc, and Alexandra Penk all made claims following the Hillsborough football stadium disaster. Which relationships fulfilled these criteria?

Rescuers are those who come to the aid of primary victims but are themselves neither primary nor secondary victims. They are not exceptions to the Alcock tests and so cannot claim – see *White v Chief Constable of South Yorkshire* (1998).

Psychiatric injury: a long-term, diagnosed mental injury which is greater than shock or grief.

Primary victim: someone in the zone of physical danger.

Secondary victim: someone not within the zone of physical danger but who witnesses horrific events.

Revision activity

Lots of these cases relate to very well-known disasters and tragedies. You can read about them on news websites, as well as looking at the specifics of the cases.

Table 3.3.8 Key cases on psychiatric injury

Case	Facts	Point of law
Behrens and Ors v Bertram Mills Circus Ltd (1957)	During a circus performance, a dog antagonised the leading elephant. Consequently, other elephants stampeded – other performers were injured and suffered shock.	Devlin J: 'I should like to award him a substantial sum ... but I am satisfied that I cannot do so except to the extremely limited extent that the shock resulted in physical or mental harm.'
Hinz v Berry (1970)	A woman suffered depression after witnessing an accident that killed her husband and injured her children.	Lord Denning MR: 'In English law no damages are awarded for grief or sorrow caused by a person's death ... Damages are, however, recoverable ... for any recognisable psychiatric illness caused by the breach of duty by the defendant.'
Hicks v Chief Constable of South Yorkshire (1992)	Parents of Hillsborough football stadium disaster victims sought damages for the fear they suffered prior to death.	Lord Bridge: 'It is perfectly clear law that fear by itself, of whatever degree, is a normal human emotion for which no damages can be awarded.'
Page v Smith (1996)	A car accident (caused by D's negligence) triggered a recurrence of C's ME. The illness was chronic and permanent, so that he was unable to work.	Provided some kind of personal injury was foreseeable, it did not matter whether the injury was physical or psychiatric.
McFarlane v E. E. Caledonia (1994)	D was on board a rescue vessel at the time of an oil rig disaster.	He was not in the zone of physical danger despite his belief and therefore was not a primary victim.
Alcock v Chief Constable of South Yorkshire (1992)	Friends and family claimed for shock they suffered as a consequence of the Hillsborough football stadium disaster.	This case set the tests for secondary victims.
Sion v Hampstead Health Authority (1994)	After being involved in an accident, C's son was negligently treated in hospital and died after a fortnight.	Death was not sudden, but expected, therefore C could not claim.
White v Chief Constable of South Yorkshire (1998)	Police officers who were on duty during the Hillsborough disaster claimed as rescuers; they were promoted to primary victims as opposed to secondary victims.	A decision based on policy; it would not be just to allow the police officers to recover compensation where relatives had been denied it. They are not promoted to primaries.

Now test yourself

TESTED

6 Why is there a restriction placed on the imposition of duty in cases involving pure economic loss?
7 Why is *Caparo v Dickman* (1990) relevant here?
8 Why did the claim in *JEB Fasteners v Bloom* (1983) fail?
9 Which standard of care is relevant if a duty is found to exist?
10 Which of the Alcock tests did the *Copocs* fail on?
11 Had *Alcock* and *Harrison* passed the 'close ties' test, would they have passed the fourth test?
12 What was the position in respect of rescuers prior to the decision in *White v Chief Constable of South Yorkshire* (1998)?

Evaluation point

To help you analyse the special duties shown here, read the Law Commission *Consultation Paper No. 137: Liability For Psychiatric Illness.*

Exam summary

In the exam, you MAY be asked:

- multiple-choice questions about individual elements of these special duties
- to apply the law relating to these special duties to a given scenario; this is likely to be a long and complex scenario, so practising spotting the relevant issues is vital
- to write an analysis of some or a part of one of these special duties, possibly linking to a topic in Chapter 1.1.

3.4 Occupiers' liability

Occupiers' liability refers to the duty owed by occupiers to those who come onto their land. There is no requirement for the occupier to also be the owner or for them to physically occupy the land.

The test applied is one of 'occupational control' and there may be more than one occupier of the same premises. A key case in this area is *Wheat v E. Lacon and Co. Ltd* (1966).

Exam tip

You will need to apply the law to given scenarios for occupiers' liability.

Liability in respect of visitors: Occupiers' Liability Act 1957

REVISED

Under s 1(3)(a), the premises occupied applies not only to land and buildings but also extends to fixed and movable structures, including any vessel, vehicle or aircraft.

The duty of care

In s 2(2), the Act imposes a common duty of care on occupiers to lawful visitors:

> 'The common duty of care is to take such care as in all the circumstances of the case is reasonable to see that the visitor will be reasonably safe in using the premises for the purposes for which he is invited or permitted by the occupier to be there.'

Visitors: in law, adult visitors are those who have been invited or licensed to enter or who have a statutory right to enter or have contractual permission.

The claimable damage under the Occupiers' Liability Act 1957 includes death, personal injury and damage to property.

Lawful visitors

Stretch and challenge

Research the relevant (and quite amusing) quote from Scrutton LJ in *The Calgarth* (1927).

This includes:

- invitees – s 1(2): those who have been invited to come onto the land and therefore have express permission to be there; the invitation must not be exceeded
- licensees – s 1(2): those who have express or implied permission to be there; this includes where a licence would be implied at common law (see below)
- those who enter pursuant to a contract – s 5(1), for example, paying visitors to see a film at a cinema
- those entering in exercising a statutory right – s 2(6), for example, a person entering to read the gas or electricity meters
- implied licence at common law, where there is repeated trespass and no action taken by the occupier to prevent it; this requires an awareness of the trespass and the danger – see *Lowery v Walker* (1911); the courts are more likely to imply a licence if there is something on the land which is particularly attractive and acts as an allurement to draw people onto the land – see *Taylor v Glasgow City Council* (1922).

Breach of the duty of care

The standard of care is of the 'reasonable occupier' (a failure to reach the given standard will amount to a breach). This is neatly illustrated by the facts of *White Lion Hotel v James* (2021).

Stretch and challenge

Look up *White Lion Hotel v James* (2021) and consider why it is different to *Geary v JD Weatherspoon* (2011).

However, there are two situations where the standard may vary, outlined in Table 3.4.1.

Table 3.4.1 Variations on the standard of care

Situation	Explanation	Key case
Section 2(3)(a) – an occupier must be prepared for children to be less careful than adults.	The court will take into account the age of the child and level of understanding a child of that age may be expected to have.	*Jolley v Sutton* (2000)
Section 2(3)(b) – an occupier may expect that a person in the exercise of his calling will appreciate and guard against any special risks ordinarily incident to it.	This applies where an occupier employs an expert to come onto the premises to undertake work. The expert is expected to know and protect themselves against any dangers that arise from the premises in relation to the calling of the expert. For example, if an occupier calls on a roofing specialist to repair a damaged roof, that roofer would be expected to know the dangers inherent in the work they are engaged to do.	*Roles v Nathan* (1963)

Warnings and warning signs

It may be possible for an occupier to discharge their duty (reach the standard of a reasonable occupier) by giving a warning of the danger.

However, s 2(4)(a) provides that a warning will not be treated as absolving the occupier of liability unless in all the circumstances it was enough to enable the visitor to be reasonably safe. The warning must cover the danger, but there is no duty to warn against obvious risks – see *Darby v National Trust* (2001).

Dangers arising from actions undertaken by independent contractors

Under s 2(4)(b), an occupier is not liable for dangers created by an independent contractor if the occupier:

- acted reasonably in all the circumstances in entrusting the work to the independent contractor, and
- took reasonable steps to satisfy themselves that the work carried out was properly done and the contractor was competent.

A key case here is *Bottomley v Todmorden Cricket Club* (2003).

Defences

There are a few defences applicable to the Occupiers' Liability Act 1957:

- *Volenti non fit injuria* – s 2(5): the common duty of care does not impose an obligation on occupiers in respect of risks willingly accepted by the visitor.
- Contributory negligence – damages may be reduced under the Law Reform (Contributory Negligence) Act 1945 where the visitor fails to take reasonable care for their own safety. See pages 130 for more detail on these defences.
- Exclusion of liability – s 2(1): allows an occupier to extend, restrict, exclude or modify their duty to visitors, in so far as they are free to do so.

Table 3.4.2 Key cases for Occupiers' Liability Act 1957

Case	Facts	Point of law
Wheat v E. Lacon and Co. Ltd (1966)	C's husband died in a fall while staying in a public house.	Both the brewery and the managers owed a duty.
Lowery v Walker (1911)	C was injured by a dangerous horse when taking a commonly used shortcut.	Licence was implied through repeated trespass, which D was aware of.
Taylor v Glasgow City Council (1922)	A child was poisoned by berries in a public park.	The council was liable: it knew children would be there and it knew the berries were poisonous.
Jolley v Sutton (2000)	Boys were injured while attempting to repair an abandoned boat in a park.	The council had failed to move the boat which was in a park and it knew would be attractive to children.
Roles v Nathan (1963)	Chimney sweeps died of carbon dioxide poisoning while unblocking D's chimney.	D was not liable, as Cs were experts.
Darby v National Trust (2001)	C's husband drowned in a pond commonly used for paddling and swimming. D had taken no steps to prevent this.	As the risk was obvious, D did not need to give warnings.
Bottomley v Todmorden Cricket Club (2003)	C was injured at a firework display held on D's land but run by a contractor.	D was still liable as they had not checked the contractor's insurance and therefore had not taken reasonable steps.
White Lion Hotel v James (2021) EWCA Civ 31	C fell out of a hotel window after sitting on the ledge. The window fastenings were broken.	A visitor's freely chosen risk does not necessarily negate an occupier's liability. So the D was still liable.

Liability in respect of trespassers: Occupiers' Liability Act 1984

REVISED 

Stretch and challenge

The origins of this Act can be found in *British Railways Board v Herrington* (1972), which overruled *Addie v Dumbreck* (1929). Can you make the link with the information on judicial precedent on page 30?

This Act imposes liability on occupiers with regard to persons other than 'visitors'. This includes trespassers (and burglars) and those who exceed their permission – see *Revill v Newbery* (1996).

Trespassers: persons on the occupier's land who have no permission or authority to be there.

Section 1(8) states that death and personal injury are the only protected forms of damage; therefore, occupiers have no duty in relation to the property of trespassers.

The duty of care

Section 1(3) states that an occupier owes a duty of care to a non-visitor if:

a) the occupier is aware of a danger or has reasonable grounds to believe that it exists, and
b) the occupier knows or has reasonable grounds to believe the other is in the vicinity of the danger or may come into the vicinity of the danger, and
c) the risk is one in which, in all the circumstances of the case, the occupier may reasonably be expected to offer the other some protection.

A key case here is *Donoghue v Folkestone Properties Ltd* (2003).

Breach of the duty of care

The standard of care is objective, so if not met it will amount to a breach.

Section 1(4) states that the duty is to take such care as is reasonable in all the circumstances of the case to see that the other does not suffer injury on the premises by reason of the danger concerned – see *Ratcliff v McConnell* (1997).

This also means that it must be the premises themselves that are dangerous, not the activity the claimant choses to engage in – see *Keown v Coventry Healthcare NHS Trust* (2006).

Revision activity

Remind yourself: what is an objective standard?

Warnings and warning signs

Under s 1(5), the duty may be discharged (reach the standard of a reasonable occupier) by giving a warning or discouraging others from taking the risk – see *Tomlinson v Congleton* (2003).

Stretch and challenge

Research *Westwood v Post Office* (1973) and apply s 1(5) to them.

Defences

There are some defences applicable to the Occupiers' Liability Act 1984:

- *Volenti non fit injuria* – s 1(6): the common duty of care does not impose an obligation on occupiers in respect of risks willingly accepted.
- Contributory negligence – damages may be reduced under the Law Reform (Contributory Negligence) Act 1945 where the visitor fails to take reasonable care for their own safety. See pages 130 for more detail on these defences.

Exclusion of liability is not expressly forbidden by the Act so it may be possible.

Stretch and challenge

Apply the defence of *volenti* to the facts of *Ratcliff v McConnell* (1998).

Table 3.4.3 Key cases for Occupiers' Liability Act 1984

Case	Facts	Point of law
Revill v Newbery (1996)	C was a burglar, shot by D.	D was liable, but contributory negligence was taken into consideration and reduced the damages.
Donoghue v Folkestone Properties Ltd (2003)	C was seriously injured by diving into Folkstone harbour on Boxing Day.	It would be reasonable to guard against that in the summer but not at that time of year, so D was not liable.
Ratcliff v McConnell (1997)	C was seriously injured by diving into a college pool late at night.	Locks and warnings were sufficient, so D was not liable.
Keown v Coventry Healthcare NHS Trust (2006)	C, a child, fell from a fire escape he had been climbing.	The premises were not dangerous; therefore D was not liable.
Tomlinson v Congleton (2003)	C was seriously injured by diving into a lake.	The state of the premises was not inherently dangerous; what the claimant chose to do in them was. D was not liable.

Typical mistake

Do not carelessly lose marks by forgetting to deal with breach, damage and defences. There will be more to the questions than just the duty owed by the occupier.

Now test yourself

TESTED

1 Why are there different statutory provisions for occupiers' liability?
2 Show all the different ways in which children are taken into account by these statutory provisions.
3 How is the claimable damage different between these statutory provisions?
4 Why was Todmorden Cricket Club liable, even though the injuries were caused by an independent contractor?
5 When might a trespasser be treated as a visitor for the purpose of these statutory provisions?

Exam tip

Look out for scenarios where children trespass regularly and the occupier knows about them. Have they become visitors?

Revision activity

There is no obligation in relation to the warning to enable the visitor to be reasonably safe. How does this contrast with the provision under the 1957 Act?

Exam summary

In the exam, you MAY be asked:

- multiple-choice questions about individual elements of the statutory provisions for occupiers' liability
- to apply the law relating to these statutory provisions to a given scenario; this is likely to be a long and complex scenario combining both types, so practice spotting the relevant issues is vital
- to write an analysis of some or a part of one of these statutory provisions, possibly linking to a topic in Chapter 1.1.

3.5 Nuisance and the escape of dangerous things

Private nuisance

REVISED

Private nuisance is concerned with protecting the rights of an occupier against 'unreasonable interference with the enjoyment or use of his land'. This often involves disputes between neighbours.

Evaluation point

Does this mean protecting the value of the property? Read *Network Rail v Williams* (2018).

Exam tip

For this chapter, you need to apply the law to given scenarios in Paper 2. This topic also links well with 'balancing conflicting interests', which is assessed in Paper 3.

The courts attempt to balance the competing rights of the landowner to use their land as they choose and the rights of the neighbour not to have their use or enjoyment of land interfered with.

In order to bring a claim in private nuisance, a claimant must have an interest in the land in which they claim their enjoyment or use of has been unreasonably interfered with. This means a legal interest, but not necessarily ownership. Key cases here include *Malone v Laskey* (1907) and *Hunter v Canary Wharf* (1997).

However, the defendant – the creator of the nuisance – does not need to own or occupy the land that the nuisance is emitting from; they just need to have used the land. A key case here is *Jones Ltd v Portsmouth City Council* (2002).

'Interference' can be:

- flooding – *Sedleigh-Denfield v O'Callaghan* (1940)
- smells – *Wheeler v JJ Saunders* (1996)
- encroachment – *Lemmon v Webb* (1894)
- noise – *Kennaway v Thompson* (1981)
- cricket balls – *Miller v Jackson* (1977)
- a brothel – *Thompson-Schwab v Costaki* (1956)
- physical damage – *St Helen's Smelting Co. v Tipping* (1865).

Stretch and challenge

Research these cases online.

Do you think the use of the land in *Miller v Jackson* (1977) was unreasonable?

Unlawful interference

This means an unreasonable use of land by the defendant which leads to an unreasonable interference with the claimant's use or enjoyment of their own land – see *London Borough of Southwark v Mills* (1999).

In determining whether or not the use of the land and the interference were reasonable or not, the courts will consider:

- nature of the locality/neighbourhood
- duration
- sensitivity
- malice.

Locality/neighbourhood

The reasonableness of the use of land will depend on the nature of the locality.

Thesiger LJ stated in *Sturges v Bridgman* (1879): 'What would be a nuisance in Belgrave Square would not necessarily be so in Bermondsey.' This means that a higher level of disturbance is considered reasonable in an industrial area than would be regarded as reasonable in a residential area – see *Hirose Electrical v Peak Ingredients* (2011).

Planning permission may change the nature of the locality but cannot give permission for a nuisance – see *Coventry v Lawrence* (2012).

Where the nuisance causes physical damage, the nature of the locality is irrelevant – see *St Helen's Smelting Co. v Tipping* (1865).

Revision activity

Find and read Lord Justice Jackson's four-point summary in *Coventry v Lawrence* (2012).

Duration

Most nuisances consist of a continuing interference, so the claimant seeks an injunction to prevent the reoccurrences.

The longer a nuisance lasts, the greater the interference and the more likelihood of it being held to be an unlawful interference. Nevertheless, a temporary activity may still constitute a nuisance. A key case here is *De Keyser's Royal Hotel v Spicer Bros* (1914).

Sensitivity

If the claimant is abnormally sensitive or their use of land is particularly sensitive, the defendant will not be liable – unless the activity would amount to a nuisance to a reasonable person using the land in a normal manner.

Key cases here include *Robinson v Kilvert* (1889) and *McKinnon Industries v Walker* (1951).

Typical mistake

Do not assume that the public benefit of the thing creating the nuisance is a defence; it is not – see *Miller v Jackson* (1977). 'Coming to the nuisance', i.e. the thing creating the nuisance was there before the claimant, is not a defence either.

Malice

If the defendant's actions are malicious, they are more likely to be held unreasonable.

Key cases here include *Christie v Davey* (1893) and *Hollywood Silver Fox Farm v Emmett* (1936).

Foreseeability

The foreseeability of the type of damage is important in claims for nuisance. It applies as it does for claims based in negligence. A key case here is *Cambridge Water v Eastern Counties Leather plc* (1994).

The *Wagon Mound No. 1* case applies to determine remoteness of damage.

In *Hunter v Canary Wharf* (1997), the judges, in holding that a claimant must have an interest in the land affected by the nuisance, appear to have ruled out the possibility of a claim for purely personal injury arising from nuisance.

Table 3.5.1 Key cases on private nuisance

Case	Facts	Relevant area of nuisance	*Ratio decidendi*
Malone v Laskey (1907)	C was injured when the cistern fell on her in the lavatory.	Legal interest in land	She was unsuccessful in her claim as she did not have a proprietary interest in the house.
Hunter v Canary Wharf (1997)	Cs lived in the Isle of Dogs and complained that the erection of Canary Wharf Tower interfered with their television reception.	Legal interest in land	Many Cs had no proprietary interest. Some were children living with parents, relations, lodgers or spouses of the tenant or owner of the property. The claim failed.
Jones Ltd v Portsmouth City Council (2002)	The roots of trees encroached on C's property and led to subsidence of the property.	Legal interest in land	Portsmouth City Council was liable as it had lawful exercise of control over the trees, even though it did not own the land.
London Borough of Southwark v Mills (1999)	Complaints related to the lack of soundproofing, meaning they could hear the day-to-day activities of their neighbours.	Must be unreasonable	There was no nuisance. Nuisance is based on the concept of a reasonable user.
Hirose Electrical v Peak Ingredients (2011)	D manufactured ingredients for curries in an industrial estate, close to C's business manufacturing parts for mobile phones. C complained about the smells from D's premises.	Neighbourhood	Significance to the location of the premises and the character of the industrial estate. D's food additive manufacturing was permitted.
Coventry v Lawrence (2012)	Motor sports expansion was becoming noisier.	Planning permission changing the neighbourhood	If the character of a locality is changed as a consequence of planning permission, then: (a) nuisance must be decided against the background of its changed character (b) otherwise offensive activities in that locality cease to constitute a nuisance.
St Helen's Smelting Co. v Tipping (1865)	Damage was caused by smelting works to crops, trees and foliage.	Physical damage	Where there is physical damage to property, the locality principle has no relevance.
De Keyser's Royal Hotel v Spicer Bros (1914)	Building work at night.	Duration/timing	Interference was considered unreasonable, since it interfered with C's sleep.
Robinson v Kilvert (1889)	D's business of making paper boxes required a warm, dry atmosphere. He let out the ground floor of the premises to C, who used it to store brown paper. The heat generated from D's work damaged the brown paper belonging to C.	Sensitivity	D was not liable.

Case	Facts	Relevant area of nuisance	*Ratio decidendi*
McKinnon Industries v Walker (1951)	Noxious fumes and smuts had deposited over C's shrubs, trees, hedges and flowers, causing them to die.	Sensitivity	Although the flowers were sensitive, the others were not, so there was still unlawful interference.
Hollywood Silver Fox Farm v Emmett (1936)	D objected to a fox farm. He fired a gun on his own land with the intention to scare the foxes and impede breeding.	Malice	D was liable despite the abnormal sensitivity of the foxes, because he was motivated by malice.
Cambridge Water v Eastern Counties Leather plc (1994)	Solvents seeped through the floor of the building into the soil below. They made their way to the water company borehole.	Foreseeable type of damage	It was not reasonably foreseeable that the spillages would result in the closing of the borehole.

Now test yourself

TESTED

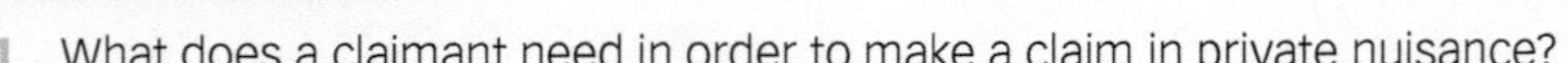

1 What does a claimant need in order to make a claim in private nuisance?
2 What is interference?
3 What can make interference unreasonable?

Exam summary

In the exam, you MAY be asked:

- multiple-choice questions about individual elements of private nuisance
- to apply the law to a given scenario, which is likely to be a long and complex scenario, so practice spotting the difference is vital
- to write an analysis of some or a part of this law, possibly linking to a topic in Chapter 1.1.

Rylands v Fletcher

REVISED

Although named after a case, this is now a tort in its own right. It is a form of strict liability, because the defendant may be liable without being negligent.

Consequently, it is controversial and therefore a restrictive approach has been taken to imposing liability under *Rylands v Fletcher*.

Rylands v Fletcher: where the escape of non-naturally stored material onto adjoining property damages or destroys that property.

Case details: *Rylands v Fletcher* (1868)

The defendant constructed a reservoir on his land, above a disused mine. Water from the reservoir filtered through to the disused mine shafts and then spread to a neighbouring working mine owned by the claimant, causing extensive damage.

Lord Cranworth said:

> 'If a person brings, or accumulates, on his land anything which, if it should escape, may cause damage to his neighbour, he does so at his peril. If it does escape, and cause damage, he is responsible, however careful he may have been, and whatever precautions he may have taken to prevent the damage.'

Therefore, the requirements for an action in *Rylands v Fletcher* are:

- accumulation on the defendant's land
- a thing likely to do mischief if it escapes

- escape
- non-natural use of land
- the damage must not be too remote.

Table 3.5.2 Elements of the requirements for an action in *Rylands v Fletcher*

Element	Explanation
Accumulation	The defendant must bring a hazardous thing onto their land and keep it there – *Giles v Walker* (1890), *Ellison v Ministry of Defence* (1997). The thing must be accumulated for the defendant's own purposes – *Dunne v North West Gas Board* (1964). The thing that escapes need not be the thing accumulated – *Miles v Forest Rock Granite* (1918).
A thing likely to do mischief if it escapes	The thing need not be inherently hazardous. It need only be a thing likely to cause damage if it escapes, for example: + a flagpole – *Shiffman v The Grand Priory of St John* (1936) + branches from yew trees – *Crowhurst v Amersham Burial Board* (1879) + a fairground ride – *Hale v Jennings Bros* (1938) + electricity – *Hillier v Air Ministry* (1962). However, in *TransCo. v Stockport* (2004), Lord Hoffmann referred to the fact that claims for personal injury had been admitted in the past but stated: 'The point is now settled by [Cambridge Water] which decided that *Rylands v Fletcher* is a special form of nuisance and *Hunter v Canary Wharf* ... which decided that nuisance is a tort against land. It must, I think, follow that damages for personal injuries are not recoverable under the rule.'
Escape	There must be an escape from the defendant's land. An injury inflicted by the accumulation of a hazardous substance on the land itself will not invoke liability. A key case on escape *is Read v Lyons* (1947). In *British Celanese v AH Hunt Ltd* (1969), the judge said the escape should be 'from a set of circumstances over which the defendant has control to a set of circumstances where he does not'.
Non-natural use of land	This means the use must be 'extraordinary and unusual'. A use may be extraordinary and unusual at one time or in one place, but not so at another time or in another place. A key case for this is *TransCo. v Stockport MBC* (2004).
Remoteness of damage	As in nuisance, liability is subject to the rules on remoteness of damage – see *Cambridge Water v Eastern Counties Leather* (1994) above.

There is no liability for pure economic loss under *Rylands v Fletcher*. A key case here is *Weller v Foot and Mouth Disease Research Institute* (1966).

Table 3.5.3 Key cases for *Rylands v Fletcher*

Case	Facts	Relevant area of *Rylands v Fletcher*	*Ratio decidendi* (if not stated above)
Giles v Walker (1890)	Thistles from D's land blew into neighbouring land and damaged C's crops.	Accumulation	D had not brought the thistles onto his land and there can be no liability for a thing which naturally accumulates on land.
Ellison v Ministry of Defence (1997)	Bulk fuel installations at an airfield caused rainwater to run off and flood neighbouring land.	Accumulation	The rainwater accumulated naturally and was not kept there artificially.

Case	Facts	Relevant area of *Rylands v Fletcher*	*Ratio decidendi* (if not stated above)
Dunne v North West Gas Board (1964)	Gas escaped from a gas main caused by a burst water main. It travelled along a sewer and was ignited, causing explosions which resulted in injuries.	Accumulation	The Gas Board had not accumulated gas for its own purposes.
Miles v Forest Rock Granite (1918)	D was blasting rocks using explosives. Some rocks flew onto the highway, injuring C.	Accumulation	The explosives were accumulated and caused the rocks to escape.
Shiffman v The Grand Priory of St John (1936)	D's flagpole fell and hit C.	Mischief	This amounted to an escape.
Read v Lyons (1947)	C worked in D's factory making explosives for the Ministry of Supply. An explosion killed a man and injured C. There was no evidence that negligence had caused the explosion.	Escape	There was no escape.
TransCo. v Stockport MBC (2004)	Water supply pipes leaked and caused damage to gas supply pipes.	Non-natural	Although strictly speaking they are not natural, in this day and age they are not extraordinary and unusual either, so D was not liable.
Weller v Foot and Mouth Disease Research Institute (1966)	A virus escaped, affecting cattle and making them unsaleable.	Remoteness	No liability for pure economic loss.

Defences

There are some defences applicable to nuisance and *Rylands v Fletcher*, including the following (but see Chapter 3.7 for more detail):

- act of stranger
- wrongful act of a third party
- act of God
- statutory authority
- consent/benefit.

Exam tip

To prepare for exam questions in this area, use the IDEA method outlined in Chapter 3.3 on page 113.

Now test yourself TESTED 

4 Does the 'thing' need to be dangerous in *Rylands v Fletcher*?

5 What does 'escape' mean in *Rylands v Fletcher*?

Exam summary

In the exam, you MAY be asked:

- multiple-choice questions on the elements of *Rylands v Fletcher*
- questions requiring short to mid-length answers explaining the meaning of the elements in relation to one of the concepts, most likely 'fault-based liability'
- long-answer questions that require you to apply these elements to a scenario.

3.6 Vicarious liability

For the topic of vicarious liability, you will need to apply the law to given scenarios in Paper 2. Vicarious liability is usually assessed alongside negligence and not on its own.

Vicarious liability: a third person has legal responsibility for the unlawful actions of another.

Typical mistake

This area of law changes frequently – it is 'on the move', according to Lord Phillips in *Various Claimants v Catholic Child Welfare Society* (2012), often referred to as the *Christian Brothers* case. Do not take the law for granted: check on new developments, as they happen all the time.

Exam tip

For this topic, you will need to apply the law to given scenarios in Paper 2. Vicarious liability is usually assessed alongside negligence and not on its own.

Stretch and challenge

Two significant new cases are *WM Morrison Supermarkets plc v Various Claimants* (2020) and *Barclays Bank plc v Various Claimants* (2020). Read these cases and identify how the law has continued to develop.

Nature and purpose of vicarious liability

REVISED

Employers are vicariously liable for the torts of their employees that are committed during the course of employment. The reasons for this were reiterated by Lord Phillips (these are sometimes referred to as 'the five incidents'):

- The employer is more likely to have the means to compensate the victim than the employee and can be expected to have insured against that liability.
- The tort will have been committed as a result of activity being performed by the employee on behalf of the employer.
- The employee's activity is likely to be part of the business activity of the employer.
- The employer, by employing the employee to carry on the activity, will have created the risk of the tort committed by the employee.
- The employee will, to a greater or lesser degree, have been under the control of the employer.

Three questions must be asked in order to establish liability:

1. Was a tort committed? (For the purposes of this course it is likely to be negligence, but the same principles can also be used in criminal law.)
2. Was the tortfeasor an employee?
3. Was the employee acting in the course of employment when the tort was committed?

Testing employment status

REVISED 

The traditional test is known as the 'Salmond Test'.

Evaluation point

How and why has the Salmond Test developed?

An employer will only be liable for torts which the employee commits in the course of employment.

An employer will usually be liable for:

- wrongful acts which are actually authorised by the employer, and
- acts which are wrongful ways of doing something authorised by the employer, even if the acts themselves were expressly forbidden by the employer.

Where there is doubt about this, the courts use the 'close connection test'. This examines the closeness of the connection between the work the employee was employed to do and the tortious conduct:

1. What function or field of activities have been entrusted by the employer to the employee (what was the nature of the job)? This is to be viewed broadly.
2. Was there a sufficient connection between the position in which the employee was employed and the wrongful conduct, to make it right for the employer to be held liable?

In *Morrison Supermarkets v Various Claimants* (2020), the Supreme Court found that:

- An employee's conduct did not meet the 'close connection test' when it amounted to pursuing a personal vendetta.
- The employee's personal motive meant that he was not acting on his employer's business.

Where a defendant is held to be acting outside of the course of employment, they are described as being 'on a frolic of their own' – Parke, B in *Joel v Morison* (1834).

Revision activity

In light of the decision in *Morrison Supermarkets v Various Claimants* (2020), examine these older cases and decide whether the employees would now be held to be acting in the course of their employment or on a frolic of their own:

- *Limpus v London General Omnibus Co.* (1862)
- *Smith v Crossley Brothers* (1951)
- *Rose v Plenty* (1976)
- *Lister v Helsey Hall* (2001)
- *N v Chief Constable of Merseyside Police* (2006)
- *Mohamud v WM Morrison Supermarkets plc* (2016).

Other areas of vicarious liability

REVISED

Deduction of wages

If the tort is committed by an employee acting in the course of employment, the employer will be liable to pay compensation to the injured person.

By the Civil Liability (Contribution) Act 1978, the employer can recover any compensation paid out from the employee by, for example, deduction from wages.

Vicarious liability and fault

The principle of vicarious liability is clearly where no fault has to be proved by the claimant on the employer at the time of the commission of the tort.

If the person who commits the tort is employed and acting in the course of employment, the employer will be liable without further proof.

It could be said that the employer is at fault in two or more ways:

1. The employer has chosen an employee who is liable to, or who could, commit a tort at work.
2. The training for the job may be inadequate or inappropriate.
3. The employer should have supervised the employee more effectively.

However, on this last point, employers are likely to want to allow employees, especially more experienced ones, greater freedom to do their work, as otherwise an army of supervisors will have to be employed to closely monitor every employee for every minute of work.

Liability for independent contractors

Traditionally, employers will only be liable for the torts of their employees, not for the torts of their independent contractors. However, this has been developed in a series of recent cases, notably *Christian Brothers*, *Cox v Ministry of Justice* (2016), *Armes v Nottinghamshire County Council* (2017) and *Barclays Bank plc v Various Claimants* (2020). In the latter, Lady Hale stated (at para 27):

> 'Where it is clear that the tortfeasor is carrying on his own independent business it is not necessary to consider the five incidents.'

This gives clarity that where the person committing the tort is part of a business entirely independent of the defendant's business, vicarious liability will not apply.

Table 3.6.1 Key cases for vicarious liability

Case	Facts	Relevant area	*Ratio decidendi*
Various Claimants v Catholic Child Welfare Society (2012) known as *Christian Brothers* case	Children were abused while in the care of a residential institution.	Wholescale review of the current law	Laid the foundations for the more detailed principles in *Cox* and *Mohamud* – see below.
Cox v Ministry of Justice (2016)	C worked in a prison kitchen and was injured by the negligence of a prisoner 'working' in the kitchen.	Was the prisoner an 'employee' of the MoJ for this purpose?	Yes – see above.
Mohamud v WM Morrison Supermarkets plc 2016	C was assaulted by a member of staff in a Morrison's petrol station.	Was the employee acting in the course of his employment?	Yes. It does not matter whether he was motivated by personal racism rather than a desire to benefit his employer's business.
Joel v Morison (1834)	Joel was struck down by a horse and cart, whose driver was Morison's agent. The driver had detoured to visit a friend when the accident occurred.	Was the employee acting in the course of his employment?	The driver was doing Morison's business, so he was not on a 'frolic'.
Morrison Supermarkets v Various Claimants (2020)	An employee who held a grudge against his employer deliberately leaked the personal information of thousands of other employees.	Was the employee acting in the course of his employment?	Personal motive meant the 'close connection' test was not satisfied.

Now test yourself

TESTED 

1. What does a claimant need in order to establish vicarious liability?
2. What is the close connection test?
3. What is a 'frolic of his own'?
4. If my employer asks me to collect some provisions from warehouse A, but I decide I prefer warehouse B, will my employer be liable for any torts I commit while in warehouse B?
5. Why does the identity of the defendant in *Cox v Ministry of Justice* (2016) make this interesting in light of *Caparo v Dickman* (1990) and *Hill v Chief Constable of West Yorkshire* (1988)?

Exam summary

In the exam, you MAY be asked:

- a multiple-choice question about the rules of vicarious liability
- a mid-length question (10–15 marks) about the meaning of vicarious liability, which then goes on to ask about either fault, morality or law reform
- a maximum-length question (30 marks), part of which requires the application of vicarious liability, but part of which goes on to question whether it is fair to impose fault in this way.

3.7 Defences

Evaluation point

This is a great example of balancing conflicting interests and substantive justice (see Chapter 1.1).

Exam tip

You will need to apply the law for defences to given scenarios in Paper 2. Defences will not be assessed on their own, but with the most appropriate substantive tort.

Contributory negligence

REVISED

The Law Reform (Contributory Negligence) Act 1945 provides that contributory negligence is a partial defence. That means the courts can apportion loss between the parties, making a fairer outcome than a complete defence. A key case here is *Revill v Newbery* (1996).

Section 1(1) of the Law Reform (Contributory Negligence) Act 1945 provides that 'where a person suffers damage as a result partly of his own fault and partly the fault of another(s), a claim shall not be defeated by reason of the fault of the person suffering damage'.

Requirements of contributory negligence

The burden of proof is on the defendant to demonstrate the following:

1. The claimant failed to take proper care in the circumstances for their own safety. Lack of proper care for own safety is not the same as 'breach of the duty of care'. It varies, and all circumstances are taken into account, including the age of the claimant. A key case here is *Gough v Thorns* (1966).
2. The failure to take care was a contributory cause of the damage suffered. This has included:
   - failure to wear a seat belt – *Froom v Butcher* (1976)
   - failure to wear a helmet on a motorcycle – *O'Connell v Jackson* (1971)
   - failure to fasten a helmet on a motorcycle – *Capps v Miller* (1989)
   - exposing oneself to danger by inappropriate use of a vehicle – *Davies v Swan Motor Co.* (1949) and *Jones v Livox Quarries* (1952)
   - suicide – *Reeves v Commissioner of Police of the Metropolis* (2000)
   - failure to follow safety instructions – *Stapley v Gypsum Mines* (1953).

There is a considerable overlap between contributory negligence and consent (below) which is a complete defence. However, since 1945 the courts have been less willing to make a finding of consent. Instead, they prefer to apportion loss between the parties rather than taking the 'all or nothing' approach of consent.

Revision activity

Research these case details online.

Now test yourself

1. Why do the courts favour contributory negligence over consent?
2. What does 'partial defence' mean?
3. Who carries the burden of proof in contributory negligence?

TESTED 

Exam summary

In the exam, you MAY be asked:

- a multiple-choice question about the effect of contributory negligence
- a mid-length question (10–15 marks) about the meaning of contributory negligence, which then goes on to ask about one of the concepts such as fault or law reform
- a maximum-length question (30 marks), part of which requires the application of contributory negligence alongside the substantive law of negligence.

Consent

REVISED

Consent, also known as *volenti non fit injuria*, is a complete defence. To absolve the defendant of all legal consequences of their actions, it requires a freely entered and 'voluntary agreement by the claimant, in full knowledge of the circumstances'.

Elements of consent

Table 3.7.1 Explaining the elements of consent

Element	Explanation
Voluntary	+ The agreement must be voluntary and freely entered. + If the claimant is not in a position to exercise free choice, the defence will not succeed. + This element is most commonly seen in relation to employment relationships, rescuers and suicide.
Agreement	+ This may be express or implied. An implied agreement may exist where the claimant demonstrates a willingness to accept the legal risks as well as the physical risks. + Lord Denning in *Nettleship v Weston* (1971) said: 'Knowledge of the risk of injury is not enough. Nothing will suffice short of an agreement to waive any claim for negligence. The [claimant] must agree expressly or impliedly to waive any claim for any injury that may befall him due to the lack of reasonable care by the defendant: or more accurately due to the failure by the defendant to measure up to the duty of care which the law requires of him.' + A key case here is *Smith v Charles Baker and Sons* (1891).
Knowledge	+ The claimant must have had knowledge of the full nature and extent of the risk that they ran – see *Morris v Murray* (1991). + A rescuer is not regarded as having freely and voluntarily accepted the risk – see *Haynes v Harwood* (1935). + A participant in sporting events/games is taken to consent to the risk of injury which occurs in the course of the ordinary performance of the sport – see *Condon v Basi* (1985).

Consent and occupiers' liability

Section 2(5) of the Occupiers' Liability Act 1957 and s 1(6) of the Occupiers' Liability Act 1984 provide that occupiers owe no duty in respect of risks willingly accepted by a person. There is no need to establish an agreement. A key case here is *Titchener v British Railways Board* (1983).

Table 3.7.2 Key cases for consent

Case	Facts	Relevant area	*Ratio decidendi*
Revill v Newbery (1996)	C shot a burglar and sued for damages relating to his injuries.	Contributory negligence	C was two-thirds responsible for own injuries.
Gough v Thorns (1966)	A lorry slowed down so that children could cross a road. D's car came through the gap and crashed into a child, causing serious injury.	Contributory negligence	A very young child cannot be guilty of contributory negligence. An older child may be, but it depends on the circumstances.
Smith v Charles Baker and Sons (1891)	Workers were putting stones into a steam crane which swung where C was working. A stone fell out of the crane and struck him on the head.	Consent – agreement	C may have been aware of the danger of the job, but had not consented to the lack of care. In an employment situation, knowing a danger exists is not to be equated with agreeing to it.

Case	Facts	Relevant area	*Ratio decidendi*
Morris v Murray (1991)	C and D had been drinking all day. D, a pilot, suggested they took an aircraft for a flight. They took off but crashed shortly after. C was seriously injured.	Consent – knowledge of the risk	The risk in accepting a ride in an aircraft from an obviously heavily intoxicated pilot was so glaringly dangerous that C could be taken to have voluntarily accepted it.
Haynes v Harwood (1935)	D left a horse-drawn van unattended in a crowded street. The horses bolted. A police officer was injured when he tried to stop the horses to save a woman and children in their path.	Consent – rescuers	A rescuer does not 'freely' accept risk.
Condon v Basi (1985)	C's leg was broken after a tackle in a football match.	Consent – sports injuries	A participant accepts the risks of injury in sporting activities, but not if this occurs outside the rules of the game.
Titchener v British Railways Board (1983)	C was injured while trespassing on a train line.	Consent and Occupiers' Liability Acts 1957 and 1984	C was fully aware of the danger of crossing a train line, so she must be taken to have consented to assuming the risk.

Stretch and challenge

Consider and make notes on how effective these defences are at creating balance between the competing interests of the parties

Now test yourself

4 What is the Latin name given to consent?
5 How may 'agreement' be communicated?
6 Why is a rescuer not regarded as having freely and voluntarily accepted the risk?
7 How much injury does a boxer consent to?

Exam summary

In the exam, you MAY be asked:

- a multiple-choice question about the effect of consent
- a mid-length question (10–15 marks) about the meaning of consent, which then goes on to ask about one of the concepts, possibly fault
- a maximum-length question (30 marks), part of which requires the application of consent to the substantive law of negligence.

Defences to private nuisance

Ordinary use of the land

In *Southwark London Borough Council v Mills* (2001), the claimant testified:

> 'I can hear ... normal conversation, singing, arguments, the television, snoring, coughing, bringing up of phlegm, sneezing, bedsprings, footfalls and creaking floorboards, the pull-cord light switch in the bathroom, taps running in the bathroom and kitchen, the toilet being used ... the vacuum is clearly audible as is any music played on the stereo.'

This was not a nuisance, as the noises complained of were merely ordinary.

Statutory authority

Many 'nuisances' are caused by public authorities acting under statutory powers, for example, road works to improve the access to a water main.

This will be a defence provided the 'nuisance' does not exceed that which was authorised. A key case here is *Allen v Gulf Oil Refining Ltd* (1981).

Typical mistake

Remember that planning permission does not authorise nuisance, but it may change the nature of the 'locality'.

Act of God and nuisances arising naturally

This means an event that happens independently of any human action, for example, a storm. It is a complete defence – see *Nicholls v Marsland* (1875).

However, once the occupier becomes aware of the nuisance and fails to remedy it within a reasonable time, they may be liable for any damage it may cause – see *Goldman v Hargrave* (1967).

Now test yourself

8 What is the effect of planning permission?

9 How would Heathrow airport defend itself against a nuisance claim regarding the building work?

10 How long does it take to acquire a prescriptive right?

TESTED

Prescription

This rarely succeeds in practice.

If a defendant can show that they have been committing the nuisance for 20 years and that the claimant has been aware of this and done nothing about it, then the defendant has a defence. This is because the defendant has acquired the prescriptive right to commit the nuisance. A key case here is *Coventry v Lawrence* (2014).

The 20 years will not start to run until the claimant becomes aware of the nuisance – see *Sturges v Bridgman* (1879).

Exam summary

You may be asked:

+ a multiple-choice question about the effect of private nuisance defences
+ a mid-length question (10–15 marks) about the meaning of private nuisance defences, which then goes on to ask about either fault, morality or law reform
+ a maximum-length question (30 marks), part of which requires the application of private nuisance defences to a scenario, and then goes on to question whether it is fair to avoid fault in this way.

Defences to *Rylands v Fletcher*

REVISED 

Table 3.7.3 Defences to *Rylands v Fletcher*

Defence	Explanation	Key case
Act of a stranger	D has a complete defence if the escape was caused by the act of a stranger over which D had no control and whose actions could not have been reasonably foreseen.	*Perry v Kendricks Transport Limited* (1956), in contrast with *Ribee v Norrie* (2000)
Act of God	This has the same meaning as under private nuisance, but there is a different case example.	*Carstairs v Taylor* (1871)
Statutory authority	This has the same meaning as under private nuisance, but there is a different case example.	*Green v Chelsea Waterworks Co.* (1894)
Consent/benefit	If C receives a benefit from the thing accumulated, they may be deemed to have consented to its accumulation.	*Peters v Prince of Wales Theatre* (1943)

Revision activity

Create a grid showing which defences are appropriate for each tort.

Table 3.7.4 Key cases for defences to nuisance

Case	Facts	Relevant area	*Ratio decidendi*
Southwark London Borough Council v Mills (2001)	C complained about normal household noises.	Ordinary use of land defence to nuisance	It was not a nuisance, as the noises complained of were merely ordinary.
Allen v Gulf Oil Refining Ltd (1981)	C lived near an oil refinery and claimed the operation of the refinery was a nuisance.	Statutory authority defence to nuisance	Gulf Oil was entitled to statutory immunity in respect of nuisance. The refinery conformed with Parliament's intention in the Gulf Oil Refining Act 1965.
Nicholls v Marsland (1875)	D made a reservoir by damming a stream. An extraordinarily heavy rainstorm caused the dam to burst and wash away C's bridges.	Act of God defence to nuisance	The defence applied.
Goldman v Hargrave (1967)	A tree growing on D's land was struck by lightning and set on fire. D was aware of this but failed to extinguish the fire. The fire spread to C's property and caused damage.	Act of God defence to nuisance	The defence did not apply.
Coventry v Lawrence (2014)	Speedway and stock-car racing had taken place since the 1970s.	Prescription as a defence to nuisance	This established a prescriptive right.
Sturges v Bridgman (1879)	D's premises adjoined those of a doctor. For over 20 years, D had used noisy machinery which had not interfered with the doctor's land. The doctor then built a consulting room at the bottom of his garden and at that point complained of the noise.	Prescription as a defence to nuisance	It failed, since the nuisance commenced only when the new building was erected. Before then, there was no right of action as there had been no nuisance.
Perry v Kendricks Transport Limited (1956)	D kept an old coach. C, a young boy, approached two other boys on the wasteland close to the coach. As he got close, the boys lit a match and threw it into the petrol tank of the coach. This caused an explosion, which left C injured.	Act of stranger defence to *Rylands v Fletcher*	An occupant of land cannot be held liable under the rule if the act bringing about the escape was the act of a stranger.
Ribee v Norrie (2000)	C's neighbouring property was owned by D and had been converted into a hostel. A fire broke out in the hostel, caused by a discarded cigarette, which spread to C's home. She suffered personal injury and damage to her property.	Act of stranger defence to *Rylands v Fletcher*	It was within the power of the defendant to prohibit smoking on the property, so he had control over the third party's actions.
Carstairs v Taylor (1871)	C stored rice in the ground floor of a warehouse which he leased from D, who used the upper floor. A rat gnawed through a gutter box draining water from the roof of the warehouse. Heavy rainfall then caused the roof to leak, damaging C's rice.	Act of God defence to *Rylands v Fletcher*	The defendant was not liable under *Rylands v Fletcher*. The heavy rain and actions of the rat were classed as an act of God.
Green v Chelsea Waterworks Co. (1894)	A water main burst, causing damage to C's land. D was under a statutory obligation to maintain high pressure in the water main. Any escape would inevitably cause damage.	Statutory authority as a defence to *Rylands v Fletcher*	D was not liable under *Rylands v Fletcher* as they had the defence of statutory authority.
Peters v Prince of Wales Theatre (1943)	C's shop was damaged when pipes from the theatre's sprinkler system burst.	Consent/benefit as a defence to *Rylands v Fletcher*	The sprinkler system was equally for the benefit of C.

Exam summary

You MAY be asked:
- a multiple-choice question about the effect of *Rylands v Fletcher* defences
- a mid-length question (10–15 marks) about the meaning of *Rylands v Fletcher* defences, which then goes on to ask about one of the concepts, possibly fault
- a maximum-length question (30 marks), part of which requires the application of *Rylands v Fletcher* defences to a scenario.

Now test yourself

11 What is the impact of an act of a stranger?

12 What amounts to an act of God?

13 Why were the Chelsea Waterworks not liable under *Rylands v Fletcher* to Green?

TESTED

3.8 Remedies

Damages

REVISED

Exam tip

This area requires you to apply the law to given scenarios in Paper 2. It will not be assessed on its own, but with the most appropriate substantive tort.

Revision activity

Create a grid showing which remedies are appropriate for each tort.

Compensatory damages

The aim of damages in tort is to put the claimant back in the position they would have been in if the tort had not been committed, in so far as it is possible to do so with money. In Latin, this is known as *restitutio in integrum*.

Physical injury to people

This includes all types of injury, including, where the claim has been successful, psychiatric harm.

Lord Blackburn in *Livingstone v Rawyards Coal Company* (1880) said:

> 'It being a general rule that where any injury is to be compensated by damages ... you should as nearly as possible get at that sum of money which will put the party who has been injured, or who has suffered in the same position as he would have been in if he had not sustained the wrong.'

In *British Transport Commission v Gourley* (1956):

> 'It is manifest that no award of money can possibly compensate a man for such grievous injuries as the Respondent in this case has suffered ... in fixing such damages the Judge can do no more than endeavour to arrive at a fair estimate, taking into account all the relevant considerations.'

These considerations are also known as the 'heads of damage'.

Typical mistake

Do not confuse 'damage' and 'damages'. The former is the 'harm' that the tort has caused; the latter is monetary compensation for the loss or harm suffered.

General damages

These are 'unliquidated' or 'non-pecuniary'. This means that they cannot be calculated exactly and it is for the judge to decide how much to award.

These damages are awarded for:
- pain and suffering: this covers past, present and future physical pain and mental anguish, including fear of future treatment or anguish caused by life expectancy being shortened; however, the claimant must be aware – see *Wise v Kaye* (1962)
- loss of amenity: the loss of things a claimant used to enjoy doing, for example, where a claimant had a particular skill or hobby, including loss of senses and reduced marriage prospects
- future loss, for example, pension rights and future expenses such as nursing care

Exam tip

It is probably wisest to think of the heads of damage as headings under which different types of damage can be assessed.

- specific injuries: there is a standard tariff for most types of injuries supplied by the Judicial Studies Board called the Kemp and Kemp Quantum of Damages.

Special damages

This is loss which can be assessed with some accuracy, for example:

- medical expenses (these are not limited to NHS)
- loss of earnings.

Pre-trial loss of earnings is considered special damages, as the precise figure of pre-trial loss of earnings can be calculated.

Post-trial loss of earnings is considered general damages, as it is not possible to calculate the amount precisely, so a formula has been developed by the courts:

Multiplicand × multiplier = future loss of earnings

Multiplicand is the court's assessment of the claimant's net annual loss; multiplier is the period of future loss.

If C's life expectancy is shortened by the accident, future loss of earnings is adjusted.

A key case here is *Pickett v British Rail Engineering Ltd* (1980).

Pre-trial expenses

The claimant may claim special damages for loss of earnings up to the date of the trial and for special damages covering expenses up to the date of trial, for example, medical or travel expenses.

Damage to property

Where property is destroyed, damages are generally assessed by reference to the market value of the property at the time of its destruction.

Where property is damaged but not destroyed, damages are usually assessed by reference to the cost of repair, unless the repair cost is greater than the market value, when the latter is then used.

Economic loss

In the very few cases where a claim purely for economic loss is successful, the nature of the claim means the loss can be calculated exactly.

Where economic loss is as a result of a personal injury or damage to property as identified above (for example, loss of earnings), it is more likely to be successful and again, as can be exactly calculated, will be included in the overall claim.

Interim and periodical payments

Damages are generally awarded in a lump sum, although not always.

Table 3.8.1 Interim and periodical payments

Type of payment	Explanation
Interim payments	+ Part 25 of the Civil Procedure Rules provides for interim payments, i.e. payments made before the full settlement is awarded. + These are most commonly used in personal injury claims and most especially so in claims for substantial damages arising out of catastrophic injuries. + In such cases, immediate money is required before the final calculation of the claim, in order to pay for things such as adapted housing, equipment or expensive care.
Periodical payments	+ Section 2 of the Damages Act 1996 provides that a court awarding damages for future pecuniary loss in respect of personal injury 'may order that the damages are wholly or partly to take the form of periodical payment', i.e. regular payments in the future.

Types of damages (other than compensatory)

- Nominal damages: often paid when no damage has been suffered, for example, £1.
- Contemptuous damages: awarded where the court feels that the action should never have been brought, often because a claimant's behaviour has been reprehensible.
- Aggravated damages: awarded if the court feels that the claimant's injury has been aggravated by the defendant's conduct and may therefore increase the amount of damages.

Mitigation of loss

It is a general principle of the law of damages that the claimant must do everything reasonable to mitigate their loss. The defendant will not be liable for damage resulting from the claimant's unreasonable failure so to do.

Table 3.8.2 Key cases on damages

Case	Facts	Relevant area	*Ratio decidendi*
British Transport Commission v Gourley (1956)	An eminent civil engineer suffered severe injuries while travelling in a train.	*Restitutio in integrum*	Judicial comment showed how difficult it can be to 'restore' C.
Wise v Kaye (1962)	C was left permanently unconscious and unaware of her surroundings.	Pain and suffering	C can only claim for pain and suffering if aware of their injuries (subjective test). There was no claim for the period when C was unconscious.
Pickett v British Rail Engineering Ltd (1980)	C, a 51-year-old, inhaled asbestos causing mesothelioma.	Reduced life expectancy	C's life expectancy was one year. Damages were calculated on the basis that C would have been expected to work until 65 years old.

Now test yourself

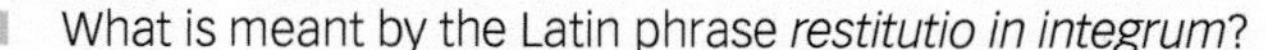

1. What is meant by the Latin phrase *restitutio in integrum*?
2. What 'head of damage' would you claim for a new phone if yours had been damaged by someone's negligence?
3. How are lost earnings calculated?

Exam summary

You MAY be asked:

- a multiple-choice question about the types of damages
- a mid-length question (10–15 marks) about the calculation or purpose of damages, which then goes on to ask about either fault, morality or law reform
- a maximum-length question (30 marks), part of which requires the application of a specific tort and the damages that are relevant should the claimant be successful.

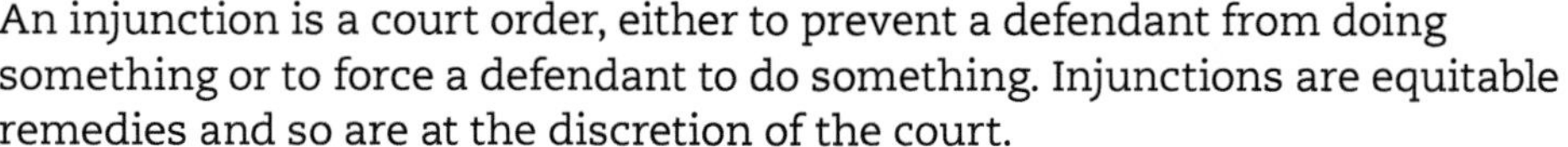

Injunctions

REVISED

An injunction is a court order, either to prevent a defendant from doing something or to force a defendant to do something. Injunctions are equitable remedies and so are at the discretion of the court.

Injunctions are most commonly used in torts such as nuisance and trespass, in order to stop the tort from continuing.

There are a number of different types of injunction, but the ones you need to be aware of are outlined in Table 3.8.3.

Table 3.8.3 Types of injunction

Type of injunction	Explanation	When used	Key case
Prohibitory injunction	An order from the court preventing D from committing a tort or from continuing it.	Usually sought in nuisance cases where C wants the activity to stop.	*Watson v Croft Promo-Sport Ltd* (2009)
Mandatory injunction	An order from the court to compel D to act in a particular way.	Usually sought where C wants D to rectify the damage caused.	*Jacklin v Chief Constable of West Yorkshire* (2007)
Partial injunction	An order to limit D's activities or reduce them.	Usually granted where the tort has some public benefit.	*Kennaway v Thompson* (1981)

Where the public interest outweighs the claimant's interest, the court may decide to award damages in lieu of an injunction – see *Miller v Jackson* (1977).

Lord Neuberger in *Coventry v Lawrence* (2014) set out when this would be appropriate, updating the original tests from *Shelfer v City of London Electric Lighting Co.* (1895).

Evaluation point

This area is closely associated with balancing conflicting interests, so ensure you can make the link.

Also, be aware that damages may be awarded in addition to an injunction.

Table 3.8.4 Key cases on injunctions

Case	Facts	Relevant area	*Ratio decidendi*
Watson v Croft Promo-Sport Ltd (2009)	Cs complained about the noise from a motor-racing circuit.	Prohibitory injunction	An injunction (and damages) was granted.
Jacklin v Chief Constable of West Yorkshire (2007)	C owned land which gave him a right of way over a stretch of land owned by D. D placed a container across the relevant stretch that prevented C's passage of vehicles.	Mandatory injunction	A mandatory injunction was granted to remove the container.
Kennaway v Thompson (1981)	C owned property next to a lake used for water sports. The frequency of the races increased over time and the lake was often used as a venue for both national and international races.	Partial injunction	The injunction granted limited the frequency of the use of the lake for competitions without preventing it completely.
Miller v Jackson (1977)	See page 5.	Damages in lieu of an injunction	The public interest prevailed over C's private right to quiet enjoyment.

Stretch and challenge

Boost your knowledge of this area by reading the Law Commission Report, *Aggravated, Exemplary and Restitutionary Damages* (1997), available online.

Now test yourself TESTED

4 Why were damages preferred over an injunction in *Miller v Jackson* (1977)?
5 What type of injunction would you seek if your neighbour was playing very loud music at 3 a.m. every day?

Exam summary

In the exam, you MAY be asked:

- multiple-choice questions on the types or requirements of injunctions
- short or mid-length questions about the value and/or purpose of injunctions
- to apply injunctions as a remedy in a long-answer scenario question.

Exam practice

In Paper 2 you will answer:

- five multiple-choice questions – at least two of these will be tort questions
- two short 5-mark scenario questions – one of these will be a tort question
- two mid-length questions – one will be a scenario and the other may be an essay requiring an extended answer which shows a clear, logical and sustained line of reasoning and leads to a valid conclusion
- an extended scenario, worth 30 marks, where you will need to comprehensively apply the law to facts and present a valid conclusion.

Multiple-choice questions (1 mark each)

1 If established by the defendant, the defence of consent has the following effect on a claim brought by the claimant:

   A Damages are reduced according to the level of fault demonstrated by the claimant.
   B Damages are reduced by half.
   C Damages are reduced without taking account of the level of fault demonstrated by the claimant.
   D No damages will be awarded.

2 Claimants have a duty to mitigate their losses when seeking damages in negligence. Which of the following accurately describes the duty to mitigate?

   A Only claim for losses which are foreseeable.
   B Cannot claim for pure economic loss.
   C Establish a link between negligence and loss.
   D Take reasonable steps to minimise losses.

3 In relation to a claim for vicarious liability made against an employer, which of the following is false?

   A An employer cannot be vicariously liable for any negligence on the part of an employee.
   B An employer may be vicariously liable for an injury caused by an employee to someone who is not an employee.
   C An employer may be vicariously liable for an injury caused by one employee to another employee.
   D An employer need not be personally at fault to be vicariously liable.

4 In a claim for psychiatric injury, which of the following is not a characteristic of a secondary victim?

   A Being in personal danger.
   B Having a close tie of love and affection with a person killed, injured or imperilled.
   C Possessing reasonable fortitude.
   D Sustaining psychiatric injury through a sudden shock.

'Short answer' 5-mark questions

5 Zeena's property was damaged by Yannick's negligence. Most of the damage was of a kind that might have been expected, but some of the damage was much more extensive than might have been expected.

   Apply the remoteness of damage principle to Zeena's claim against Yannick for compensation in an action in negligence, suggesting why she is likely to recover compensation for some, but perhaps not for all, of the damage.

6 Andy owned a car wash. Beth was digging up the road outside Andy's car wash. Beth had been given the plans for the road showing the location of the water pipes, but she had not bothered to look at them. Consequently, when Beth used her digger, she broke the water pipe leading to Andy's car wash. The car wash was not damaged, but Andy did lose an afternoon's earnings as he had no water to wash customers' cars.

   Suggest why any claim made by Andy in respect of his economic loss would not succeed in court.

7 Cameron bought a bungalow in a quiet residential area. Dianne, the owner of a neighbouring house, ran a community radio station from the shed in her back garden. Despite being warned of this before purchasing the house, Cameron became increasingly irritated by the music and noise.

   Suggest whether Cameron has the basis of a claim.

15-mark questions

8 On an ice rink owned by NICE-ICE, some figure skaters were in the habit of skating in an area clearly marked out for speed skating only. While doing so, Jon (a figure skater) skated into the path of Kylie (a speed skater). In the resulting collision, Jon suffered severe facial injuries and Kylie was knocked out.

   Advise Jon and Kylie as to their rights and remedies against NICE-ICE.

9 Explain the importance of fault-based liability, in particular in relation to *Rylands v Fletcher*.

10 Evie was walking to collect her children from school. A coach carrying children back to school from a trip suddenly hit a nearby tree and burst into flames. Although her children were not on that coach, Evie did not know this and went to help some of the survivors to escape from the wreckage and she was lucky not to suffer serious injury. It was proved that the accident was caused by negligence on the part of the coach

driver, Freya. For several months after the accident, Evie suffered depression and severe anxiety attacks.

Advise Evie as to her rights and remedies against Freya.

30-mark questions

11 Previously a quiet lake overlooked by a few cottages, Linacre Lake has recently been developed by its new owner, Wetlife Developments, to provide extensive leisure facilities, including swimming and powerboating. In consequence, Ingrid, a cottage owner has experienced a large increase in noise, especially at weekends and during frequent competition weeks. Additionally, damage to a diesel oil storage tank owned by Wetlife Developments resulted in a leak which caused extensive contamination of Ingrid's vegetable garden.

Some swimmers were in the habit of swimming beneath the surface in an area of Linacre Lake clearly marked out for powerboating only. While doing so, Jon surfaced into the path of a powerboat being driven by Kylie. In the resulting collision, Jon suffered severe facial injuries and Kylie was knocked out of the boat and had her arm severed by the propeller. Kylie's friend, Rachel, who was in another boat, dragged her out of the water to safety. The experience caused Rachel deep emotional disturbance.

Consider the rights and remedies of Ingrid, Jon, Kylie and Rachel against the owners of Linacre Lake.

12 Leila owned a book shop in the centre of town. She had recently asked Pritamjit, the brother of a friend of hers, to install some new shelves along one of the walls.

Ninder was a customer in the book shop and he wanted to look at a book on the top row of the new shelves. Ninder stood on a small stool provided for the use of customers to reach the book. Despite the fact that he could see that the top shelves were loose and coming away from the wall, he held onto the top shelves to reach the book. The shelves collapsed and Ninder fell to the floor, suffering a broken arm.

At the back of Leila's book shop was a storeroom with a door out onto the next street. Customers frequently went through the storeroom when they left the shop as it provided a convenient short cut. Leila was concerned because some wiring had come loose in the storeroom. Leila therefore put up a notice on the door to the storeroom saying, 'Strictly no admittance'. Maddie saw the notice, but she was late for an appointment with her bank and decided to use the short cut anyway. Maddie brushed against the loose wiring and received a severe electric shock. She suffered bad burns and her mobile phone was smashed when she fell to the floor.

Consider the rights and remedies of Ninder and of Maddie against Leila in relation to their injuries and losses.

End-of-unit summary

- Understand and recognise the procedural and substantive differences between tort and crime, and tort and contract.
- Understand the aims and principles of tort.
- Recognise actionable negligence in respect of personal injury and damage to property.
- Explain and apply duty of care.
- Explain and apply breach of that duty.
- Explain and apply the rules on foreseeability and causation in respect of the damage.
- Explain and apply the relevant defences.
- Recognise when occupiers' liability legislation is relevant.
- Understand and apply the differences between a visitor and a trespasser.
- Explain and apply the duties to each, with reference to section numbers of the acts and cases.
- Explain and apply how these duties can be breached, with reference to section numbers of the acts and cases.
- Explain and apply the relevant defences.
- Explain who can make a claim in private nuisance, and against whom.
- Explain and apply what amounts to a nuisance.
- With reference to cases, recognise what amounts to an unreasonable interference.
- Explain and apply the relevant defences.
- Select and explain appropriate remedies.
- Identify when a claim in *Rylands v Fletcher* is appropriate, including the type of damage suffered.
- Explain and apply the elements the claimant must show.
- Recognise and explain the 'non-natural use of land' element.
- Explain and apply the relevant defences.
- Understand the nature and purpose of vicarious liability (this will include evaluation points).
- Explain and apply the tests for establishing the tortfeasor is an employee.
- Explain and apply the tests for establishing the tortfeasor is acting in the course of employment.
- Explain and apply the principles of *volenti non fit injuria* and select when its use is appropriate.
- Explain and apply the principles of contributory negligence and select when its use is appropriate.
- Explain and apply the basis of compensatory damages, including mitigation of damage.
- Explain in which torts an injunction might be more appropriate.

4 Law of contract

4.1 Rules of contract law

Contract law is an optional unit and assessed by AQA on Paper 3A.

This is an area of private law concerned with agreements (contracts) between:
- one person and another person
- one person and a business, or
- a business and a business.

Rules and principles

REVISED

This chapter relates to the basic rules and principles of contract law:
- formation of a contract
- terms of a contract
- vitiating factors
- discharge of a contract
- remedies available.

Formation of a contract

A contract is an agreement between two parties who are bound by law to carry out the obligations under the contract which can be enforced or compensated in court.

As such, when a valid contract is formed, both parties have rights that can be enforced. If either party fails to carry out their part of the agreement, then they may be in breach of contract.

In civil law, when there is a breach of a contract the 'injured' party (claimant) will either ask for the other party (defendant) to carry out the agreement or ask for compensation for any losses in a court of law.

However, to fill the courts with cases concerning 'broken promises' would be ridiculous. Therefore, contract law has established a series of steps or rules and principles in the formation of a contract. In basic terms:
1. There must be an intention to create legal relations.
2. There must be a valid offer and a valid acceptance of that offer.
3. There must be 'consideration' to support the acceptance of the offer (normally the price paid for goods and services).

Revision activity

Think about this morning or a typical day in your life. Identify all the agreements you have entered into, for example, paying for a bus or train journey. Which are legally enforceable?

Exam tip

You will need to correctly define each important term in contract law. For example, definitions of a contract or an offer and acceptance are crucial in securing marks and providing a foundation for you to explain or analyse a topic for an exam question.

Revision activity

Using a decided case, identify and memorise a definition of a contract.

Contract: an agreement between two parties which is binding in law and therefore enforceable in court.

Breach of contract: when a party fails to carry out any of their obligations under the agreement; or in carrying it out they fail to do what they are supposed to do.

Contract terms

A contract's terms are the individual statements made by the contracting parties which form the contents or subject matter of the contract. Consider the following:

Jamil says to Kate that he will sell his electric scooter to her for £500. The contract's basic terms would be:
- It is an electric scooter.
- The price is £500.

Revision activity

Think about any agreements you have entered into with close family and friends this week, for example, agreeing to meet someone at the cinema. Which are legally enforceable?

Once agreed upon, the terms are the binding part of the contract of which the parties agree to perform in order for the contract to be fulfilled. If either party fails to carry out the term, then they will be in breach of contract. So in the above case, if:

- the scooter is a non-electric, push or kick scooter, or
- the price changes to £600 after the acceptance,
- then, *prima facie* there is a breach of contract.

Terms can either be:

- express (from the parties themselves)
- implied (as a presumption of agreement by the parties) or
- 'imputed' by process of law, for example, under consumer protection law.

Terms can be:

- conditions, which go to the root of the contract, or
- warranties, which are lesser terms and are generally descriptive.

Vitiating factors

Even if a contract has all of the necessary constituent parts in its formation – offer, acceptance, consideration and intention – there can still be other defects in the contract unknown to either party.

These defects are called vitiating factors and can invalidate a contract, even if both parties are happy with the terms of the agreement at the time the contract is made.

Vitiating factors come into operation through either:

- a void contract – the contract was not valid from the start, or
- a voidable contract – the contract may be avoided by either party.

Revision activity

Start a contract dictionary. Under V, write 'void' and 'voidable', together with their definitions.

Discharge of a contract

Discharge refers to the ending of a contract. In the majority of cases, contracts are discharged when both parties complete their obligations under the contract. This is called discharge by performance.

However, a contract can also be discharged through frustration. Here, the contract cannot be performed due to events outside of the party's control. Although there are limits to this, in effect the contract will end as soon as the intervening event occurs.

Remedies for breach of contract

There are two types of **remedy** available for breach of contract: common law remedies and equitable remedies. The type used depends on factors in the case.

Typical mistake

When discussing remedies, do not assume that all remedies are available to the injured party. Common law damages are available as of right, but equitable remedies are at the discretion of the judge.

Common law remedies

Damages are the most common remedy in contract law. They involve a payment of money to compensate the other for their loss. If the case is proven, then damages are granted as of right.

There are three basic types of damages:

- unliquidated
- liquidated
- *quantum meruit*.

Discharge (of a contract): the ending of a contract.

Remedy: in contract law, this is a way of providing a solution to a breach of contract.

Quantum meruit: a reasonable sum of money that is to be paid for services in contracts where an exact sum of money is not stipulated.

Equitable remedies

These have developed due to the inadequacies of common law remedies. If the case is proven, then equitable remedies are at the court's discretion but are not automatically granted.

There are two main types of equitable remedy, which have been developed to assist specific situations:

- specific performance (see page 177–8)
- rescission (see page 178).

Revision activity

Think about the different types of remedy, both common law and equitable. Identify situations where each type would be appropriate.

Now test yourself TESTED

1. Give a definition of a contract.
2. List the main constituent parts of a contract.
3. What is a vitiating factor? Name the two types on the AQA specification.
4. How can a contract be discharged?
5. What are the three basic types of damages available for a breach of contract under the common law?
6. What are the two main types of equitable remedy available for a breach of contract on the AQA specification?

Exam summary

In the exam, you MAY be asked:

- multiple-choice questions about individual rules of contract law or how contracts are discharged
- to explain, in broad terms, the individual rules of contract law, such as what a contract is and how a contract is formed, and how a contract can be discharged by performance, breach or frustration
- to write an analysis of some of the individual rules of contract law such as the formation of a contract, the terms of a contract, a contract's potential vitiating factors and the differences between legal and equitable remedies.

4.2 Theory of contract law

This chapter relates to the analysis and evaluation of the purpose of rules of contract, why the law has insisted upon the voluntary nature of a contract and the principles that oversee the law.

Typical mistake

Do not explain at great length your historic knowledge of the growth of contract law in your exam responses when such knowledge is not required.

Evaluation point

See the past exam papers available on the AQA website for a thorough, but not prescriptive, response.

Freedom to contract: the voluntary nature of agreements

Modern contract law has its origins in the nineteenth-century theory of *laissez-faire* economics, where transactions between parties were free from regulation.

While foundations of modern contract law were developed during the nineteenth century, in particular during the Industrial Revolution in Great Britain, its origins can be traced back to the Middle Ages and beyond.

The fundamental basis of contract law is the issue of voluntariness, the freedom to contract. Rules and principles have developed to formalise these voluntary arrangements.

Protection for the consumer

Contracts are not uniquely formed as part of a business arrangement. Many contracts are formed during the normal routine of life.

In most instances, we do not make such agreements formally in writing. For example, on the way to school or college, you may travel by bus or train, buy a chocolate bar or a can of fizzy drink. In each of these cases, without paying much attention to these acts, a contract is formed.

But what if:

- you were injured on the bus due to the fault of the driver
- the chocolate bar had a foreign body in it
- the can was empty or contained another liquid other than a fizzy drink?

Over time, the courts began to develop contractual rules to protect consumers and Parliament introduced legislation – statute law – to formalise this protection. After the UK joined what is now the European Union, further protection was provided for consumers as part of EU membership. These consumer rights remain valid post Brexit, as most have been incorporated into UK law.

Revision activity

Read the introductory chapter of a contract law textbook that considers the origins or historic formation of contract law and familiarise yourself with the contents.

The common law's distinction between the constituent 'parts' of a contract

REVISED

The common law has established three key parts in the formation of a contract:

1. Agreement: where a valid offer is followed by a valid acceptance (see below).
2. Consideration: something is given in return for something promised, proving that the agreement exists (see below).
3. The intention to create legal relations: a clear intention to be bound by the agreement from both sides (see Chapter 4.3).

Exam tip

Do not forget that a contract must follow the basic requirements of agreement, consideration and intention to create legal relations.

Agreement

Table 4.2 1 Agreement

Offer	Acceptance
An offer is a statement made by one party, the offeror, which sets out the terms that they agree to be bound by.	There is no contract formed until an offer is accepted. There must be a valid offer to enable valid acceptance.
An example of an offer in a unilateral contract is an advertisement which can operate as a kind of reward. Here, the person reading the advertisement does not need to make an offer to comply, but simply needs to comply with the reward's terms. Sometimes an offer is only made after an invitation to treat. This is passive conversation which invites another person to make an offer.	Various rules on acceptance have been developed to accommodate specific situations. Examples include: + The postal rule in *Adams v Lindsell* (1818) – if the post is an accepted method of acceptance, then the acceptance is made on posting the letter, even if the letter is never received. + More modern communication methods, such as text, email or other electronic means, have had to be regulated and rules formed as a result; acceptance is usually upon 'receipt' of the offer.

Stretch and challenge

Using the AQA website find any 10-mark scenario questions that examine offer and acceptance. Using a similar word count, create your own question that models the style of the AQA question.

Revision activity

Identify a basic definition of:

- offer
- acceptance.

Consideration

Rationale for consideration

In the absence of agreements under seal, a method of enforcing informal contracts was required. This led to the creation of the doctrine of consideration.

Consideration was born out of the need to grant a favour or an advantage in return for something promised: in other words, *quid pro quo*. The usual form of consideration is therefore the price paid for goods or services.

While defining consideration specifically remains a problem, its most common evidence is in the offeree agreeing to pay money to the offeror in return for goods and services.

Exam tip

Latin terms are used throughout contract law. Include them in the exam to enhance your answer and demonstrate your familiarity with contract law.

Consideration and privity

Consideration must come about as a result of a promise to do something. For example:

- I'll mow your lawn (promise).
- In return, I want you to pay me £20 (consideration).

Only the person who has provided, or agreed to provide, the consideration (for example, the £20 for mowing the lawn) can enforce the promise (to mow the lawn).

It is therefore argued that only those persons who are privy (parties) to the contract can sue if they are denied the agreed benefit (for example, the £20).

Consideration and economic duress

In some cases, contracting parties realise that their obligation will not be fulfilled for a variety of reasons, notably in building and construction works. A failure to complete on time could have further implications, which could be catastrophic.

In order to fulfil the contract, one of the parties may ask for extra money (more than originally agreed) to complete the contract on time. The promise to pay the extra money will only be binding if the party promising the extra money obtains any further benefit and not simply the original fulfilment of the contract – see *Williams v Roffey* (1990).

However, the promise to pay the extra money will only be enforceable if the promise was given freely and without economic duress (a 'threat' to damage someone's financial interest).

The nature and effectiveness of exclusion/ exemption clauses

REVISED

An exclusion or exemption clause is a term in a contract which excludes the liability of the party inserting it from certain contractual breaches that may occur at a later time.

Historically, exclusion clauses operated unfairly against the other party, especially where the parties entered the contract on an unequal footing with different bargaining strengths.

The law has developed so that there is more judicial and statutory control over exemption clauses, but with mixed results for parties relying on these clauses.

The nature and effectiveness of remedies

REVISED

The effectiveness of remedies depends very much on the opinion of the injured party. There is no real way to compensate an injured party unless the contract is carried out as per expectations.

If there is a breach, compensation in the form of common law or equitable remedies may provide some, or all, satisfaction. However, the disappointment and the requirement to seek legal redress in court can only add to the suffering and irritation for such breaches.

Consumers often have to face up to businesses who fail to carry out their contractual obligations. Seeking redress against such companies has led to protection for consumers in the form of domestic or EU law.

The Consumer Rights Act 2015 was introduced to simplify the law in relation to consumers and their rights in the purchase of goods and services.

Now test yourself TESTED

1. List any agreements or contracts you have entered into so far today.
2. How many of the agreements that you have identified in Q1 would you consider to be legally enforceable?
3. Give a definition of an offer.
4. Give a definition of an acceptance.
5. What is the purpose of the doctrine of consideration?
6. Explain one valid purpose for using an exclusion/exemption clause in a contract.

Revision activity

Identify any contracts you have entered into today or during the last week. Assume that there was a breach in each case; what would you consider to be an appropriate remedy for each breach?

Exam summary

In the exam, you MAY be asked:

- multiple-choice questions about the voluntary nature of contract, principles governing contract law and the constituent parts of a contract
- to explain theories of contract law, such as the voluntary nature of contract law and requirements of a binding contract
- to write an analysis of the voluntary nature of contract and of principles governing contract law (for example, the theory of freedom of contract or of the rationale behind the doctrine of consideration) and some of the theories of contract law (such as the rationale behind the doctrine of consideration, or the effectiveness of remedies for consumers).

4.3 Essential requirements of a contract

This part of the AQA specification looks at:

- an agreement (offer and acceptance)
- consideration (including privity of contract), and
- intention to create legal relations.

Agreement (offer and acceptance)

REVISED

For an agreement (contract) to be made, there must be a valid offer followed by a valid, unconditional acceptance of the offer.

Offer: an expression of one party's willingness to contract on certain terms, made with the intention that it will be legally binding upon acceptance.

The offer

The party making the offer is known as the offeror.

The party to whom the offer is made is known as the offeree.

The offeror will usually state verbally or in writing that they will be bound by the terms of the offer following a valid acceptance and that they have an intention to create legal relations.

The contract will not be formed until the offeree accepts the terms in the offer. A simple example of an offer would be if I said to a friend:

- 'I'll sell you my car for £5000.' Or,
- 'Do you want to buy my car for £5000?'

Offeror: the person making an offer to the offeree.

Offeree: the person accepting an offer.

Typical mistake

Do not confuse an invitation to treat (no offer) with its exceptions, for example, a unilateral offer sometimes referred to as a reward.

Revision activity

Start to develop and practise your contractual vocabulary by using terms such as 'offeror' and 'offeree', rather than 'buyer' and 'seller'.

Invitation to treat

Where problems have arisen is in the difference between a valid offer and what the law calls an 'invitation to treat'. An offer will most likely lead to a binding contract, but an invitation to treat is simply an invitation to make offers and can be seen in the early stages of contractual negotiations.

The most common example of an invitation to treat is having items on display on a shop's shelf or advertised in a magazine.

Goods on display in shops or the internet

Such items will not be considered to be an offer. Otherwise, simply picking up an item in a shop could be seen as making an acceptance!

The law says that the display of goods is an invitation to treat and by picking up the item, and taking it to the till, the customer makes an offer to buy and the shop owner can choose whether to accept the offer to buy or not – see *Pharmaceutical Society of Great Britain v Boots Cash Chemists Ltd* (1953).

The same approach has been taken with goods on display in shop windows. It is for the customer to come into the shop to make the offer to buy. At this point, the shopkeeper can decide whether or not to accept the offer to buy and therefore sell the goods – see *Fisher v Bell* (1961).

Goods or services advertised in newspapers, magazines and other media

Again, the advertisement is not an offer but instead an invitation to treat. It is up to the person who acts on the advertisement to make an offer to buy what is advertised. This can then be accepted by the advertiser, forming a contract – see *Partridge v Crittenden* (1968).

Nevertheless, there are some exceptions to this rule in advertisements:

- If an advertisement is made where a reward will be paid, for example, to find a lost cat, and the cat is returned, then the person making the advertisement cannot rely on the reward being an offer to treat.
- Instead, the law will treat it as what is called a unilateral offer – see *Carlill v Carbolic Smoke Ball Co.* (1893).

Traditional coin-operated machinery

Historically, coin-operated machinery such as car parking meters themselves would be seen as the 'offer' and the inserting of the coins would be seen as the acceptance. *Thornton v Shoe Lane Parking* (1971) confirmed this rule and stated that a ticket generated after the insertion of coins came after the acceptance.

So, if the ticket contained an unfavourable term or condition, this would not be legally enforceable. However, this may not be the case in the more modern world.

Evaluation point

Try to understand the reasons why situations like 'goods on display in a shop' are not offers but seen as invitations to treat.

Communication of offers

One of the basic rules of contract is that an offeree cannot accept an offer that has not been communicated to them. Clearly, it would be impossible to accept an offer if the offeree has no knowledge of it – see *Taylor v Laird* (1856).

Termination of offers

1 An offer may be terminated by a counter-offer.

   If an offeree decides they would like to change the terms of an offer (for example, by trying to negotiate/change the price of an item), then this would be called a counter-offer.

   A counter-offer, in effect, ends the original offer and becomes an offer in itself, making the offeree become the offeror. Therefore, the counter-offer can be accepted or rejected by the person making the original offer – see *Hyde v Wrench* (1840).

   A modern example of a counter-offer would be in using internet selling sites, such as eBay. A seller can place an item on eBay with a 'Buy it now or best offer' label. Here, the potential buyer can offer a lower price than the 'Buy it now' price, and it is up to the seller to accept the lower offer or counter-offer with a higher price at which they are happy to sell.

2 Death of either the offeror or offeree.
3 Lapse of time – see *Ramsgate Victoria Hotel v Montefiore* (1866).
4 Revocation: an offer can be revoked (cancelled) at any time before acceptance – see *Dickinson v Dodds* (1867).

Revision activity

Try to find an example of a 'buy it now' item on an internet auction website.

Table 4.3.1 Key cases on offers

Case	Facts	Element of offer	Legal point
Pharmaceutical Society of Great Britain v Boots Cash Chemists Ltd (1953)	The court was asked to clarify if controlled drugs displayed in a self-service pharmacy were offers (an offence) or invitations to treat (no offence).	Goods on display	The display was an invitation to treat. The contract was formed when the goods were presented at the till.
Fisher v Bell (1961)	D had a flick knife on display in his shop window. Statute made it an offence to 'offer' for sale such an item.	Goods on display	It was not an offer, but an invitation to treat.
Partridge v Crittenden (1968)	P was charged with 'offering for sale' several wild birds, which was a criminal offence, after placing an advertisement in a newspaper.	Goods or services advertised in the media	His advertisement was an invitation to treat and therefore no offer to sell had been made.
Carlill v Carbolic Smoke Ball Co. (1893)	C bought and used a medical product correctly but still caught the 'flu. She sued for £100.	Goods or services advertised in the media	The advert was not a true offer: it was an example of a unilateral offer.

Case	Facts	Element of offer	Legal point
Hyde v Wrench (1840)	W offered to sell his farm for £1000 and rejected H's offer of £950. W then refused H's higher offer of £1000 and sold to another party.	Counter-offers	The original offer of £1000 had been rejected by H's counter-offer of £950.
Taylor v Laird (1856)	T had commanded L's ship but resigned command and worked as an ordinary crew member. On his return to England, T tried to claim his wages.	Communication of offers	T was unable to claim since he had not communicated his offer. There was therefore no contract.
Ramsgate Victoria Hotel v Montefiore (1866)	M offered to buy shares in the hotel. Six months later the hotel owners 'accepted' the offer, by which time the share price had fallen.	Lapse of time of offer	Although the offer had not been withdrawn, the sheer length of time between offer and acceptance was extreme and had lapsed after a reasonable amount of time.
Dickinson v Dodds (1867)	X offered to sell his house to Y, promising to keep the offer open until Friday. On Thursday he sold the house to Z and communicated this fact to Y. Y pretended not to know and 'agreed' to buy the house on Friday morning.	Revocation of offer	An offeror is free to withdraw an offer at any time before acceptance. (In addition, there had been no 'consideration' from Y to keep the offer open until Friday.)

The acceptance (of the offer)

In order for a contract to be formed, the offer must be validly accepted by the offeree and that acceptance communicated back to the offeror. It is important, therefore, that the acceptance must:

- 'mirror' the offer and be certain – see *Sudbrook Trading Estate v Eggleton* (1983)
- not change the terms of the offer
- be communicated properly back to the offeror.

Exam tip

You might be faced with a scenario question which involves an enquiry being made after an offer is made. This generally will not be a counter-offer, so the offer will still stand.

Acceptance must be unconditional

It is clear that an acceptance must be unconditional – see *Hyde v Wrench* (1840) above.

However, making enquiries about the offer may not amount to a counter-offer and therefore may not be taken as rejecting the original offer – see *Stevenson v McLean* (1880).

Battle of the forms

In the commercial world, businesses will often make the same type of offers to sell their products or services, and other businesses will agree to buy their products or services.

With the similarity of such offers, companies draw up 'standard forms' with the terms and conditions that they wish to contract on. This is usually to their own advantage.

However, if two businesses contract together and both use their own standard forms, one standard form which makes the offer and the other standard form containing the acceptance, the question is – which standard form is to be used if there is a conflict of terms? See *Butler Machine Tool Co. Ltd v Ex-Cell-O Corp.* (1979).

Revision activity

Using the internet, identify a typical business contract from a large high-street shop and read through its terms and conditions.

Communication of the acceptance

If a valid offer has been made, then the contract can only be formed if the acceptance is communicated back to the offeror. Only the offeree can make the acceptance.

The general principle of 'silence does not amount to an acceptance' makes common sense. In general terms, an acceptance can be made in any form. However, if a specific method of acceptance is stipulated, then the acceptance must follow that format to be valid.

Usually the offer is accepted through conduct (see *Carlill v Carbolic Smoke Ball Co.* above) or through an agreed method, and this method is communicated to the offeror.

The 'postal' rule

Historically, using the post via the Royal Mail was a commonplace method of communication and was deemed an exception to the rule that an acceptance had to be communicated to the offeror. This is known as the postal rule – see *Adams v Lindsell* (1818): an acceptance is valid and the contract is formed when the acceptance letter is posted and not when it is received by the offeror.

Although it remains an antiquated method of communication given the digital age of email, cloud-managed file-sharing services such as Box or Dropbox and other file transfer protocols, the postal rule appears to morph alongside. It still appears that the rule only operates where such acceptance is agreed upon or is in the normal manner that the offeror conducts their business. If this is not stated in the contract, nor is it a common-sense approach to accept, then the courts will look at whether it was reasonable to accept in such a way.

The High Court has considered the validity of the rule in two cases: *Pretty Pictures v Quixote Films Ltd* (2003) and *Greenclose v National Westminster* (2014):

- An exchange of emails would not amount to a binding contract where the parties intended their agreement to be concluded by post (*Pretty Pictures v Quixote Films Ltd* (2003)).
- But, on balance, emails should not be subject to an equivalent of the postal acceptance rule (*Greenclose v National Westminster Bank plc* (2014)).

If it is clear that the acceptance must be communicated to the offeror before a contract is formed, by excluding the rule in the terms of the contract, then the postal rule will not suffice – see *Holwell Securities v Hughes* (1974).

In more modern times, the Electronic Commerce Directive 2000 provides that where a contract is formed by electronic means, an offer is made when a consumer makes or sends an order. It is therefore most likely that when the consumer receives an 'acknowledgment screen', this will constitute the acceptance.

Stretch and challenge

Given the recent High Court decisions on the 'postal rule' and the issue of 'snail mail' versus email, if you were a Supreme Court judge, how would you decide a modern version of the postal rule in an electronic age of email, WhatsApp, Facebook and SnapChat?

Table 4.3.2 Key cases on acceptance

Case	Facts	Element of acceptance	Legal point
Stevenson v McLean (1880)	M offered to sell S some iron and S agreed the price and quantity. S asked for four months of credit instead of paying cash. Hearing nothing from M, S sent a letter of acceptance.	Acceptance must be unconditional	The enquiry for credit was not a counter-offer but was instead an enquiry for information. The offer was still able to be accepted.
Butler Machine Tool Co. Ltd v Ex-Cell-O Corp. (1979)	B's standard form of contract contained a price variation clause. E accepted the offer on their own standard form which had conflicting terms and no price variation clause.	Battle of the forms	Lord Denning controversially suggested replacing contested terms by implying reasonable ones.
Adams v Lindsell (1818)	D wrote to C offering a quantity of wool and requiring an acceptance via the post. D's letter was incorrectly addressed, causing delay. C accepted the offer and posted it the same day, but D had already sold the wool.	Communication of the acceptance	The court held that the contract began on the day that the acceptance was returned via the post.

Consideration

REVISED

Unless explained properly, consideration remains the greatest misunderstood concept in contract law.

In ordinary terms, consideration is the price an offeree pays for the goods or services that are offered. For example:

- X offers to sell Y her car for £3000.
- Y accepts the offer to pay £3000 for the car.
- The £3000 is the 'consideration' for X's offer to sell the car: 'I will pay you the asking price of £3000'.

Consideration is a backing, a securing of an offer, proof that the agreement exists. In contract law, if someone offers you something and you don't do something to secure that offer, even if you accept the offer but don't provide any 'consideration', then the offer is unenforceable, despite a valid offer!

In *Currie v Misra* (1875), consideration was defined as being in terms of 'benefit and detriment'. The parties both must receive benefit and suffer a detriment. The benefit or detriment is known as the consideration. In the example above:

- X gains the benefit of £3000 but to the detriment of releasing his ownership of the car to Y.

Nevertheless, despite the common law's requirement of consideration, the courts have blindsided this requirement and have invented, on the facts, consideration. In such cases, the law of equity has invented consideration despite there not being any through the doctrine of 'promissory estoppel'.

Consideration was defined in *Dunlop v Selfridge* (1915) as:

> 'an act or forbearance of one party, or the promise thereof, is the price for which the promise of the other is bought, and the promise thus given for value is enforceable'.

A contract is not fully formed simply because there is an intention to create legal relations and an agreement (a valid offer and a valid acceptance of the

Revision activity

Identify and memorise a typical definition of consideration, such as that from *Dunlop v Selfridge* (1915).

offer). Historically, consideration was developed to provide further evidence that the parties to an agreement intended a legally binding contract by contributing something in return for the promise of the other party.

However, contracts may be formed without a cash transaction, so consideration can take other forms. For example:

- X offers to give her car to Y if Y promises to mow her lawn every week during the summer months for three years.

Typical mistake

Remember that consideration does not necessarily have to be a cash amount.

Rules for consideration

As with all parts of contract law, judges have developed a series of rules in relation to consideration.

Exam tip

Explain the rationale of the judges' decisions in the consideration cases you use in an exam question, to demonstrate your understanding of the law.

1 Consideration must be sufficient

The consideration must be in a form which the courts have accepted as 'sufficient'. This means it must be real, be tangible and have some inherent value – see *Ward v Byham* (1956).

2 Consideration need not be adequate

The courts are not necessarily interested in whether parties to the agreement have made a bad or poor agreement. They are more interested in the freedom of contract.

Therefore, if the price for goods or services does not reflect the value of the goods, then in the absence of duress or undue influence, the courts will seek to enforce the original agreement's terms – see *Thomas v Thomas* (1842).

3 Consideration must not be past consideration

The general rule is that past consideration is unenforceable. So, if a voluntary agreement is struck and there was no mention of payment, then a later promise to pay is unenforceable. For example:

- If A agrees to give B his car for free, then later B agrees to give A £100 for the car, the £100 consideration is not enforceable – see *Re McArdle* (1951) and *Roscorla v Thomas* (1842).

Note the exception to this rule in *Lampleigh v Braithwaite* (1615): when a party has requested a service where there is a reasonable implication that a payment be made, even though such has not been stated in the agreement.

Stretch and challenge

The rule that consideration must not be past consideration and is unenforceable is outdated and in need of a rethink. What do you think?

4 Consideration must move from the claimant

It is common sense that only the person who has provided the consideration can sue if they feel the agreement has been broken from the other side. So, third parties to the agreement are unlikely to be able to enforce a contract if they have provided no consideration.

Following the passing of the Contracts (Rights of Third Parties) Act 1999, it is now possible, in certain cases, that a third party which has provided no consideration for the agreement may sue to enforce the contract.

Therefore, it is possible in the *Tweddle v Atkinson* (1861) case in Table 4.3.3 that X could now sue, provided the case conforms to the 1999 Act.

5 Performance of existing obligations: an existing duty will not amount to valid consideration

The general rule is that if a party is under an existing obligation to carry out something, they cannot use that promise as consideration for a new agreement – see *Stilk v Myrick* (1809) but compare *Hartley v Ponsonby* (1857).

This rule also applies to persons who are under a legal obligation to carry out an act. In *Collins v Godefroy* (1831), the court rejected a police officer's claim that he was entitled to a payment promised by a defendant in a court case if the police officer gave evidence. The officer was under a legal obligation to attend and no further consideration was present.

However, there are some exceptions to the general rule about performing existing obligations. If a party does something extra than what was required in the original agreement, then that may be considered to be new consideration in return for the new agreement – see *Hartley v Ponsonby* (1857).

Revision activity

Summarise the judicial rules that have been developed in relation to consideration.

Table 4.3.3 Key cases on consideration

Case	Facts	Element of consideration	Legal point
Dunlop v Selfridge (1915)	D sold tyres to X, a dealer, who then resold the tyres to S, a retailer, at a price below the agreed price enforced by D.	Definition	This case provided the legal definition of consideration (see page 153).
Ward v Byham (1956)	The father of an illegitimate child agreed with the mother to pay her £1 a week to keep the child 'well looked after and happy'. He then refused to pay.	Consideration must be sufficient	The court held that as the mother was under no legal obligation to keep the child 'happy', this was sufficient consideration for the £1 per week.
Thomas v Thomas (1842)	A widow was allowed to stay in the matrimonial home for a very low rent of £1 per year.	Consideration need not be adequate	This was sufficient consideration for the agreement for her to stay in the house.
Roscorla v Thomas (1842)	T sold a horse to R, stating that it was 'free from vice'. In fact, the horse was violent. R sued for breach of contract.	Consideration must not be past consideration	There was no consideration for the later promise that the horse was fine. The only consideration, the £30, was in the past, and therefore not relevant to the later promise.
Lampleigh v Braithwaite (1615)	B asked L to get him a King's pardon after B had been accused of killing a man. L did so, at his own expense. B later agreed to pay L £100, which he failed to do.	Rule in *Lampleigh v Braithwaite*	It was implicit that a payment would be made at the time of the agreement, and L was entitled to the £100.
Tweddle v Atkinson (1861)	A father and future father-in-law (D) agreed to pay a sum of money to X. D died before he made the payment. X sued the executors of his estate for the money promised.	Consideration must move from the claimant	Because X had provided no consideration to the original agreement, he could not enforce it.
Stilk v Myrick (1809)	When two members of a ship deserted, the captain promised the remaining crew a share of the deserters' wages if they got the ship home. Once home, the captain refused to pay any extra wages.	Performance of existing obligations	The court rejected C's argument that he was entitled to the extra wages, since he was simply doing what he was contractually obliged to do and had provided no further consideration for the new promise.
Hartley v Ponsonby (1857)	19 ship crew members were left when 17 others deserted. Only four were 'able seamen' on this dangerous voyage. The captain promised to pay the remaining crew extra money if they agreed to sail, but later refused to pay.	The performance of existing obligations	By agreeing to continue in such dangerous circumstances, the remaining crew had provided further consideration to the new agreement.

Privity of contract

Generally, a contract is only enforceable by the parties to the contract – see *Dunlop v Selfridge* (1915). Therefore, the common law prevents a person who is not party to the contract from enforcing the contract even if it was for their benefit: this is privity of contract.

The basic rule follows common sense, since a third party would generally not wish to be bound by an agreement they had not agreed upon. However, if a benefit is bestowed from such a contract onto a third party, then the basic rule may seem unfair – see *Tweddle v Atkinson* (1861). Again, the rules of consideration would apply, since there was no further act or forbearance to enforce the offer.

Exceptions to the rule of privity

Exceptions to the general rule include:

- statute: for example, application of s 56 of the Law of Property Act 1925 in *Beswick v Beswick* (1968)
- restrictive covenants; see *Tulk v Moxhay* (1848)
- collateral contracts: see *Shanklin Pier v Detel* (1951)
- The Contracts (Rights of Third Parties) Acts 1999.

It seems unfair that a third party is unable in contract law to claim the benefit that is intended for them. This led to calls for reform and led to the 1999 Act which provides:

> 'A person who is not a party to a contract may in his own right enforce a term of the contract if ... the contract expressly provides that he may, or ... the term purports to confer a benefit on him.'

Table 4.3.4 Key cases on privity of contract

Case	Facts	Element of privity	Legal point
Tulk v Moxhay (1848)	C sold land with a restrictive covenant attached, which prevented the land from being built upon. The land was sold several times, until D bought it and wanted to build on the land.	Exception to basic rule: restrictive covenants	D argued there was no privity of contract, but the court held that the covenant was enforceable in equity, as an injunction, and not damages, was sought by C.
Shanklin Pier v Detel (1951)	S employed X to paint a pier. D said a particular paint was suitable. Within three months, the paint began to peel off.	Exception to basic rule: collateral contracts	Established the doctrine of collateral contracts, where a contract may be given as consideration by simply agreeing to enter into another contract.
Beswick v Beswick (1968)	P agreed to sell his coal business to his nephew, D, in return for a sum of money each week, then £5 per week to P's wife after he died. D agreed, but after P died, D made one payment then refused to pay any more.	Exception to basic rule: s 56 of the Law of Property Act 1925	P's wife was able to sue in her capacity as her late husband's administratrix in enforcing D's promise to pay.
Nisshin Shipping Co Ltd v Cleaves & Co Ltd (2003)	N's cargo ship was hired out to various companies to transport their goods. A clause in each contract stated that a commission was to be paid to C who 'brokered' the hiring but was not a signatory of the actual contract.	Enforceability under the 1999 Act	The 1999 Act placed the burden of proof on N to show that the parties did not intend the term to be enforceable by C, the third party. N failed to do this and therefore the clause was enforceable by C.
Avraamides v Colwill (2006)	A had hired X Ltd, a bathroom company, to refurbish his two bathrooms. The work was not satisfactory but A didn't sue X as they had no assets. Instead, he sued C who had taken over X Ltd and had taken over their assets.	Enforceability under the 1999 Act	The CA held that A did not qualify under the Act as he was not specifically identified under C's contract to buy X Ltd.'s assets and C's agreement to fulfil their customer orders.

Intention to create legal relations

REVISED

There is a basic requirement that both parties to a contract must intend to form a legally binding agreement and have an intention to create legal relations (ITCLR). This intent is important, as the courts will only enforce agreements that need support and filter out gratuitous promises that do not require court action.

Typical mistake

Do not assume that since there seems to be an agreement with all its constituent parts, there must be a contract. This may not be the case where there are one or two rebuttable presumptions in social or business arrangements.

Exam tip

Look closely at scenario questions and take note of the parties to an agreement. Are the parties related? If so, could the rebuttable presumption apply? Similarly, a business 'agreement' could fail if there was no intention to create legal relations.

Consider the following two situations:

1. Nigel says he will meet his girlfriend, Robyn, at the gym at 6 pm. Robyn agrees and goes to the gym, but Nigel stays at home to watch TV. Robyn is furious.
2. Nigel agrees to buy his girlfriend Robyn's mobile telephone from her for £100. The next day he changes his mind. Robyn is furious.

In both of these situations, there is an agreement struck between Nigel and Robyn. However, the courts would be unlikely to enforce situation (1) as there is little likelihood that either party had an intention to create legal relations. In situation (2), it is more likely that there was an intention to create legal relations.

Intention to create legal relations: both parties intend to be legally bound by the terms of the contract.

Rebuttable presumption: an assumption in law unless a contrary view is expressed.

Contract law distinguishes between two key types of contract in determining whether there is an intention to create legal relations. In both, the types are formed with a rebuttable presumption:

+ Social and domestic agreements: there is a presumption in agreements between families and friends that there is no intention to create legal relations unless the contrary can be proved – the rebuttable presumption, see *Merritt v Merritt* (1970) and *Errington v Errington* (1952). Such promises or agreements are not legally enforceable – see *Balfour v Balfour* (1919) and *Jones v Padavatton* (1969).
+ Commercial or business agreements: there is a presumption that there is intention to create legal relations. Unless the contrary can be proved – the rebuttable presumption, see *Jones v Vernons Pools* (1938), such agreements are legally enforceable – see *Edwards v Skyways* (1964).

Table 4.3.5 Key cases on intention to create legal relations

Case	Facts	Element of intention to create legal relations	Legal point
Balfour v Balfour (1919)	While married, Mr B, who was working abroad, agreed to send maintenance payments which eventually stopped. Mrs B sought to enforce the payment.	Social/Domestic arrangement or otherwise.	As the agreement was social and domestic there was a presumption against an intent to be legally bound.
Merritt v Merritt (1970)	Mr and Mrs M had separated and Mr M agreed to pay Mrs M £40 per month. Mr M agreed that Mrs M should pay off the mortgage and that he would transfer the home into her sole name when it was paid off. Later he refused to do so.	Social/Domestic arrangement or otherwise.	When parties are separating or are separated there is a presumption of an intention to create legal relations.
Jones v Padavatton (1969)	A mother persuaded her daughter to give up a job in the USA to study for the Bar in England. A house was provided by the mother, but later they both quarrelled and the mother sought possession of the house.	Social/Domestic arrangement or otherwise.	As there was no formality in the agreement, there was no intention to create legal relations and the mother could reclaim the house.

Case	Facts	Element of intention to create legal relations	Legal point
Jones v Vernons Pools (1938)	J claimed to have won a competition run by D. D refused as the form, called 'a coupon', contained the phrase 'binding in honour only'.	'Gentleman's' agreement' or legally enforceable business agreement	No contract as the agreement to pay was based purely upon the honour of the parties.
Edwards v Skyways (1964)	E was told he would receive an *ex gratia* payment as part of a redundancy payment.	'Gentleman's' agreement' or legally enforceable business agreement	Presumption that the agreement, being a business agreement, was binding. *Ex gratia* simply meant 'no pre-existing liability' and not to prevent any liability.
Wilson v Burnett (2007)	A woman won a prize of £100,000 in bingo and refused to share it with two other women although they had agreed beforehand they would split winnings.	Social agreement	The trial judge and the Court of Appeal dismissed any binding agreement: chat about sharing winnings was not an intention to create legal relations.
MacInnes v Gross (2017)	Over a meal in a restaurant, M and G had discussed a deal which would have benefitted each other.	Oral contracts	The case was dismissed by the Court as the parties had not manifested an ITCLR, specifically there was no certainty as to terms.
Wells v Devani (2019)	D had contacted W, the owner of a number of flats, stating that he would introduce buyers for the flats to W for a commission. D said W agreed and using their contacts, introduced a housing association who bought the flats. W refused to pay the commission.	Business arrangement	The Supreme Court held that although the agreement had been 'vague', a court would be more likely to find an intent if the parties had acted upon the words.

Now test yourself

TESTED

1. How would the courts distinguish between an offer and an invitation to treat?
2. What is the difference between a unilateral offer and an invitation to treat?
3. What impact on the original offer does a counter-offer have?
4. Why were the cases of *Stilk v Myrick* (1809) and *Hartley v Ponsonby* (1857) decided differently?
5. Explain the rule that consideration need not be adequate.
6. Explain the rule in *Lampleigh v Braithwaite* (1615).
7. How do the courts decide if there is an intention for an agreement to be legally binding?
8. What were the reasons for the cases of *Balfour v Balfour* (1919) and *Merritt v Merritt* (1970) to be decided differently?

Revision activity

What area of law making is the answer to Q8 relevant to? Make the link.

Exam summary

In the exam, you MAY be asked:

- multiple-choice questions about the law on offer, acceptance, consideration or ITCLR in contract law
- to examine and discuss, in part or in whole, offer, acceptance, consideration and ITCLR in contract law through extended answer questions
- to apply the law on offer, acceptance, consideration and ITCLR in contract law problem/scenario situations.

4.4 Contract terms (1): General

In negotiations to form a contract, both parties may discuss a variety of issues before committing to the agreement.

Many of the issues that are discussed will form the basis of the contract's terms. However, some of the issues discussed may not. Therefore, contract law makes a distinction between what are called:

- terms, which form part of the contract, and
- mere representations – statements of opinion/fact or what are known as trade 'puffs', which are unlikely to form part of the contract.

When problems arise after the contract is made and a party wishes to rely on a matter discussed before the agreement, the courts will have to decide whether the issue is:

- a term – which will create contractual obligations, or
- a non-contractual (mere) representation – which simply encourages one party to enter into the initial agreement and is not binding.

Therefore, the terms are the subject matter of the contract and bind both parties to perform them in order for the contract to be complete.

Terms are decided upon during negotiations or inserted into the contract, for example, on a party's standard form contract. They can be expressly stated and therefore included into the contract by the parties or implied as a matter of fact from what was the intention of the parties or by statute law. An example of a statute that implies terms into a contract is the Consumer Rights Act 2015.

Revision activity

Create a contract, including all of its terms, for the following situation: you agree to buy your friend's A-level Law revision guide. Tip: include who, what, why, where and how.

Representations: statements made before the contract which may or may not become one of the main terms of the contract.

Revision activity

In order to understand trade puffs, watch advertisements on television and read advertisements in magazines or newspapers and pick out any boasts or pretention that the business makes which would be unlikely to be legally binding.

Express terms

REVISED 

If matters that were discussed at the negotiation stage are clearly written into a contract, this makes it easier to understand and therefore determine which matter becomes a term of the contract.

However, if this is not the case, the common law has created a series of tests to determine whether a matter previously discussed is included in the contract.

Table 4.4.1 Determining whether a term is included in a contract

How important was the representation?	Clearly, if either party attaches great importance to a statement made during negotiation, then it is more than likely it will be considered a term – see *Birch v Paramount Estates* (Liverpool) Ltd (1956).
A party relies on the skill of the other making the representation.	If one party makes a specific representation due to their level of expertise and the other party relies upon it, this is more likely to become a term of the contract – see *Dick Bentley Productions Ltd v Harold Smith (Motors) Ltd* (1965) and *Oscar Chess Ltd v Williams* (1957).
Was the written agreement signed?	If a written contract is signed, the courts will usually take it that both parties have read and agreed its contents. The courts agreed in *L'Estrange v Graucob* (1934) that the term was 'in regrettably small print but quite legible'. Such terms would nowadays be subject to scrutiny under the Unfair Contract Terms Act 1977.
A representation is not a term unless the parties are aware of it when making the contract.	Generally, if a party is unaware of a 'term' which is relied upon later by one of the parties who knew of the term, then the term is unlikely to be actionable. This depends on the term and the likely impact of its operation.

Exam tip

An express term will be a clear point that expresses the subject matter of the contract. However, remember that terms can be implied by the presumed intention of the party and by statute.

Table 4.4.2 Key cases on express terms

Case	Facts	Element of express terms	Legal point
Birch v Paramount Estates (Liverpool) Ltd (1956)	A married couple bought a house on the basis that they were told it would be 'as good as the show house'. They sued when it was not so.	How important was the representation?	The Court of Appeal stated that the statement was so crucial to forming the contract that it became a term.
Dick Bentley Productions Ltd v Harold Smith (Motors) Ltd (1965)	C asked D to find him a 'well-vetted' Bentley car. D found a car, but falsely stated it had done 20,000 miles, when in fact it had done 100,000 miles.	Where a party relies on the skill of the other making the representation	The Court of Appeal held the mileage was a term of the contract and C could successfully sue for breach in relying on D's expertise.
Oscar Chess Ltd v Williams (1957)	W, a motorist, sold his car to O, a motor dealer. Without any specialist knowledge, W stated it was a 1948 Morris 10. However, it was a 1939 Morris 10. O sued W.	Where a party relies on the skill of the other making the representation	W's statement was an innocent representation and as a dealer, O should have spotted the error. The statement was held not to be a term of the contract.
L'Estrange v Graucob (1934)	L bought a cigarette-vending machine from G. L signed the written contract without reading its exclusion term. The machine stopped working, so L sued under the Sale of Goods Act as to the fitness of purpose.	Was the written agreement signed?	G was held to be protected by the clause and L failed in her action since she had signed the contract.

Implied terms

REVISED

Not all terms may have been expressed or written in the contract. It could be that an event occurs where the express terms do not cover the eventuality and therefore terms can be implied into a contract to cover such – see *Grant v Australian Knitting Mills Ltd* (1936).

The law implies terms into a contract in one of three possible ways:

- implied through custom
- implied by fact during a dispute to see what the unexpressed intentions of the parties were, or
- implied by statute, regardless of what either party may have intended.

Typical mistake

Do not ignore presumed implied terms and statutory implied terms in the rush to consider only what a scenario question has made explicit.

Exam tip

Support any description or evaluation of the law with relevant and accurate case citations.

Terms implied by custom

In such cases, over a long period of time common practices will allow an actual and enforceable implied term – see *Hutton v Warren* (1836).

Terms implied by fact

There are many ways such terms are incorporated into the contract, where the courts, through the common law, attempt to give the presumed intention of the parties in cases of dispute. These are:

- through common trade practices: specific to the type of industry and how that commonly operates through professional custom
- through the 'officious bystander' test: had an officious bystander been present at the time of the contract and had suggested such a term so that both parties would have agreed to it – see *Shirlaw v Southern Foundries Ltd* (1939)

- to preserve business efficacy: where two parties contract, the effectiveness of the agreement must be adhered to and terms can be implied to allow this to operate – see *The Moorcock* (1889).

The courts will not simply imply a term because the term is reasonable.

In *Liverpool City Council v Irwin* (1977), Lord Cross, in the House of Lords, stated that the insertion of such a term had to be 'necessary'.

In *Marks and Spencer v BNP Paribas* (2015), the Supreme Court laid down the leading authority on common law implied terms where a court will themselves imply a term. The Court stated:

- A term will only be implied into a contract where it is strictly necessary for business efficacy.
- It is not enough that the parties would have agreed to it had it been suggested to them.
- The test is not one of absolute necessity but whether, without the term, the contract would lack commercial or practical coherence.
- A term will not be implied where it 'lies uneasily' with the express terms of a contract.

Revision activity

What would be the implied terms in a contract for the sale of a pair of running shoes which cost £150?

Terms implied by statute

Since the rise of the consumer society and the unequal bargaining power between consumers and businesses, successive governments have introduced statutory terms that are implied into contracts to balance the parties' positions. In such cases, neither party can ignore or exclude such implied terms.

The main statute governing this area of law is the Consumer Rights Act 2015. The terms that are implied under this Act are specifically under ss 9, 10, and 11 for the supply of goods and ss 49 and 52 for the supply of services.

Stretch and challenge

In the following situation, what would you consider to be the express and implied terms of the contract?

Dennis buys a second-hand pair of designer trainers from an internet auction site for £10.00.

Table 4.4.3 Key cases on implied terms

Case	Facts	Element of implied terms	Legal point
Grant v Australian Knitting Mills Ltd (1936)	C bought woollen underpants which contained traces of chemicals. These chemicals caused a painful skin disease.	Implied term as to quality and fitness for purpose	The courts implied a term that the underpants should be fit for the purpose bought, that they could be worn without discomfort or pain.
The Moorcock (1889)	D owned a wharf and allowed the C to dock their ship at a jetty. Both parties knew the ship would be damaged at low tide if it were to remain at the jetty. The ship was badly damaged at low tide.	To preserve business efficacy	The court held that since both parties were aware of the tidal situation, C was simply taking advantage of the situation, and to award damages would not promote business efficacy.
Poussard v Spiers and Pond (1876)	P, a famous opera singer, was hired for three months. When she was taken ill and unable to perform, her lead role was given to an understudy. P sued for breach of the contract.	Significance of terms	P was in breach of contract as her inability to perform on the first night was crucial as the critics and a full audience would have been guaranteed.

Evaluation point

Ensure you are familiar with the differences between express and implied terms, in particular, how implied terms are incorporated into contracts.

Conditions, warranties and innominate terms

REVISED

When parties are negotiating before formalising a contract, some matters are left as mere representations and others form the terms of the contract. So, important matters will invariably become terms of the contract, which are either expressly incorporated or implied into the contract.

When the terms are incorporated into the contract, some may have more importance than others. Therefore, the law applies certain weightings to the terms.

Some terms will have vital significance to the contract, since a failure to stick to the terms will mean the contract cannot be carried out. Other terms may be part of the contract but a failure to stick to them will still allow the contract to be carried out, although not in precisely the way the parties desired.

The type of term breached dictates the type of remedy or resolution to which the injured party is entitled. The courts have determined that there are three types of term:

1. A condition is a term that is fundamental in carrying out the purpose of the contract fully. Breach of a condition gives the injured party the right to reject the contract – see *Poussard v Spiers and Pond* (1876).
2. A warranty is any other term of the contract. It is normally a term that is descriptive or 'ancillary' to the contract. Breach of a warranty does not allow the injured party to reject the contract – instead, they are allowed to claim damages to compensate them for any loss.
3. An innominate term is neither a clear condition nor a clear warranty and is decided upon by the courts, depending on the level of 'injury' following a breach – see *Grand China Logistics v Spar Shipping* (2016).

Revision activity

Using the internet, find a contract for the sale of goods from a high-street shop and decide which of its terms are conditions and which are warranties.

Exam tip

In exam questions which include identifying terms, the decision on whether a term is a condition or warranty may be self-evident. However, where this may not be the case, ask yourself whether the term is integral to the contract (condition) or incidental to the contract (warranty).

Stretch and challenge

In the following situation, what would you consider to be the condition, the warranty and the innominate term?

- Jill orders a takeaway from an online restaurant.
- She orders a spicy Mexican 10-inch pizza with chips.
- She orders extra jalapeños which are 'subject to availability' and for the pizza to be delivered 'as soon as possible'.
- The pizza is delivered, but there are no chips, extra jalapeños and five hours after the order was placed.

Now test yourself

TESTED

1. Why are mere representations, statements of opinion or trade 'puffs' not automatic terms under a contract?
2. Why was the *ratio decidendi* in *Oscar Chess Ltd v Williams* (1957) important in setting clear rules on incorporating representations into a contract?
3. What is the difference between an express term and an implied term?
4. Explain three ways in which terms are implied into a contract by fact.
5. How has Parliament, through statute law, created implied terms into a contract?
6. Why was the decision in *Grant v Australian Knitting Mills Ltd* (1936) unsurprising?
7. Explain the difference between a condition and a warranty.
8. What is an innominate term?

Exam summary

In the exam, you MAY be asked:

- multiple-choice questions about the law on express or implied terms in contract law
- to examine and discuss, in part or in whole, express or implied terms in contract law through extended answer questions
- to apply the law on express or implied terms in contract law problem/scenario situations.

4.5 Contract terms (2): Specific terms implied by statute in relation to consumer contracts

In contracts for the sale of goods and supply of services, certain basic consumer rights are implied by the Consumer Rights Act 2015. It was passed to simplify the law relating to consumers' rights and help to resolve disputes quickly and cheaply.

The Act sets out, in clearer terms, the distinction between a consumer's rights and a trader's rights. For the first time, rights on digital content are included, such as online movies and games and downloaded or streamed music.

Exam tip

Make sure you are comfortable with the section numbers of this Act and understand the implied terms to which they relate.

Terms implied into a contract to supply goods

REVISED

Sections 9, 10 and 11 are implied terms of the Consumer Rights Act 2015.

Typical mistake

It is easy to muddle the section numbers of the Consumer Rights Act 2015 or refer to the old law and definitions under the Sale of Goods Act, the Unfair Terms in Consumer Contracts Regulations and the Supply of Goods and Services Act.

Section 9: satisfactory quality of goods

Every contract for the supply of goods is treated as including a term that the quality of the goods is satisfactory (s 9(1)).

The test is objective (s 9(2)) and the quality of the goods must meet the standard that a reasonable person would consider satisfactory, including fitness for purpose, be free from minor defects and be safe (s 9(3)).

Deciding whether or not the quality of the goods is satisfactory must take into account their description, their price (or consideration) and any other relevant circumstances. The quality of goods includes their state and condition.

The implied term as to quality does not cover any defect brought to the consumer's attention before the contract.

Section 10: fitness for particular purpose of goods

The contract for the supply of goods is treated as including a term that the goods are reasonably fit for purpose, even if they are not the specific purpose for their supply.

If the consumer makes it clear to a trader the purpose for which the goods are to be used, and they are supplied as such, then the goods must be fit for that particular purpose. Examples could include hiking boots, outdoor lights, waterproof coats.

The implied term does not apply if the consumer does not rely, or it would be unreasonable to rely, on the opinion of the trader.

Section 11: description of the goods

The contract for the supply of goods by description is treated as including a term that the goods will match that description (s 11(1)).

This applies to goods bought by sample, even if the majority of the goods match the sample but some do not (s 11(2)).

Stretch and challenge

Make a list of five types of goods that could apply to sections 9, 10 and 11 of the Consumer Rights Act 2015. For example, under s 9: underpants, felt-tipped pens, etc. This will help you understand which goods might be used in an exam scenario question.

Evaluation point

Ensure you have a clear understanding of sections 9, 10 and 11 of the Consumer Rights Act 2015 and the differences between the three sections.

Remedies for the breach of a term implied into a contract to supply goods

REVISED

If there is a breach of one of the terms in ss 9, 10 and 11, then the consumer is entitled to seek redress, if applicable, under the following sections.

Section 20: short-term right to reject

The consumer has a short-term right to reject goods, normally 30 days from the purchase and/or delivery of the goods to the consumer.

The consumer has the right, under certain circumstances, to reject the goods and treat the contract as at an end.

Section 23: right to repair or a replacement

If the consumer has the right to repair or a replacement of the goods within six months, the trader must do so within a reasonable time without significant inconvenience to the consumer (s 23(2)(a)).

The trader must bear any necessary costs in doing so (s 23(2)(b)).

The consumer cannot insist on a repair or a replacement if this is impossible, or disproportionate to either a repair or replacement (s 23(3))

A consumer who agrees to a repair cannot require the trader to replace the goods or exercise the short-term right to reject, unless the trader is given a reasonable time to repair them.

Revision activity

For the five items listed in the Stretch and challenge activity (page 161), identify the most appropriate remedy for a potential breach of an implied term.

Section 24: right to a price reduction or a final right to reject

This section usually applies after the consumer has accepted a repair or replacement under s 23 but the repair or replacement does not conform to the contract.

In such cases under s 24, the consumer has the right to require a business to reduce, by an appropriate amount, the price the consumer is required to pay under the contract, or to receive a refund from the trader for any monies paid by the consumer for goods bought. The amount of the reduction may be the full amount.

Terms implied into a contract to supply services

REVISED

Section 49: reasonable care and skill to supply of services

Every contract to supply a service includes a term that the trader must perform the service with reasonable care and skill.

Section 52: performance within a reasonable time to supply of services

This section applies where the contract does not fix the specific time for which the service is to be performed, or how the time is to be fixed.

Every contract to supply a service includes a term that the trader must perform the service within a reasonable time. What is a reasonable time is a question of fact in each case.

Revision activity

Make a list of five services that could apply to each section of the Act concerning terms implied into a contract to supply services, so that you can understand which services might be used in a scenario question. For example, under s 49 hairdresser, window cleaner etc.

Exam tip

Terms implied into contracts to supply services are different to the supply of actual goods. Do not confuse them.

Remedies for the breach of a term implied into a contract to supply services

REVISED 

Section 55: right to repeat performance for the supply of services

The right to repeat performance requires:

- the trader to perform the service again, to the extent necessary to complete its performance
- conformity with the original contract.

Section 56: right to a price reduction for the supply of services

The right to a price reduction is the right to require the trader to reduce the price to the consumer by an appropriate amount.

The amount of the reduction may, if appropriate, equal the full amount of the price.

Now test yourself

TESTED 

1 Why was the Consumer Rights Act 2015 introduced?
2 Explain the implied term into a contract to supply goods under s 9.
3 Explain the implied term into a contract to supply goods under s 10.
4 Explain the implied term into a contract to supply services under s 49.
5 Explain the implied term into a contract to supply services under s 52.
6 What are the two main remedies for the breach of a term implied into a contract to supply services?

Exam summary

In the exam, you MAY be asked:

- multiple-choice questions about your understanding of specific contract terms implied by statute in relation to consumer contracts
- to explain or analyse your understanding of specific contract terms implied by statute in relation to consumer contracts under the Consumer Rights Act 2015
- to apply your understanding of specific contract terms implied by statute in relation to consumer contracts to a scenario situation, in order to consider the rights and remedies of the parties.

4.6 Contract terms (3): Exclusion clauses

For this topic you will need to have a basic understanding of the nature of exclusion clauses and limitation clauses and their common law and statutory controls.

The nature of exclusion clauses and limitation clauses

REVISED

Exclusion or exemption clauses are one of the most controversial types of terms in a contract, sometimes referred to as an unfair term.

Exclusion clauses may be inserted into a contract in order to reduce or eliminate the liability of either party where certain events may occur. They can operate perfectly legitimately where both parties are of equal bargaining power.

However, it is common that the parties may have unequal bargaining power, particularly where consumers are involved.

Businesses will generally operate on standard form contracts. Here, the business will use a contract that is standard to its business purposes. In many cases, businesses may seek to take the upper hand and wish to tip the balance of the contract in their favour.

Exclusion or exemption clauses: clauses which seek to exclude from liability one party for a breach of contract, or even for a tort.

Revision activity

Identify an exclusion clause that might be written into a contract for the sale of a concert ticket.

Typical mistake

Do not assume that every exclusion clause will be invalid. In many cases, the clause will be valid and a show of tough or shrewd business acumen, rather than being unfair on the other party.

Evaluation point

Ask yourself, how many times have you ticked 'agree' to the 'terms and conditions' on a company's website while ordering goods on the internet without actually reading the thirty-odd pages of such terms and conditions?

Common law control of exclusion clauses

REVISED

Where one party is more dominant (usually the business) and seeks to rely on an exclusion clause to the detriment of the other party (usually the consumer), then the courts have devised two rules which indicate whether to accept the clause's operation or deny it:

1. The clause must be incorporated into the contract as part of the contract.
2. The clause will be constructed by the courts and it operates to protect the party wishing to rely upon it from damage caused and not seek to gain an undue advantage from it.

Incorporation of the clause

The general rule is that the exclusion clause must be brought to the attention of the party before or at the time the contract was formed. The exclusion clause is generally included in the contract either by signature or if the other party had knowledge of the clause.

Revision activity

Collect five examples of exclusion clauses that can be found on the back of tickets, for example, a bus ticket or a receipt from a fast-food restaurant.

Revision activity

Collect five examples of notices that purport to exclude liability, for example, 'Caution – wet paint'.

Where the parties sign the contract, then the maxim *caveat emptor* applies. Here, the general rule is that you:

- agree to what you sign for
- are bound by the exclusion clause whether or not you've read the contract in full or not – see *L'Estrange v Graucob* (1934).

Where the contract is not necessarily signed, but the clause should have been brought to the other party's notice (for example, by a sign or on a document given to a party), the exclusion clause will only be binding if the parties had express knowledge of it at the time of the contract – see *Olley v Marlborough Court Hotel* (1949). A ticket with an exclusion clause on the reverse is generally insufficient – see *Chapelton v Barry UDC* (1940).

However, if there is a misrepresentation of the clause, then it is unlikely the clause will be binding.

The general rules for knowledge of the exclusion clause to be enforced are:

- Did the party have knowledge of the clause (perhaps they had contracted before and were understood to have such knowledge)? or
- Were reasonable steps taken to bring the exclusion clause to the attention of the party?

The clause can be incorporated through the parties' previous dealings. So, if the parties have traded before, the clause will be binding on the basis of previous knowledge even if the clause was not brought to the attention of the other party this time – see *Hollier v Rambler Motors (AMC) Ltd* (1972).

Also, the term can be incorporated through trade custom so that the parties are aware that such terms are commonplace and they both trade in the same or similar markets.

Exam tip

Remember that while a party may have signed the agreement, an exclusion clause may still be invalid. To be valid, the clause must be validly incorporated into the contract and stand up to statutory regulation.

Construction of the clause

The exclusion clause must be interpreted, or constructed, by the courts to see if it will achieve what it is meant to do without unduly penalising the other party.

The main rule of construction here is the *contra proferentem* rule:

- Any ambiguity with regard to the clause must be interpreted against the party proposing or having drafted the clause and wishing to rely upon it – see *Hollier v Rambler Motors (AMC) Ltd* (1972).
- Where an exclusion clause is held to be valid in situations where the claimant alleges negligence, very clear words must be used.

Statutory control of exclusion clauses

REVISED

Before the enactment of the Unfair Contract Terms Act 1977 (UCTA), there was little statutory regulation of exclusion clauses and the common law decisions of judges were used to decide whether or not the exclusion clause should stand in a contract.

Unfair Contract Terms Act 1977

UCTA was introduced to give consumers greater protection. The Act makes certain exclusion clauses void and makes others only valid if they satisfy the test for reasonableness.

Stretch and challenge

Using your five examples from the revision activities above, apply UCTA to each clause to see if it is valid or void under the Act.

Void exclusion clauses

Section 2(1) – a party cannot rely on an exclusion clause that tries to exclude or restrict their liability for death or personal injury resulting from negligence.

Valid if reasonable

Section 2(2) – in the case of other loss or damage, a person cannot exclude or restrict their liability for negligence except when the term or notice satisfies the requirement of reasonableness.

Section 3 – where a consumer deals on a business's standard form of contract, the business cannot exclude its liability for breach, or provide a substantially different performance, or no performance at all, of the contract unless its actions satisfy the requirement of reasonableness.

The test for reasonableness is not specifically defined in the Act, but certain sections provide assistance.

Section 11(1) states 'the term shall have been a fair and reasonable one to be included having regard to the circumstances which were, or ought reasonably to have been, known to or in the contemplation of the parties when the contract was made.

Consumer Rights Act 2015

Section 31: liability that cannot be excluded or restricted (goods)

A term of a contract under ss 9, 10 and 11 to supply goods cannot be excluded or restricted by a trader.

Section 57: liability that cannot be excluded or restricted (services)

A term of a contract under s 49 to supply services cannot be excluded or restricted by a trader.

Section 65: the bar on exclusion or restriction of negligence liability

Traders cannot rely on a term inserted into a consumer contract or notice which excludes or restricts liability for death or personal injury resulting from negligence.

Where a term of a consumer contract or notice intends to exclude or restrict a trader's liability for negligence, a person is not to be taken to have voluntarily accepted any risk merely because they agreed to or knew about the term or notice.

Evaluation point

Ensure you have a clear understanding of ss 31, 57 and 65 CRA 2015 and the differences between the three sections.

Table 4.6.1 Key cases on exclusion clauses

Case	Facts	Element of exclusion clauses	Legal point
L'Estrange v Graucob (1934)	D's contract contained an exclusion clause stating D would not be responsible if the machine broke. The machine did break and stopped working.	Incorporation of the exclusion clause	As L had signed the contract, she was bound by its terms even though she hadn't read them.
Olley v Marlborough Court Ltd (1949)	O booked into M's hotel as a guest. A sign in her room stated the hotel would not be held responsible for any articles lost or stolen. O left a fur coat in the bedroom which was later stolen.	A representation is not a term unless the parties are aware of it when making the contract	Since the contract was made at the reception desk, the notice in the bedroom was too late to become a term of the contract.
Chapelton v Barry UDC (1940)	C hired a deckchair at the beach. He paid 2p and was given a ticket which said on the back the council would not be liable for any accident or damage. When the chair collapsed and C was injured, he sued for damages.	Incorporation of the clause	The court held that the clause was not incorporated into the contract since it was a mere receipt given after the contract was made.
Hollier v Rambler Motors (AMC) Ltd (1972)	C's car was damaged in a fire at D's garage. On previous occasions, the standard form contained an exclusion clause excluding liability for fire damage. On this occasion, the standard form had not been signed.	Construction of the clause	The Court of Appeal stated that the standard form was not incorporated into the contract simply because of previous dealings.

Now test yourself

TESTED 

1. Explain what is meant by an exclusion/exemption clause.
2. What are the two common law rules for whether an exemption clause will be accepted or denied by the courts?
3. How have the courts approached exclusion clauses that appear on notices, tickets or receipts?
4. How has the *contra proferentem* rule helped claimants in contractual disputes over exclusion clauses?
5. Explain the implied term under s 65 of the Consumer Rights Act 2015.

Exam summary

In the exam, you MAY be asked:

- multiple-choice questions about your understanding of exclusion clauses as contractual terms
- to explain or analyse your understanding of exclusion clauses as contractual terms, for example, what they are and how they are controlled under the common law or through statutory intervention
- to apply your understanding of exclusion clauses as contractual terms to a scenario situation, in order to consider the rights and remedies of the parties.

4.7 Vitiating factors

The AQA law specification looks at two vitiating factors (reasons) that potentially vitiate (invalidate) a contract: misrepresentation and economic duress.

Vitiating: invalidating; a vitiating factor makes the contract null and void.

Misrepresentation

REVISED

The nature of misrepresentation

If a party is encouraged to enter into a contract because of a false statement of material fact which later turns out to be untrue, then the untrue statement or misrepresentation may provide a remedy to the injured party. *Inntrepreneur Estates Ltd v Holland* (2000) provides a straightforward and modern example of an 'untrue statement'.

A misrepresentation cannot be:

1 a mere opinion – see *Bissett v Wilkinson* (1927)
2 an expression of future intent – see *Edgington v Fitzmaurice* (1885)
3 a mere trade puff – see *Carlill v Carbolic Smoke Ball Co.* (1893), case details on page 148.

A misrepresentation can arise from conduct rather than from a verbal or written statement – see *Spice Girls Ltd v Aprilia World Service BV* (2000), but not from mere silence – in *Hamilton v Allied Domecq* (2007) Lord Rodger stated 'a failure ... to speak might be regarded as morally questionable. But that is different from saying [there is] a legal duty to speak'.

A statement made after the formation is not actionable – see *Roscorla v Thomas* (1842), case details on page 153.

Types of misrepresentation

Misrepresentations cover many different types of statement. They may be blatant lies or innocent telling of inaccurate information. Once it has been established that a statement made was false and that this statement induced the other party into signing a contract, it will be necessary to establish:

+ the type of misrepresentation, and
+ the relevant remedy to that type of misrepresentation.

Exam tip

It is vital for you to appreciate the three main types of misrepresentation.

Stretch and challenge

Identify five statements that could be considered misrepresentations in the sale of a car, for example, the engine size is 1.3 when it is a 1.1.

There are three types of misrepresentation:

1 Fraudulent misrepresentation is a statement made knowingly or deliberately or being reckless as to whether it is true or not.

   See Lord Herschell's full test of fraudulent misrepresentation in *Derry v Peek* (1889), where he stated that a statement is a fraudulent misrepresentation if it was made:
   + knowing it to be false
   + without belief in its truth
   + reckless, or careless as to whether it be true or false.
2 Negligent misrepresentation can be actioned at common law where the loss is financial – see *Hedley Byrne and Co. Ltd v Heller and Partners Ltd* (1963). But here, liability for the misrepresentation will only arise where there is a 'special relationship' and the party making the misrepresentation owes a duty of care to the other party.

In contrast, s 2(1) of the Misrepresentation Act 1967 allows an action where a misrepresentation is made and a loss occurs as a result of relying on the misrepresentation. That person will be liable unless they can show they had reasonable grounds to believe the statement – see *Howard Marine v Ogden* (1978).

3 (Wholly) innocent misrepresentation: here an untrue statement is made, but the party making it can demonstrate reasonable grounds for believing the truth of the statement.

Evaluation point

Ensure you have a clear understanding of the three types of misrepresentation and the differences between them.

Remedies for misrepresentation

This depends upon the type of misrepresentation. For all three types of misrepresentation on the AQA specification, rescission is available. However, rescission may not always be appropriate in each individual case.

Rescission: a contractual remedy which places both parties back into the pre-contractual position and as if it never actually happened.

Fraudulent misrepresentation

Here, the innocent party can rescind the contract and claim damages.

- Damages are based on the tort of deceit and therefore there is no requirement that the injuries are foreseeable.
- The injured party is entitled to reparation for 'all the damage flowing from the fraudulent inducement' – see *Doyle v Olby (Ironmongers)* (1969).
- The defendant is responsible for all damages and consequential loss where there is a causal link between the misrepresentation and the damage – see *Smith New Court Securities Ltd v Scrimgeour Vickers Ltd* (1996).
- A loss of profit can also be claimed.
- The injured party can still affirm the contract (insisting on its continued performance) or disaffirm the contract (and refuse any future performance).

Typical mistake

The remedies available to each type of misrepresentation are different and sometimes candidates get confused when asked to explain or apply the remedies for a specific type of misrepresentation.

Negligent misrepresentation

Section 2(1) of the 1967 Act states that the same remedies are available here as if a statement is made fraudulently.

- Damages are available under the 1967 Act and at common law.
- Common law damages are based on foreseeable loss under tort law.
- Contributory negligence can reduce the amount of damages.

Innocent misrepresentation

Here, s 2(2) of the 1967 Act states the remedies are rescission or damages in lieu of rescission. A successful claimant cannot claim both.

- There is no automatic or absolute right to damages.
- There is a discretionary right to damages.
- Rescission is possible.

Economic duress

REVISED

Definition and rules

Threats to coerce a party into a contract have long been recognised at common law as a vitiating factor. The courts appreciate an innocent party's lack of real consent. To establish a case of economic duress, the victim must prove two things:

- coercion of the will
- illegitimate pressure.

Economic duress: where one party makes threats to a person's financial situation in order to form or change an agreement.

A contract agreed under economic duress cannot be recognised as a true or real agreement between the parties.

The concept of economic duress was first supported by Kerr J in *The Siboen and The Sibotre* (1976), where he described economic duress as 'such a degree of coercion that the other party was deprived of his free consent and agreement'.

Pressure to negotiate and enter into contracts are a fact of business life. Sometimes it may be difficult to identify the line between necessity to contract and coercion. Commercial pressure is simply not enough to invalidate a contract.

The rules are fairly *ad hoc* as cases arise:

- Coercion of will: the courts will take into account whether the injured party protested, whether there was an alternative route available, were they independently advised or whether they took steps to avoid it – see *Pao On v Lau Yiu Long* (1980).
- Illegitimate pressure: coercion caused by pressure in itself is not enough. A hard-driven bargain is exactly that, otherwise every toughly fought deal would be at risk of being voided.
- Threats by a union to blacklist a ship were decided to be economic duress – see *The Universal Sentinel* (1983): 'submission arising from the realisation that there is no other practical choice open to them.'
- A threat to a small firm by a larger firm that they would breach a contract can be economic duress – see *Atlas Express v KafCo.* (1989).
- There was no economic duress in *Williams v Roffey Bros* (1991), as the builders had made a reasonable choice.

Revision activity

Identify five instances that could be considered economic duress in the formation of a contract to supply football boots to an independent sports shop by a major sports label.

Remedies for economic duress

The effect of economic duress would be to make a contract voidable.

An injured party will, therefore, be entitled to have the contract put aside, unless they have expressly or impliedly asserted it. The injured party must seek rescission as soon as possible after the original economic duress has stopped.

As economic duress is similar to the tort of intimidation, a remedy for damages would lie in tort.

Table 4.7.1 Key cases on misrepresentation

Case	Facts	Element of vitiating factor	Legal point
Derry v Peek (1889)	D's prospectus said they had permission to use steam-powered trams. They didn't have permission but genuinely believed they were going to.	Fraudulent misrepresentation	Statement was not a misrepresentation as the company honestly believed they would have permission. Lord Herschell defined the test.
Bissett v Wilkinson (1927)	A statement was made without expert knowledge as to how many sheep an area of land could hold.	A statement alleged to be a misrepresentation must be a statement of material fact.	The statement was speculation and mistaken so could not be relied upon.
Edgington v Fitzmaurice (1885)	Directors of a company borrowed money allegedly to repair buildings but paid off debts, which was their intention from the start.	A statement alleged to be a misrepresentation must be a statement of material fact.	This was a false statement of material fact and a clear actionable misrepresentation.

Case	Facts	Element of vitiating factor	Legal point
Spice Girls Ltd v Aprilia World Service BV (2000)	In signing a contract to promote scooters, the group failed to notify the manufacturer that one of them was about to leave and did so.	Silence is generally not a representation since no statement is made, but there are exceptions.	The presence of the group member during filming and signing of the contract was a representation that no one in the group was about to leave.
The Siboen and The Sibotre (1976)	Charterers of ships during a world recession demanded renegotiation of their contracts with ship owners.	Definition	Economic duress is such a degree of coercion that the other party was deprived of free consent and agreement.
Pao On v Lau Yiu Long (1980)	C refused to complete the main contract unless certain subsidiary agreements were met by D. D was anxious for the main contract to be fulfilled.	Validity of claim	The validity of claims depends upon whether the injured party protested, had an alternative course open to them, were independently advised or took steps to avoid duress.
The Universal Sentinel (1983)	The ship was blacklisted unless a release fee was paid to a shipping workers' federation.	Where was pressure from?	Economic duress can also include pressure from trade unions or federations.
Inntrepreneur Estates Ltd v Holland 2000	A brewery misrepresented the amount of beer a pub sold to its new tenants – 'the pub is ticking over on 480 barrels' but the reality was 372.	Untrue statement	A contractual clause where a lessee acknowledges no reliance placed on pre-contractual statements would have fallen within scope of s 3 Misrepresentation Act 1967.
Idemitsu Kosan v Sumitomo Corp (2016)	IK purchased a company X from SC. The contract to buy contained several warranties as to X's liabilities, which IK later claimed were deliberately undervalued by SC.	Terms versus representations under s 2(1)	A warranty is a contractual term or promise that comes into existence once the agreement has been concluded, whereas a representation is simply a pre-contractual statement.

Table 4.7.2 Key cases on economic duress

Case	Facts	Legal point
The Atlantic Baron (1979)	H agreed to build a tanker for N. H later insisted that the price would increase by 10%. N reluctantly agreed the new price increase, but later argued economic duress to recover the extra 10%.	While the court held that there had probably been economic duress, waiting eight months had simply affirmed the contract.
Atlas Express v Kafco (1989)	K had won a contract to supply handbaskets to W. During the contract, supplier A raised its prices and threatened to stop the delivery unless K agreed to pay. K reluctantly agreed.	K was not bound by the agreement to pay the increase, especially as A raised the price just before Christmas and K would be unable to find an alternative supplier.
DC Builders v Rees (1965)	D had carried out work on R's house. R knew that D was in financial trouble and said they would pay £300 against an agreed sum of £462 that was owed. D agreed in order to avoid bankruptcy.	The CA said that R had used coercion and that there was no true accord between the parties.

Now test yourself TESTED

1 What is a misrepresentation under contract law?
2 What are the three different types of misrepresentation?
3 Explain the remedies available for one type of misrepresentation.
4 What is economic duress?
5 According to Lord Scarman in *Pao On v Lau Yiu Long* (1980), what must be checked before the validity of a claim of economic duress can be established by the courts?

Exam summary

In the exam, you MAY be asked:
- multiple-choice questions about your understanding of misrepresentation or economic duress
- to explain or analyse your understanding of vitiating factors to a contract, specifically through misrepresentation or economic duress
- to apply your understanding of misrepresentation or economic duress to a scenario situation, in order to consider the rights and remedies of the parties.

4.8 Discharge of a contract

Discharge of a contract refers to the point at which a contract comes to an end. In such a case, both parties are 'freed' from their contractual obligations. The AQA specification looks at three ways a contract can be discharged:
- performance
- breach (actual and anticipatory), and
- frustration.

Performance

A contract is not discharged until all of the obligations are performed. This general rule requires that performance must match exactly and completely the contract's obligations – see *Cutter v Powell* (1795).

Therefore, if one party fails to fully perform their contractual obligations, the other party should in theory be able to sue for breach of contract.

Exam tip

Unless asked to do so by the question, you do not have to suggest ways that a contract can come to an end if your answer suggests there is a problem with the contract in a scenario.

Modification of the general rule

The general rule can be modified or avoided in several ways:
- Divisible/severable contracts are those where obligations are divisible, whereby each separate obligation can be singularly enforceable – see *Taylor v Webb* (1937).
- Acceptance of part-performance, if genuine, can be acceptable by both parties and payment for what is performed can be enforceable – see *Sumpter v Hedges* (1898).
- Where substantial performance is achieved and a party has largely performed their obligations, it may be possible to enforce the appropriate payment – see *Daken v Lee* (1916).
- If either party is prevented from performing the obligations under the contract, then the general rule will not apply – *Condor v Baron Knights* (1966).

Typical mistake

If a question clearly leads you to a particular type of discharge of contract, for example, breach, it will be unnecessary for you to discuss all the other ways a contract can come to an end. Keep your answer relevant to the scenario.

Time of performance

In many cases, a failure to perform on time is a breach of warranty, which then allows damages but not a repudiation of the contract.

Where time is of the essence, repudiation can follow from a breach if:

- both parties had made this clear
- the subject matter dictates such
- a time extension is given on the proviso that repudiation will occur if this deadline is not met.

Breach

REVISED

A breach occurs where a party fails to perform their obligations under the contract. It arises where there:

- is non-performance, or
- is a defective performance, or
- are repudiating obligations without any justification.

A common example would be a breach of a condition under a consumer contract which would allow the injured party to repudiate the contract, whereas a breach of a warranty wouldn't.

Types of breach

Types of breach include:

- breach of an actual term of the contract, allowing an action for damages
- breach of a condition which is either expressed or implied, including an innominate term, where the breach is sufficient to allow the repudiation of the contract – see *The Hong Kong Fir Case* (1962)
- an anticipatory breach, where one party notifies the other of an intention to breach their obligations under the contract – see *Hochester v De La Tour* (1853).

Revision activity

Research online the cases of *The Hong Kong Fir Case* (1962) and *Hochester v De La Tour* (1853).

Frustration

REVISED

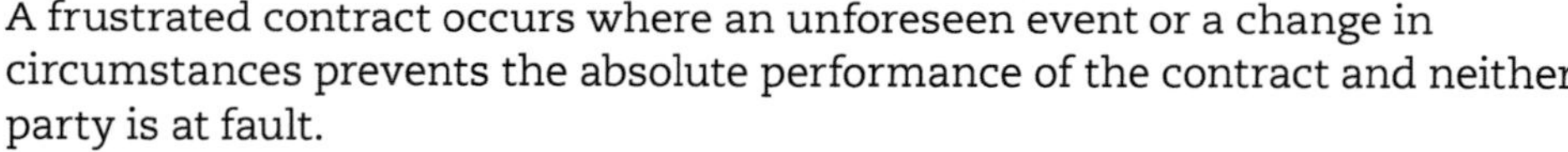

A frustrated contract occurs where an unforeseen event or a change in circumstances prevents the absolute performance of the contract and neither party is at fault.

The doctrine of frustration was developed to provide a remedy for situations that arise during the duration of the contract which make future performance:

- illegal – see *Fibrosa Spolka v Fairbairn* (1943)
- impossible, or
- fundamentally different.

Table 4.8.1 Doctrine of frustration

Illegal	Both parties are ready and willing to perform, but a change in the law prevents performance. This can be a change in the law in another country or the outbreak of war making trade with a hostile country illegal – see *Metropolitan Water Board v Dick Kerr* (1915).
Impossible	The contract ends in one of four ways: + subject matter is destroyed – see *Taylor v Caldwell* (1863) + subject matter is unavailable – see *Morgan v Manser* (1943) + one of the parties dies + there is a risk of the contract being unable to be performed completely.
Fundamentally different	The central purpose of the contract is destroyed by a frustrating event. The development essentially, and famously, arose due to the postponement of a coronation. The result of the frustration depends upon whether the commercial purpose of the contract is destroyed, as per *Krell v Henry* (1903), or if that purpose actually continued, as per *Herne Bay Steamboat Co. v Hutton* (1903).

Stretch and challenge

Research online the cases of *Taylor v Caldwell* (1863) and *Morgan v Manser* (1943).

Evaluation point

Ensure you have a clear understanding of the three situations that can arise to frustrate a contract.

Limits of the doctrine of frustration

Certain restrictions or limitations are imposed by the courts, as it may be unfair on one of the parties to simply set aside the contract. Instead, obligations remain:

- where one party induces the frustrating event (then the contract will be breached)
- if the event is expressly provided for in the contract (then the frustration does not apply)
- where the actual event was or should have been foreseen.

Impact of the Law Reform (Frustrated Contracts) Act 1943

This Act was created to address some of the unfairness of the common law doctrine. It states:

- any money already paid before the frustrating event is recoverable
- any money payable before the frustrating event is no longer owed
- where any expenses have occurred, payment can be ordered by the court
- if any valuable benefit has been obtained, payment may be ordered by the court.

Table 4.8.2 Key cases on discharge of contract

Case	Facts	Element of discharge	Legal point
Cutter v Powell (1795)	Correct goods were delivered in wrong size cases.	Performance	Part performance is no performance.
Taylor v Webb (1937)	A seaman died so performance was not complete.	Avoiding the strict rule on performance	If the contract has divisible obligations, a fair payment for each part completely performed can be expected.
Daken v Lee (1916)	A builder completed a contract but some of the work was unsatisfactory, so D refused to pay.	Substantial performance	If performance is substantial, then recovery is possible.
Startup v Macdonald (1843)	The contract was to deliver at the end of March, which the seller did at 8:30 p.m. on 31 March (a Saturday).	Avoiding the strict rule on performance	If a party offers to perform and is refused by the other party, then payment is recoverable.
Williams v Roffey (1990)	Extra money was promised to builders if they would simply complete their contractual obligations on time.	Agreement to end a contract	Consideration must be provided to end a contract.
Frost v Knight (1872)	D promised to marry his fiancée when his father died. D broke off the engagement before he died.	Consequence of an anticipatory breach	Fiancée successfully sued D, even though the actual breach had not yet arrived.
Taylor v Caldwell (1863)	A music hall central to a contract was destroyed in a fire.	Frustration of contract	Frustration by impossibility.

Case	Facts	Element of discharge	Legal point
Morgan v Manser (1943)	An actor was contracted for ten years but conscripted into the army for six of those years.	Frustration of contract	Due to obvious and important frustration, both parties were excused performance.
Metropolitan Water Board v Dick Kerr (1915)	A contract to build a reservoir was stopped by the government due to the outbreak of war.	Frustration of contract	This was a clear frustrating event, as it was impossible for the parties to continue.
Krell v Henry (1903)	A room was booked to observe the coronation procession of King Edward VII. The coronation was postponed due to the King's illness.	Frustration of contract	The central purpose was to observe the procession and therefore the contract was frustrated.
Herne Bay Steamboat Co. v Hutton (1903)	As part of the coronation celebrations, D hired a boat to watch the King. The coronation was postponed due to the King's illness.	Frustration of contract	The central purpose of the contract (a trip around the Solent) remained, so there was no frustration.
The Hong Kong Fir Case (1962)	A ship was chartered for two years but was not seaworthy and was lost after 18 weeks.	Breach of innominate term	CA said the term was a warranty which only entitled the claimants to sue for damages.
Hochester v De La Tour (1853)	D agreed to employ H at a future date, but then wrote to H saying his services were no longer required. H sued D for breach of contract.	Anticipatory breach	The Court held (1) D was liable for breach. (2) This removed H's obligation to perform the contract.
Canary Wharf v EMA (2019)	The European Medicines Agency sought to end its 25-year lease on a London building because of Brexit: EU law required EU agencies to be based in EU countries.	Frustration of contract	HC rejected the argument. A 'break clause' could have been negotiated in the first place and the lease allowed the EMA to sub-let to another tenant.

Now test yourself

1. How does the case of *Williams v Roffey* (1990) modify the rule on discharge of contract by agreement?
2. Define the different types of breach.
3. What is meant by frustration of contract?
4. What are the main ways a contract can be frustrated?
5. Why was the case of *Krell v Henry* (1903) decided differently to the case of *Herne Bay Steamboat Co. v Hutton* (1903)?
6. Explain one of the limits to the doctrine of frustration of contract.

Exam summary

In the exam, you MAY be asked:

- multiple-choice questions about your understanding of how a contract is discharged, for example, through performance
- to explain or analyse your understanding of how a contract is discharged, specifically through performance, breach or frustration
- to apply your understanding of how a contract is discharged by performance, breach or frustration to a scenario situation, in order to consider the rights and remedies of the parties.

4.9 Remedies

This final topic on the AQA contract law specification examines:

- compensatory damages
- equitable remedies of specific performance and rescission
- termination of contract for breach.

Exam tip

Unless a question asks for a discussion of remedies, there is generally no reason to discuss this topic in an exam question.

Typical mistake

In a scenario question, do not list all types of common law and equitable remedies, defining and explaining them before discounting those that are irrelevant. This wastes time, as not all remedies will be necessarily available or relevant to the scenario. Pick, define and apply only those that are relevant.

Compensatory damages

REVISED

The main type of common law remedy for breach of contract is damages. This is an award of money in order to compensate the injured party.

The aim is to place the party into the position they would have been in if the contract had been performed.

Damages: normally in the form of a cash compensation payment, to put the injured party financially into the position they would have been in had the contract been performed.

Categories of recoverable loss

The two main categories of damages available here to the injured party are:

- liquidated damages, and
- unliquidated damages.

Liquidated damages

Liquidated damages operate when both parties to the contract have, at the time of contracting, fixed an amount of damages in a clause in the contract that would be paid should there be a breach of contract – see *Dunlop Pneumatic Tyre Co. v New Garage and Motor Co.* (1914).

However, the amount fixed could be ignored by the court unless it represents a fair and proper assessment of any loss.

If the amount is a proper reflection of the loss, the courts will enforce the agreed amount of damages.

If, however, the amount is seen as a penalty, that is to say an amount of money that far exceeds the breach of contract, this will be unenforceable.

The courts will not enforce a penalty clause where it seeks merely to punish the defendant for a minor breach.

Unliquidated damages

Where there is no fixed amount of damages in the contract, the courts can fix an amount based on the actual loss called unliquidated damages. Here, the courts look closely at the principle of placing the party in the position they would have been in if the breach had not occurred.

The main tests for unliquidated damages can be seen by looking at the issue of causation, the remoteness of loss and the duty to mitigate loss in order to fix the amount.

Causation

The courts will simply look at the breach to see whether it was factually caused by the actions of the defendant – see *The Monarch Steamship* (1949).

Remoteness of loss

It is not practical for every consequence that follows a breach of contract to be compensated for. Here, the courts will look at what consequence should be compensated for and how much compensation should be paid. The classic case is *Hadley v Baxendale* (1854).

In *Hadley v Baxendale* (1854), Alderson, B stated in court:

> 'Where two parties have made a contract which one of them has broken, the damages which the other party ought to receive in respect of such breach of contract should be such as may fairly and reasonably be considered either arising naturally, i.e., according to the usual course of things, from such breach of contract itself, or such as may reasonably be supposed to have been in the contemplation of both parties, at the time they made the contract, as the probable result of the breach of it.'

This is known as the rule in *Hadley v Baxendale*. See Table 4.9.1 for the case details.

The court decided that the carrier was not liable for the loss for two reasons:

1. The absence of a mill shaft would not normally cause a loss since the mill owner could have a spare.
2. The carrier was not aware that the claimant could not restart production until a new mill shaft was made.

Mitigation of loss

Common sense should prevail that following a breach, the injured party should, as best as possible, try to lessen or mitigate any actual or potential loss – see *Pilkington v Wood* (1953).

The courts will take a dim view if the defendant simply sat back and allowed the consequences of the breach to get worse, when they could have done something to prevent further loss. The basic principle here is that the injured party must act reasonably in relation to the breach.

If the alternative is to take an unreasonable course of action, for example, to buy substandard goods in replacement, then the courts will not require them to do so.

It is up to the defendant to prove that the claimant failed to follow a reasonable path to mitigate any loss.

Stretch and challenge

Consider the following situation:

Jimmy owns a car repair garage. His hydraulic lift used to raise a car off the ground has stopped working. He contacts LiftZRepairZ, who say they can fix the lift 'by the end of next week'. However, three weeks later LiftZRepairZ have not been to fix the lift.

Jimmy sues the company, who says they thought he would have had another spare hydraulic lift he could use.

Equitable remedies

REVISED

Unlike common law remedies, equitable remedies are not 'as of right' and instead are at the discretion of the courts. The two key equitable remedies on the AQA specification are:

+ specific performance, and
+ rescission.

Specific performance

Specific performance requires the defendant to carry out their agreed obligations under the contract.

The court can order specific performance and/or damages. Orders for specific performance are rare: the courts are reluctant to force defendants to carry out their obligations, usually because it would be impossible or difficult for them to do so. If the courts believe that damages will be more appropriate, they will not order specific performance.

However, it may be that damages will not compensate the injured party, since the goods or services may have a distinctive characteristic.

Whether or not a court will exercise its discretion in granting an order for specific performance centres on the principle as to whether it would be fair to do so – see *De Francesco v Barnum* (1890).

Also, if the order of specific performance would mean excessive hardship on the party, the court will not order such – see *Dyster v Randall and Sons* (1926).

Evaluation point

Consider five examples of a breach of contract, for example, sending apples instead of oranges to an orange juice manufacturer, and decide the most appropriate equitable remedy to compensate the breach.

Rescission

Rescission is an attempt to place the parties to the contract, as best as possible, in the position they were in before they entered the contract. It is an attempt to unpick the contract.

Rescission is available where a contract is voidable as a result of a vitiating factor, such as misrepresentation or economic duress (see Chapter 4.7).

However, the right to rescind the contract may be lost where:

- the claimant affirms the contract
- a third party acquires the rights of the goods – see *Car & Universal Credit v Caldwell* (1964)
- time has lapsed – see *Leaf v International Galleries* (1950), or
- *restitutio in integrum* is impossible.

Restitutio in integrum: the restoration of an injured party back to the original, pre-contractual situation.

Termination of contract for breach

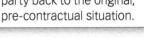

A breach of contract occurs when:

- a party to the contract does not perform their obligations, or
- the party fails to reach the standards set or expected in the contract, or
- the party unlawfully repudiates the contract.

The breach can be of any term of the contract – condition, warranty or an innominate term – or could be an anticipatory breach where one of the parties notifies the other that they will be breaching a condition.

The consequences of a breach depend upon the type of term breached:

- Breach of a condition: the injured party can sue for damages and/or repudiate the contract.
- Breach of a warranty: the injured party can sue for damages only.
- Breach of an innominate term: the injured party can sue immediately or wait until the contract performance date, then sue.

Stretch and challenge

Research the following cases on termination by breach: *Photo Productions v Securicorp* (1980) and *The Hansa Nord* (1976).

Table 4.9.1 Key cases on remedies

Case	Facts	Element of remedies	Legal point
Dunlop Pneumatic Tyre Co. v New Garage and Motor Co. (1914)	D sold tyres to X, a dealer, who then resold the tyres to S, a retailer, at a price below the agreed price enforced by D.	Liquidated damages	Case sets out a test to differentiate between liquidated damages and penalties.
Hadley v Baxendale (1854)	There was a delay in transporting a mill shaft. C sued D for the losses as a result of the delay.	Remoteness of damage	Test established for remoteness of damage.
Pilkington v Wood (1953)	C sued a solicitor for damages after receiving negligent advice when buying a house. The solicitor said he should have sued the vendor to mitigate the loss.	Mitigation of loss	This argument was rejected. The court said that the duty to mitigate did not require C to 'embark on a complicated and difficult piece of litigation against a third party'.
Globalia v Fulton (2017)	G chartered a ship from F but G terminated the agreement two years early. F accepted the breach of contract and sold the ship on, but then sought to claim damages from G for the two years' loss of revenue.	Mitigation of loss	The sale of the ship was not an actual mitigation of loss, since F could have sought an alternative charter of the ship and over time would have been better off financially.
De Francesco v Barnum (1890)	A young dancer entered into a contract of apprenticeship which paid her no money and disallowed her from taking on any paid employment elsewhere.	Specific performance	The contract was so disadvantageous to the dancer that the court would grant neither an injunction nor require specific performance of the contract.
Dyster v Randall and Sons (1926)	C, who had been made bankrupt, could not find the financial means to purchase a house he had agreed to buy.	Specific performance	The court refused an order of specific performance.
Car & Universal Credit v Caldwell (1964)	N bought a car from C and paid using a fraudulent cheque. C contacted the police and the AA when he discovered this the next day. N meanwhile sold the car to T.	Rescission – third party	C had done enough to rescind the contract and was entitled to his car back from T.
Leaf v International Galleries (1950)	L bought a painting from D. Both believed it was by a famous painter but five years later it was discovered to be a fake. L sued D for misrepresentation.	Rescission – lapse of time	The claim for innocent misrepresentation was successful, but because it had been such a long time, L had lost the right to rescind.
Photo Productions v Securicorp (1980)	S provided security services for P. One of S's staff accidentally burnt the factory down. P sued S, who said an exclusion term in the contract excluded their liability.	Termination by breach	HL held that the doctrine of fundamental breach was not at issue here. The exclusion clause covered the damage and S was not liable for the damage.
The Hansa Nord (1976)	G agreed to sell D 12,000 tons of cattle feed pellets, all of which 'to be made in good condition'. Some of the pellets were not so, but all of the cargo was still usable for its intended purpose.	Termination by breach	Only a breach of a condition (one that goes right to the root of the contract) allows an injured party to repudiate the contract. This was not the case here as all of the cargo could be used for its intended purpose.

Now test yourself

TESTED

1 Using examples, what is the difference between common law and equitable remedies?
2 How do the courts distinguish between a penalty and liquidated damages?
3 How do the courts decide whether to allow a claim for unliquidated damages?
4 For what reasons is a claimant expected to mitigate their loss following a breach of contract?
5 How would specific performance provide a remedy for a claimant, and in what circumstances would an order for specific performance be denied?
6 How would rescission provide a remedy for a claimant?

Exam summary

In the exam, you MAY be asked:

+ multiple-choice questions about your understanding of contractual remedies
+ to explain or analyse your understanding of contractual remedies, specifically through damages, specific performance, rescission or for breach
+ to apply your understanding of contractual remedies, specifically through damages, specific performance, rescission or for breach, to a scenario situation, in order to consider the rights and remedies of the parties.

Exam practice

There are a mix of:

+ multiple-choice questions (MCQs) requiring the candidate to identify whether a statement is true or false
+ problem/scenario questions worth 5, 10 and 30 marks and
+ a 15-mark extended answer question asking the candidate to discuss a statement based on a specific area of contract law.

In 15-mark and 30-mark questions, you are required to provide an extended answer which shows a clear, logical and sustained line of reasoning leading to a valid conclusion.

Multiple-choice questions (1 mark each)

1 Which of the following is an accurate statement concerning the postal rule for the purposes of forming a contract?
  - **A** The postal rule applies to all forms of communication, including email.
  - **B** The postal rule applies when the letter is received, not posted.
  - **C** An offer cannot be revoked after an acceptance is posted.
  - **D** The postal rule cannot be excluded in the terms of the offer itself.

2 Select the false statement about the Unfair Contract Terms Act 1977 (UCTA).
  - **A** UCTA applies to both consumer and business-to-business contracts.
  - **B** A contractual term cannot exclude liability for death.
  - **C** UCTA uses the test for reasonableness in identifying unfair terms.
  - **D** If a term is found to be unfair, UCTA will make the term void.

3 Which of the following is not a suitable way for an exclusion clause to be validly included into a contract?
  - **A** Through the application of the maxim *caveat emptor*.
  - **B** If the parties had express knowledge of the clause at the time of the contract.
  - **C** Reasonable steps are taken to bring the clause to the attention of the other party.
  - **D** Using a ticket with the clause on the reverse.

4 Choose the best description of misrepresentation as a form of vitiating factor in contract law.
  - **A** It can be a mere opinion.
  - **B** It can be an expression of future intent.
  - **C** It can be a mere trade puff.
  - **D** It can be a false statement of material fact.

5 Select the true statement about the doctrine of consideration.
  - **A** Consideration does not have to be sufficient.
  - **B** Consideration must be adequate.
  - **C** Past consideration is accepted by the courts.
  - **D** Consideration can only be in the form of money.

Short answer 5-mark questions

6 Explain the contractual remedy of recission and how it can benefit an injured party.

7 Explain why the breach an express term leads to different remedies available to the parties.

8 Paige is employed as a taxi driver and agrees to drive her sister, Hope, to the cinema on Friday night. Hope says she will let Paige borrow her expensive shoes for a party later that month if she does. Paige drives Hope to the cinema but Hope later refuses to let her borrow her shoes.

Applying the rules of intention to create legal relations, suggest why Paige would probably have no rights and therefore no remedies against Hope.

9 Adam is shopping online. He notices a pair of expensive headphones advertised on a well-known brand's website for £3.99. The headphones normally retail at £399.99. He clicks the image which adds a pair of headphones into his 'shopping basket'. However, when he goes to pay for the headphones, the price is £399.99.

Suggest why Adam would probably have no rights against the website's owners to insist on the lower price.

10-mark questions

10 Dorothy needs to pay for her car parking in a city-centre car park. She has no coins, but a sign on the parking meter says she can 'Pay by phone'. Dorothy rings the number and an automated message explains the price per hour and that by paying the parking fee by phone, she agrees to the car park's terms and conditions. One of the conditions is that the car park owner will not be responsible for damage to her car caused by the negligence of other users of the car park. Dorothy's car is badly damaged by another customer of the car park who drives off without leaving their details.

Advise Dorothy as to whether she has any rights and remedies against the car park owner.

11 Belinda is shopping on U-Trade, an internet auction site. She wants to buy the DVD of an old film that she can't easily buy elsewhere when she comes across one advertised for sale by Charles for '£20.00 – Buy it Now or Best Offer'. Belinda messages Charles and says she will give him £10.00 as a 'Best Offer'. He rejects this, messaging her back saying he would take £15.00. Belinda instantly pays Charles £15.00 through the website. However, later Charles says he's sold it to another person for the full amount.

Advise Belinda as to whether she has any rights and remedies against Charles in offer and acceptance.

15-mark questions

12 Examine the relationship between the doctrines of consideration and privity of contract.
Discuss the extent to which the doctrine of privity is necessary in contract law.

13 There are various ways in which an offer can be terminated.

Examine the termination of an offer in contract law. Discuss the various ways, using case examples, how contract law allows an offer to be terminated prior to acceptance.

30-mark questions

14 Joe is a student in the final year of studying A-levels. In his spare time, he designs and makes decorative greetings cards. Joe can supply ready-made cards from his catalogue and 'made to order' cards at the request of a buyer. Joe has just received an enquiry for 100 ready-made cards and 100 'made to order' cards from his father, who runs a newsagent's shop.

However, Joe has told his father that he is going to give up his studies in order to become a professional skateboarder. Alarmed at this, Joe's father places the order for the cards and says he will pay him £200 per month to finish his studies in six months' time. Joe says that this is not enough and he would need at least £500. His father says he will only pay Joe £300 per month: 'Take it or leave it'. Joe reluctantly agrees to continue with his studies and accepts his order for the cards. Joe's father pays on time for the order for the cards, but after three months he stops paying £300 monthly and refuses to continue to do so. In fact, his father says that he only had enough money for three months and had no intention of paying Joe after that.

Consider the rights and remedies of Joe against his father.

Assess the extent to which the rules that you have applied in the case of Joe and his father achieve an appropriate balancing of interests between the parties.

15 Tegan runs a carpet-cleaning service. She hears that Neil, a nightclub owner, needs his carpets cleaned after a 24-hour rave. She rang Neil telling him that she would clean the whole nightclub's carpets for £1000. Neil said the most he would pay would be £900. Tegan says she will think about it. A week later, Neil rings Tegan and says he'll pay her the £1000 after customers were refusing to stay because of the smell of the carpet. However, Tegan has agreed another job with another company to clean their carpets.

Tegan buys a new carpet cleaner form KleenaZ, an industrial cleaning machine supplier. When she removed it from its packaging, she noticed that one of the wheels was loose. When she used the cleaner, the loose wheel became distracting and difficult to use. After a week the loose wheel fell off and it was impossible to use as a cleaner.

Consider the rights and remedies of Neil against Tegan and of Tegan against KleenaZ.

Assess the extent to which the rules that you have applied in the case of Tegan and Neil and KleenaZ achieve an appropriate balancing of interests between the parties.

End-of-unit summary

You should have an understanding of:

- The rules and principles of contract, specifically formation, terms, vitiating factors, discharge and remedies.
- The theory of contract.
- The essential requirements of contract: offer.
- The essential requirements of contract: acceptance.
- The essential requirements of contract: consideration.
- Contractual terms including implied, express and innominate terms.
- The Consumer Rights Act 2015.
- Exclusion clauses and how they are controlled by the common law and statute.
- Vitiating factors of misrepresentation and economic duress.
- Discharge of contract through performance, breach or frustration.
- Remedies of contract including compensatory damages, equitable remedies and termination of contract for breach.

5 Human rights

5.1 Rules in human rights law

Human rights law is an optional unit and assessed by AQA on Paper 3B.

Human rights are a collection of fundamental entitlements that exist in our legal system simply because we are human beings. In the UK, it does not matter where you are from, nor your gender, race, religion or sexuality: these rights exist and apply to all in equal measure. Or, rather, they are meant to apply equally.

Human rights refer to a series of key rights that cannot be removed from citizens, although they can, and have been, restricted for good and sometimes not-so-good reasons.

The Human Rights Act 1998 was passed into law by the UK government in 2000. As case law has developed, the idea and awareness of having basic human rights has become a crucial part of the way society operates.

While the intention of Parliament should prevail, the courts MUST take into consideration two guiding factors in interpreting the law:

1 All laws must be interpreted in a way that is compatible with the Human Rights Act 1998 under s 33, and
2 No law is to be in contravention with any Article under the European Convention on Human Rights.

The Human Rights Act brought into law, for the first time, many rights in a single document that citizens thought already existed but largely did not.

The law under the Act, and the consequent case law, has been seen as both a benefit and a detriment to UK citizens.

Revision activity

Explain the difference between a 'right' and a 'freedom'.

Rights: rules or laws which are believed to belong to every person without discrimination.

Typical mistake

It is easy to become muddled with the different Acts and Conventions, so make sure that you understand the differences between each important piece of law.

European Convention on Human Rights

REVISED 

Until the Human Rights Act 1998 was passed, UK citizens were protected under the European Convention on Human Rights. The Convention had been drawn up after the Second World War, following the atrocities perpetrated by the Nazis, in order to avoid such trauma from occurring in Europe again. It marked a turning point for peace and European diplomacy.

Championed by Winston Churchill and drafted in 1950 by the newly formed Council of Europe, the Convention came into force in 1953. The Convention has its own specific court, the European Court of Human Rights (ECtHR), which is based in Strasbourg, France.

Exam tip

To help prepare for the exam, draw up a timeline of the different pieces of human rights legislation – domestic, European and international – and make sure that you can explain why each piece was specifically passed.

Rules and principles of law under the Convention

REVISED 

The original Convention is divided up into Articles (similar to sections of an Act of Parliament) which guarantee certain important rights and freedoms. These include, for the AQA specification:

+ Article 2 – the right to life
+ Article 5 – the right to liberty and security of person
+ Article 8 – the right to privacy where there is a respect for private and family life, home and correspondence
+ Article 10 – freedom of expression
+ Article 11 – freedom of peaceful assembly and association.

Evaluation point

If there is a right to life, should there be a right to death, for example, to allow assisted suicide. Discuss whether English law strikes a fair balance between those in health and those with a terminal illness.

Stretch and challenge

Using A3 paper, begin to create mind maps on the main five Articles of the European Convention on Human Rights.

Recognition by the UK

REVISED

While a signatory of the ECHR, the UK courts were not bound by it, but it remained strongly persuasive. Until 2000, UK citizens had to exhaust domestic laws on human rights (if they existed) before they could gain access to those rights under the Convention. This was a complicated and expensive process.

The Human Rights Act enshrined the Convention into domestic law in the UK, albeit with restrictions. The government introduced the 1998 Act to streamline access to the basic human rights and freedoms under the Convention, so that citizens could access these rights as a first line of uncomplicated protection in any domestic court.

However, many of the rights allow the imposition of restrictions, generally asserted as being for the purpose of protecting national security.

The introduction of the 1998 Act has been controversial. Dubbed a 'burglar's charter', many argued it vastly overprotects criminals rather than assisting the victims of crime.

Stretch and challenge

Using the internet, research the case of *Thompson and Venables v United Kingdom* (1999).

Table 5.1.1 Key case on human rights law

Case	Facts	Outcome
Thompson and Venables v United Kingdom (1999)	The two child-killers of Jamie Bulger argued there had been a breach of Article 6 of the ECHR (the right to a fair trial) due to the media frenzy that surrounded the case.	Their lawyers successfully argued that the trial and the surrounding media attention undermined the chance of a fair trial. No compensation was paid to the applicants as a result, but the court awarded their legal costs to be paid.

Now test yourself

TESTED 

1. Using key dates from this chapter, draw a timeline in the formulation of human rights law that has impacted the UK.
2. What do you think is meant by 'the right to life'? Should there be any restrictions, such as a right to die?
3. What do you think is meant by 'the right to liberty and security of the person'? Should there be any restrictions, such as detaining suspected criminals?
4. What do you think is meant by 'the right to a respect for a private life'? Should there be any restrictions, such as media scrutiny of celebrities?
5. What do you think is meant by the term 'freedom of expression'? Should there be any restrictions, such as when religion is criticised?

Exam summary

In the exam, you MAY be asked:

+ multiple-choice questions about the law on a specific topic under human rights law
+ to examine and discuss, in part or in whole, a specific topic in human rights law through extended answer questions.

5.2 Theory of human rights

This chapter looks at:

+ the different theories of rights
+ rights contrasted with civil liberties, and
+ the scope of 'fundamental human' rights.

Typical mistake

This topic concentrates on the **theories of human rights**. As these are theoretical concepts only, make sure that you do not quote them as being legal fact as opposed to being legal theory (especially natural rights and legal rights). As they are theories, there is room for debate, conjecture and challenge in your answers.

Exam tip

This topic is more a sociological area than a legal area, but nevertheless it is an important one to understand. The topic underpins the 'why do we have rights?' rather than the 'what rights do we have?' concept.

Theories of rights

REVISED 

Table 5.2.1 Different theories of human rights

Theory of rights	Explanation
Natural rights	+ Each citizen from birth to death has certain fundamental rights that cannot be removed by their government. This theory follows John Locke's writings. + Natural rights developed from the law of nature, natural order and selection. + They form the basis of a peaceful and co-existing society, focusing on the rights of individuals. + This theory relies upon the citizens being independent from one another and having a government or state which respects such individualism.
Legal rights	+ Rights come from the state and not society or the individual or **natural law**. + These rights are formulated by the state in order to run and maintain order in society. + This is a common theory in countries run by despotic regimes or autocrats as opposed to democracies.
Societal rights	+ Societal rights depend very much upon the beliefs, views and autonomy of that society, so may differ as beliefs or religions differ. + To be a societal right, the right must be socially useful and achieve the greatest social benefit for the majority of the citizens in order to be accepted. + Society must find some social utility of the right – a right must be valuable or beneficial to society.
Historical rights	+ This theory applies to the English legal system especially. Custom creates a system of laws common to the country, which evolve, develop and spread with common usage. They are considered valuable as they are tried and tested, and therefore accepted, by society. + Following the English Civil War and eventually the 'Glorious Revolution' (1688), there was a reaffirmation of the rights, liberties and customs that the English had enjoyed since ancient times but which had been gradually eroded or changed by successive monarchs and not through democratic means. + Many historical rights have their basis upon religious beliefs, and then socio-economic beliefs through trade and such practice.
Economic rights	+ Karl Marx argued that rights are maintained by laws which simply protect and prop up the dominant group or groups in society who control the production of goods and services. + A class system and division are created and maintained by these economic rights – society is split into the exploiters and the exploited. + The most economically powerful group becomes the main influence on the government, or in fact becomes the government. + Such rights are not from natural law or custom but made and developed to assist the powerful to the detriment of the weak. This leads to inequality and discrimination. + Marx argued against such capitalism as being fundamentally wrong and an affront to democracy. He held that rights can only truly operate in a classless society.

Theories of human rights: systems of ideas proposed to explain the rationale of having rights based on general principles.

Natural law: rules which are not necessarily written down as laws but are nevertheless followed by citizens.

Evaluation point

Compare and contrast any two theories of human rights. For example, compare and contrast legal rights with economic rights.

Revision activity

Using the internet, research in greater detail John Locke's theory of natural rights.

Rights contrasted with liberties

REVISED

There is a slight difference between rights and liberties:

- Rights are considered universal to all human beings regardless of origin, whereas liberties (or civil liberties) are those specific to a particular country.
- Liberties represent the things that we are free to do in our countries, provided that there is no law against such activities.
- Liberties have been part of our society for centuries and evolve or change as society changes.
- Liberties are 'allowed' in certain societies, whereas rights are guaranteed in certain societies.

In the UK, the Human Rights Act came into law in 2000 and gave effect to the European Convention on Human Rights (ECHR). This guaranteed a certain number of fundamental rights.

Scope of 'fundamental human' rights

REVISED

In order for there to be fundamental human rights, there has to be an understanding that they come with responsibilities and restrictions:

- Every right has a responsibility – citizens cannot expect to have total use of a right unless they respect that others also have the same right.
- In order to use a right, it must not be to the detriment of other citizens who coexist at the same time.
- It may be necessary to restrict our fundamental human rights such as to life, liberty, etc., in order to make a society run smoothly.

There are three main ways to categorise rights that are based on restrictions:

1. Absolute rights cannot be restricted in any way, nor can they be removed. For example, we have the right not to be tortured during the investigation of a crime or for any other purpose.
2. Limited rights are more common and there are many examples under the Human Rights Act 1988. For example, we may have the freedom of movement in the UK, but this can be restricted if a person is lawfully arrested or imprisoned.
3. Qualified rights need to be balanced against the needs of other people and will be restricted, generally temporarily, for the benefit of society. For example, the police may restrict the freedom of movement in order to stop people from entering a certain area during a protest, to avoid public order issues.

Revision activity

Begin a human rights dictionary by adding 'absolute rights', 'limited rights' and 'qualified rights', together with their definitions.

Evaluation point

Make a list of five absolute rights, five limited rights and five qualified rights held by UK citizens.

Now test yourself

TESTED

1. Explain what is meant by the term 'natural law'.
2. How did Karl Marx explain the theory of economic rights?
3. Explain how the right to freedom of movement, for example, going for a walk with a friend, has to be balanced with other citizens' rights.
4. Explain how the right to the freedom of expression, for example, writing a newspaper article, has to be balanced with other citizens' rights.
5. Explain what is meant by an 'absolute right' and how it might be restricted.
6. Explain what is meant by a 'limited right' and how it might be restricted.
7. Explain what is meant by a 'qualified right' and how it might be restricted.

Exam summary

In the exam, you MAY be asked:

- multiple-choice questions about the law on the theory of human rights
- to examine and discuss, in part or in whole, the law on theories of human rights through extended answer questions.

5.3 Human rights in international law

This chapter looks at:

+ the Second World war and its aftermath
+ The United Nations and the Universal Declaration of Human Rights 1948
+ The Council of Europe and The European Convention on Human Rights 1953.

The Second World War and its aftermath

REVISED

The Second World War (1939–45) erupted as a culmination of many grievances and demands, most notably from Germany, that had been festering in Europe ever since the Great War ended in 1918. Germany had been made to pay reparations to the Allied forces as punishment for losing the war. This had left Germany impoverished, which led to the rise of nationalism calling for the end of foreign control.

One of the main national political parties was the National Socialist Party, the Nazi Party. It quickly took control of government and set its own laws and rights to 'benefit' those it felt were the 'master race'. It restricted the rights of those it felt were undermining Germany – most notably Germany's Jewish population.

During the lead up to war, and most notably during the war, ethnic groups in Germany and the countries it controlled (such as Poland) were forced to leave their homes, moved to concentration camps and either forced to work or exterminated.

Exam tip

This topic is more a historical area than a legal area, but nevertheless it is important as it explains the reason for the rush to enforce human rights after the Second World War.

Revision activity

Explain why Adolf Hitler and the Nazi Party were able to carry out crimes against humanity and war crimes with relative impunity.

Evaluation point

Watch or read J.B. Priestley's retrospective play *An Inspector Calls* written in 1945, or any YouTube summary. Discuss how Priestley, a socialist, supported specific human rights that were later championed by Winston Churchill in the United Nations.

The Second World War in Europe ended on 7 May 1945, when Germany surrendered to the Allied forces. This formally ended hostilities in Europe. It marked the end to the atrocities perpetrated by Nazi Germany against the human rights of its own citizens and of those across Nazi-occupied Europe. At its conclusion, Europe was devastated, millions were dead and human rights atrocities were committed that shocked the world.

The discovery of the **Holocaust** and the ease with which one nation was able to remove or deny basic rights to its citizens was seen as an affront to basic human rights.

Holocaust: the name given to the genocide of over six million Jews by Adolf Hitler's Germany and its allies.

The United Nations

The League of Nations was formed after the First World War to resolve international disputes, but its decisions were largely ignored by Nazi Germany.

The **United Nations** (UN) was formed in 1945 to replace the ineffectual League of Nations. It was tasked with maintaining international order, promoting human rights and with providing dispute resolution between Member States. In 2017, there were 193 Member States.

The UN has six primary 'organs' or parts, which include the General Assembly, the Security Council and the International Court of Justice.

United Nations: the purpose of this organisation is to achieve international order, and it has a representative from most sovereign nations. It also has a peace-keeping force which is sent to military zones during times of conflict. Its main offices are in New York and Geneva.

Due to the experiences from both world wars, and keen to avoid further atrocities, the United Nations produced the Universal Declaration of Human Rights in 1948.

Stretch and challenge

Using the internet, familiarise yourself with the current role of the UN.

Universal Declaration of Human Rights 1948

This document was created by the United Nations from its representatives of many different countries, faiths and beliefs from all over the world.

It set out common expectations and standards that countries who signed up to the Declaration were to allow their citizens in enforcing basic human rights.

The Declaration was voluntary and not, however, binding on those countries who signed up.

Revision activity

Using the internet, find an original copy of the Universal Declaration of Human Rights 1948 and create your own facsimile copy of the relevant sections.

The Council of Europe and the European Convention on Human Rights 1953

REVISED

For similar reasons to the establishment of the United Nations, the Council of Europe was established on a more geographically local level. It was formed to provide greater unity between European countries, to promote cooperation between the states and to avoid the ravages of war. Championed by the British Prime Minister, Winston Churchill, during the Second World War, the Council was founded in 1949.

The European Convention on Human Rights was drafted in 1950 by the Council of Europe and formally came into force in 1953.

The Council established the European Court of Human Rights. This was formed to enforce the European Convention on Human Rights and draws its inspiration from the Universal Declaration of Human Rights.

The UK signed the Convention in 1950, but it was not until 2000, when the Human Rights Act 1998 came into effect, that the Convention became part of UK law.

Typical mistake

Do not spend too long discussing the causes of the Second World War and the background to Adolf Hitler and the Nazi Party. Questions will centre on outlining the reasons for the establishment of the United Nations and the consequent European developments from the Council of Europe and the European Convention on Human Rights.

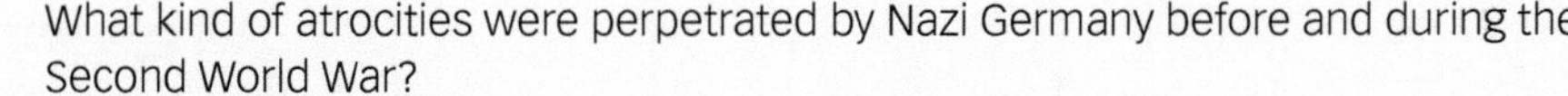

Now test yourself

TESTED

1 What kind of atrocities were perpetrated by Nazi Germany before and during the Second World War?
2 Explain why the United Nations was established and for what purposes.
3 Explain the purpose of the Universal Declaration of Human Rights in 1948.
4 What is the purpose of the Council of Europe?
5 Explain the history behind the European Convention on Human Rights.

Exam summary

In the exam, you MAY be asked:

- multiple-choice questions about human rights in international law
- to examine and discuss, in part or in whole, human rights in international law through extended answer questions.

5.4 Human rights in the UK

This chapter looks at human rights in the UK before and after the Human Rights Act 1998 (HRA 98).

Prior to the Human Rights Act 1998

REVISED

Status of the European Convention on Human Rights in the UK

Until 2000, the human rights and freedoms of UK citizens were mainly protected by the European Convention on Human Rights.

The Convention was drawn up and signed by European countries after the Second World War in order to prevent the wartime atrocities from happening again. The UK signed and ratified the Convention, but it was not until 2000 that it became law.

If a citizen felt that one of the rights under the Convention had been breached, they had to endure a long, expensive and gruelling process to challenge it. This process would first require exhausting domestic routes of redress by testing existing laws, arguing that they were incompatible with the Convention's rights. Citizens would then have to bring a claim to the European Court of Human Rights. This again was a lengthy process without guaranteed success.

This led to calls by civil rights groups and politicians to draw up a 'Bill of Rights' to incorporate the Convention into the UK's domestic law. This eventually became the Human Rights Act 1998.

Evaluation point

Explain why the European Convention on Human Rights, signed by the UK in 1953, did not become binding upon the UK's courts until 2000.

Exam tip

When answering a question on this topic, it is important to understand that rights and freedoms did not begin in the UK with the passing of the Human Rights Act. The Act simply codified much of the European Convention into UK law.

Impact of decisions of the European Court of Human Rights

The European Court of Human Rights (ECtHR) is a very important and powerful court. However, despite its unique purpose, it has been criticised for a variety of reasons:

- It can take years for a case to reach the Court, so some breaches of the Convention can simply be abandoned before reaching the Court.
- Judges must be independent but can be accused of acting in their own state's interests.
- Usually, having a panel of seven judges in order to avoid bias can slow down the decisions of the Court.
- While the Court does have sanctions available, such as finding a state in breach of the Convention and ordering compensation to be paid, there is no real way of enforcing their decision.
- A decision of the Court relies mainly on the co-operation of the state in breach of the Convention, who could in theory refuse to accept its decision.

Typical mistake

Do not mix up the European Convention on Human Rights with the Human Rights Act 1998, or the European Court of Human Rights with the European Court of Justice. You need to understand the different purposes of each.

Breaches of the Convention by the UK

Table 5.4.1 below gives details of case law where the European Convention on Human Rights was breached by the UK.

Stretch and challenge

Using an online video sharing and social media platform such as YouTube, watch a documentary on the background of the *Thompson and Venables* (1999) case. See if you agree with the decision of the ECHR.

Revision activity

Using the internet, research the case of *Sunday Times v United Kingdom* (1979).

Table 5.4.1 Cases where the ECHR was breached by the UK

Case	Facts	ECHR Article breached	Held
Sunday Times v United Kingdom (1979)	The government wanted to prevent publication of the thalidomide scandal under the UK's contempt laws.	Article 10	There was an absolute breach. Publication was allowed.
Thompson and Venables v United Kingdom (1999)	See page 184.	Article 6	The Article was breached.
Lustig-Prean and Beckett v United Kingdom (2000)	Applicants were discharged from the Royal Navy for being homosexuals.	Article 8	There was an absolute breach of right to privacy. The UK changed the law.
Wilson and Palmer v United Kingdom (2002)	Applicants failed to secure pay rises because they were members of trade unions.	Article 11	There was a clear breach of Article 11. The law changed in 2004, outlawing such action.

Now test yourself TESTED

1 Identify which rights or freedoms are covered by Articles 2, 5 and 10.
2 Explain why the European Convention on Human Rights was drawn up.
3 Identify and explain one problem with the decisions of the European Court of Human Rights.
4 Explain the decision in *Sunday Times v United Kingdom* (1979).

Evaluation point

Discuss how human rights or freedoms were maintained in the UK before the passing of the Human Rights Act 1998.

Exam summary

In the exam, you MAY be asked:
- multiple-choice questions about the European Convention on Human Rights 1953
- to explain the background and the purpose of the European Convention on Human Rights 1953
- to analyse the background and the purpose of the European Convention on Human Rights 1953.

After the enactment of the Human Rights Act 1998

REVISED

This section looks at the domestic impact of the UK's first designated piece of human rights law, which has been controversial since its enactment.

Human rights law: laws governing fundamental rights and freedoms that exist in our legal system simply because we are human beings.

Typical mistake

Do not confuse section numbers of the Human Rights Act 1998 with the Article numbers of the European Convention on Human Rights. Neither document's section/Article numbers correspond with each other.

Incorporation and interpretation of the European Convention on Human Rights

Revision activity

Using the internet, research the timescale of the Human Rights Act 1998 from Green Paper to Royal Assent.

Incorporation

The Human Rights Act 1998 was passed by the UK government in 1998 and became law in 2000. It was the first specific Act passed in the UK that solely enforced basic human rights for its citizens.

The Act incorporates *inter alia* Articles 2 to 12 and 14, as well as Articles 1 to 3, of the First Protocol (see Chapter 5.5) of the European Convention on Human Rights into domestic law.

Interpretation

The purpose of HRA 1998 is declared as being primarily:

> 'to give further effect to rights and freedoms guaranteed under the European Convention on Human Rights'.

Section 3 of the 1998 Act states that 'so far as it is possible to do so, primary legislation and subordinate legislation must be read and given effect in a way which is compatible with the Convention rights'. Therefore, any UK legislation should be harmonious and not contravene the Convention's rights.

However, this compatibility is only 'so far as it is possible to do so' which, in effect, allows the UK government to avoid the Convention's rights.

It is interesting to note that English courts had given precedence to the Convention even before the 1998 Act was passed – see *R v DPP ex parte Kebilene* (1999).

Exam tip

You do not need to memorise the sections of the Human Rights Act 1998. Just make sure that you have a broad understanding of the purpose of the sections, as outlined below.

Revision activity

Using the internet, research the case of *R v DPP ex parte Kebilene* (1999).

Impact of the Human Rights Act 1998 on UK constitutional arrangements and law

Table 5.4.2 Impact of the Human Rights Act 1998 on UK constitutional arrangements and law

Sections from HRA 1998	Quote from statute	Impact on UK law
Section 6	'It is unlawful for a public authority to act in a way which is incompatible with a Convention right.'	The term 'public authority' is fairly broad, covering organisations and persons in the public sector, but it does not include government ministers or those connected to Parliament while exercising functions connected to Parliamentary business.
Section 7	'A person who claims that a public authority has acted (or proposes to act) in a way which is made unlawful by section 6 may (a) bring proceedings against the authority under this Act in the appropriate court or tribunal, or (b) rely on the Convention right or rights concerned in any legal proceedings.'	Therefore, if an individual believes that a public authority is acting in breach of a Convention right, they can bring proceedings against them in a court or tribunal.
Section 2	'A court or tribunal determining a question which has arisen in connection with a Convention right must take into account any ... judgment, decision, declaration or advisory opinion of the European Court of Human Rights.'	Decisions and opinions of the European Court of Human Rights must be taken into account by UK courts, even if there is a conflicting decision of a UK court.
Section 19	'A Minister of the Crown in charge of a Bill in either House of Parliament must, before Second Reading of the Bill ... make a statement to the effect that in his view the provisions of the Bill are compatible with the Convention rights.'	This is a statement of compatibility. However, s 19 also states that the minister can nevertheless make a declaration of incompatibility and still proceed with the Bill, thus avoiding Convention rights.
Section 4	'if the court is satisfied that the provision is incompatible with a Convention right, it may make a declaration of that incompatibility'	Therefore, a court can make a declaration of incompatibility. This brings the specific incompatibility to the attention of the government but does not affect either party to that present action.

Under s 10(1), if an Act is incompatible under s 4, a statutory instrument can be used to amend the Act to comply with the Convention.

But see 10(2), where the relevant government minister 'may by order make such amendments to the legislation as he considers necessary to remove the incompatibility'. This means that they do not have to amend the law to comply with the Convention.

The HRA98 and devolutionary settlement in Scotland and Northern Ireland

In both Scotland and Northern Ireland, the ECHR is written into the legislation that created the devolved administrations – the Scotland Act 1998 and the Northern Ireland Act 1998, respectively. As such, the HRA98 is enforceable.

Despite successive Conservative governments promising to repeal the Act, it remains uncertain how this would apply to the devolved governments in Scotland and Northern Ireland.

Repeal of the HRA 98 in either country would be complicated, particularly as religious conflict between the political parties in Northern Ireland has created challenges for power-sharing devolution.

Criticisms of the Human Rights Act 1998

+ There are so many loopholes in the Act which allow avoidance of the rights under the Convention, that the Act seems no more than an altruistic paper-exercise which only benefits the UK's citizens if the government so wishes.
+ The Act removes the sovereignty of the Supreme Court and replaces it with a European Court of Human Rights, which allows non-UK judges to decide on UK domestic issues.
+ If found incompatible, the UK government does not have to amend UK laws to make them compatible with the Convention.
+ The Act relies on individuals, not organisations, to bring an action for a declaration of incompatibility.
+ There is no overarching scrutiny committee which monitors an Act's adherence to the Convention. Instead, the Act relies on individuals (or organisations bringing the attention to individuals) pointing out any incompatibilities.

Revision activity

From your knowledge of the Human Rights Act 1998, can you think of any other criticisms of the Act?

Table 5.4.3 Key cases on human rights law

Case	Facts	Outcome
R v DPP ex parte Kebilene (1999)	Three defendants were charged with terrorist offences, but the trial judge stated that s 16A of the Terrorism Act 1989 was contrary to Article 6 of the European Convention on Human Rights.	The House of Lords agreed with the trial judge.
Re: Medicaments (No. 2), Director General of Fair Trading v Proprietary Association of Great Britain (2001)	See page 207.	
R v A (2001)	See page 207.	
H v Mental Health Review Tribunal (2001)	See page 207.	

Now test yourself

TESTED

5 What was the purpose of the Human Rights Act 1998?

6 What is the main objective of s 2 of the Human Rights Act 1998?

7 How can s 19 of the Human Rights Act 1998 be criticised?

8 In what way does it seem that s 10(2) defeats the overall purpose of s 10(1)?

9 Explain one criticism of the Human Rights Act 1998. Use evidence to support your answer.

Exam summary

In the exam, you MAY be asked:

+ multiple-choice questions about human rights in the UK after the enactment of the Human Rights Act 1998
+ to explain, in broad terms, human rights in the UK after the enactment of the Human Rights Act 1998, such as its impact on subsequent legislation or where incompatibility is found in statute law
+ to write an analysis of some of the human rights in the UK after the enactment of the Human Rights Act 1998, in particular criticisms of human rights.

5.5 European Convention on Human Rights 1953

The European Convention on Human Rights is divided into Articles and Protocols which protect an individual human right. The main Articles are:

- Article 2: the right to life
- Article 3: freedom from torture or inhuman or degrading treatment
- Article 4: freedom from slavery
- Article 5: the right to liberty
- Article 6: the right to a fair trial
- Article 8: the right to respect for private and family life, home and correspondence
- Article 9: freedom of thought, conscience and religion
- Article 10: freedom of expression
- Article 11: freedom of peaceful assembly and association
- Article 12: the right to freely marry
- Article 13: the right to an effective remedy in a national court
- Article 14: freedom from discrimination.

It is important to note that while the Convention guarantees these rights, a state can still restrict them, even if that state has signed the Convention, ratified the Convention and incorporated the Convention into domestic law.

Article 2: the right to life

REVISED 

Article 2(1): the right to life

The **right to life** is certainly one of, if not the most, important and fundamental rights that we have in the UK. Again, this is a **restricted right** and is not absolute. Life here means human life.

Article 2(1) states:

> 'Everyone's right to life shall be protected by law. No one shall be deprived of his life intentionally save in the execution of a sentence of a court following his conviction of a crime for which this penalty is provided by law.'

This Article protects the most fundamental right that we may take for granted – the right to stay alive and not be killed.

The Article has been used, unsuccessfully, by citizens in the UK who have argued the contrary – if there is a citizen's right to life, then there must be a citizen's right to end their life. Article 2 protects life – it does not allow a right to die.

A key case here is *Pretty v United Kingdom* (2002). The applicant was suffering from motor neuron disease. As a result, she was paralysed but could make lucid decisions. She wanted her husband to assist in her suicide and sought clarification that he would not consequently be prosecuted under the Suicide Act 1961. Her argument *inter alia* was under Article 2, that if there was a right to live there must be a subsequent right to die. Having been unsuccessful in her argument in the domestic courts, she appealed to the European Court of Human Rights.

In dismissing her appeal, the Court stated:

- Article 2 ensured that a citizen's life could not be readily taken by countries in which they lived.
- That while there was a right to life, there is no express or implied corresponding allowance to take life under this Article.

Right to life: this means that no one can take another's life without just cause. There may be exceptions, such as the death penalty or acting in self-defence.

Restricted right: a right that for valid reasons is not an absolute right. Exceptions to the right can be put in place to remove it as a total right.

Typical mistake

Article 2 can be confusing. Suicide and assisting a suicide are both criminal offences in the UK. Those citizens who take loved ones to countries such as Switzerland where assisted suicide is allowed (under strict rules) can still be prosecuted upon their return.

Exam tip

When evaluating this right, try to understand why it is so important and why this in particular was incorporated into human rights law.

Paradoxically, this Article expressly allows the continuance of the death penalty for those convicted of applicable crimes in countries who maintain such a punishment.

Revision activity

Using the internet, research the case of *Pretty v UK* (2002).

Stretch and challenge

What offence would a person commit if they helped the suicide of a terminally ill person, who gave their consent to their suicide?

Article 2(2): justified exceptions

The right to life can be restricted under Article 2(2) in limited 'justified' circumstances.

Article 2(2) states:

> 'Deprivation of life shall not be regarded as inflicted in contravention of this Article when it results from the use of force which is no more than absolutely necessary:
>
> (a) in defence of any person from unlawful violence
>
> (b) in order to effect a lawful arrest or to prevent the escape of a person lawfully detained
>
> (c) in action lawfully taken for the purpose of quelling a riot or insurrection.'

Evaluation point

Despite the right to life, it appears that the police are given an ambiguous right to kill as justifiable exceptions to the rule. Discuss the validity of this statement.

Revision activity

Using the internet, research the case of *Re A (Conjoined Twins)* (2001).

These exceptions are justified to effect arrests and control public disorder:

- Clause (a) would cover the situation where necessary force is used, for example, to help someone being attacked but where the attacker is killed in the process.
- Clause (b) would cover the situation where necessary force is used, for example, by the police or a private citizen while arresting someone or impeding someone from escaping lawful detention.
- Clause (c) would cover the situation where necessary force is used, for example, to subdue a riot or similar violent uprising.

The most obvious restriction is where countries use the ultimate penal sanction of the death penalty. The UK suspended the death penalty for murder in 1965 and finally abolished it in 1969. The death penalty was abolished in 1973 in Northern Ireland.

The right to life can be restricted during war time and within the rules of engagement in battle. The military, police or prison service may use lethal force in certain, justified circumstances.

Revision activity

Using the internet, research how many EU countries maintain the death penalty as a criminal sanction.

Table 5.5.1 Key cases on Article 2 of the European Convention on Human Rights

Case	Facts	Outcome
Re A (Conjoined Twins) (2001)	Twins were born conjoined. If an operation was not carried out to separate them, both would die. The operation, however, would 'kill' one twin to allow the other to survive.	The criminal law's defence of necessity was available to a surgeon in such situations, but with clear and specific guidelines set by the courts.
Pretty v United Kingdom (2002)	See page 193 for details.	There is no right to death or to assist a death, even for people with such debilitating conditions.
Airedale NHS Trust v Bland (1993)	B was kept alive only by a life-support machine following injury at the Hillsborough football stadium disaster. His parents and the hospital applied for permission to remove him from the machine.	To avoid criminal sanction there must be no duty to treat the patient if this was not in their interests. As B's hope of improvement was futile, permission was granted.
Armani Da Silva v UK (2016)	C's cousin was mistakenly shot by police thinking he was a terrorist. An independent report concluded there had been mistakes in the killing, but the CPS decided not to prosecute any of the police involved.	The ECtHR held there was no breach of Article 2 as there was insufficient evidence to prosecute any individual officer.

Now test yourself

TESTED 

1. Why is it important to have a right to life?
2. If we have a right to life, should there be a right to death/commit suicide or to assist in a suicide? If so, why?
3. What are the justified exceptions to the right to life? Do you agree with them?
4. Explain whether you believe that following an expulsion order, a citizen's right to life should take priority over the possibility of their life being threatened in the destination country.
5. Do you agree or disagree with the decision in *Pretty v United Kingdom* (2002)? Explain your answer.

Article 5: the right to liberty and security of the person

REVISED

Article 5 covers the **right to liberty and security of person**.

In essence, this Article protects citizens when they are outside their homes. This is neatly complemented by Article 8, which in essence protects citizens inside their homes.

Liberty refers to an individual's physical movement without interference by the state or otherwise.

Security of person refers to an individual's physical and emotional self and their right not to be interfered with.

Right to liberty and security of person: this means that no one without just cause can interfere with your right to live a free life. There may be exceptions, such as arrest or imprisonment.

Exam tip

When evaluating this right, try to understand that there are two separate, but closely linked, rights:

1. A citizen is allowed to be 'at liberty' – free to conduct their day-to-day business such as going to college or work.
2. A citizen has the right not to have their body touched, held or restrained without just cause.

Article 5(1): The right to liberty and security of person

Article 5(1) states:

> 'Everyone has the right to liberty and security of person. No one shall be deprived of his liberty save in the following cases and in accordance with a procedure prescribed by law.'

Liberty means autonomy or independence from arrest or detention and is a fundamental right in a free and democratic society.

Security of person means that an individual cannot have their body, their physical or mental health interfered with if there is no just cause.

Therefore, despite having such a right to liberty under Article 5, it is restricted in cases where the law allows arrest or detention.

Revision activity

Make a list of activities that the right to liberty allows you to do during a typical school or college day.

Article 5(1)a–c: justified deprivation of liberty – lawful arrest or detention

Article 5(1)(a)–(c) provides that a deprivation of liberty is justified in the following cases:

> '(a) The lawful detention of a person after conviction by a competent court.
>
> (b) The lawful arrest or detention of a person for non-compliance with the lawful order of a court or in order to secure the fulfilment of any obligation prescribed by law.
>
> (c) The lawful arrest or detention of a person effected for the purpose of bringing him before the competent legal authority on reasonable suspicion of having committed an offence or when it is reasonably considered necessary to prevent his committing an offence or fleeing after having done so.'

Examples of what these clauses cover:

+ Clause (a): lawful imprisonment in an adult prison or secure children's home, a secure training centre or a young offender institution. This must be in a 'competent' court and not a 'kangaroo' court or lynch mob.
+ Clause (b): where the police arrest someone who has 'jumped' or 'skipped' bail while awaiting trial.
+ Clause (c): where the police can arrest a suspect who is about to, or is in the process of, or has committed an offence. Again, such an arrest must be in order to bring them before a 'competent' court.

Typical mistake

This is a more specific right than the general right of freedom of movement, as Article 5 protects an individual against unlawful arrest, detention or imprisonment.

Evaluation point

Despite the right to liberty and freedom of person, it appears that the judicial system is given an ambiguous right to avoid the rule. Discuss the validity of this statement.

Revision activity

There are various methods of deprivation on the right to liberty. Do you agree with them? If so, why?

Article 5(2)–5(5): additional requirements to justify deprivation of liberty in cases of lawful arrest or detention

Article 5(2)

Article 5(2) states:

> 'Everyone who is arrested shall be informed promptly, in a language which he understands, of the reasons for his arrest and of any charge against him.'

Therefore, a person must be informed as soon as possible that they are or have been arrested, the reason for the arrest and all in a language they understand.

Article 5.2 allows, for example, the police time to find a translator if required, or if there is a struggle in order to arrest a suspect, time to provide the information.

Article 5(3)

Article 5(3) states:

> 'Everyone arrested or detained in accordance with the provisions of paragraph 1 (c) of this Article shall be brought promptly before a judge or other officer authorised by law to exercise judicial power and shall be entitled to trial within a reasonable time or to release pending trial. Release may be conditioned by guarantees to appear for trial.'

An arrested person must be brought to trial, bailed (with or without conditions) to appear at a trial or released within a reasonable period of time.

Article 5(4)

Article 5(4) states:

> 'Everyone who is deprived of his liberty by arrest or detention shall be entitled to take proceedings by which the lawfulness of his detention shall be decided speedily by a court and his release ordered if the detention is not lawful.'

An arrested person is entitled to a swift trial to decide their innocence or guilt. This includes any appeals against conviction and/or sentence.

Article 5(5)

Article 5(5) states:

> 'Everyone who has been the victim of arrest or detention in contravention of the provisions of this Article shall have an enforceable right to compensation.'

For an arrested person who is lawfully arrested, but found not guilty, there will be little, if any, possibility of compensation.

However, if any of the rights under Article 5 are infringed, the arrested person is entitled to compensation, usually in the form of a financial reward.

Revision activity

Using the internet, research the case of *HL v UK* (2004).

Table 5.5.2 Key cases on Article 5 of the European Convention on Human Rights

Case	Facts	Outcome
Stafford v UK (2002)	S served a life sentence for murder, then was convicted of fraud when on licence. He returned to prison but was not released after serving the full sentence for the second crime. He sought damages.	Breach of Article 5. The ECtHR held there was no sufficient connection between his original conviction for murder and a threat to commit further violent crimes after his release.
HL v UK (2004)	H, who was autistic, had lived with carers for three years. He became aggressive and was detained under the Mental Health Act 1983 (MHA83). He was denied contact for three months with his carers and argued a deprivation of liberty.	Breach. Despite being compliant during his detention, the ECtHR held that H had been deprived of his liberty as he had no recourse against being held under the MHA83 such as challenging his detention or treatment given.
Austin v UK (2012)	A, a protester, B a shopper and C an office worker out for lunch had been 'kettled' by the police in Oxford Circus in London for seven hours following the May Day protest in 2001. They all argued breach of Article 5.	No breach. The ECtHR said that while the situation of holding the applicants for between 5 and 7 hours was regrettable, it was proportionate to the avoidance of the risk of harm.

Case	Facts	Outcome
MH v United Kingdom (2013)	A woman with Down's Syndrome was placed in a secure hospital for her own safety under s 2 MHA83. The woman's mother had applied for her release, which was refused, and triggered an automatic detention for a further six months.	Breach. The EctHR held that the inability of the woman (or her mother) to challenge her detention under s 2 MHA83 had violated her human rights under Article 5. Lack of remedies (that would be available to a 'competent' patient) breached Article 5(4).
R (Roberts) v Commissioner of Police of the Metropolis (2015)	C was detained by the police after giving a false name in order to avoid paying her bus fare. The area was known to be violent.	No breach. The ECtHR held that the interference with her rights were proportionate to the police's legitimate aim of the prevention of disorder.

Now test yourself

TESTED 

6 Why is it important to have a right to liberty and security of the person?
7 What does security of person mean?
8 What are the justified exceptions to the right to liberty and security of the person?
9 Do you agree with the justified exceptions to the right to liberty and security of the person?
10 Do you agree or disagree with the decision in *MH v United Kingdom* (2013)? Explain your answer.

Article 8(1): the right to respect for family and private life, home and correspondence

REVISED

Article 8 protects citizens when they are at home. It protects their freedom to pursue activities, within reason, within their own place of residence without state interference.

This Article covers a broad range of rights which were not specifically or satisfactorily covered by statute or the common law, before the passing of the Human Rights Act 1998.

This has meant that many Acts of Parliament have had to be passed in order to comply with this Article, for example, the Data Protection Act 1998 and the Freedom of Information Act 2000.

Specifically, the Article protects citizens from interference with their privacy and can, in certain circumstances, impose obligations on public bodies, such as the government or local authorities to promote such privacy.

Under Article 8(1) every person has a right to respect of privacy, family life, home and correspondence, as shown in Table 5.5.3.

Right to respect for family and private life: this means that no one without just cause can interfere with your right to live a free life.

Typical mistake

Despite being a fundamental right, this is one of the most heavily restricted. Exam questions will often give clues, sometimes implied, as to a legitimate restriction or restrictions. You must give responses that are based on the law and not what you feel personally is a correct restriction or not.

Table 5.5.3 Rights under Article 8(1)

Rights	Explanation
Privacy	+ A citizen has the right to live their own life in a way that they choose to do so in private. + For example: choosing their own sexuality, or how that sexuality is demonstrated, appearance (clothes, hair style, having tattoos or piercings, or not so having) or the right not to be interfered with by the media without public interest. + See *Douglas v Hello! Ltd* (2001) below and *Lustig-Prean and Beckett v United Kingdom* (2000).
Family life	+ A person's choices on how they conduct their family relationships must be respected. + For example: sexual activity, being married or unmarried, having children within or outside of marriage, allowing those families seeking immigration or settlement to live together until status is granted.
Home	+ This covers homeowners, tenants and landlords. A person's right to access and occupy their home without interference from public authorities must be respected. + For example, people cannot be evicted without just cause. + This includes peaceful enjoyment of one's home without noise or other types of pollution – see *Hatton v United Kingdom* (2001).
Correspondence	+ A person's post, email, phone calls, texts etc. must be respected.

Prior to the Human Rights Act 1998, there was no general right to privacy. Homes were generally protected under tort law, while several Acts of Parliament protected correspondence in different ways.

Stretch and challenge

Under what circumstances do you think the right to privacy of a person's correspondence should be ignored by the state?

Exam tip

Remember that there are four similar, but specifically distinct, parts to this Article: privacy, family life, home and correspondence.

Compare the different outcomes of the cases in Table 5.5.4.

Table 5.5.4 Key cases on Article 8

Case	Facts	Outcome
Douglas v Hello! Ltd (2001)	Actors Michael Douglas and Catherine Zeta-Jones sued *Hello!* magazine and sought an injunction when it published unauthorised photographs of their wedding.	The Court of Appeal upheld the couple's right to privacy but had to balance this with the magazine's freedom of expression under Article 10.
Hatton v United Kingdom (2003)	H sought a declaration that the increase of noise, caused by aircraft landing and taking off from Heathrow Airport in London, was a breach of Article 8.	The EctHR held the applicant's right to respect his family and private life had not been breached. House prices had not been adversely impacted and only 2–3% of residents reported sleep disturbance.
Laskey, Jaggard and Brown v United Kingdom (1997)	A group of homosexual males performed consensual sadomasochistic acts upon each other and were convicted with several offences against the person. They argued that their rights under Article 8 had been violated.	ECtHR held there was no violation of Article 8, as state law dictates the level of consensual activity between individuals, and as the activities were filmed and distributed among many participants, questioned their concern for privacy.
R (AR) v Chief Constable of Greater Manchester Police (2018)	A had been accused and acquitted of rape by jury. However, when he later applied to be a teacher and a taxi driver, the police checks included the original allegation of rape.	The Supreme Court held that there had been no breach of Article 8. The requirement to protect potential young and vulnerable victims outweighed the potential prejudicial effect of disclosing the original allegation.
R (Bridges) v South Wales Police (2019)	C challenged the South Wales Police's use of automatic facial recognition (AFR), under Articles 8(1) and (2), that on two occasions they allegedly had recorded his image.	It was held that the Article had not been breached: the AFR was used for a limited time, for a specific purpose, covered a limited area and had led to the detection of criminals.
Gaughran v UK (2020)	G was convicted in 2008 for drunk driving and released in 2013. His photograph, fingerprints and a DNA sample were taken. The police intended to indefinitely keep all G's samples.	The ECtHR felt that the police (the State) had overstepped its margin of appreciation of retaining evidence and, as such, its actions in keeping the samples was disproportionate interference with G's right under Article 8.

Now test yourself TESTED

11 Using examples, explain the meaning of the right to respect privacy.
12 Using examples, explain the meaning of the right to respect a family life.
13 Using examples, explain the meaning of the right to respect a home life.
14 Using examples, explain the meaning of the right to respect for correspondence.
15 Research further the case of *Laskey, Jaggard and Brown v United Kingdom* (1997). Do you agree with the ECHR's decision? Explain your answer.

Article 10: freedom of expression

REVISED

This Article protects an individual's right to express themselves and in consequence to hold an opinion without state interference. This could be:

- temporarily, for example, by speech, or
- permanently, for example, in written or electronic form.

Exam tip

Remember that ideas, views and opinions can be expressed not just by individuals in domestic situations but by religions, political organisations, the media and through artistic expression. Exam questions may focus on a less common group of citizens (such as painters or dancers expressing opinion) than someone writing for a newspaper.

Typical mistake

In a democratic society, allowing a broad basis to the freedom of expression means accepting another's right to express a view that may be unpopular or unpleasant. Such views may be acceptable and you cannot simply discount them as offensive in an exam.

Freedom of expression is achieved by different means:

- being able to freely converse with each other on topics or issues
- publishing newspaper or magazine articles or broadcasting television or radio programmes or via the internet
- through artistic mediums, such as painting or drawings or via theatrical performances.

Freedom of expression: this freedom promotes and encourages healthy debate and challenge so that citizens can express ideas, views and opinions.

This is even the case where views may 'offend, shock or disturb the State or any sector of the population' – see *Handyside v United Kingdom* (1976) and *The Observer and the Guardian v United Kingdom* (1991).

Article 10(1) states:

> 'Everyone has the right to freedom of expression. This right shall include freedom to hold opinions and to receive and impart information and ideas without interference by public authority and regardless of frontiers. This Article shall not prevent States from requiring the licensing of broadcasting, television or cinema enterprises.'

Revision activity

Look through a magazine or newspaper, particularly one aimed at teenagers and above. Consider whether any of the content, in your opinion, may 'offend, shock or disturb the state or any sector of the population'.

Freedom of expression is commonly misunderstood as being an existing right before the enactment of the Human Rights Act 1988. It is also commonly misunderstood as giving UK citizens the freedom of speech, which it does not due to its restrictions.

The freedom is massively restricted by domestic laws, for example, those covering racial hatred and criminalising homophobia. Nevertheless, this residual freedom allows a person to:

(a) receive information and ideas – for example, allow citizens to read/view publications by a free press
(b) communicate information and ideas – for example, allow a free press to report on issues that it felt were newsworthy and in the public interest.

Compare the different outcomes of the case examples in Table 5.5.5.

Table 5.5.5 Key cases on Article 10

Case	Facts	Outcome
Handyside v United Kingdom (1976)	H published in the UK, *The Little Red Schoolbook*, with a chapter on pupils containing information on sex. He was charged and convicted with having in his possession an obscene publication for gain.	ECtHR held there was no violation of Article 10, as the UK's right to interfere with H's freedom of expression was allowed by its domestic law.
The Observer and the Guardian v United Kingdom (1991)	This was called the '*Spycatcher*' case, after the name of a book written by a former member of MI5 which revealed theories and tactics of that organisation which the UK government tried to ban.	ECtHR ruled that the UK government had breached Article 10 by preventing the newspapers serialising the book since it was freely available in other countries (e.g. Scotland) and therefore contained no secrets to suppress.
Steel and Morris v United Kingdom (2005)	Known as the McLibel case, two environmental activists published a leaflet criticising fast-food chain McDonald's. Some accusations were false and others true. The UK courts ordered the pair to pay compensation for libel.	ECtHR ruled that UK laws breached Article 10 and did not protect the public's right to criticise companies whose business practices affect people's lives and the environment.

Now test yourself

TESTED

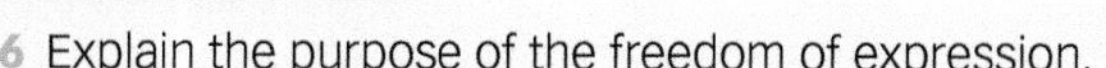

16 Explain the purpose of the freedom of expression.

17 Explain how drawings or paintings can contain a freedom of expression.

18 Explain why it is acceptable to say or publish information that, to some, may 'offend, shock or disturb the State or any sector of the population'.

19 Explain the purpose of 'requiring the licensing of broadcasting, television or cinema enterprises' as a restriction of Article 10.

20 Research further the case of *Steel and Morris v United Kingdom* (2005). Do you agree with the ECtHR's decision? Explain your answer.

Article 11: freedom of peaceful assembly and freedom of association with others

REVISED

This freedom under Article 11, was directly born out of the restrictions of movement and peaceful protest that were disallowed by the Nazi Party in Germany, before and during the Second World War, and in order to crush any opposition to its government and policies.

In more modern times, the Article allows citizens to come together for peaceful protest and to form groups and associations for a common cause. But, see the restrictions below.

Conversely, it disallows forcing people to join an organisation, such as a trade union, or to take part in a protest against their will. This is something which some despotic Middle Eastern countries propagate, as did the Nazis.

Article 11(1) states:

> 'Everyone has the right to freedom of peaceful assembly and to freedom of association with others, including the right to form and to join trade unions for the protection of his interests.'

'Assembly' means that citizens can meet and gather with other citizens as a group for lawful purposes.

Right to freedom of assembly and association: being able to assemble (gather) with other people for peaceful purposes and associate with (be in the company of) others for the same reasons.

Exam tip

Be aware that there are two similar but specifically distinct parts to this Article:

1. the freedom to come together
2. the freedom to come together with individuals of their choosing.

'Association' means that citizens can form lawful groups, organisations or clubs for their own interests. This freedom included the forming of trades' unions to protect workers' rights, their freedoms and their interests.

Compare the different outcomes of the cases in Table 5.5.6.

Stretch and challenge

Explain the arguments relied upon by the excluded members of the trade union in *ASLEF v United Kingdom* (2007).

Typical mistake

This is not an absolute right, although it is often assumed that this is the case. Also, remember that there are reciprocal rights under this Article, so people cannot be forced to associate and assemble.

Table 5.5.6 Key cases on Article 11

Case	Facts	Outcome
Wilson and Palmer v United Kingdom (2002)	See page 190.	
ASLEF v United Kingdom (2007)	A, the trade union, expelled one of its members for being an activist for the British Nationalist Party. The member successfully took the union to an employment tribunal and rejoined the union.	ECtHR stated there was a violation of Article 11: 'just as a person has a right to join a union, a union has a right not to admit a person for legitimate reasons, especially when the views of a member are fundamentally at odds with the union.'

Now test yourself

TESTED 

21 Explain the meaning of freedom of assembly.
22 Explain the meaning of freedom of association.
23 Explain the purpose of a trade union.
24 Research further the case of *Wilson and Palmer v United Kingdom* (2002). Do you agree with the ECtHR's decision? Explain your answer.
25 Research further the case of *ASLEF v United Kingdom* (2007). Do you agree with the ECtHR's decision? Explain your answer.

Exam summary

In the exam, you MAY be asked:

- multiple-choice questions about Articles 2, 5, 8, 10 or 11 in human rights law
- to examine and discuss, in part or in whole, these Articles in human rights law through extended answer questions
- to apply the law on these Articles in human rights law problem/scenario situations.

5.6 Restrictions

Exam tip

Your response should always balance the rights or freedoms under Articles 8, 10 and 11 against the potential scenario or exam question's suggested restriction. Sometimes, you might need to make a judgement call if a clear outcome is not possible.

The rights under Articles 8(1), 10(1) and 11(1) mean that no one without just cause can interfere with your right to live a free life. However, for each of the rights or freedoms under these Articles, there are consequent and necessary restrictions under Articles 8(2), 10(2) and 11(2).

Individual freedoms must be balanced with the rights or freedoms of other people, so none of these three Articles are absolute rights.

Controversial issues such as euthanasia, publishing newspaper articles damning government actions and banning certain 'radical' groups have been the subject of much discussion and challenges under the Human Rights Act.

The restrictions are similar in their objectives but differ slightly in their individual aims. Therefore, each of the Articles are known as 'qualified rights'.

Remember:

+ Article 8: the right to respect for family and private life
+ Article 10: the freedom of expression
+ Article 11: the freedom of assembly and association.

Restrictions: key limitations on an absolute right or freedom. Each of the three Articles 8, 10 and 11 are legitimately restricted to prevent disorder, and are created to be lawful, necessary and proportionate.

Typical mistake

Do not assume that an exam question or exam scenario's restriction is automatically valid or will apply. This may not necessarily be the case, and you need to think about the restriction from your own knowledge of its lawfulness, necessity and proportion.

Article 8(1): the restrictions under Article 8(2)

REVISED

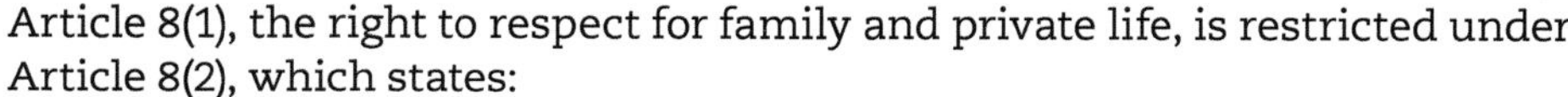

Article 8(1), the right to respect for family and private life, is restricted under Article 8(2), which states:

> 'There shall be no interference by a public authority with the exercise of this right except such as is in accordance with the law and is necessary in a democratic society in the interests of national security, public safety or the economic well-being of the country, for the prevention of disorder or crime, for the protection of health or morals, or for the protection of the rights and freedoms of others.'

This means that the right to respect for family and private life can be restricted if there is a law, required in a democratic society and it:

(a) benefits national security, the public's safety or the financial safety of the country, or
(b) prevents disorder or crime, or
(c) protects health or morals of its citizens, or
(d) protects the rights and freedoms of others.

Evaluation point

'Despite the right to respect for family and private life, it appears that the authorities are given an ambiguous right to ignore this as a result of the justifiable exceptions to the rule.' Discuss the validity of this statement.

Revision activity

In your opinion, identify some examples of lawful restrictions under Article 8(2).

Article 10(1): the restrictions under Article 10(2)

REVISED

Article 10(1), the freedom of expression, is restricted under Article 10(2), which states:

> 'The exercise of these freedoms, since it carries with it duties and responsibilities, may be subject to such formalities, conditions, restrictions or penalties as are prescribed by law and are necessary in a democratic society, in the interests of national security, territorial integrity or public safety, for the prevention of disorder or crime, for the protection of health or morals, for the protection of the reputation or rights of others, for preventing the disclosure of information received in confidence, or for maintaining the authority and impartiality of the judiciary.'

Thus, the freedom of expression can be restricted if there is a law, required in a democratic society and it:

(a) benefits national security, the country's boundaries or the public's safety – see *R v Ponting* (1985), or
(b) prevents disorder or crime, or
(c) protects health or morals of its citizens – see *R v Lemon and Gay News* (1979), or
(d) protects the reputation or rights of citizens who are affected by a person exercising their freedom under Article 10(1), or
(e) prevents the revelation of information gained under trust, or
(f) maintains the authority and neutrality of the judiciary.

Stretch and challenge

In your opinion, identify some examples of lawful restrictions under Article 10(2).

Table 5.6.1 Key cases on restrictions of Article 10

Case	Facts	Outcome
R v Ponting (1985)	D gave opposition MPs documents stating that the government had lied about the sinking of an Argentinian battleship during the Falklands War.	Despite the clear direction of the judge that D's conduct did amount to an offence, the jury found D not guilty.
R v Lemon and Gay News (1979)	A poem was published in an issue of *Gay News* describing various sexual acts performed on the body of Christ after the crucifixion, including acts of fellatio.	The magazine and its editor were convicted with the common law offence of blasphemous libel.

Further restriction of Article 10: Section 12 Human Rights Act 1998

Section 12 HRA98 was specifically incorporated into the Human Rights Act in relation to freedom of expression and adds a further restriction to Article 10.

The section requires courts when granting 'relief' to have particular regard to the importance of the freedom of expression. A court should not impose, for example, an injunction without the respondent being notified, unless there is a strong justification for doing such.

Evaluation point

'Despite the right to freedom of expression, it appears that the authorities are given an ambiguous right to ignore this as a result of the justifiable exceptions to the rule.' Discuss the validity of this statement.

Article 11(1): the restrictions under Article 11(2)

REVISED

Article 11(2), the right to freedom of peaceful assembly and to freedom of association with others is restricted under Article 11(2), which states:

> 'No restrictions shall be placed on the exercise of these rights other than such as are prescribed by law and are necessary in a democratic society in the interests of national security or public safety, for the prevention of disorder or crime, for the protection of health or morals or for the protection of the rights and freedoms of others. This Article shall not prevent the imposition of lawful restrictions on the exercise of these rights by members of the armed forces, of the police or of the administration of the State.'

Thus, the freedom of assembly and association can be restricted if there is a law, required in a democratic society and it:
(a) benefits national security or the public's safety, or
(b) prevents disorder or crime, or
(c) protects health or morals of its citizens, or
(d) protects the rights and freedoms of others.

The important point added here is that a restriction can be placed on this freedom, for example, by a curfew, by the country's armed forces, police or similar organisations, necessary in a democratic society.

Revision activity

In your opinion, identify some examples of lawful restrictions under Article 11(2).

Now test yourself

TESTED 

1. Explain one reason why it is important that Article 8(1) is restricted under Article 8(2).
2. Explain one reason why it is important that Article 10(1) is restricted under Article 10(2).
3. Explain one reason why it is important that Article 11(1) is restricted under Article 11(2).
4. Explain the jury's decision in *R v Ponting* (1985).
5. Explain the purpose of s 12 of the Human Rights Act 1998.

Exam summary

In the exam, you MAY be asked:

- multiple-choice questions about the main restrictions under the European Convention on Human Rights
- to examine and discuss, in part or in whole, restrictions in human rights law under the European Convention on Human Rights through extended answer questions
- to apply the law on restrictions in human rights law in problem/scenario situations.

5.7 Enforcement

This chapter looks at how the rights and freedoms are implemented in the UK through:

- claims before the European Court of Human Rights
- the role of domestic courts
- the effect of decisions on states and claimants
- judicial review.

Having rights and freedoms is important in a democratic society and there must be consequent mechanisms of enforcement. Unless a restriction applies, most rights and freedoms can be enforced through the UK's courts.

More recently, the process of judicial review has allowed citizens to challenge the decisions of public bodies, such as the government, local authorities or their officials.

If a human rights issue is in question, and domestic law does not provide a solution, then a claim can be brought before the ECtHR.

Exam tip

You need to understand the process of bringing a case to the ECtHR and the potential conflict between domestic courts and the decisions of the ECtHR.

Typical mistake

Do not confuse the ECHR (Convention) with the Human Rights Act 1988. Also, make sure that you understand how the ECtHR fits into the hierarchy of the English courts.

Claims before the European Court of Human Rights

REVISED 

The ECtHR includes judges representing various European states, many of which are not part of the European Union. The ECtHR is not a European Union institution and the EU-UK Trade and Cooperation Agreement (colloquially termed 'Brexit') contains a number of provisions that 'locks in' the UK's continued adherence to the European Convention on Human Rights.

The judges act independently and not in the interests of their own states.

There is usually a panel of seven judges to hear a case. Even if the case is sent to the Court, a panel of three judges will first hear its merits before agreeing, or not, to fully hear the complaint.

If they find that a member state has breached an Article then they have the power, although difficult to enforce, to award compensation or other 'just satisfaction' to the complainant.

The Court relies heavily on the cooperation of the member states to be bound by its decisions, but the Court cannot in principle force the state to change its domestic law.

Bringing a claim

Once the citizen has exhausted all means of redress for their complaint in their domestic courts, they can make a petition to the European Commission of Human Rights.

The Commission will investigate whether the citizen's petition has any merits before agreeing to pass the petition on to the full Court.

The petition must be made within a specific period of time (usually six months) from being denied redress from the last court in their state (generally the Supreme Court in the UK).

If the Commission feel that there is a legitimate petition, it will seek to resolve the issue amicably with the cooperation of the member state's government.

If the complaint cannot be resolved amicably, the case will be sent to the Court to decide whether the citizen's rights have been breached.

Also, a member state is able to bring a claim for an alleged breach of the Convention committed against another member state.

Stretch and challenge

Consider some of the problems for an individual in bringing a claim to the European Court of Human Rights.

Role of domestic courts

REVISED

In some situations, UK law, both common and statute, already protected the rights and freedoms of its citizens before the introduction of the Human Rights Act 1998. However, large parts of the European Convention on Human Rights had not been covered by UK domestic law before the Act.

If a complainant is unsuccessful with domestic law or feels that such laws are incompatible with the Convention, a claim can be made by petition to the European Court of Human Rights.

Under the Human Rights Act 1998, citizens can bring a claim in the domestic courts to argue that a public body has breached one or more of their rights under the Convention and seek redress. If the court agrees that there is a breach, an appropriate remedy can be issued.

If there is an existing domestic law which covers a human right, for example, under the Equality Act 2010, then this method of redress must be used first, before being challenged.

The cases in Table 5.7.1 demonstrate the conflict between domestic law and the Convention.

Revision activity

Which groups have their rights protected under the Equality Act 2010?

Revision activity

Explain the arguments relied upon by the court in the decision in *R v Gough* (1993).

Table 5.7.1 Conflict between English domestic law and ECHR

Case	Conflict between domestic law and ECHR
Re: Medicaments (No. 2), Director General of Fair Trading v Proprietary Association of Great Britain (2001)	The case involved an alleged breach under Article 6 and the test of bias in UK court cases. Domestic law in relation to bias (a jury member had been the neighbour of one of the defendants) had been set in *R v Gough* (1993). However, *Gough* was incompatible with several cases decided by EctHR, so the Court of Appeal refused to follow the House of Lords' decision in *Gough*.
R v A (2001)	Lord Steyn stated that 'the interpretative obligation under s 3 of the 1998 Act is a strong one. It applies even if there is no ambiguity in the language in the sense of the language being capable of two different meanings'. He also said that it may be necessary under s 3 to 'adopt an interpretation which linguistically may appear strained' and that a declaration of incomparability was a 'measure of last resort'.
H v Mental Health Review Tribunal (2001)	The Court of Appeal held that certain sub-sections of s 72(1) of MHA83 were incompatible with the Convention's Articles 5(1) and 5(4). However, the Court could only state this and could not change the law. That was for Parliament to amend.

Effect of decisions on states and claimants

REVISED

The irony is that while the decisions of the domestic courts are binding upon the parties to a human rights case, the effect of a decision from the ECtHR, while binding, is difficult to enforce. Nevertheless, decisions have these effects:

+ For states – the ECtHR may decide the state is in breach and award compensation to a claimant. However, it cannot make the state change its laws, but relies upon the state voluntarily amending its domestic laws.
+ For claimants – if successful, the most appropriate decision would be to award them compensation, but this is not guaranteed. As with decisions against the state, the ECtHR has no means of enforcing that the state makes the compensation payment.

Process of judicial review

REVISED

This process reinforces the canon that everyone is equal before the law, and that includes public bodies or their officials.

The decisions of the lower courts, in particular the Magistrates' Courts, can be challenged under judicial review.

Judicial review is carried out by the Queen's Bench Division of the High Court.

Judicial review: process allowing certain decisions of government or other public bodies to be challenged by citizens to see if they are 'reasonable'.

Table 5.7.2 Principles and remedies of judicial review

Principles	There are three main challenges under judicial review: 1 Illegality: the decision by the public body has included a mistake of law or has gone beyond that which the law allows the public body to act. 2 Irrationality: the decision by the public body is so unreasonable that no reasonable public body would have made such a decision. 3 Irregularity: the decision by the public body has not followed the correct procedure.
Remedies	Remedies are possible under private law, e.g. injunction or compensation. Under public law, the following remedies are available by court order: 1 Prohibition – prevents or prohibits the public authority from continuing with the decision or from doing the same act in the future. 2 Certiorari – the High Court can quash a decision made by the public body. 3 Mandamus – forces a public body to do something, e.g. to hear a case or argument that it has refused to hear.

Table 5.7.3 Key cases on judicial review

Case	Facts	Outcome
Associated Provincial Picture Houses v Wednesbury Corporation (1948)	A cinema was granted a licence to open seven days per week, but on Sundays no one under 15 was to be admitted. The cinema sought a declaration that the condition was unfair.	This case established the 'Wednesbury' unreasonableness test: a decision will be deemed unreasonable, and struck out, if it was so unreasonable that no reasonable public body could have reached the same decision.
Council of Civil Service Unions v Minister for the Civil Service (1984)	The government had banned workers of GCHQ (part of the UK's security service) from being members of a trades' union.	Known as the 'GCHQ' case, this case set out and summarised the three challenges or principles for judicial review, above.

Now test yourself

TESTED

1 Describe the features of the European Court of Human Rights.
2 How does a citizen bring a case to the European Court of Human Rights?
3 What is meant by judicial review?
4 Explain the three main challenges available under judicial review.
5 Explain the remedies available under judicial review.

Stretch and challenge

Research what is meant by GCHQ and explain the purpose behind it.

Evaluation point

Discuss the importance of judicial review and how it provides a balance between the 'establishment' and the UK's citizens.

Exam summary

In the exam, you MAY be asked:

+ multiple-choice questions about enforcement of rights and freedoms under the European Convention on Human Rights
+ to examine and discuss, in part or in whole, enforcement of rights under the European Convention on Human Rights through extended answer questions
+ to apply the law on enforcement of rights and freedoms in human rights law in problem/scenario situations.

5.8 Human rights and English law

For this topic, the AQA specification looks at how the ECHR translates into the rights and freedoms within the English legal system:

+ the right to life under civil and criminal provisions
+ the deprivation of liberty
+ privacy and communication
+ expression, assembly and association.

English law and the right to life under Article 2

REVISED

Outline of criminal and civil law provisions and investigatory procedures

Article 2 of the ECHR provides that a citizen's right to life must be protected by law. The Convention places an obligation on the state not to take life, except in extremely limited and defined circumstances. In such situations, the police must take reasonable steps to protect life where there is a real and immediate risk.

If there is a death in these situations, then there is an obligation under Article 2 to ensure there is an official investigation.

As discussed on page 193–4, UK citizens have the right to life under Article 2 of the ECHR, which is guaranteed under the Human Rights Act 1998, albeit with certain restrictions.

Evaluation point

Discuss whether the death penalty for murder should be reintroduced in the UK.

Exam tip

This chapter provides some examples you can use to demonstrate restrictions to freedoms. Using actual examples to support your analysis or explanation will boost your answers.

Homicide and associated offences

In English common law, homicide is defined as the unlawful killing of a human being and is categorised for our purposes as either murder or manslaughter.

Murder and manslaughter are both crimes in the UK. Whether a defendant commits murder or manslaughter depends upon the circumstances of the death – in particular, how the death occurred and what was going through the mind of the defendant at the time of death.

There are certain situations which provide a defence to a killing whereupon a homicide offence is 'committed', but the defence of self-defence or the prevention of crime prohibits a defendant's criminal responsibility (see Chapter 2.8).

Typical mistake

Remember that Parliament cannot restrict the Articles without redress. Judicial review is one way for citizens to test the legality of any restrictions.

Obligations on police and others in planning dangerous operations/protective policing

As a core value, the police have a fundamental obligation to protect the life of citizens in the UK. However, Article 2(2) appears heavily balanced in the police's favour should a life be taken during an arrest.

When planning an operation, for example, a raid on a suspected 'drugs den' or policing a demonstration, the police's commanders must have a clear understanding of the role of the police during the operation.

If the police operate outside this core value, and therefore outside either the police's common law or statutory rules, then the commanders may be held liable for their subordinates' action. A chief constable could, in certain situations, be held personally responsible.

The police, as a public authority, have to act in a way that is compatible with the Human Rights Act 1988. When the police use force, even lethal force, they must have a primary concern for human life unless it is unreasonable to do so, for example, in self-defence where a suspect is shot dead.

Stretch and challenge

Explain the argument that the police should be given extra rights under self-defence while carrying out their role.

Civil law negligence

Where the criminal law does not provide a remedy for a breach of Article 2, then civil law negligence may provide a form of recourse following a death.

Negligence is a 'modern' tort, established in English law in 1932 by Lord Atkin in *Donoghue v Stevenson* (1932) – see Chapter 3.3. It covers a wide range of situations where a death occurs, for example, in a car crash, during poorly performed surgery or in police custody.

A successful claim in negligence requires the establishment of a duty of care, the breach of such duty and foreseeable damage caused by the defendant's actions.

The burden of proof in a negligence claim is that on a balance of probabilities the defendant's negligent act caused the death of the victim.

Independent investigation of deaths in custody or attributable to agents of the state

Where a death occurs in police custody, the Independent Police Complaints Commission (IPCC) is used to investigate the death.

The IPCC began its remit in 2004 and is part of the UK's obligation to enforce Article 2. It was formed following complaints and concerns of a lack of an independent organisation overseeing, *inter alia*, deaths of suspects in police custody.

As well as an obligation to protect life, there is an obligation to carry out an investigation under Article 2 which must be independent, effective, open to public scrutiny, prompt and reasonably expeditious, and any next of kin must be involved where necessary.

The IPCC's involvement is part of the state's involvement. It is used to complement other investigatory processes, such as criminal prosecutions and inquests into death, which again must be independent, robust and effective.

The Court of Protection was established under the Mental Capacity Act 2005 as a jurisdictional court over the personal and financial matters of citizens who lack the mental capacity to make rational decisions for themselves.

English law and the deprivation of liberty under Article 5

REVISED

In addition to a citizen's freedom of liberty being restricted by the police or other authorised agents, for example, during arrest, liberty can be restricted where mental capacity is brought into question.

'Deprivation of liberty' is concerned with a restriction under Article 5 of the ECHR – the right to liberty and security of the person.

The acid test for 'deprivation of liberty' was defined by the Supreme Court in *P v Cheshire West and Chester Council and another* (2014) and *P and Q v Surrey County Council* (2014). The test stated that an individual is deprived of their liberty under Article 5 if they:

- lack the capacity to consent to their care/treatment arrangements
- are under continuous supervision and control, and
- are not free to leave.

All three parts of the acid test must be satisfied.

A 'deprivation of liberty' must be in accordance with government standards, the Court of Protection or under the Mental Health Act 1983.

English law and privacy and communication: protecting or restricting rights under Article 8

REVISED 

Under Article 8(1) of the ECHR, citizens in the UK have the right to respect for private and family life, homes and correspondence.

Under Article 8(2), these rights are restricted, which has led to criticism.

In consequence, provisions have been passed by Parliament that protect and restrict rights under Article 8. Some examples are given in Table 5.8.1 and Table 5.8.2.

Revision activity

Use the internet to research the case of *S and Marper v United Kingdom* (2008).

Table 5.8.1 Provisions to protect and restrict rights under Article 8: criminal law

Provision under criminal law	Restriction of right to privacy	Protection of right to privacy
1 The Police and Criminal Evidence Act 1984 (PACE 84)	Under Part II of PACE 84, the police are given powers to: + enter premises + search premises, and + seize items at premises.	Under Part II of PACE 84, the public are given safeguards: + police must have reasonable grounds + items or persons sought must be identified as practicably as possible.
2 The Investigatory Powers Act 2016 (IPA 16)	Part II of the IPA 16 gives the British security services the power to: + intercept items sent through the post + intercept electronic communications.	Under Part I of the IPA 16, there are general privacy protections under the criminal law as: + it provides guidance to the security services + it creates offences if the security services breach guidelines.

Table 5.8.2 Provisions to protect and restrict rights under Article 8: civil law

Provision under civil law	Restriction of right to privacy	Protection of right to privacy
1 The Freedom of Information Act 2000 (FOIA)	Under Part II of the FOIA, information held by a public authority is exempt from disclosure where it is: + in the interest of national security + in the defence of the country + to assist law enforcement.	Under Part I of the FOIA, information held by a public authority is available for public disclosure – this is subject to guidelines.
2 The Investigatory Powers Act 2016 (IPA 16)	Part II of the IPA 16 gives the British security services the power to: + intercept items sent through the post + intercept electronic communications.	Under Part I of the IPA16, there are certain privacy protections under the civil law as: + it provides guidance to the security services + citizens are able to sue if a communication is intercepted without lawful authority.

English law and expression, assembly and association under Articles 10 and 11

REVISED 

There must be a balance between privacy and the right to freedom of expression, assembly and association and the state's duty to maintain a peaceful society.

The public have a right to communicate discontent or disagreement or even protest, but this has to be balanced with the state's right to maintain lawful order.

Freedoms under Articles 10(1) and 11(1) are restricted under Articles 10(2) and 11(2) respectively.

Table 5.8.3 Restriction of freedoms under Articles 10(1) and 11(1) in English law

Restrictions under Article 10(2)	+ Under the common law, breach of the peace prevents citizens from causing a disturbance in a public place. + The Racial and Religious Hatred Act 2006 creates an offence of using words, behaviour or written material to create racial hatred. + The Obscene Publications Act 1959 creates offences relating to the publication of obscene matter such as articles in newspapers or magazines.
Restrictions under Article 11(2)	+ Under the common law, the police can arrest and move on protesters for breaching the peace. + Under s 14 of the Public Order Act of 1986, senior police officers are allowed to impose conditions on public assemblies. This is in regard to the numbers taking part, the location and duration of the protest. + The Criminal Justice Public Order Act of 1994 created an offence of trespass in the criminal law called aggravated trespass.

Now test yourself

1. Explain Article 2 of the European Convention on Human Rights.
2. Which criminal offences penalise a person who unlawfully kills another human being?
3. Explain what is meant by the police's 'core value' in relation to Article 2.
4. Explain how the civil law through tort law can provide a remedy for a breach of Article 2.
5. Explain the role of the Independent Police Complaints Commission (IPCC).
6. Identify the case which established the acid test for 'deprivation of liberty'.
7. Explain what is meant by the acid test for 'deprivation of liberty'.
8. Explain how a citizen's right to privacy under Article 8 can be restricted by the Police and Criminal Evidence Act 1984.
9. Explain how a citizen's right to privacy under Article 8 can be restricted by the Investigatory Powers Act 2016 under civil law.
10. Explain how a citizen's right to privacy under Article 8 can be protected by the Police and Criminal Evidence Act 1984.
11. Explain the term 'assembly'.
12. Explain the term 'association'.
13. Explain one way in which a citizen's freedom of expression under Article 10 is restricted by an Act of Parliament.

Exam summary

In the exam, you MAY be asked:

+ multiple-choice questions about human rights and English law in relation to the rights granted by the ECHR Articles
+ to examine and discuss, in part or in whole, human rights law and English law under the ECHR Articles through extended answer questions
+ to apply the law on human rights and the English legal system in problem/scenario situations under the ECHR Articles.

5.9 Reform of the protection of human rights in the UK

This chapter examines reform of the protection of human rights in the UK. To reform the law means to update, change or repeal (remove) it. There may be various reasons for reform, for example, society no longer agrees with the law.

Exam tip

If a question asks you to analyse a particular Article of the ECHR, remember to include criticism or support for the Article. This could include any reform proposals relevant to the question.

Typical mistake

There are very many criticisms and proposals for reform for the Human Rights Act 1998. It would be impossible to know and articulate them all. Instead, research common proposals or develop sensible ones yourself.

For many citizens, the enactment of the Human Rights Act 1998 was long overdue. It was introduced as a means to 'bringing rights home'. However, its enactment and subsequent enforcement has been heavily criticised. For the first time, the provisions of the ECHR were made directly enforceable in the UK.

The Act was given cross-party support in Parliament when it was passed, and it remains not a political tool, but rather an Act supporting mutual respect and consideration of others.

The horrors of the Second World War led to the European Convention on Human Rights as a means to prevent such atrocities from occurring again. It is unarguable that human rights and freedoms form the foundation of a democratic society.

As legislation in the UK must be compatible with the Act, it not only provides rules and considerations for policymakers but also provides rules and safeguards for citizens.

Revision activity

Using your previous knowledge of human rights, summarise the importance of the Human Rights Act 1988.

Is there a real need for reform of the Human Rights Act 1988?

REVISED

Despite support for the Act, laws and rights must move with a changing society. While the fundamental tenets of rights and freedoms remain the same, the laws that support such tenets must move with the times.

Criticism of the Human Rights Act

- The Act is seen by many as not 'British', since it introduces 'foreign' rules which have removed Parliament's sovereignty.
- By its very application and interpretation by the courts, the Act is seen as enforcing 'foreign' rules.
- It is generally misunderstood by the public and misrepresented in the media.

Proposals for reform

Table 5.9.1 Proposals for reforming the Human Rights Act 1998 (HRA 98)

Date of reform proposal	Origin and name of proposal	Purpose of proposal
2006	Department for Constitutional Affairs: Review of the Implementation of the Human Rights Act	The review stated that the HRA 98 had been widely misunderstood by the public and had been misused in a number of situations.
2006	David Cameron, then leader of the Opposition	The Conservatives proposed a British Bill of Rights and Responsibilities to 'define the core values which give us our identity as a free nation', along with a repeal of the HRA 98.
2007	The Labour Government published a Green Paper: The Governance of Britain	This included a proposal for a British Bill of Rights and Duties, providing explicit recognition that 'human rights come with responsibilities and must be exercised in a way that respects the human rights of others'.
2009	Labour Government report: Rights and Responsibilities: developing our constitutional framework	Labour felt HRA 98 had been an important move towards the incorporation of rights and freedoms but that an incorporation of UK values alongside the Convention rights would endorse a stronger guarantee of rights and freedoms.
2008	Joint Committee on Human Rights	A report emphasised a need for public consultation before plans were drawn up.
2010	General election manifesto promises	The Conservatives were to replace the HRA 98 with a Bill of Rights, while Labour and the Liberal Democrats were committed to protecting the Act.
2011	The Commission on a Bill of Rights was established	Established to investigate the creation of a Bill of Rights.
2012	The Commission of 2011 published its report: A UK Bill of Rights? The Choice Before Us	As the Commissioners could not agree on a common position, each one published their own findings under the one report.
2013	2013 Conservative Party Conference, Home Secretary Theresa May	'The next Conservative manifesto will promise to scrap the Human Rights Act ... the Conservative position is clear – if leaving the European Convention is what it takes to fix our human rights law, that is what we should do.'
2015	Conservative Party General Election Manifesto 2015 (coalition government in office)	Promise to scrap the HRA 98 and replace it with a Bill of Rights.
2017	Conservative Party General Election Manifesto 2015 (government in office)	The manifesto stated that while Brexit is in process, the HRA98 would not be replaced and the UK would remain signatories of the ECHR for the duration of the Parliament.
2020	Independent review of the Human Rights Act 1998	Following the election of the Conservative Government in 2019, and as part of its manifesto, the review will take a 'fresh look at the Act' to 'ensure it continues to meet the needs of the society it serves' (see below).

Stretch and challenge

Using the internet, research the purpose of the independent review of the Human Rights Act in 2020.

A Bill of Rights

The UK Bill of Rights was essentially a Conservative Party election promise in 2010 and afterwards.

- It would be a legal document to replace the Human Rights Act 1998, as a solution to criticisms of the Act.
- If passed into law, it could be changed by a UK government without being challenged by any EU country.

- The contents of the Bill were largely unknown, unwritten and certainly unratified by public consultation.
- Decisions of the ECHR would not be directly applicable or enforceable upon the UK.

Proposals for a UK Bill of Rights were, however, scrapped before the 2017 General Election.

Revision activity

Create your own Bill of Rights. What rights and freedoms would it include?

Evaluation point

'Human rights in the UK are simply a fantasy and not a reality.' Using one specific Article of the HRA98, discuss whether you agree or disagree with this statement.

The 2020 independent review of the Human Rights Act 1998

While the Government has stated that the UK remains committed to the ECHR, it launched an independent review, limited to looking at the structural framework of the Human Rights Act (HRA) rather than limiting or expanding the rights and freedoms themselves.

The review will *inter alia* consider:

1. The relationship between the domestic English courts and the EctHR, specifically:
   - how the duty to 'take into account' ECtHR case law has been applied in practice
   - whether dialogue between the domestic courts and the ECtHR works effectively
   - whether there is any room for improvement.
2. The impact of the HRA on the relationship between the judiciary, executive and Parliament.
3. Domestic courts – are they being unduly drawn into areas of policy?

Now test yourself TESTED 

1. Explain why the Human Rights Act 1998 was introduced into UK law.
2. Explain one reason why the Human Rights Act 1998 is arguably in need of reform.
3. How did the Department for Constitutional Affairs in 2006 criticise the Human Rights Act 1998?
4. Explain why the Commission set up in 2011 did not produce definite reform proposals.
5. Explain what is meant by a UK Bill of Rights.
6. Why did the Conservative Government in 2017 decided to suspend its proposals for a UK Bill of Rights?

Exam summary

In the exam, you MAY be asked:

- multiple-choice questions about reform of human rights for UK citizens
- to explain, in broad terms, reform of human rights in relation to each Article of the Convention and of the Human Rights Act 1998
- to write an analysis of the reform of human rights in relation to each Article of the Convention and of the Human Rights Act 1998.

Exam practice

The topic is examined in a number of ways. There is a mixture of:

- multiple-choice questions (MCQs) where you need to identify whether a statement is true or false
- problem/scenario questions worth 5, 10 and 30 marks and
- a 15-mark extended answer question asking you to discuss a statement based on a specific area of human rights law.

In 15-mark and 30-mark questions, you are required to provide an extended answer which shows a clear, logical and sustained line of reasoning leading to a valid conclusion.

Multiple-choice questions (1 mark each)

1 Select the one true statement about the theory of natural law.

A Each citizen has certain fundamental rights which can be removed or restricted by its government.

B Developed from the law of nature, natural order and selection, the theory of natural law forms the basis of a peaceful and co-existing society.

C John Locke's writings disputed that individuals are entitled to the right of life, liberty and property.

D This theory relies upon the citizens being co-existent with each other while controlled by the government or state.

2 Select the one false statement. Article 2 covers the right to life, but:

A capital punishment via the death penalty is authorised

B taking a loved one to a country where assisted suicide is tolerated prevents prosecution in the UK

C the police can take the life of an individual providing they have reason to do so

D it is a qualified right and not an absolute right.

3 Select the one true statement. Article 11 of the European Convention on Human Rights covers the freedom of assembly and association, however:

A organisations can lawfully form for any reason whatsoever

B organisations can form legally but are not allowed the right to protest

C employees can be forced to join trades' unions under this Article

D this is a qualified right and not an absolute right.

4 Select the one false statement. Article 8(1) of the European Convention on Human Rights protects the right to respect for family and private life. However, Article 8(2) restricts this right where:

A there is a benefit to national security

B the restriction prevents disorder or a crime

C medical treatment is necessary for vulnerable citizens

D the neutrality and authority of the judiciary are maintained.

5 Select the one false statement. Article 11(1) of the European Convention on Human Rights protects the right of peaceful assembly and the freedom of association. However, Article 11(2) restricts this right where:

A there is a benefit to national security

B the restriction prevents disorder or a crime

C medical treatment is necessary for vulnerable citizens

D the neutrality and authority of the judiciary are maintained.

5-mark questions

6 Explain how Article 8 of the European Convention on Human Rights can be restricted.

7 Information received by prison officers has suggested that six prisoners are planning to escape from a high-security prison. The information also suggests that the prisoners have homemade weapons and that a handgun has been smuggled into the prison to be used in the escape. On the morning of the escape, members of a specialist police firearms team raid the cells. Three of the prisoners are shot dead and a banana wrapped in tin foil is found in one of the prison cells.

Suggest whether it could probably be a violation of the prisoners' rights to life under Article 2 of the European Convention on Human Rights following the actions of the police.

8 Charles is a keen birdwatcher and on weekends he takes his binoculars and long-lensed camera to a local wildfowl park to watch and photograph rare birds. Charles' ex-wife Teresa has told the police that he is taking photographs of children at a nearby school and of residents in their bedrooms in a nearby housing estate. Both accusations are untrue and made out of spite by Teresa. The police arrest Charles, he is denied bail and kept on remand for nine months at a local prison.

Suggest whether it could probably be a violation of Charles' rights to liberty and security of person under Article 5 of the European Convention on Human Rights following the actions of the police.

10-mark questions

9 A local police force has been criticised for not doing enough to stop the activities of a football hooligan gang at the city's football club on matchdays. Information is received by the police indicating that a huge fight has been arranged with another gang from a visiting team. On match day, determined to avoid further criticism, the police use twice as many officers than usual and instruct them to stop any hooligan activity at all costs. During a scuffle with both sets of fans the police are described by onlookers as 'heavy-handed'. The police use a lot of force during the fight and two of the gang die as a result.

Advise the police as to how the provisions of Article 2 of the European Convention on Human Rights might apply to these facts.

10 Taylor has been diagnosed with autism, a specific learning difficulty. As a result of her condition, she can become angry and agitated. One day, while out shopping, a police officer sees Taylor shouting at a shop assistant and arrests her, mistakenly believing that she is under the influence of drugs or alcohol. She is held on remand for 18 months before being released with no charge.

Advise Taylor as to how the provisions of Article 5 of the European Convention on Human Rights might apply to these facts.

15-mark questions

11 Examine the relationship between the common law and the development of human rights. Discuss the extent to which the common law is founded on moral rules.

12 Examine the purpose of Article 2(1) of the European Convention on Human Rights. Discuss the extent to which the restrictions under Article 2(2) are justified.

13 Examine the purpose of Article 5(1) of the European Convention on Human Rights. Discuss the extent to which the restrictions under Article 5(2) are justified.

30-mark questions

14 One afternoon, a supermarket store detective detained Mika, who is from Poland, for three hours in the manager's office. The store detective detained Mika because she believed she had stolen a bottle of whisky and some baby milk. When the police arrived, Mika was arrested and had her rights read to her. However, Mika does not speak much English and did not understand what was happening.

Mila was put on remand and her trial date was set for six months' time. She was refused access to a solicitor for the first two weeks. When the date arrived for her trial, the judge was ill, so the trial date was postponed for another six months. At Mika's trial, she was sent to prison for two years.

Consider what rights and remedies Mika may have against the supermarket and whether her rights or liberties were breached while on remand or during the trial.

15 Belinda is a professional football player and plays for her national team. In January, she finds out that she is pregnant, but because the team has qualified for the World Cup in June, she decides to have an abortion in order to play. An online newspaper, *GuffMail* wants to publish the details. However, on the run up to the previous World Cup, where Belinda had also had an abortion in order to play, the website had been prevented from publishing the details by the courts.

Belinda's brother, Christian, is a lead member of a performance-art dance troupe. Having heard of her second abortion, he decides to turn her life into a piece of performance art. Here, together with his dance troupe, they plan to expose the two abortions in their dance performances.

Consider what rights and remedies Belinda may have against *GuffMail* and Christian arising out of these incidents.

End-of-unit summary

- Understand the theories of rights in human rights law.
- Appreciate the differences between rights and liberties.
- Understand what is meant by the scope of 'fundamental human' rights.
- Appreciate human rights in international law in the context of post WW2.
- Explain the status of the European Convention on Human Rights in the UK.
- Explain the impact of decisions of the European Court of Human Rights.
- Understand and explain Article 2 and its restrictions.
- Understand and explain Article 5 and its restrictions.
- Understand and explain Article 8 and its restrictions.
- Understand and explain Article 10 and its restrictions.
- Understand and explain Article 11 and its restrictions.
- Explain the enforcement of human rights.
- Understand the process of judicial review.
- Be able to explain human rights in English law via the criminal and civil law.

Glossary

Acceptance: an unconditional agreement to all the terms of an offer. Page 141

Actus reus: a guilty act. Page 61

ADR: alternative dispute resolution, one of the key Woolf reform recommendations. Page 33

Appropriation: any assumption by a person of the rights of an owner, including where they have come by the property (innocently or not) without stealing it, any later assumption of a right to it by keeping or dealing with it as owner. Page 82

Assault: where the defendant intentionally or recklessly causes the victim to apprehend immediate unlawful personal violence. Page 32

Automatism: an act done by the muscles without any control by the mind, such as a spasm, a reflex action or a convulsion; or an act done by a person who is not conscious of what they are doing, such as an act done while suffering from concussion or sleepwalking. Page 32

Autonomous: legally capable of making one's own decisions and therefore legally responsible for their consequences. Page 64

Bail: a form of security, either a sum of money or a promise in exchange for the freedom of an arrested person as a guarantee that they will appear in a criminal court when required. Page 44

Balance of probabilities: the civil standard of proof which means the claimant must satisfy the court that their version of events is more likely than not. Page 2

Battery: the intentional or reckless application of unlawful force upon a victim. Page 78

Belonging to another: belonging to any person having possession or control of property or having any proprietary right or interest in it. Page 82

Bilateral discharge (of contract): both parties discharge the contract. See *discharge* (of contract), page 142

Bill of Rights: a document which sets out the civil rights of citizens. Page 189

Binding precedent: a case from a senior court that must be followed in future cases. Page 30

Breach of contract: when a party fails to carry out any of their obligations under the agreement; or in carrying it out, they fail to do what they are supposed to do. Page 141

Burden of proof: a defendant is innocent until proven guilty. Page 62

Civil courts: courts that deal with non-criminal matters. Page 41

Claimant: legal term for a person or organisation starting a civil claim in the courts. Page 2

Conditional fee agreements (CFAs): 'no win, no fee' arrangements. Page 55

Constitutions: sets of rules which state how a country is to be run and the specific rights of its citizens.

Contract: an agreement between two parties which is binding in law and therefore enforceable in court. Page 141

Criminal courts: two levels – the Magistrates' Court deals mainly with summary offences and the Crown Court deals mainly with indictable offences. Page 44

Custody: where a person is under arrest or on remand in prison awaiting trial or while serving a custodial sentence in prison. Page 44

Damages: normally in the form of a cash compensation payment, to put the injured party financially into the position they were in before the breach. Page 176

Defendant: legal term for a person defending or responding to a legal claim (called a respondent in some aspects of civil law). Page 2

Delegated legislation: secondary legislation – laws passed in a specific area by a secondary body to which Parliament has passed its power. Page 22

Diminished responsibility: a partial defence, reducing a murder conviction to one of manslaughter. Page 70

Discharge (of a contract): the ending of a contract. Page 142

Doctrine: for judicial precedent, doctrine means the 'principle, operation and rules' of precedent. Page 30

Duress by threats: a common law defence whereby someone commits a crime because they were subject to a threat of death or serious injury. Page 99

Duress of circumstances: a common law defence whereby someone commits a crime because of the circumstances in which they found themselves. Page 101

Economic duress: where one party makes threats of an economic nature to the other party in order to form or change an agreement. Page 169

The Executive: the UK's democratically elected government. Page 53

Exclusion or exemption clauses: clauses which seek to exclude from liability one party for a breach of contract or even for a tort. Page 164

Factual causation: but for the defendant's action, the victim would not have suffered that consequence. Page 65

First instance courts: courts where trials are initiated, rather than held on appeal. Page 41

Freedom of expression: this freedom promotes and encourages healthy debate and challenge so that citizens can express ideas, views and opinions. Page 200

Golden rule: where judges decide that the literal rule produces absurd results when interpreting statute. Page 26

Gross negligence manslaughter: an offence requiring the death to have been caused by the defendant's gross negligence, rather than deliberately. Page 74

Guilty: legally responsible for a specified wrongdoing. Page 2

Holocaust: the name given to the genocide of over six million Jews by Adolf Hitler's Germany and its allies. Page 187

Horizontal direct effect: directives give an individual rights against other people, provided they have been implemented. Page 39

Human rights law: laws governing a collection of fundamental entitlements that exist in our legal system simply because we are human beings. Page 190

Intention: a decision to bring about the criminalised act. Page 66

Intention to create legal relations: both parties intend to be legally bound by the terms of the contract. Page 155

Judicial review: process allowing certain decisions of government or other public bodies to be challenged by citizens to see if they are 'reasonable'. Page 208

Judiciary: collective term for all the different types of judge in the English legal system. Page 51

Lay people: in the criminal justice system, either magistrates or juries; 'lay' in this circumstance means legally 'unqualified'. Page 47

Legal moralism: immoral conduct is criminalised for better social cohesion. Page 63

Legal personnel: a collective term which includes solicitors, barristers and legal executives. Page 49

Liable: held to be legally responsible for a breach of the civil law. Page 2

Litigation: the process of taking action, normally in a civil dispute. Page 54

Literal rule: where judges use the exact meaning of words when interpreting statute, no matter how absurd the outcome. Page 26

Loss of control: a partial defence, reducing a murder conviction to one of manslaughter. Page 70

Magistrates: volunteer citizens who work as unpaid (except for expenses) judges in the Magistrates' Court and the Youth Court. They deal with the vast majority of criminal cases. Page 47

Mens rea: a guilty mind. Page 61

Mischief rule: a rule of statutory interpretation used to prevent the mischief an Act is aimed at. Page 26

Murder: the unlawful killing of a human being with malice aforethought. Page 69

Natural law: rules which are not necessarily written down as laws but are nevertheless followed by citizens. Page 185

Novus actus interveniens: where a subsequent intervening act breaks the chain of causation. Page 66

Obiter dicta: 'other things said'. Page 32

Offer: an expression of one party's willingness to contract on certain terms, made with the intention that it will be legally binding upon acceptance. Page 146

Paternalism: the state is justified in protecting individuals from harm. Page 63

Persuasive precedent: usually in the form of *obiter dicta*, persuasive precedent is part of the judgment that should be followed in similar cases but is not binding. However, a reason for deciding not to follow it must be given. Page 30

Primary victim: someone in the zone of physical danger. Page 115

Property: includes money and all other property, real or personal, including things in action and other intangible property. Page 82

Prosecutes: legal term for bringing a criminal charge against a defendant. Page 2

Psychiatric injury: a long-term, diagnosed mental injury which is greater than shock or grief. Page 115

Purposive approach: where judges look to see what is the purpose of the law when interpreting statute. Page 26

Quantum meruit: a reasonable sum of money that is to be paid for services in contracts where an exact sum of money is not stipulated. Page 142

Ratio decidendi: 'the reason for the decision'. Page 32

Reasonable doubt: the criminal standard of proof which means the prosecution must provide sufficient evidence for the jury or magistrates to be certain of the defendant's guilt – if they do not, then they have reasonable doubt. Page 32

Reasonable person: sometimes known as the 'man on the Clapham omnibus', the reasonable person is a hypothetical ordinary person, used by the courts to decide whether a party has acted as a reasonable person would do. The reasonable person is a reasonably educated, intelligent but nondescript person, against whom the defendant's conduct can be measured. Page 5

Rebuttable presumption: a conclusion that a judge will take in court unless the contrary is raised and proven. Page 44

Regulation: a process whereby the actions of individuals or a collective are overseen and governed by an authorised organisation. Page 50

Remedy: in contract law, this is a way of providing a solution to a breach of contract. Page 142

Representations: statements made before the contract which may or may not become one of the main terms of the contract. Page 157

Restitutio in integrum: the restoration of an injured party back to the original, pre-contractual situation. Page 178

Restricted right: a right that for valid reasons is not an absolute right: exceptions to the right can be put in place to remove it as a total right. Page 193

Restrictions: key limitations on an absolute right or freedom to prevent disorder. Each of the three Articles 8, 10 and 11 are legitimately restricted to prevent disorder and are created to be lawful, necessary and proportionate. Page 203

Right to freedom of assembly and association: this means you are able to assemble (gather) with other people for peaceful purposes and associate with (be in the company of) others for the same reasons. Page 201

Right to liberty and security of person: this means that no one without just cause can interfere with your right to live a free life. There may be exceptions, such as arrest or imprisonment. Page 195

Right to life: this means that no one can take another's life without just cause. There may be exceptions, such as the death penalty or acting in self-defence. Page 193

Right to respect for family and private life: this means that no one without just cause can interfere with your right to live a free life. Page 198

Rights: rules or laws which are believed to belong to every person without discrimination. Page 183

Robbery: where someone steals, and immediately before or at the time of doing so, and in order to do so, uses force on any person or puts or seeks to put any person in fear of being then and there subjected to force.

Rylands v Fletcher: where the escape of non-naturally stored material onto adjoining property damages or destroys that property. Page 124

Secondary victim: someone not within the zone of physical danger but who witnesses horrific events. Page 115

Self-defence: using reasonable force in order to defend oneself. Page 97

Standard of proof: the defendant's guilt must be proved 'beyond all reasonable doubt'. Page 62

Stare decisis: 'let the decision stand'. Page 32

Subjective recklessness: the defendant commits an act knowing there is a risk of the consequence happening. Page 66

Sue: take civil legal proceedings against a defendant. Page 2

Theft: the dishonest appropriation of property belonging to another with the intention of permanently depriving the other of it. Page 82

Theories of human rights: systems of ideas proposed to explain the rationale of having rights based on general principles. Page 185

Tort law: an area of the law that allows a person to claim compensation when they have been injured or their property has been damaged. Page 105

Trespassers: persons on the occupier's land who have no permission or authority to be there. Page 119

Ultra vires: a Latin term meaning 'beyond the powers' – the secondary body has exceeded the powers given to it by the parent Act. Page 23

Unilateral discharge (of contract): only one party discharges the contract. See *discharge* (of contract), page 142

United Nations: the purpose of this organisation is to achieve international order and it has a representative from most sovereign nations. It also has a peace-keeping force which is sent to military zones during times of conflict. Its main offices are in New York and Geneva. Page 187

Unlawful act manslaughter: an offence requiring the death to have been caused by the defendant's unlawful conduct, rather than deliberately. Page 73

Vertical direct effect: an individual can claim against the state even if the directive is not yet implemented. Page 39

Vicarious liability: a third person has legal responsibility for the unlawful actions of another. Page 127

Visitors: in law, adult visitors are those who have been invited or licensed to enter, or who have a statutory right to enter or have contractual permission. Page 117

Vitiating: invalidating; a vitiating factor makes a contract null and void. The two most common vitiating factors are misrepresentation and economic duress. Page 168

Index

absolute liability offences 6
absolute rights 186
Acts of God 133
Acts of Parliament 3, 19–20, 21
 and crime 61
 and privacy rights 198, 199
 repeal of 36
actual bodily harm (ABH) 79, 95, 96
actus reus (AR) 61, 62, 65–6, 67
 of assault/battery 77, 78, 79
 of attempt 88–9
 contemporaneity rule 68
 of manslaughter 73
 of murder 69
 of robbery 86
 of theft 82–3
 of wounding and GBH 80
advertisements 147
Alcock v Chief Constable of South Yorkshire 115, 116
alternative dispute resolution (ADR) 41, 42, 43
appeals
 civil courts 42, 52
 criminal courts 46, 52
Aquinas, St Thomas 9
Aristotle 9
arrest
 and justified deprivation of liberty 196–7, 210
assault 77, 78–9, 95, 96
association, freedom of 183, 201–2, 205
attempted crimes 88–91
attempting the impossible 90
automatism defence 91, 93–4, 96
autonomous adults 64
Bagehot, Walter 18
bail 5
barristers 49, 50
basic intent crimes 95, 96
battery 78–9
Bentham, Jeremy 5, 9
binding precedent 30
breach of contract 141, 173
 anticipatory 173, 174, 175
 breach of a condition 160
 failure to perform 172
 remedies for 142–3, 146, 162, 176–9
 compensatory damages 176–8
 equitable remedies 142–3, 146, 169, 177–8
 supply of goods 162
 supply of services 162–3
 termination of contract for 178
 time of performance 172–3
Brexit 38, 39, 40, 144, 206
burden of proof
 of diminished responsibility 73
 in tort law 106
by-laws 22
capacity defences 91–6
Caparo test 110
cautions 5
circuit judges 52, 53
circumstances, duress by 101–2
Citizens Advice 55
civil courts 2, 41–2, 52
civil law 2, 4, 13, 16–17
 employment law 1, 41, 105
 family law 41, 105
 see also contract law; fault; tort law
Civil Legal Advice Service 56, 57
Civil Liability (Contribution) Act (1978) 128
close connection test 127, 128
coin-operated machinery 147–8
Coke, Edward 61, 69
common law 3, 8, 30, 61
 breach of the peace 212
capacity defences 91–7
contract law 144–5
control of exclusion clauses 164–5
 remedies in 142, 146, 176–7
 terms of contract 158
 necessity defences 97–102
 and tort law 105, 107
community sentences 47
conditional fee agreements (CFAs) 55–6
conflicting interests 4–5, 130
consent 5, 105, 131–2, 133
consideration
 in contract law 144, 145, 151–3
Constitution of the United Kingdom 18
Constitutional Reform Act (2005) 15, 22, 53
consumer protection 144
Consumer Rights Act (2015) 157, 159, 161, 166
contra proferentem rule 165
contract law 17, 41, 105, 141–82
 agreement 144, 146–51
 acceptance 149–51
 invitation to treat 144, 147, 148
 termination of offers 148
consideration 144, 145, 151–3
 and privity 145, 154
 rules for 152–3
contract terms 141–2
 discharge of a contract 142, 172–5
 doctrine of frustration 173–5
 exclusion or exemption clauses 145–6, 164–7
 formation of a contract 141
 intention to create legal relations (ITCLR) 144, 155–6
 non-contractual representations 157
 terms of contract 157–67
 conditions, warranties and innominate terms 160, 178
 exclusion or exemption clauses 164–7
 express terms 157–8
 implied terms 158–9, 161–3
 theory of 143–6
 consumer protection 144
 freedom to contract 143
 vitiating factors in 142, 168–72
 void contracts 142
 voidable contracts 142
 see also breach of contract
Contracts (Rights of Third Parties) Act (1999) 152, 154
contributory negligence 6, 105, 118, 120, 130
corrective justice 11
correspondence principle 64
Council of Europe 188
County Courts 41, 49
 judges 52
Court of Appeal 42
Civil Division 31
Criminal Division 31
 judges 52, 53
Criminal Attempts Act (1981) 62, 88, 90
criminal convictions
 disclosure of 5
criminal courts 2, 5, 44–9
 appeal system 46
 bail 44, 47
classification of criminal offences 45
Crown Prosecution Service (CPS) 45
 either-way offences 45, 47
 guilty verdicts 62
 indictable offences 44, 45
 judges 52
 juries 48
 rebuttable presumption 44
 role of lay people in 47–8
 sentencing 6, 13, 47, 48, 61, 92
 summary offences 44, 45, 47, 77
 trial processes 5, 45
 see also Crown Court; Magistrates' Court
Criminal Justice Act (1988) 77
Criminal Justice Act (2003) 64
Criminal Justice and Courts Act (2015) 37, 61
Criminal Justice and Immigration Act (2008) 98
Criminal Justice Service (CJS) 2
criminal law 1, 2, 16, 61–104
 aim of 4
 attempted crimes 88–91
 defences 91–102
 capacity defences 91–6

necessity defences 97–102
defining crime 61
fault in 5, 6, 64–7
formulating rules of 64
liability 62, 64, 65–8
offences against the person
fatal 69–76
non-fatal 77–87
property offences 82–7
reform 35, 36
rules of 61–3
substantive justice in 11, 13
theory in 63–4
Crown Court 44, 45, 48, 49
judges 51, 52
Crown Prosecution Service (CPS) 45, 49
custody, deaths in 210
customs 3
damages 105, 106, 135–7, 138
for breach of contract 142, 176–8
mitigation of loss 137
death penalty 194
defences
in criminal law 91–102
in tort law 105, 106, 126, 130–5
delegated legislation 22–5
Devlin, Lord 9
Dicey, A.V. 15–16, 21
difference principle 11
digital content, consumer rights on 161
diminished responsibility 72–3
direct intent 66, 67
discharges 47
dishonesty 84, 86
dispute resolution 41–3
district judges 52, 53
diversity 8
divorce law 1
duress
by threats 99–101
of circumstances 101–2
duty of care 107, 110–12, 114
breach of 111–12, 113, 120
Caparo test 110
and human rights 210
'neighbour' principle 110
to lawful visitors 117–18
to non-visitors 119–20
warnings and warning signs 118, 120
economic duress 145, 169–70, 171
economic loss
damages for 136
liability for 108, 114, 125
economic rights 185
Electronic Commerce Directive (2000) 150
employers
liability of 109, 127–9
testing employment status 127–8
employment law 1, 41, 105
equality before the law 15, 54
equitable remedies
for breach of contract 142–3, 146
rescission 143, 169, 178
specific performance 143, 177–8
European Commission 38
European Communities Act (1972) 21–2, 38, 39–40
European Convention on Human Rights (ECHR) 183–4, 188, 193–202
Article 2 (the right to life) 183, 193–5, 209
justified exceptions 194
Article 5 (the right to liberty and security of person) 183, 195–8
deprivation of liberty 196–8, 210
Article 8 (the right to privacy) 183, 198–200, 203, 211
Article 10 (freedom of expression) 183, 200–1, 204, 211–12
Article 11 (freedom of peaceful assembly and association) 183, 201–2, 205, 211–12
and the Human Rights Act (1998) 184, 186, 190–1
restrictions 203–5
in the UK 189–90, 207, 213
European Council 38
European Court of Human Rights (ECtHR) 183, 188
claims before 206
and the right to life 193–4
in the UK 189, 192, 207, 215
European Court of Justice 30, 39, 42
European Parliament 38
European Union 3, 38–40
consumer protection laws 144, 146
EU law and statutory interpretation 28
impact of EU law on the law of England and Wales 39
sources of EU law 39
exclusion or exemption clauses in contract terms 164–7
fair labelling 64
family law 41, 105
family life, right to 198–200, 203
fault 5–7, 64–7
in civil law 5, 6, 7
in criminal law 5, 6, 7, 64–7
fault or no fault 106
and vicarious liability 128
see also strict liability offences (SLOs)
fines 47
first instance courts 41
Fitzjames-Stephens, James 9
formal justice 11
fraudulent misrepresentation in contract law 168–9
freedom of expression, assembly and association 200–1
restrictions on 204, 211–12
frustration of contract 173–5
Fuller, Lon 9
funding legal services 54–7
golden rule 26, 27, 29
goods
implied terms of contract to supply 161–2
government
Green and White Papers 19
and the judiciary 52, 53
grievous bodily harm (GBH) 80–1, 96
gross negligence manslaughter 6, 74–5
Hadley v Baxendale rule 177, 179
harm and criminal conduct 63
Hart, H.L.A. 9, 63
helplines 55
High Court 31, 41
Chancery Division 31
civil litigation claims 41
criminal appeals 46
Family Division 31
judges 51, 52, 53
Queen's Bench Division 31, 46, 208
historical rights 185
homicide law 209
House of Commons 3, 18, 19
House of Lords 3, 18–19, 25, 31
householders and self-defence 98
human rights 4, 41, 183–217
and English law 209–12
in international law 187–8
judicial review 208
qualified rights 203
restrictions 193–4, 203–5
rights contrasted with liberties 186
scope of 'fundamental human' rights 186
theories of 185–6
in the UK 189–92
enforcement 206–8
English law 209–12
reform of the protection of 213–15
UK Bill of Rights 214–15
see also European Convention on Human Rights (ECHR)
Human Rights Act (1998) 3, 8, 21, 28, 183, 184
criticism of 192, 213
enforcement of 207
and English law 209
and the European Convention on Human Rights 184, 186, 190–1, 198, 199, 200, 204
impact on UK constitutional arrangements and the law 191–2
independent review of (2020) 215
reform proposals 213–15
and restricted rights 203, 204
implied terms of contract 158–9
consumer contracts 161–3
imprisonment 47
independent contractors
dangers created by 118
liability for 128–9
injunctions 106, 109, 137–8
innocent misrepresentation 169
insanity defence 91–3
insurance 55

intention
in criminal law 66–7
to permanently deprive 84–5, 86
see also mens rea (MR)
interests/rights 4–5
international law
human rights in 187–8
intoxication defence 94–6
involuntary intoxication 95
involuntary manslaughter 73–4
Jhering, Rudolf von 4, 5
judicial precedent 30–4
advantages and disadvantages of 33
key cases for 34
law reporting 32
obiter dicta 30, 32
practice statement 31
ratio decidendi 32
stare decisis 30, 32
judicial review 208
judiciary 51–4
independence of 16, 52–4
types and roles of judges 51–2
juries 47, 48
justice and law 11–15
failures in achieving justice 13
key cases regarding 14
miscarriages of justice 13
land-based torts 105
LASPRO 13, 17
law centres 55
Law Commission 21, 35–7, 64
reform proposals
automatism defence 94
duress 100
insanity defence 93
intoxication defence 96
law making 18–40
delegated legislation 22–5
judicial precedent 30–4
law reform 35–7
parliamentary 18–22
statutory interpretation 25–9
Law Reform (Frustrated Contracts) Act (1943) 174
Legal Aid Agency 56
legal executives 49, 50
legal moralism 63
Legal Ombudsman 51
legal rights 185
Legal Services Board 50
legal system 41–57
access to justice 54
dispute resolution 41–3
funding legal services 54–7
judiciary 51–4
personnel 49–51
see also criminal courts
liability 107, 117–21
in contract terms 166
in criminal law 62, 64, 65–8
for economic loss 108, 114
and exclusion clauses in contracts 164
occupiers' liability 106, 117–21
and consent 131–2
defences 118, 120
trespassers 119–21
for psychiatric injury 106, 108, 114, 115–16, 135
strict liability offences 6, 8, 67–8, 124
vicarious liability 6, 106, 109, 127–9
see also negligence
limited rights 186
liquidated damages 176
in contract law 142
literal rule 26, 27, 28
litigation 54–7
lobbyists 21
loss of control
and voluntary manslaughter 70–1
magistrates 47–8
Magistrates' Court 44, 45, 46, 49, 208
judges 52
offences tried in 77, 78
mandatory injunctions 138
manslaughter 96, 209
gross negligence 6, 74–5, 77
involuntary 73–4
voluntary 70–3
maximum certainty 64
media and law making 20
mediation 42, 43
mens rea (MR) 61, 62, 65, 66–7
of assault/battery 77, 78–9
of attempt 89–90
automatism defence 93
contemporaneity rule 68
intoxication defence 94, 94–5, 96
of manslaughter 74–5
of murder 70
of robbery 86–7
of theft 83–5
of wounding and GBH 81
Mental Capacity Act (2005) 210
Mill, John Stuart 9, 63
mischief rule 26, 27, 29
misrepresentation 168–9, 170
Misrepresentation Act (1967) 169
mitigation of loss 177
monarchy 18
moral rules 4
morality and law 7–11, 63
murder 6, 7, 61, 69–70, 96, 209
insanity verdict 92
natural law 9, 10, 185
natural rights 185
nature of law 1–15
Nazi Germany
and human rights 187, 201
necessity defences 97–102
negligence 5, 6, 105, 107, 110–16
contributory 6, 105, 118, 120, 130
damage 113
fault or no fault 106
gross negligence manslaughter 6, 74–5
human rights and English law 210
misstatements 106, 114
negligent misrepresentation 168–9
objective standard of care in action for 108–9
see also duty of care
negotiation 42, 43
Northern Ireland Act 192
Northern Ireland Assembly 3
novus actus interveniens 66
nuisance 5, 105, 106, 109, 121–6, 137
defences 126, 132–3
private nuisance 121–4
oblique intent 66, 67
Obscene Publications Act (1959) 212
occupier's liability 106, 117–21
and consent 131–2
Occupiers' Liability Act (1957) 117–18, 131
Occupiers' Liability Act (1984) 119–21, 131
Offences Against the Person Act (1861) 79–81
officious bystander test 158
Parliament (UK) 3, 16
and the judiciary 53
law making 18–22
delegated legislation 23
sovereignty 21–2, 64
partial injunctions 138
peaceful assembly, freedom of 183, 201–2, 205, 211–12
performance of a contract 172–3, 174
specific performance 177–8
persuasive precedent 30
pluralist societies 8
police 1, 2, 3, 5
human rights and English law 209, 210, 211
Police and Criminal Evidence Act (1984) 1, 23
political parties 18, 20
positivism 9, 10
postal rule 150
Pound, Roscoe 4, 5
pre-emptive strikes 98
precedent 3, 30, 64
judicial precedent 30–4, 61
pressure groups 20
Pretty v UK 193, 195
prevention of crime
and self-defence 98
privacy rights 183, 198–200, 203, 211
private law 1, 105
private nuisance 121–4
foreseeability of 122–3
interference 121–2
privity of contract 145, 154
Privy Council (PC) 22
judicial committee 30
procedural justice 13
procedural law 1, 4
key areas of 5
and rule of law 16–17
procedural UV 23, 24
prohibitory injunctions 138

promissory estoppel 151
property offences 82–7
psychiatric damage 106, 108, 135
psychiatric injury
  liability for 106, 108, 114, 115–16
Public Defender Service 56, 57
public laws 1, 2
public opinion 21
Public Order Act (1986) 212
purposive approach
  to statutory interpretation 26, 27, 29
qualified rights 186
quantum meruit 142
Racial and Religious Hatred Act (2006) 212
Raz, Joseph 16
reasonable person test 5, 109, 111
rebuttable presumptions
  in contract law 155
remoteness of loss 176–7
rescission 143, 169, 178
retrospective liability 64
rights/interests 4–5
risk
  and duty of care 112
robbery 86–7, 96
Robinson v Chief Constable of West Yorkshire 108, 110
rule of law 15–17, 64
Rylands v. Fletcher 105, 106, 124–6
  defences to 133
Salmond Test 127–8
Scotland Act (1998) 192
Scottish Parliament 3, 21
Second World War
  and human rights 187, 189, 201
self-defence 97–9
self-induced automatism 94
sentencing 6, 47, 61, 92
  Magistrates' Court 48
  substantive justice in 13
Sentencing Code 35, 36
services
  implied terms of contract to supply 162–3
shops, display of goods in 147
Simonds, Viscount 9
social contract 11
social engineering 5
societal rights 185
society and law 4–7
solicitors 49, 50
specific intent crimes 95, 96
standard of proof
  in tort law 106
stare decisis 30
state of affairs offences 65
statute law 3
  contract terms in
  exclusion clauses 165–6
  implied terms 159
  see also Acts of Parliament
statutory authority and nuisance 133
statutory instruments (SIs) 22, 23, 24
statutory interpretation 25–9
  aids to 26–7
  key cases for 27
  rules of 25–6, 27–9
strict liability offences (SLOs) 6, 8, 67–8, 124
'struggle for law' 5
subjective recklessness 66, 67
substantive justice 11, 13, 130
substantive law 1, 2, 4
  key areas of 5
  and rule of law 17
substantive UV 23, 24
Supreme Court 22, 42, 192
  judges 52, 53
  judicial precedent 30, 31
Supreme Court of Judicature Act (1925) 109
Terrorism Act (2006) 4
theft 82–5, 96
Theft Act (1968) 82, 84, 86
Thompson and Venables v United Kingdom 184, 189, 190
threats, duress by 99–101
tort law 17, 41, 105–40
  claimants 105
  defences 105, 106, 126, 130–5
  defendants 105
  defining 105
  policy decisions 107–8
  remedies 106–7, 135–8
  damages 105, 106, 135–7, 138
  injunctions 106, 137–8
  rules of 105–6
  Rylands v. Fletcher 105, 106, 124–6, 133
  see also liability; negligence; nuisance
trade unions 55, 201, 202
transferred malice 67
trespass 109, 117, 137
  aggravated 212
  liability in respect of 119–21
tribunals 42, 52
ultra vires (UV) 23, 24
Unfair Contract Terms Act (1977) 165–6
United Nations (UN) 187–8
Universal Declaration of Human Rights (1948) 188
unliquidated damages 142, 176
utilitarianism 5
vicarious liability 6, 106, 109, 127–9
victims of negligence
  primary and secondary 115
vitiating factors in contract law 168–72
  economic duress 145, 169–70, 169–72, 171
  mispresentation 168–9, 170
void exclusion clauses 166
volenti non fit injuria 118, 120
voluntary intoxication 95
voluntary manslaughter 70–3
von Hayek, F.A. 16
war crimes 8
Welsh Government 3
White v Chief Constable of South Yorkshire 115, 116
wills 49
Wolfenden Report (1978) 9
wounding and GBH 80–1, 96
Youth Court 44